DARK
AND
LIGHT

DARK
AND
LIGHT

The Story of the Guinness Family

Derek Wilson

Weidenfeld & Nicolson
LONDON

First published in Great Britain in 1998
by Weidenfeld & Nicolson

A CIP catalogue record for this book is available
from the British Library.

ISBN 0 297 81718 3

Typeset by Selwood Systems Limited, Midsomer Norton

Set in ITC Stone Serif

Printed in Great Britain by Butler & Tanner Ltd, London and Frome

Weidenfeld & Nicolson

The Orion Publishing Group Ltd
Orion House
5 Upper Saint Martin's Lane
London, WC2H 9EA

CONTENTS

ILLUSTRATIONS

Frontispiece
The first Arthur Guinness (1725–1803) (*Guinness Limited, Park Royal, London;* Signature © *Guinness Ireland Group*)

Between pages 176 and 177
The 'Second Arthur Guinness' (1768–1855)
His first wife Anne (née Lee 1774–1817) with their youngest child, Rebecca.
Arthur Lee Guinness.
Richard Samuel Guinness.
Arthur Edward, Benjamin Lee and Edward Cecil Guinness.
Arthur, Baron Ardinlaun.
Edward, Viscount Iveagh.
A 1901 shooting party with George V.
Arthur Eustace (1865–1955) (*Courtauld Institute, London*)
Arthur's wife's sister, Eva (b. 1868) (*Courtauld Institute, London*)
Henry Grattan Guinness.
His second wife, the 26-year-old Grace Hurditch.
Cartoon from the *Southend and Westcliff Graphic* in March 1912.
Walter Guinness, the adventurer of the family (*James Sant RA*)
Walter in New Guinea with pygmies.
In Walter's steam yacht, the converted ferry *Rosaura*.
Kenwood, on Hampstead Heath, during the First World War.
Self-Portrait (1663) by Rembrandt which hangs in Kenwood (*English Heritage Photographic Library, London*)
An early Guinness poster with a text provided by one of S. H. Buson's talented copywriters – Dorothy L. Sayers, 1935 (*Guinness Limited, Park Royal, London*)
Benjamin 3rd Lord Iveagh (1937–1992), the last member of the family to preside over Arthur Guinness Son and Co. Ltd.

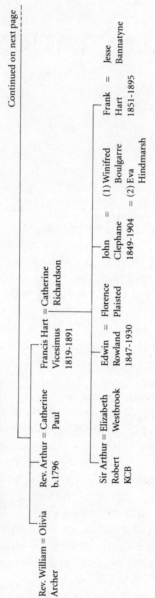

The Guinnesses: Select Pedigree

The New Zealanders

Continued on next page

Rev. William = Olivia Archer

Rev. Arthur = Catherine Paul
b.1796

Francis Hart = Catherine Richardson
Vicesimus
1819-1891

Sir Arthur = Elizabeth Westbrook
Robert
KCB

Edwin = Florence Plaisted
Rowland
1847-1930

John = (1) Winifred Boulgarre
Clephane = (2) Eva Hindmarsh
1849-1904

Frank = Jesse Bannatyne
Hart
1851-1895

The Brewers

Continued on next page

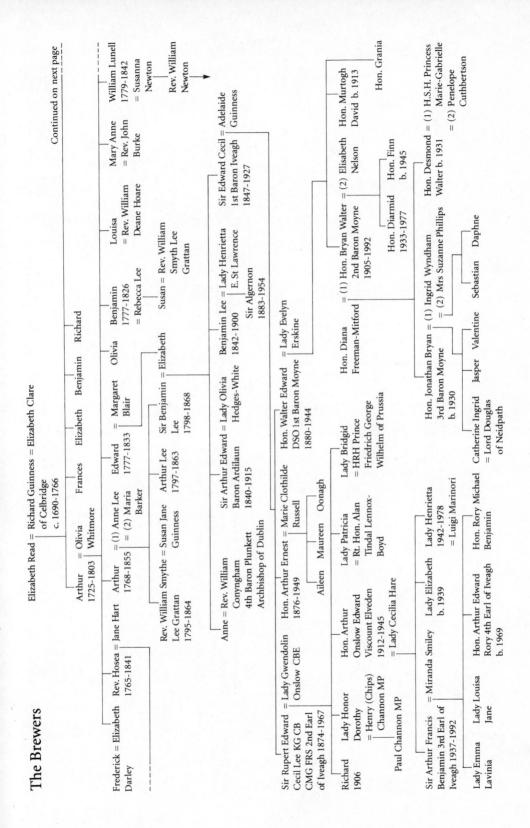

The Missionaries

Continued on next page

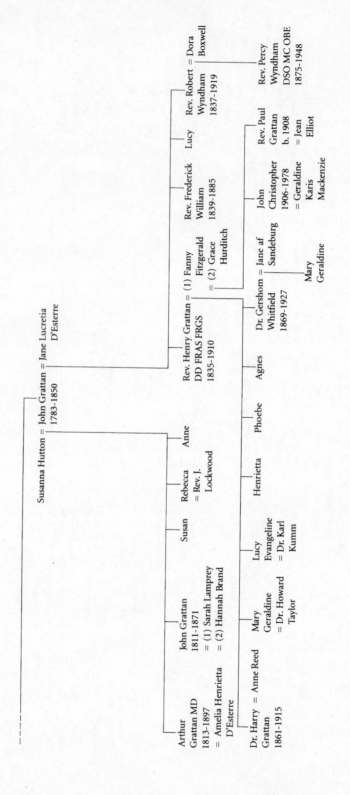

The Bankers

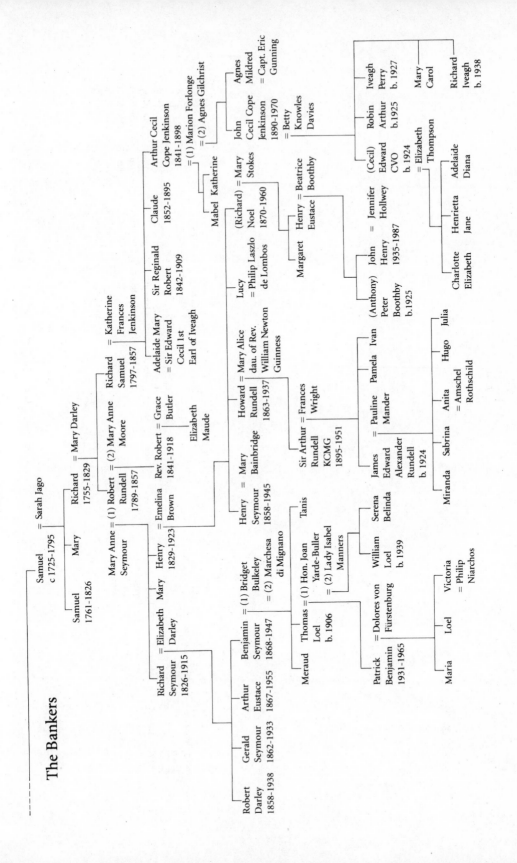

1

INTRODUCTION

When, a dozen years ago, I set myself the task of writing a history of the Rothschild family I did not envisage the project growing into a trilogy. It was as I worked on *Rothschild: A Story of Wealth and Power* that I realised that, though unique, the remarkable banking family had something in common with a few other great commercial dynasties – something, that is, beyond industriousness and entrepreneurial flair. Each grasped the unprecedented opportunities provided by technical innovation and expanding markets to found a great fortune. Each wrestled with the social implications of being *nouveau riche* in the nineteenth century when 'trade' was elbowing its way into the ranks previously dominated by 'land' and 'ancestry'. Each maintained its dominance well beyond 1900 but had to reinvent itself in a world of changing social and political conventions and ultimately had to face the ruthless commercial realities of international conglomerates, takeovers and mergers. It occurred to me that by looking closely at three very different family businesses to see how they were able to ride the roller coaster of history it might be possible to discern interesting common features and points of difference. *Rothschild: A Story of Wealth and Power* explored the rise of a great finance house against the background of European Jewry and anti-semitism. *The Astors: Landscape with Millionaires* looked at Anglo-American relations from the viewpoint of a leading transatlantic family. *Dark and Light: The Guinness Story* considers how a great brewing and banking dynasty established and maintained for itself a respected position on both sides of the Irish Sea throughout decades when political and ideological conflict dragged Britain and Ireland apart. By relating the lives of individuals – businessmen, preachers, playboys, politicians, philanthropists, poets, artists and society hostesses – against the changing cloudscape of great events, I have tried to tell a story which is fascinating in itself while at the same time adding something to our understanding of two and a half centuries of history.

Such an endeavour inevitably relies heavily on the help provided by those who possess personal memories or are the custodians of private or public archives. Among those to whom I am especially indebted for their assistance are: the Earl of Iveagh, Mr C. E. Guinness CVO, Mrs Michele Guinness, Ms Susan Garland, Archivist of Guinness Brewing, Great Britain, Ms Annie Oatley, Head of Information, Guinness Mahon Group, Ms Jill Springall of the National Portrait Gallery and the staffs of The Iveagh Bequest, Kenwood, Guinness Publishing Ltd, Irish National Archives, the National Library of Ireland, Essex Record Office, Southend-on-Sea, Suffolk Record Office, Bury St Edmunds, North Devon Record Office, Barnstaple, and Cambridge University Library. The information contained in the following pages is the result of many minds: any faults can only be ascribed to one.

Derek Wilson
May 1998

1

DUBLIN'S FAIR CITY

On Sunday, 12 July 1691 a Dutchman defeated a Frenchman and thus ensured the continued mastery of Englishmen over Irishmen. The Battle of Aughrim lasted from 11 a.m., when forces loyal to James II emerged from mass, to nightfall, by which time the marshy ground was white with the bodies of the slain. Charles Chalmont, Marquis de St Rhue (usually anglicised to St Ruth) had chosen his battlefield wisely. His Irish troops, led by French and Irish Catholic commanders, defended a soggy terrain between the castle of Horse Ridge (*Eachdhruim* or Aughrim) on his left flank and a causeway on his right. For hour after hour, Godert de Ginkel (subsequently ennobled as Baron Aughrim and Earl of Athlone), brought over from Holland by King William, vainly attempted to demolish the enemy by hurling against them his German–Dutch–English–Irish Protestant cavalry and artillery. In the end it was a lucky chance that turned the fortunes of the day. As the afternoon frustratingly lengthened into evening Ginkel ordered a desperate attack on Aughrim Castle. While repulsing it St Ruth was felled by a chance cannon shot. His left cavalry wing immediately crumbled and fled the field. 'In the long and bloody strife, both on the field of bravery and in the accidental retreat, there were slain of the Irish officers and soldiers about two thousand, and six hundred wounded. Amongst the slain was the great General St Ruth ... the noble youth the Lord Bourk, Viscount of Galway, Brigadier Connell ... Brigadier Henry McJohn O'Neil, Colonel Charles Moor of Kildare ...' Plunkett's *Jacobite Narrative* unrolls a mournful catalogue of death.[1] The outcome of this, the last pitched battle fought in the British Isles* was devastatingly simple:

---

*The routs and skirmishes of 1715 and 1745 bear no comparison in military terms.

'After Aughrim Irish Protestants, whether Cromwellian newcomers or older settlers, could be confident that for the foreseeable future they would govern Ireland'.[2]

About the time that the Battle of Aughrim was contested a boy was born to one of those settler families who would be well placed to take advantage of the triumph of the Protestant 'Ascendancy' and whose progeny would constitute its greatest success story. Their names would appear on the troubled pages of Anglo-Irish affairs, at first as footnotes but thereafter with increasing frequency and prominence. At the same time they would make their mark on a wider world by their commercial success, their philanthropy and their religious zeal.

The story begins unsatisfactorily with the appearance, unverified in any extant baptismal register, of Richard Guinness, in Oughterard, Co. Kildare. Decades later, when the family was passing through its *nouveau riche* phase, attempts were made to trace an august, ancient lineage (see below pp.28–9). Of Richard they spoke or wrote little. However, two facts about this indistinct progenitor do seem clear: he was a member of the Church of Ireland and he was landless. Richard Guinness belonged to the Protestant Anglo-Irish underclass. Any settler society has within its ranks a proportion of downwardly mobile families and Ireland was no exception. Major colonisation schemes had been engineered by the governments of Elizabeth I, James I and Cromwell, and these involved making grants out of confiscated lands to the soldiers of conquering armies and to adventurers prepared to essay a new start beyond the sea. Inevitably, there were those who failed to make a success of farming, or who sold lands for quick profit or who, as younger sons, enjoyed no workable share of their patrimony. Some moved to Dublin, Cork or one of the handful of small towns to try their hands at trade – Richard's younger brother, William, took up an apprenticeship with a Dublin gunsmith around the turn of the century. Others became the paid employees of major landowners and wealthy members of the Protestant Ascendancy. Some of them were no better off than the more successful members of the despised majority population of the island, but they still belonged to a superior caste, enjoying social status and legal rights denied to their Catholic neighbours. The colourful legends overlaying Guinness origins may or may not have substance; what is important for an understanding of the family's rise to prominence is an appreciation of its modest beginnings.

The Ireland in which Richard was fortuitously born was entering the first century of peace in a history dominated by clan feuds and conflicts with England. It was these changed conditions and the growing prosperity of eighteenth-century Ireland which created the ambience for determined and energetic Guinnesses to elbow their way into a prominent place in Anglo-Irish society. By the beginning of the 1800s their wealth and influence were unchallengeable and when the Ascendancy's era of gilded irresponsibility finally passed, this family, unique among the landed clans of Anglo-Irish squiredom, were seen to have exchanged Hibernia's hunting fields and levees for the watering holes of the international élite. There would not be a city or sizeable town anywhere in the civilised world where the name 'Guinness' was unknown.

The hilltop parish of Oughterard, Co. Kildare, was a brisk hour's ride from Dublin over indifferent roads when the enterprising and industrious Richard Guinness began to make his mark. Romantic legend has the young man as a groom in the employ of the relatively well-to-do Read family and eloping with the daughter of the house, Elizabeth. If there is any truth in the tale it seems odd that the runaway couple 'fled' fewer than four miles and settled in Celbridge on the banks of the Liffey. And it defies explanation that the vicar of Celbridge, Feighcullen and Ballybraine would take them into his household, despite the scandal. However, one of the few record-based facts about Richard is that he was long in the employ of the Reverend Arthur Price and that he rose to be his agent and receiver, responsible for the ecclesiastical holdings in the area. From this meagre information we may assume that Richard was landless or that he possessed property inadequate to the maintenance of a wife and family, suggesting that he was a younger son. Price was a career cleric from a family of career clerics well established in the hierarchy of the Irish church. He had taken his degree at Trinity College, Dublin and, by the first decade of the eighteenth century, was striding purposefully along the broad highway of ecclesiastical preferment. This involved him spending much time in the privileged circles of city society that revolved around Dublin Castle (rebuilt in the eighteenth century as a powerful yet elegant symbol of English authority) – or, at least, did so on the fairly rare occasions when the current lord-lieutenant took the trouble to cross the water and see for himself the country he was supposed to be administering for the crown.

As a land agent Richard was at the sharp end of English Protestant oppression of Catholic Irishmen. He had to collect the tithes that supported the clergy of a church whose ministrations were not esteemed by the people and which was denounced as heretical by the pope. He had to oversee the inheritance laws, which provided that lands and tenancies must pass to any sons who declared for the faith of the established church, bypassing if necessary any Catholic heirs. He kept an eye on the running of SPCK (Society for the Propagation of Christian Knowledge) schools, set up with the express intention of winning over Irish children to the reformed religion. He may even have organised the expulsion of Catholic tenants in favour of land-hungry Protestant neighbours, for this was a common practice in a province where the government's main objective was to eviscerate the culture and break the spirit of the majority population. Ireland lay compressed under the weight of the penal laws, which denied its ancient people the right to vote, to buy land or to join the professions.

It was a policy heartily endorsed by most of the Ascendancy. Scintillating Dublin society members used the income from cheaply run Irish estates to build themselves classical palazzos and mansions. The up-and-coming mercantile class, recently swelled by Huguenot and Flemish master craftsmen, occupied the precisely proportioned terraces and squares that were rapidly transforming Dublin into the second city of the British Isles. Though they had their own battles to fight, they had every-thing to gain from endorsement of the *status quo*. As in every settler society from the plantation caballeros of South America to the home-steaders of the veld, attitudes to the natives varied from frank exploitation to self-justifying paternalism. The existence of two unequal nations was accepted by the ruling class as so obviously natural as to require no explanation or defence. The Irish were a backward, uncivilised people wallowing in superstition and they were potentially dangerous because (until 1766) Rome continued to uphold the Stuart claim to the English throne.

There were always a few liberal constitutionalists who could not stomach the injustices of the system and far-sighted pragmatists who warned of the dangers inherent in the subjection of a numerically superior population. Alan Brodrick, Lord Midleton, George I's first Lord Chancellor of Ireland, fought against both the Dublin and London parliaments for repeal of some anti-Catholic legislation and John Bowes, a later holder of the same office, observed that existing law did not 'presume an Irish Papist to exist in the Kingdom, where they are only supposed to breathe by the connivance of the government'.[3] Jonathan Swift was the most effective voice of satirical indignation. He bitterly lampooned attitudes prevalent among Dublin's equivalent of aristocratic Parisian society: 'I have been assured', he declared in *A Modest Proposal for Preventing the Children of Ireland from being a Burden to their*

Parents or Country (1729), 'that a young healthy child well nursed is at a year old a most delicious, nourishing and wholesome food, whether stewed, roasted, baked, or boiled, and I make no doubt that it will equally serve in a fricassee or a ragout.'

No such sentiment troubled the mind of the Reverend Arthur Price. He was an establishment man through and through. Resolutely he ascended the Church of Ireland's *scala di seta*. As a reactionary who always put the interests of England and the Protestant faith first, his appointment to the episcopal bench in 1724 drove Lord Midleton to the verge of apoplexy. Thereafter Price spent much of his time in London, where he vigorously supported the rigged casino that was Walpole's administration, thus ensuring further favours. He reached his career summit in 1744 with his accession to the archbishopric of Cashel.

Richard Guinness rose with his patron and was loyal to the cleric's principles as well as his person. Dr Price's long and frequent absences left his agent in a position of ever-increasing authority. The ecclesiastic entertained a considerable affection for Celbridge and it was there that he built his country house, Oakley Park. He relied heavily on his agent and reposed complete trust in him. When Guinness's first son was born in 1725 he stood godfather to the child, who was christened Arthur in his honour. Richard prospered, even though his wife died in 1742, leaving him sole parent to six children. He was ideally placed to acquire property in the area and to begin to be a landowner in a very modest way. It may be that he grew his own barley, for tradition has it that Richard originated that distinctive strong beer, sometimes referred to as porter, which became the basis of the family's fortune.

Brewing in Ireland was something between a hobby and a cottage industry, as it had been on both sides of the water for centuries. Cask beer had a relatively short shelf life and this would inhibit the growth of large-scale home and export businesses, until the Industrial Revolution brought the necessary technological breakthrough. Barley was plentiful in the Dublin area, thanks to the low acidity of the soil, so that farmers could set aside from good and average harvests sufficient grain for their household brewing and distilling, or for sale to small, local commercial concerns. Every householder had his own recipe for beer, which dictated the drying time of the barley and the quantities of hops and herbs which were added. Fathers passed on to sons those secrets which made their brews more flavoursome or potent. Richard Guinness, it seems, developed a drink which found favour with his patron, his neighbours and friends for three reasons. By adding a quantity of highly roasted malt to the mash he produced a dark beer that had strength, rich taste and longevity. How

original Guinness's porter* was and what similarities it may or may not
have had to other beers consumed in the area we cannot know. There are
missing links in the evolutionary chain but some time in the early
decades of the Hanoverian century, this *homo erectus* of beers emerged,
which was destined to become the commercially dominant strain of its
entire species.

The first discoveries in the archaeological strata upon which we can
pronounce with authority date from 1752. In that year the Most
Reverend and Right Honourable the Lord Archbishop of Cashel died and
was buried in St John's, the church he had designated as his cathedral
after having had the ancient minster of St Patrick, symbol of the old faith,
dismantled. In his will Price remembered most handsomely the agent
who had served him faithfully for most of his adult life. Richard received
the considerable legacy of £100, probably equivalent to about four times
his annual salary. Now, he wasted no time in marrying again and investing in a local coaching inn, which he and his second wife, Elizabeth
Clare, ran for many years.

The archbishop's posthumous generosity extended to his godson;
Arthur Guinness also received £100 under the old man's will. This fact has
been seized on by those who like to identify simple reasons for the
accumulation of immense riches. Arthur's legacy has become the
'millionaire's dime' upon which a fortune was based. Such stories may be
comforting in that they suggest that we, too, given a lucky break, could
become inordinately wealthy, but they do scant honour to the industry
and entrepreneurial flair upon which most commercial empires are, in
reality, founded. Certainly Arthur's legacy was a boost to his prospects but
he and his brothers had already started on successful careers and
possessed sound business instincts.

All four of them were well-motivated entrepreneurs and they looked to
fast-growing Dublin as the place where real money was to be made. Their
uncle William had become a freeman in 1719 and was by then running
his own business in Dame Street, which must have prospered since his
son Richard was able to take it over on his father's retirement. Of Arthur's
brothers, Benjamin, who lived and died a bachelor, set up in business as
a grocer. Samuel, the youngest, was apprenticed to a goldsmith, learned
to be a skilled goldbeater, married the daughter of a joiner and became
the founder of a dynasty which would include barristers, bankers,
merchants and politicians. Richard, the youngest, went into brewing with

*Strictly speaking, the word 'porter' originated rather later in London when extra-strong stout became
popular with market porters.

Arthur (see below). Shortly before the mid-point of the century one of their sisters, Frances, married into the established Darley clan of builders and brewers, and the links between the two mercantile families were, thereafter, very close. Thus it is clear that well before the days of the great brewery the Guinnesses had begun to make their mark in Dublin society.

That society was clearly stratified, but also open to fresh blood. Colonial capitals are particularly prone to snobbery of the 'Lowells talk only to Cabots and Cabots talk only to God' variety. The lords and ladies, gentlemen and gentlewomen who set the tone in Dublin made much of their fashionable English connections and some of them lived in a style they could not have afforded in London or Bath. They built, dressed and behaved ostentatiously. Dublin, for example, was recognised as the duelling and gambling capital of Europe. Unlike their English counterparts, the majority of them had no sense of responsibility for their tenants whom, by and large, they despised. It followed that this arrogance of the 'top' people displayed itself in maintaining their distance from the Anglo-Irish bourgeoisie. At the same time they were increasingly dependent on the bankers, builders, lawyers, merchants and financiers of that rising middle class.

The mercantile community occupied an uneasy position between their Ascendancy masters and the Catholic majority. They aped their social superiors, but resented the economic restraints those superiors imposed through the Dublin parliament at the behest of Westminster (see below pp.20–23). Religion and culture separated them from the mass of the Irish people but, as a class, they did not feel contempt for the depressed multitude and were, indeed, committed to the economic improvement of Ireland, which would involve advancing the condition of at least some of its people. It was their ongoing campaign to improve their own and, as it seemed to them, the country's interests that imparted a certain flexibility to Dublin's middle class. They recognised and welcomed talent and enterprise. At the same time they constituted a solid edifice supported upon the main pillars of ancient families and buttressed with their own brand of exclusivism. These were the men who, through their trade guilds, elected the oligarchy which ran the city.

There can be little doubt that Arthur's sights were also set upon Dublin, but he was prepared to take a longer-term view of his prospects. Every born entrepreneur is an opportunist, able to recognise a viable commercial proposition and take advantage of it while rivals are still weighing up the pros and cons. Arthur would become a Dublin businessman, but only when the right opening presented itself. Meanwhile he would build his capital base. He was twenty-seven when he came into his inheritance, had moved to Leixlip, four miles down the Liffey towards Dublin, and was learning the brewing trade. With the Archbishop's money he did what most Anglo-Irish men with spare cash did: he bought land. Land was cheap because Catholics were not allowed to purchase it. They were, however, desperate to rent and Arthur would have obtained an attractive return on his investment. By September 1756 he was sufficiently experienced to divert some of his income to securing the lease on a small Leixlip brewery, which he then ran with his brother Richard. It was a modest beginning to a stunningly successful career, marking Arthur Guinness's entry to the fluctuating fellowship of 800 small-time Irish brewers, many of whom survived in business only a few years.

The chance to move to Dublin was not long in coming. In 1759 Arthur grabbed the opportunity of acquiring cheaply the lease of a brewery at St James's Gate. The premises belonged to the Rainsfords, a family prominent in the civic life of Dublin. The business, a modest one by the standards of the city, had been run by the owner or tenants until 1750, but thereafter had fallen into disuse on the failure of the last lessee. The plant needed renovation and improvement, but the premises had two major advantages. In the first place, they were adjacent to the city's water-course. A plentiful supply of soft water was vital to the production of good-quality beer and a cluster of breweries had been established in this quarter of Dublin. With good Liffey water, with better equipment, with a sizeable market on his doorstep and with his own expertise Arthur doubted not that he could turn a handy profit. But the site had another, personal, attraction: it incorporated a commodious house, useful out-buildings, spacious gardens and a summer-house. All this was located, if not in a fashionable part of the city, certainly in a respectable area. At thirty-four years of age the land agent's son from Celbridge had established himself in the capital as a man of property.

Within two years he brought a bride to his substantial town house. Olivia Whitmore was quite a catch. She was an heiress with a personal fortune of £1000 and her family connections were impressive. Her father, a member of the Dublin mercantile élite with a fine house on Essex Street, had died, leaving his daughter in the care of the banker William Lunell. Her mother was a Grattan, a name to be conjured with in political circles and one destined to enjoy a greater celebrity in the person of Olivia's cousin, Henry (see below pp.20–23). Her extended family included parliamentarians and a chief justice, as well as several wealthy merchants. It would certainly not have been difficult to find a suitable match for the girl, so it is significant that those responsible for locating someone sufficiently substantial, capable and caring to be entrusted with young Olivia considered that Arthur Guinness fitted the bill.

It is difficult to form an understanding of most husband–wife relationships in an age when the conventions surrounding matrimony, not to mention the position of women, were far different from those of our own day. Financial and dynastic considerations played a greater part than affection in pre-nuptial negotiations. In the absence of any personal letters we only have the bare facts of a lifelong partnership (Olivia outlived her husband by eleven years) and the rearing of ten children upon which to base any assessment of the inner harmony of the Guinness household. When Arthur brought his courtship to a successful conclusion Olivia Whitmore was nineteen and he not far short of twice her age.

It must have been about this time that Arthur Guinness commissioned a portrait. Now, at last we can put a face to the name. The features that look out at us from the canvas are not those of a tough, energetic, no-nonsense entrepreneur. We see a gentleman, neatly periwigged, discreetly dressed and serene of countenance. There is the suggestion of a smile about the lips and the green eyes. One could fancy that the sitter was a person of taste, culture and human sympathy. He was certainly all of those things. Yet he was also a man of contradictions. His business dealings suggest prudence, but his signature can only be described as flamboyant (see frontispiece). When his interests were threatened and he believed he had right on his side he could be forceful, even violent, as he revealed a few years later when defending his property against city municipal bureaucrats (see below p.20). Arthur was a man of many parts and from his entry to the Dublin commercial and social scene he played a prominent role in the city's life.

'My Trust is in God' – so ran the family motto when, fifty-five years later, the Guinnesses became armigerous. As far as the first Arthur was concerned the boast was not a piece of showy heraldic piety. He attended divine service at St Patrick's Cathedral along with the Dublin smart set and became a generous benefactor to the dean and chapter. Of itself, this signified little in terms of sincerity of belief. When John Wesley attended holy communion in the fashionable church in 1758 he was shocked by the irreverent behaviour of the congregation and apostrophised in his journal, 'Oh, who has the courage to speak plain to these rich and honourable sinners!'.[4] However, Arthur's religion went beyond formalism. He supported several charities, was on the board of Meath hospital (and ultimately its governor) and was a member of the Friendly Brothers of St Patrick, among whose philanthropic aims was the abolition of duelling, an upper-class foible for which he had no sympathy. In the 1780s when, largely due to the energetic proselytising of Robert Raikes, Sunday schools were seen as the answer to illiteracy and unruly behaviour among children of the poorer classes, it was Arthur Guinness who set up the first such institution in Ireland. Add to this that his eldest son felt the call to holy orders and declined to take his place in the brewery, and that two of his daughters married clergymen, and it becomes apparent that Christian faith was an important ingredient in the household over which Arthur presided.

Arthur Guinness was a living advertisement for the Protestant work ethic advocated by Wesley and other religious 'enthusiasts' during the years of the first great evangelical awakening. Evangelicals regarded Ireland as a very specific challenge: they were battling not only against the haughty indifference of the Protestant establishment, but also the obduracy of the Catholic majority, regarded by the gospel-mongers as brainwashed by their priests. When the evangelist George Whitefield contended against the demonic hosts of ignorance and papistry on Dublin's Barrack Square in 1751 his words provoked a hail of stones. He never returned, but Wesley made frequent visits over forty years and lived to see dramatic changes in the religious life of the Irish capital. At two of his meetings on Barrack Square in the summer of 1765 crowds listened respectfully and many responded. By 1789 the Methodist Society, of whose survival he had often despaired, had a membership of over a thousand, which made it second only to London in size. Several of these Christian enthusiasts had by then separated from the Anglican church and worshipped in elegant new chapel buildings provided, as the preacher ironically noted, 'for those rich and honourable sinners who will not deign to receive any message from God but in a genteel way'.[5]

The meeting house of which Wesley wrote was Bethesda Chapel, built by William Smyth with money inherited by his wife, who came from a family of leading goldsmiths. The Smyths were a respectable Church of Ireland family – William's uncle was Archbishop of Dublin – but William and his ordained brother Edward came under evangelical influences and caused a sensation by travelling, via Methodism, to out-and-out non-conformity. Bethesda Chapel became *the* great centre of Irish evangelicism for several decades and the Reverend Edward Smyth accompanied Wesley on several of his campaigns. William regarded his ministry as offering hospitality to the servants of the Gospel and particularly as seeking the conversion of Ireland's élite. He was the means of introducing Wesley to several prominent Dubliners. Among the latter

Arthur Guinness must have featured, for Mrs Smyth was his wife's cousin. It is, therefore, no wild flight of fancy to imagine the brewer among the elegant congregation to which Wesley preached, in 1787, with somewhat muted enthusiasm: 'Mr Smyth read prayers, and gave out the hymns, which were sung by fifteen or twenty fine singers; the rest of the congregation listening with much attention and as much devotion as they would have done to an opera. But is this Christian worship? Or ought it ever to be suffered in a Christian church?'[6] The Smyths were quite open in their desire to win worshippers away from the moribund established church. Wesley himself deplored separation and instructed his followers to present themselves at St Patrick's for communion once a month. Most of them did so and the impact of several hundred earnest souls on the normal, polite cathedral congregation was profound.

Respectability and affective religion seldom sit easily together. Arthur Guinness was certainly jealous of his social status and his increasing prominence in Dublin society. Yet it would have been surprising if his family had been totally immune to this strain of personal piety introduced into that society and, indeed, they were not. Arthur's eagerly awaited eldest son (their first child was a daughter, named Elizabeth after her step-grandmother) was born in the year of Wesley's triumphant 1765 tour of Ireland and was christened Hosea, 'Jehovah has saved'. Whether the name indicated a general allegiance to evangelical biblicism or was an acknowledgement of the baby's survival of a difficult birth is not recorded, but it is significant that the name 'Arthur' given subsequently to every elder son in the senior line of the family was, on this occasion, withheld until the birth of the brewer's second boy three years later. Hosea grew up with a sense of his dedication to God, was educated as a scholar rather than a businessman and proceeded to take holy orders. All these snippets of information contribute to an image of the head of the clan Guinness as a respected and respectable Dubliner of more than conventional piety.

Arthur's kindred connections via Olivia included not only the Smyths, who had provided the Irish church with several bishops and archbishops, and who could trace their ancestry back to an Elizabethan lord mayor, but also the Darleys, responsible for erecting many of the city's finest buildings, the La Touches, whose banking dynasty was founded by an officer in one of William of Orange's Huguenot regiments, and the Grattans and Marlays who had been active in Anglo-Irish politics and administration for over a century. These were the people at whose salons and dinner-tables the Guinnesses were entertained.

Arthur could not have held his own in such company without money.

His wife's capital helped and it may be that some of it went towards the purchase of Beaumont, a fine, recently built country house overlooking Dublin Bay. However, it was remarkable business success which financed his gentleman's life-style. The equipping of two homes with fine furniture, pictures, silver and porcelain in order to entertain in a suitable fashion and the maintaining of a high social profile could not have been achieved without a substantial and growing income. Arthur turned the St James's Gate brewery into one of the city's leading manufactories of beer and ale. He was an active and respected member of the Dublin Corporation of Brewers, serving as warden in 1763, master in 1767 and representing the guild for several years on the Common Council of the city. However, he was far from being at the very top of the Irish brewing fraternity. After ten years Guinness's was not even half-way up the league table of Dublin's forty breweries. Even in 1790, when he had recently been appointed official purveyor of beers and ales to Dublin Castle, Arthur was not the most eminent member of the trade; that accolade was given to James Farrell, who boasted extensive business premises in Black Pitts and a fine town mansion in Merrion Square East. But what Arthur's enterprise lacked in output its owner more than made up in influence. In 1773 the House of Commons sought the advice of three leading experts when they were conducting an inquiry into Irish brewing. These informants were George Thwaites, master of the guild, 'Mr Andrew, a considerable brewer' and Arthur Guinness, 'another considerable brewer'.

Arthur Guinness was always described as a brewer and as such he considered himself, but he was far too shrewd a financial manager to base his fortune on the manufacture of alcoholic beverages alone. He steadily increased his holdings in a buoyant property market and derived a significant part of his income from rents. In 1780 he went into partnership with his brother Samuel to found the Hibernian Insurance Company, the first such enterprise in Dublin, and in 1782 he built a flour mill (the Hibernian) at Kilmainham, which was then just outside the western boundary of the city. Eventually the sale of flour accounted for a quarter of Arthur's total profits.

However, it was beer upon which his financial vessel floated. Beer was everyone's friend. It was even popular with the guardians of public morality. Working-class alcoholism was a problem on both sides of the Irish Sea. Dublin, no less than London, had its equivalent of Gin Lane. Respectable citizens steered clear of the 'working manufacturers, the labouring poor and beggars' who thronged 'the low taverns and bagnios, eating houses and whiskey shops of the overcrowded area between Dame Street and the waterfront'.[7] For the poor, the depressed and the hopeless the transport to euphoria and oblivion was whiskey and the fare was cheap, especially for potheen, the product of illicit home stills. Some evangelicals called for total abstinence. In fact, the British temperance movement, which would gather momentum in the next century, had its beginnings in 1770s Dublin. More pragmatic liberal reformers argued from the premiss that it was impossible to change ingrained habits. Just as modern political correctness promotes contraceptive advice for the young, rather than the urging of self-restraint, so perceived wisdom two hundred years ago advised and encouraged the diverting of drinkers from spirits to beer. Arthur Guinness and his colleagues in the Corporation of Brewers could thus present themselves as major contributors to social well-being and claim that increased output leading to lower prices was an expression of civic responsibility.

Arthur was by no means so profit-driven as to favour excessive consumption. Loyal son of the Anglican establishment though he was, he yet had a Nonconformist conscience in such matters. Once, believing that the city fathers should set an example, he tried to put a stop to the aged custom of feasting the election of a new alderman. Such occasions invariably involved gluttony and carousing. Guinness urged the Dublin Council to abandon them and, instead, to make commensurate donations to the Blue Coat Hospital. The proposal was rejected.

Guinness's customers were located almost exclusively in Dublin. The city provided a healthy, expanding market for a product popular with most sections of the community, from the sailors and dock workers who frequented the harbour pubs, the garrison soldiers, students at the university, the members of parliament in whose house tables were permanently laid out with victuals while the assembly was in session, the tradespeople of the buzzing commercial apiary around Smithfield, to the denizens of the elegant squares and crescents on both sides of the river from Sackville Street to College Green, linked, after 1796, by Carlisle Bridge. If city brewers were slow to exploit Dublin's hinterland it was partly because rural drinkers were loyal to their local suppliers, but also because transport facilities for the conveyance of bulk cargoes scarcely existed. The Grand Canal, begun in 1772 carving a watery highway from Dublin to the River Shannon and thus the west coast, had, by 1800, still not reached its destination and the Royal Canal, headed towards Roscommon and the north-west, had come to a virtual halt with its backers facing bankruptcy.

Frustrations attended the endeavours of Ireland's businessmen. Across the sea industrial revolution was revitalising commercial life. In Ireland the potential for commercial expansion existed, but as long as the

Westminster government loaded manufacturers and entrepreneurs with legal and fiscal chains they could not display their mercantile athleticism. The legitimate development of business was, inevitably, caught up with politics. In the last troubled quarter of the century Anglo-Irish politics meant, not just demonstration against or accommodation with the government in London, but holding to a responsible course, while being buffeted by the winds of religious dogma, republicanism, radicalism, reaction, unenlightened self-interest and revolution. In the tumultuous years spanning the eighteenth and nineteenth centuries, the Guinnesses were still primarily concerned with commercial survival and social standing in Dublin, but theirs was a name increasingly heard in the clubs and drawing-rooms of the nation's capital.

2

ARTHURIAN LEGENDS

When Arthur Guinness married Olivia Whitmore his in-laws presented him with a silver loving cup on which were engraved the arms of bride and groom. There was nothing unusual about that – except that Arthur had no right to the heraldic devices he claimed. They were those of the ennobled Magennises of Co. Down and the Dublin brewer possessed no proof of his descent from this ancient family. Legends and theories persisted among and around later Guinnesses, but no incontrovertible evidence was ever advanced to establish an exalted Irish lineage. Indeed, within the family there persisted another story linking the brewers with a Cornish progenitor, one of Cromwell's invading soldiery. At the end of the nineteenth century Henry Seymour Guinness commissioned extensive genealogical research, none of which succeeded in illuminating the family's path farther back than Richard of Celbridge.[1]

While the Guinness lineage is of little more than academic interest, Arthur's heraldic borrowings do have an important bearing upon his feelings and thoughts about his Irish identity within the complexities of late-eighteenth-century politics. The claim to distinguished ancestry was about more than family ambition and status; it concerned the nature of the Ireland that was emerging in the second half of the eighteenth century. The clan Arthur chose to associate himself with was not only Catholic, it was officially regarded among Dublin's socio-political élite as traitorous. When James I ennobled the head of the clan as Viscount of Iveagh in 1623 he was rewarding a loyal Ulsterman, and one to whom he looked to ensure the eradication of 'papistry', and obedience to the crown throughout his estates. The Magennises certainly remained true to the

Stuarts or, to state the case more accurately, they were among those land-owners of the Pale who, in the bitter conflicts of the mid-seventeenth century, covered their bid for greater independence from Westminster with the cloak of adherence to the king's cause. They were tainted with involvement in the great rebellion of 1641 and, though they survived Commonwealth and Protectorate, it was as a family with Catholic and nationalist sympathies, and one intermarried with the notorious O'Neils. Inevitably they supported James II against Protestant William and, in doing so, they brought about the collapse of their position in Ireland. The fifth viscount followed the pretender into exile and was stripped of his peerage. By the time Arthur Guinness was using the devices of 'lion rampant or' coupled with the bloody hand of Ulster 'on a chief ermine' the senior members of the Magennis clan were living in France and Spain, never to return.*

The Guinnesses were neither the first nor the last *arriviste* family to apply the gilding of spurious ancient lineage to the base metal of com-mercial success, but in the unique social and political atmosphere of eighteenth-century Dublin such activity had a specific significance. With the exception of a handful of families such as the Kavanaghs, O'Briens and Plunketts, who could trace their origins back beyond 1066, the top families were all descended from land grabbers, whether Norman, Elizabethan or Cromwellian. They were, therefore, intent on maintaining their superiority, not only over the majority population, but also over those they perceived as being further down the social evolutionary chain.

'They will follow me wherever I go' – so the Earl of Kildare responded when, in the middle of the century, he was chided for commissioning his new residence, Leinster House, to be built on the 'wrong' side of the Liffey. He was, of course, right. The presence of his palatial complex, which now houses the National Museum and the National Library as well as the two chambers of the Dáil, could not be ignored by the Ascendancy's leaders. Within a decade architects and builders were transforming the adjacent area into a gracious urban Arcady of elegant squares, commodious houses, private gardens and shaded walks. As Dublin steadily divested itself of its frontier-town image and donned the architectural finery which enabled it to parade without embarrassment among the fashion centres of Europe, its leading citizens spent more time in its theatres, clubs and ballrooms. By the 1770s Dublin had its own 'season'. Irish peers and squirearchs were increasingly inclined to come up from their country estates and establish

*Other Magennises did remain in Co. Down. A certain John Magennis was a leader of Catholic dissidents there in 1798.

a permanent base in the capital. Absentee landlords devoted a few weeks a year to the Dublin scene and maintained prestigious establishments there. The Butlers, the Fitzgibbons, the Beresfords and all who belonged to the ruling club had to maintain a very visible presence in the stylish neighbourhood of Merrion Square, Baggot Street and Fitzwilliam Square.

The assertion of superiority had to do with power as well as personal prestige. Every Ascendancy grandee would have endorsed the dictum of the greatest contemporary Irishman: 'People will not look forward to posterity who never look backward to their ancestors'.[2] Burke, writing here about the French Revolution, was no defender of a sterile *status quo* (certainly not as far as Ireland was concerned – see below p.23), but he accepted, as did most thinking men, the necessity of political hierarchies headed by those born and reared to rule. In a colonial situation such as Ireland that meant government by officials sent from London aided by a parliament representing, for the most part, families with a stake in the country and experience stretching back over several generations.

The aspirations of Dublin's middle class encouraged its members to emulate the attitudes of their betters, while rejecting the rigidities of policy which frameworked their superiority and the dominance of the English interest. They lusted after the monogrammed carriages and Continental fashions of the aristocracy. When leasing houses they edged ever closer to Dublin's fashionable districts. And they laid stress on their own ancestry, demonstrating that their families had just as long an association with Ireland as at least some of the nobility and gentry. Impressive lineage was a very definite advantage to an entrepreneur who aspired to higher things – even if that lineage was forged.

What motivated Arthur Guinness to associate himself specifically with the Magennises is not clear. It may have been nothing more profound than his familiarity with the arms of the noble family displayed on memorials in his parish church of St Catherine, Dublin, where two members of the ancient family were buried. These inscriptions would still have been very crisp in the years when Arthur first became familiar with the city, for the third and fourth Viscounts of Iveagh had died only a few years before the Glorious Rebellion. The fourth viscount bore the name Arthur and it may not be fanciful to imagine an ambitious young member of the mercantile class gazing upon his carved monument in St Catherine's, wrestling with his conscience and reflecting that the rearrangement of a few letters would be all that would be necessary to add dignity to a family newly arrived in Dublin. Perhaps it was not Arthur at all but one of his brothers who first noticed the similarity of names and decided that an implied or stated connection would be good for the prestige and trade of a Dublin newcomer.

By grafting themselves on to the stock of an older clan the Guinnesses were also affirming their Irishness. Economic and political pressures applied from London caused sentiment among the Protestant mercantile and landed classes to cohere. The substantial enfranchised minority thought of themselves, very straightforwardly, as *the* Irish people. The Catholic population were of no account and English interests were not infrequently alien. Like the colonists of New England or, paradoxically, the aristos of pre-revolutionary France, Ireland's meritocrats claimed to be the representatives of enterprise and culture, the men who held in their hands the destiny of Ireland. They were, spiritually, the heirs of the leaders of the past. Given that premise, there was a certain logic about assuming an ancient Irish name.

The years of peace and, for the upper orders, prosperity gave rise to Hibernianism, an enlightened interest in and desire to advance all things Irish. Arthur Guinness was an early member of the Dublin Society (the Royal Dublin Society after 1820) which began as an organisation dedicated to the improvement of home agriculture and industry but which steadily expanded its remit. In 1772 it set up a committee 'to inquire into the ancient state of the literature and other antiquities of Ireland' and this blazed the trail for the Royal Irish Academy, founded in 1785. Arthur was prominent among the men of public goodwill and enquiring mind who encouraged Gaelic poetry and music, set up the Dublin botanical gardens, awarded prizes for quality crops and farming stock, established an architectural school, organised concerts, corresponded with foreign innovators on matters from soil analysis and plant hybridisation to textile machinery, and met to discuss papers on subjects as diverse as the brewing of porter and the desirability of an Irish poor law. As one of Guinness's colleagues wrote in verses praising the Dublin Society,

> Soon shall Hibernia see her broken state,
> Repair'd by Arts and Industry, grow great.[3]

It is no coincidence that two of Arthur's commercial enterprises bore the name 'Hibernian'.

One of the pioneering antiquarians of the period declared that it was his aim 'to disarm persecution' by making known the literature and exploits of the Gaelic past and forging links of understanding between rulers and ruled.[4] Liberal-minded Dubliners, among whom Arthur Guinness counted himself, laboured in various ways to bridge the religious canyon which cleft Irish life. When the brewer first established himself in Dublin, Catholics were kept within political and economic bounds by the hounds of the penal laws. Only a minority of the

Protestant community would have agreed with Wesley, who recorded in his journal in August 1747 on the stubborn Catholicism of the Irish majority, 'Nor is it any wonder that those who are born Papists generally live and die such, when the Protestants can find no better ways to convert them than Penal Laws and Acts of Parliament'.[5]

Over the next half-century, until the outbreak of rebellion in 1798, Catholic disabilities were, by degrees, relaxed. As the religious wars of a previous epoch faded to a distant memory most of the restrictions seemed archaic. International papalism was no longer a political threat. With the exception of a few hotheads, Irish Catholics lived at peace with their lords and masters. Protestant landowners and businessmen found more advantage in treating their neighbours with toleration than in enforcing the letter of the law. Further than that, it was often argued in such forums as the Dublin Society that necessary commercial and agricultural develop-ment was being undermined by laws which forced talented entrepreneurs to seek their fortunes overseas and gave tenants no incentives to improve their farming methods. Prejudice and the entrenchment of privilege were still formidable obstacles to reform, but when Catholic opinion became organised and respectfully vociferous, and when the British government considered it prudent to prevent revolutionary ideas from America and France taking root in Irish soil the circumstances existed for reform. By 1782 several of the most irksome penal law provisions had been repealed. Compromise never satisfies. Catholic leaders continued to press for complete emancipation, taking advantage of England's increasing embroilment with France and the demands of moderate radicals for greater independence from Westminster (see below p.224). In 1793, after long and heated debates in the London and Dublin legislatures, Catholics were admitted to public service, membership of urban corporations and leading professions, the franchise and proprietorial freehold – in theory at least.

It was in the summer of this latter year that Arthur Guinness declared in public his views on the treatment of the majority population. What-ever the law stated, its implementation could still be hampered by the established political and commercial élites. Thus, when a prominent and popular Catholic businessman, Valentine O'Connor, applied for the freedom of the city in 1793, his appeal was rejected by sixty-six votes to twenty-nine. Following the decision someone put about the rumour – presumably to irritate or embarrass Arthur Guinness – that he had been among the blackballers. Arthur felt sufficiently strongly on the matter to publish a disclaimer. It was, he declared, his unvarying policy to uphold the rights of the religious minority to political equality. He knew about the miseries created by confessional divisions. Some of his uncle William's progeny had married outside the Protestant faith and converted to Catholicism, and this had set up family tensions.

Arthur was not afraid of being in an unpopular minority. By his middle years he was no longer too concerned about being accepted to keep silence on matters of principle. Or self-interest. In 1773 Arthur Guinness and two of his industrial neighbours had been charged by the city corporation with diverting Liffey water from the common watercourse for their own manufacturing processes. The 'culprits' claimed traditional usage based on a partisan reading of old leases. Courteous exchanges gradually gave way to defiant words, neither side being prepared to yield. In the summer of 1775 things turned nasty. Workmen sent to fill in Guinness's conduit were confronted by the proprietor himself, wielding a pick handle. Arthur and the sheriff, backed by their respective supporters, faced each other across the ditch, shouting abuse. Guinness made it clear in no uncertain terms that if the official had the watercourse filled in his men would dig it again. The standoff ended when the sheriff retreated with as much dignity as he could muster. It was now left to the lawyers to argue the rights and wrongs of the case with their customary lack of expedition. While they were doing so Arthur reinforced his position and aggravated the situation by building a wall to keep interfering council officials off 'his' property. Not until 1785 was the dispute finally resolved by arbitration, the brewery agreeing to lease from the city the ground through which the water flowed.

In 1783 Olivia Guinness gave birth to her last child, a son, christened John Grattan. The name and the date are highly significant, for, in that summer her cousin Henry Grattan was the country's leading politician and the hero of the hour in Irish mercantile and progressive circles. Only weeks before – so great was the esteem in which this thirty-six-year-old politician was held – a grateful Dublin parliament had granted him an estate of £50,000 for his services to the nation. Entering the assembly in 1775, Grattan had quickly made his mark as a passionate orator and an advocate of the leading economic interest groups. A contemporary described him as 'almost unrivalled in crushing invective, in delineations of character, and in brief, keen arguments'.[6] He fought tenaciously for the lifting of trade restrictions and financial imposts that disadvantaged Irish producers and tradesmen. At last the Protestant middle class had a golden-voiced champion who could sway parliament, unite a significant part of the population and force the Ascendancy leaders to take note. In the ensuing years his majesty's government 'graciously responded' to the 'humble requests' of his 'loyal Irish subjects'. In truth they had little alternative. Mishandling of the American colonies, the criticism this provoked and the contagion of political radicalism spreading from France inclined Westminster to self-interested conciliation.

However, what one administration gave another could take away. Grattan and his supporters knew full well that a change in the political climate which brought the sun out over London could once more bring dingy clouds to Irish skies. What was needed to ensure permanent concessions was a Declaration of Rights, which would give the Dublin parliament legislative freedom and the Irish judiciary independence from London. In May 1782 Grattan delivered his most famous speech to the Dublin House of Commons. He affirmed both Ireland's nationhood and its indissoluble links with England: 'This nation is connected with England not only by allegiance to the crown but by liberty – the crown is one great point of unity but Magna Carta is greater – we could get a king anywhere but England is the only country from which we could get a constitution'.[7] The house rose to him. The motion to end the legislative and judicial superiority of England was unanimously carried. A year later Ireland became a distinct political entity under the crown.

'Liberty' means different things to different people. To educated Catholics it was a slogan conveying their desire for a voice in the shaping of their destiny. Dublin's businessmen marched beneath the freedom banner towards the desired goal of unencumbered trade and higher profits. During the years of political ebb and flow Ireland's mercantile élite were campaigning loudly for the lifting of trade restrictions and tariff barriers between Ireland and England. In this, as in constitutional issues, Grattan was their champion. Representing the brewers' lobby throughout the nineties, he urged a variety of fiscal reforms: excise duties should be lightened; the protection of English beer imports should cease; restrictions on the import of foreign hops should be swept away and there should be harsher levies on the distilleries to inhibit the competition of cheap spirits. His arguments, aided by his considerable oratory, represented the brewers almost as social crusaders: Westminster was driving the Irish poor into the merciless clutches of a horned and hoofed John Barleycorn from which fate the manufacturers of good honest porter were struggling to deliver them. Not surprisingly, this was a version of events with which Arthur Guinness concurred. Summoned to advise the Dublin parliament in February 1792, he complained that, thanks to consumption of spirits and English beer and also to excessive duties, the brewing industry was in a worse state than it had been when he first entered the trade. Setting to one side the rhetoric and posturing, what we see is the familiar argument of free enterprise versus state control. The

English government was employing a complex of laws and imposts to preserve home industry and regulate social behaviour. The brewers saw their profits as inextricably bound up with the economic health of the country. And it was the brewers who, after two decades of campaigning, carried the day. In 1795 Pitt's hard-pressed government was obliged to acquiesce in the rescinding of beer duties and the easing of commerce across the Irish Sea.[8]

These were exciting days for progressive and wealthy Dublin families. They prospered as trade restrictions were lifted and the westward waterways opened up new markets. The trappings of wealth and increased political clout enhanced their social status. They were now full partners in the Ascendancy, but partners with a distinct Irish identity. Thus, when Arthur's eldest boy Hosea completed his studies at Winchester his father did not send him to New College, Oxford, with many of his contemporaries. Rather, he brought him back to Trinity, Dublin, to complete his training as a scholar and a gentleman. Hibernisation was firmly in fashion, so noble ancestry was a more desirable appendage than ever to the accoutrements of a master brewer. The Guinnesses were far from being the only ones to create or rediscover their roots. *Nouveau riche* and *ancien pauvre* alike eagerly exploited their muniments cupboards. In the more relaxed 1780s several dispossessed ancient families, including some Catholic exiles, petitioned for the recognition or restoration of their ancient titles, even though the lands which had supported those dignities had long since been redistributed.

Most of these aspirants were simply clamouring for a place in the sun and, by doing so, were indicating that they had come to terms with the *status quo*. They wanted to be a part of the new Ireland. However, there were those whose motivation was different. In January 1786 Roderick O'Connor, self-styled King of Connaught, led over 400 men in raids on estates in County Roscommon to reclaim properties allegedly stolen from his family in centuries past. This was just one of many lawless acts perpetrated by Catholics who espoused a nationalism very different from that of Arthur Guinness and his friends. In fact, there was a clutch of rival nationalisms competing for supremacy. They were about to come into bitter conflict.

In April 1789 the aged John Wesley preached at Bethesda Chapel for the last time. It is more likely than not that some of the Smyths' Guinness relatives would have been among those 'delicate hearers, who could not bear sound doctrine if it were not set off with ... petty trifles'.[9] who crowded the little building, conscious that this was probably their final opportunity to hear the century's greatest proclaimer of Christian truth.

Within days, other more clamorous voices were making themselves heard from afar. On 6 May the Estates General was convened in Paris. The Dublin press eagerly reported the doings and sayings of the revolutionaries. Publishers as enthusiastically issued translations of inflammatory pamphlets and of the more solidly reasoned works of Rousseau, Voltaire and Montesquieu. Before the year's end the Theatre Royal had commissioned and produced a revolutionary play, *Gallic freedom or the destruction of the Bastille*. Everyone was enthralled by the news of old tyrannies and injustices overthrown. Some feared the collapse of civilised society. For others, 'bliss was it in that dawn to be alive'. Catholic agitators clamoured for their statutory freedoms to be fully implemented and for remaining discriminatory restrictions to be abolished. But there were those for whom the eradication of grievances was not enough. Republicanism was in the air. Cautious reform of the type favoured by Arthur Guinness and Henry Grattan was being swiftly overtaken by the thundering hooves of revolution. In the autumn of 1791 the Society of United Irishmen came into being. What was ominous about it, as its name suggested, was that it merged the nationalist aspirations of Catholics and radical Protestants.

The chronicle of Ireland is punctuated with tragic full stops; moments when slow progress towards political harmony and constitutional development was suddenly halted by suspicion, prejudice and acts of violence. Within a few months everything that had been achieved since the Battle of the Boyne was overthrown. The United Irishmen demanded full civil rights for all citizens, including the franchise and eligibility for election to parliament. The horrifying prospect of majority rule reawakened Protestant paranoia. The executive in Dublin Castle and their supporters in parliament clung determinedly to cultural apartheid.

A Protestant King, to whom only being Protestant we owe allegiance; a Protestant house of peers composed of Protestant Lords Spiritual, in Protestant succession, of Protestant Lords Temporal, with Protestant inheritance, and a Protestant House of Commons elected and deputed by Protestant constituents: in short a Protestant legislature, a Protestant judicial [sic] and a Protestant executive in all and each of their varieties, degrees and gradations.[14]

So one member of the Irish Commons described his vision for the country. Now, for the first time, the cry 'Protestant Ascendancy' was taken up as a political slogan.

Although Arthur Guinness's colleagues on the Dublin council endorsed this dogma in the summer of 1792, the wisdom of age convinced the brewer that this over-reaction was potentially ruinous. His independence of spirit refused to allow him to go along with the prejudices of the élite. But he was powerless to prevent the opening up of old wounds and the inflicting of new ones. In 1793 England went to war with revolutionary France and the United Irishmen began plotting with sympathisers across the Channel. The moderate minority in parliament struggled against overwhelming odds to defuse the situation by measures of constitutional reform. At this point Grattan, disgusted with the behaviour of the government and unable to condone the actions of the United Irishmen, resigned his Commons seat. The reaction of his opponents was to denounce him as a secret supporter of insurrection and to strip him of his honours. Rabid sectarians continued to denounce the architect of Ireland's legislative independence and, in 1800, Grattan was obliged to fight a duel in defence of his honour.

Arthur felt similarly isolated. Even within his family his was a minority voice. Hosea was now a curate at St Werbergh's, the church of the Dublin establishment, and preaching politically correct sermons. Three of his brothers eagerly took up arms in defence of the Protestant Ascendancy. One response to the increasing number of acts of violence had been the raising of volunteer forces which were little more than vigilante bands and, inevitably, did nothing but add to the mounting chaos. These unofficial posses of Protestant bully boys were disbanded by order of Dublin Castle. However, in the autumn of 1796 the government, faced with an internal situation rapidly getting out of hand and the threat of French invasion, authorised the formation of yeomanry units which were little more than the volunteers under a new name. William and Edward Guinness joined up immediately. Their brothers, Arthur and Benjamin, were now involved in the running of the family business and, much to the chagrin of the younger, could not be spared. Even fifteen-year-old John Grattan clamoured for action and he was actually wounded while carrying dispatches.

The Guinness boys found themselves in a vengeful, brutish and ill-disciplined force determined to show the papists who was boss. When open insurrection broke out in early 1779 the militia turned it into a civil and, to a large extent, a religious war. Complaints against the high-handed actions, burnings, lootings and beatings inflicted by government troops were more clamorous than those against marauding rebels. The Viceroy, Charles, Earl Cornwallis, a seasoned general who had fought in America and India, complained that for the men under his command, 'murder appears to be the favourite pastime'. Militarily the tactics worked, but the ruling élite paid a high price for their victory. The administration in London, anxious to maintain a stable peace in Ireland and already moving in the direction of Catholic emancipation at home, pressed for legislative union. The cosy coterie of Protestant parliamentarians and voters were bribed, cajoled and frightened into relinquishing their power. In the summer of 1800, despite Grattan's persistent and eloquent resistance, the Dublin assembly was disbanded after only seventeen years of independence.

Political ambition would, in future, have to be channelled via Westminster. Henry Grattan was persuaded to take his seat there as a member for Dublin and he continued to fight for the rights of his Catholic countrymen to the end of his days. At the age of seventy-three, although a sick man, the great patriot set out for London once again, remarking that he was making 'my last effort for the liberty of my country'. Within weeks he was dead, his mortal remains, somewhat ironically, receiving honourable burial in Westminster Abbey. The fact that Grattan could be claimed by two nations which enjoyed a love-hate relationship points up the dilemma that Ireland's political and commercial leaders would experience throughout the new century. Closer union brought enhanced trade opportunities and greater potential profit, but it failed to resolve the deep-seated issues between the two countries. For families like the Guinnesses the challenge to define their 'Irishness' would remain.

3

BANKING, BEER AND BIBLES

A rthur Guinness died in the first cold days of 1803 and, in accordance with his instructions, was laid to rest in the churchyard at Oughterard where his parents were buried. It was his last homage to his ancestry and the last family connection with their humble origins in rural Kildare. Arthur's children and grandchildren bought country estates and became major Irish landowners, but their lives would be centred on Dublin, London and countries far afield where nineteenth-century British enterprise was establishing that progressive, Protestant culture for which Arthur Guinness, Henry Grattan, Edward Smyth and their Ascendancy friends had long contended. David Livingstone, in the second Victorian decade, defined his work in Africa as opening 'a path for commerce and Christianity'. It has long been argued how far these two were compatible, but there can be little doubt that those who sailed and marched under the Union Jack to distant markets and mission fields were convinced of the superiority of British culture and were determined to transplant it. Among their number were members of the Guinness family. In 1803 they were God-fearing Dublin merchants, no less and very little more. Yet to say that is to imply that they were missionaries – religious and commercial. Just as they believed in the quality of their merchandise and sought to enlighten a wider world with the gospel of Irish porter, so they were firm in their Protestant convictions, supporting the crusade against 'papistical error' and later carrying the Good News into the dark abodes of heathendom, at home and abroad.

Inevitably, that assessment does not hold good for every member of what became an extremely large tribe. It is still less true if we include Guinness daughters and the families into which they married. The abilities to create wealth and to use it wisely and productively are not genetically transmitted. The Guinnesses had their share of wastrels, incompetents and nonentities, who also inherited the family's wealth, system of values and a name which, during the nineteenth century spread from local to international celebrity. This heritage opened doors of opportunity in the fields of commerce, politics and philanthropy, but for those who were not equal to the expectations that went with the name it became a burden – for some a crushing one.

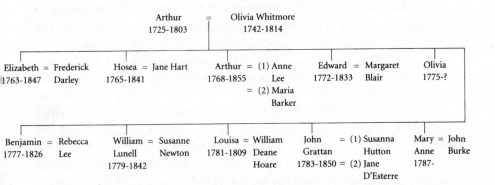

The patriarch's immediate family provides evidence of all these factors. Arthur was survived by nine children, and did his best to provide for all of them and see them well settled before his death. Of the girls Olivia had died young. The eldest, Elizabeth, was very respectably married. Her husband was the builder and quarry master Frederick Darley, to whom she was related by marriage before they came together. In 1809 she had the pleasure of becoming Dublin's first lady when Frederick was elected Lord Mayor. Darley's businesses were flourishing and his fortune grew even faster in the boom years that ushered in the new century when the needs of war boosted demand for a range of goods and services. But the inflated property prices could not last and when the inevitable trade downturn arrived Darley was caught with all his own resources and borrowed capital tied up in unsaleable buildings and materials for which there was no call. He was forced to throw himself upon the mercy of his brewing in-laws. The Guinnesses rescued him and took his son into the St James's Gate ale business.

Two more of Arthur's daughters, Louisa and Mary Anne, were bequeathed handsome jointures of £2000 each, which made them very attractive as potential brides. Both married into the ecclesiastical establishment. Louisa's husband, William Deane Hoare, a member of a prominent banking family, was Vicar-General of Limerick. As such he was the chief administrator of the diocese and the bishop's right-hand layman. He was ultimately responsible for the collection of tithes and other revenues, and for prosecuting on behalf of the established church in the civil and ecclesiastical courts. Thus he represented to the Catholic majority in the diocese the unacceptable face of Protestantism. Louisa did not long enjoy her exalted position within rural society. She died at the age of twenty-eight in the same year that her elder sister became Dublin's Mayoress.

Mary Anne married a younger son of the baronetical Burke family of Galway. John Burke was a clergyman, and he and his wife enjoyed the status of leaders of local society. However, as is not uncommon in vicarage families, their sons John and Arthur turned out badly and, though they were given their chance in the brewery, both succumbed to drink and poor company.

Arthur's first two sons represented between them their father's religious sensibilities. Hosea, who had become, in 1811, rector of St Werburgh's, a centre of that fashionable Anglicanism of which Wesley had despaired, played no part in the family businesses, yet was very conscious of his position as the senior member of the clan. He inherited the estate at Beaumont and lived there for some years in befitting style, before selling it to his brother Arthur. It was Hosea who sought to establish, legally, the Magennis link and his right to bear heraldic arms. This move should be seen in the light of the social consequences of the Act of Union. Bribery was a major weapon in the armoury of a British government determined to force constitutional change on the reluctant majority of Ireland's legislators. Ministers of the crown shamelessly lavished peerages, titles, ecclesiastical preferment, land grants and cash upon their friends and seduced their enemies with promises of similar rewards. Such was the volume of British generosity that in the spring of 1800, before the Act of Union came into effect, it was necessary to establish a college of heralds in Dublin to deal with the grants to and claims of upwardly mobile members of the Ascendancy. Hosea opposed the union and he can have had little but contempt for those who sold their principles. However, as time passed, the snobbery and arrogance of those who flaunted their newly acquired armigerous honours on banners, plate and carriage panels must have become intolerable to those with ancient claims to such dignities. Hosea undoubtedly believed that he was a cut above such upstarts and had the ancestry to prove it. In 1814 he applied to Viscount Mahon, Ulster King of Arms, for confirmation of his right to bear Magennis arms in virtue of his grandfather's descent. His application was dealt with by the herald's deputy, Sir William Betham, a young scholar who found himself in an embarrassing position. He could discover no proof of the Guinnesses' armigerous standing and so could give no permission for the use of Magennis arms. On the other hand, to refuse the claim would cause Hosea and his family enormous embarrassment. They and their associates were far too important to offend. Betham's solution was to make a new grant of arms, technically different from those of the Magennises but, to the untrained eye, indistinguishable.

We might question why a clergyman, whose concerns should be primarily with the kingdom of heaven should bother himself with securing recognition of his position within those of this world. In fact, Hosea's desire to fasten the Guinnesses into the framework of Irish hierarchy with secure heraldic rivets evidences an attitude prevalent among 'comfortable' establishment clergy, especially during the upheaval years 1789–1815. Their position in society obliged them to believe that existing structures reflected the divine order and any challenge to the one inevitably involved a weakening of the other. '... Of this we may all be well assured,' wrote the contemporary Bishop of Llandaff, 'that when religion shall have lost its hold on men's consciences, government will lose its authority over their persons, and a state of barbarous anarchy will ensue'.[1] Hosea was a student during the tumultuous years of the French Revolution and eagerly debated with friends and fellow countrymen the ferment of ideas that were causes and effects of the conflict and which gave rise to such jangling reverberations in Ireland. Later, as a clergyman of the established church whose entire ministry was devoted to the spiritual needs of Dublin's élite, he could only abhor the growth of nationalist extremism which went hand in glove with demands for the disestablishment of the Irish church. A clear-sighted member of the Dublin Castle executive writing in 1792 about Catholic emancipation had stated, 'A Catholic government could maintain itself without the aid of England and must inevitably produce a separation of the executive which would speedily be followed by a separation between the two countries'.[2] Whatever sympathy Hosea might feel for the majority population was tempered by both theological and political considerations: the papists were wrong and, given power, would force the Anglican church into becoming a self-financing sect.

As rector of St Werburgh's for thirty years Hosea was comfortably provided for, although this did not prevent him occasionally applying to the family business for subsidies. As a religious leader and an intellectual (he obtained a doctorate from Trinity College and who but a classical scholar would encumber his youngest child with the name 'Vicesimus'?)

he held aloof from the brewery, but believed that he and other family members had a legitimate claim on its profits when times were hard. This became a cause of some friction between Hosea and his brother Arthur, who had the task of steering the family business through the difficult years of the war and its aftermath. 'My dear Hosea,' Arthur began a letter in May 1821, 'I feel myself placed in a painful and delicate situation when called upon to address my Elder Brother, and a Brother who I so sincerely love and respect upon the subject of his pecuniary concerns but my situation … as the Family Banker forces me to speak plainly…'.[3] Arthur found his clergy relatives particularly tiresome in financial matters. 'May I recommend, my dear Olivia, that you keep a systematic account of all your expenditures…' So he counselled Hosea's daughter who had married the Reverend William Archer.

Hosea's wife bore him twenty children between 1794 and 1819 (if we assume that Francis Hart Vicesimus [i.e. the twentieth] was the last), of whom only six survived into adulthood. The melancholy procession of small coffins must have imparted a certain sombreness to life at the rectory and there were other strains. The eldest boy followed his father's profession and, as a humble curate in Armagh, experienced financial difficulty. Another was taken into the brewery, but succumbed to alcoholism. Olivia Archer fell beside her wits. Reading between the few lines available to us we might well conclude that Hosea's family was not an altogether happy one. Only one of Hosea's sons showed that he had inherited some of the Guinness enterprise. At eighteen, as soon as he could leave home, Francis Hart Vicesimus said goodbye to his recently widowed father and set sail for India. He spent several years in the colonial service, returning about 1850 with a wife and a young family. If he hoped for some Guinness money to help him make a new start in his own country he was disappointed. His response was to put the greatest possible distance between himself and Dublin. The government and various colonising societies were promoting the settlement of New Zealand. After a half-century of sporadic European exploitation, mission-ary involvement and conflict with the Maoris, the basis of a democratic polity was established by the New Zealand Constitution Act of 1852. Francis was among the hundreds of propertyless young men who, in that same year, ventured forth to try his fortune in the world's remotest corner. He travelled with his family on the emigration ship *Tory* under the auspices of the New Zealand Association and set up home in the frontier town of Canterbury. There he worked as a police sub-inspector, keeping order among the rough-and-ready sheep farmers of the plains. From this position he later advanced to become a resident magistrate. His son,

Arthur Robert, rose to still greater heights in the administration (see below p.94). With these exceptions the senior Guinness line rapidly faded into obscurity.

Hosea's next brother, another Arthur, called himself the 'family banker' and this he was in two senses. After 1808, when he was elected a director of the Bank of Ireland, finance became his principal avocation (see below). At the same time, as the business brains of the Guinnesses he was the family banker in that he supervised the various trusts set up by his father, advised his ever-growing colony of relatives on the handling of their investments and, when necessary, came to the aid of those of them who had inherited a taste for the good things of life, but not the commercial expertise necessary to provide them. Arthur was brought into the family business by his father as soon as he was of age and was joined, shortly before the end of the century, by his brother Benjamin. By this time the first Arthur Guinness was an old man, so that the apprenticeships of the next generation were necessarily brief. By 1800 the brothers had taken over completely. Young Arthur's first twenty years of commercial life coincided with the Napoleonic Wars and with an upturn in trade that saw St James's Gate production grow sixfold until Guinness was Dublin's premier brewery. If the dramatic increase in prosperity tempted him into euphoria he soon learned that success is neither inevitable nor irreversible.

The chances are that he was not so tempted, for Arthur grew up a Calvinistic Christian, who saw his life as falling under the providence of God. For him religious faith and sound business practice went hand in hand. Cromwell may or may not have charged his men to praise God and keep their powder dry, but Arthur's motto was certainly 'praise God and keep the books balanced'.

> ... the continued good account of our Business calls for much thankfulness to Almighty God while we humbly ask for the infinitely higher blessings of His Grace in the Lord Jesus Christ.... Surely it becomes me to speak of the Lord's patience and longsuffering towards one so utterly evil and sinful and to pray that I might be enabled through Grace to live every hour under the teaching of the Holy Spirit patiently abiding His time for calling me to that Place [of] Everlasting Rest, the purchase of the precious blood of the Lamb of God for saved sinners...[4]

Arthur wrote thus to his son in his last decade, but the principles enunciated were those he adhered to throughout a long life. Evangelical religion took root more firmly in him than in his clerical brother, perhaps because the fire of simple zeal had not been dampened by the green wood of academic study. While Hosea was a major pillar of the Church of Ireland establishment, Arthur and his family were more often to be found worshipping at Bethesda Chapel, which had become the national head-quarters of evangelicalism.

The tremors of revival were vibrating with sporadic violence through Ireland around the turn of the century and were shaking existing denominations apart. For some years Bethesda Chapel was under the sway of the ultra-Calvinist John Walker, a one-time Church of Ireland priest and fellow of Trinity, who in his zeal for 'pure' New Testament religion came to reject the concept of ordained ministry and other accretions to the faith. He rejected not only Anglicanism but also Methodism and all established denominations. Ultimately, even Bethesda was too broad for Walker. He took his disciples away to form the 'Church of God', commonly known as 'Walkerites'. He was succeeded at Bethesda in 1805 by Benjamin Mathias, a man of calmer disposition but similar theology. An eloquent preacher, Mathias occupied the pulpit in Dorset Street for thirty years, proclaiming the divine election of the saints and the iniquities of Romanism and Anglicanism. His principal ideas were left to posterity in two substantial volumes bearing the title, *An Inquiry into the Doctrines of the Reformation and of the United Church of England and Ireland, respecting the Ruin and Recovery of Mankind*. Such were the men who influenced the religious opinions of Arthur Guinness and created tensions between him and his ordained brother.

As his father's son, a respected proprietor of one of Dublin's leading industries and a man of virtuous life, Arthur was much courted by the great and the good, and frequently pressed to take high public office. On two occasions he was strongly urged to enter parliament and sitting MPs actually volunteered to stand aside in his favour. Arthur shunned the political manoeuvrings and temptations to corruption that attended such an office. He did, however, follow his father's example of serving on the city council and, in 1808, he was elected Lord Mayor.

It was a time of the making and breaking of fortunes. War provided opportunities for clear-headed and determined businessmen. Technical innovation provided the means to realise those opportunities. By the early years of the century Guinness porter was being exported across the Irish Sea in significant quantities, to be sold in the Isle of Man, Liverpool and Bristol. At least one consignment was shipped to Portugal for the sustenance of Wellington's peninsular army. In 1816 steam packets began to ply between Dublin and England, introducing faster and more reliable crossings. From the western ports an extending canal system conveyed Arthur's barrels into the English hinterland, where expanding conurbations created new, eager markets. In 1825 a Guinness agency was established in London.

The 1830s was the decade of 'railway mania', the miles of track offering fast transit and a growing volume of trade to industrialists able to expand more quickly than their rivals. But the heights of speculative enterprise were treacherous places for the careless and the ill-prepared. Over-rapid expansion, under-capitalisation, unwise investment and unscrupulous opposition produced hundreds of victims. The Guinnesses were not immune. Three family enterprises went bankrupt or were rescued from insolvency during Arthur's lifetime.

It was by no means a foregone conclusion that the head of the clan would safely negotiate the crags and glaciers of Victorian commerce. Arthur followed his father's sound principle of diversification. To brewing, flour-milling and insurance he added banking and stock-exchange speculation. It seemed wise to invest business profits in sound equities. Unfortunately, Arthur did not choose well. He put a considerable portion of Guinness money into government securities. In the aftermath of Waterloo they were riding high, but the problems of peace brought a downturn in the securities market and it was well over a decade before Arthur could release any of his holdings without incurring a loss. As a result the brewery was starved of investment and this may well have been a significant factor in the fall of beer sales by nearly a half in the immediate post-war years.

Another drain on Guinness resources at this period was caused by the disastrous career of Arthur's brother Edward. Born four years after Arthur, Edward took to the law, a profession in which two of his cousins, Samuel and Richard, were already involved. However, having been brought up in a commercial environment, being possessed of capital and a family name which opened doors, he decided to launch himself into heavy industry. It does not appear that he was totally incompetent, or that he had learned nothing from his father and brother of the rudiments of manufacture and trade. He seems to have been well thought of in Dublin. One newspaper wrote of him, 'He gave bread to several hundred fellow creatures, who prospered under his auspices ... he was candid and honourable in his dealings; highly esteemed and respected not only as a merchant but as a private gentleman'.[5] He had a largeness of spirit that compelled him to think big. His weakness lay in not appreciating that grandiose schemes succeed as a result of careful attention to minute details. His father had turned a failing brewery into Ireland's leading manufactory of strong ale. He had also opened a very successful flour mill. The principle behind both enterprises was obvious: identify a gap in the market and fill it.

Edward looked around for just such an opportunity and believed he had
found it close at hand. On the familiar road between Dublin and Leixlip
lay Palmerston and Lucan, which boasted small struggling ironworks ripe,
or so it seemed, for modernisation. Irish output of iron and steel was
minimal; her dependence on imports from across the water was just one
example of the ties that bound her to England and ensured her continued
backwardness. Yet, theoretically at least, the war provided a real
opportunity for the development of an Irish industry. The appetite for
munitions was voracious and English foundries were struggling to satisfy
it. New iron- and steelworks were springing up, stimulating, in their turn,
coal production, machine factories, transport systems, textiles mills and
credit banking. If Ireland were to share significantly in the new wealth
she would have to develop her own heavy industries. Edward determined
to take a pioneering role.

Personal pride and ambition also played a part in his thinking. His
older brothers enjoyed prominent positions in their chosen callings, but
it soon became apparent to Edward that he was unlikely to cut a very
dramatic figure at the bar. A major commercial coup, on the other hand,
would prove to everyone that he was worthy of the Guinness name. Thus
he sank all his capital in the ironworks at Palmerston and Lucan.

He borrowed heavily from bankers, giving the names of his father and
his barrister cousins as guarantors. When he needed still more money he
approached friends and relatives, assuring them of the magnificent
prospects of his enterprise. Among those persuaded by Edward's charm
and enthusiasm was his younger brother John Grattan, who parted with
his share of the family inheritance. Yet despite the favourable economic
climate of the war years, the foundries failed. By 1811 Edward was
bankrupt. The project had proved too vast both for his resources and for
his talents. Heavy industry was capital intensive. Cultivating new markets
called for patience and considerable negotiating skills. Coke had to be
imported from England. The industrial interest in the Westminster parliament was opposed to any measures which would facilitate the development of Irish competition. Edward might fool his backers and himself
with visions of booming business and high dividends. The reality was that
his industrial goose gobbled up cash and laid no golden eggs. If the would-
be ironmaster's crash had been unique we could, perhaps, write him off as
a wastrel, as earlier family chroniclers have tended to do. The fact is that
his was one of many failed ventures with whose corpses Ireland was
littered by the end of the war. A major cause of the tragedy that would
smite the country in 1847 was that for decades her economic development
had been neglected. Absentee landlords pocketed rents, but failed to

improve farming methods. Credit banking was slow to develop. Industrial enterprises were starved of investment and the Westminster government did nothing to aid them or protect them from English competition. Edward Guinness was not entirely to blame for his own humiliation.

Arthur had to dig deep into his own and company reserves in order to bail out his brother. Samuel and Richard also looked to the family banker to cover their potential losses. Arthur felt obliged to do what he could to cushion John Grattan Guinness in his hour of misfortune. All this placed a strain on the businesses at the very time when they needed fluidity. It also created a precedent. Arthur's relatives were increasing in number and many of them lacked the prudence or industry to build their own fortunes. Yet, as Guinnesses, they believed that a certain life-style was part of their birthright. Thus it was that, over the years, Arthur had to deal with cousins, nephews and even in-laws bringing their buckets to the family well. 'I have from various casualties, which have, in the Lord's Providence, fallen out, chiefly affecting the property of my many dear Relations, had several individuals and families depending on me solely or partially for support ... so that ... I have not been accumulating as you suppose, and indeed, I think I could not have done so acting as a Christian man...'.[6] So Arthur explained years later to one importunate. His sense of religious duty was not inherited by later generations. The brewing Guinnesses developed a thick skin towards the appeals of poor relatives and became very selective about the charity they dispensed within the family. This in part explains the lack of cohesiveness. The extended Guinness clan was not as close as some other famous commercial dynasties.

Unfortunately, the 'Edward problem' could not be disposed of by one donation, however large. The man's debts were massive and the head of the family could not or would not cover them all. Up to this point the failed industrialist had enjoyed the sympathy and understanding of a large section of Dublin opinion. Now, he threw all that away. He welshed on his remaining creditors and fled to the Isle of Man, where the law protected him from prosecution for debt. The family's standing was shaken. A brother of the Rector of St Werburgh's and of a director of the Bank of Ireland had left his employees and servants in the lurch and run away, rather than honourably face up to his responsibilities. The situation did not improve after Edward's flight. From his haven he continued to write begging letters: his wife was ill – driven to distraction by money worries; he had been obliged to rent an expensive house so that his children (eight survived infancy) could have a garden to play in; he had cut his household servants to a minimum, sold his carriage horse and

really could not be expected to reduce his expenditure further. The family
stood by for the remainder of his impecunious life and he survived largely
on an annuity from Arthur and occasional hand-outs from his brothers.
Benjamin, the only one to predecease him, left him a handsome legacy of
£1865. Clearly, despite everything, Edward had not forfeited the affection
of his siblings. Relations were maintained with his widow after Edward's
death in 1833. Four years later his daughter, Elizabeth (Bessie), married
Arthur's third son, who inherited the brewery.

After 1815 Arthur left the affairs of St James's Gate largely in the hands
of his brothers Benjamin and William Lunell, and devoted himself to the
world of finance. The making of a working-man's beverage carried no
social cachet and could actually involve embarrassment in some religious
circles. A recurring phenomenon in the family history is a tendency of
respectable Guinnesses to distance themselves from the business that
provided their bread and butter. It was not that they wanted to enjoy
extravagant and irresponsible life-styles; few Guinnesses have been guilty
of that; they simply preferred to use the income from beer to finance
more 'worthy' social and commercial activities. Three years after Waterloo
Arthur became Deputy Governor of the Bank of Ireland and, in 1820, he
was its governor. The bank had been established, thirty years earlier, and
fortified with exclusive privileges in order to facilitate and regulate the
flow of capital and credit, and to ensure close monitoring by London of
the Irish economy. Like all responsible financial institutions, its watch-
word was caution. The joint-stock banks whose number grew in Ireland
during the first half of the century took more risks – sometimes with
disastrous results – in order to establish businesses and keep the economy
lubricated. The Bank of Ireland, responsible for the circulation of specie,
the backing of its banknotes and the guaranteeing of promissory notes,
had to be more circumspect. For example, it was not until the 1830s that
the governors sanctioned the setting up of branch banks. It must, therefore, bear some of the responsibility for Ireland's sluggish commercial and
industrial progress.

The principal beneficiaries of the institution's activities were members
of the predominantly Protestant mercantile class. In economic terms
there was an unscalable escarpment between them and the vast bulk of
the population, who were complete strangers to banking activities. The
Catholic majority, locked into a miserable, one-crop system of subsistence
farming, conducted most of their necessary negotiations by barter. When
they needed cash they not infrequently fell into the clutches of the
'gombeen men', loan sharks whose interest could rise to forty-three and
a third per cent. It is not to be wondered at that the Bank of Ireland was

widely regarded as an agency of the Ascendancy's anti-Catholic conspiracy and there is no doubt that some of the governor's associates and
friends considered the control of capital as an important element in
preserving the *status quo*. Not so Arthur Guinness. He was no bigot. While
other members of the Dublin élite graced their enjoyment of power with
claims of divine approval Arthur, by contrast, always subjected his politics
to religious scrutiny, a practice which won him more enemies than
friends. Like his father, his outlook was liberal and he was whole-
heartedly in favour of the further extension of Catholic liberties.

After 1801 the hope for Catholic emancipation rapidly faded in Ireland.
The Ascendancy opposed it. The majority population was too preoccupied with survival to risk angering their landlords. The Roman
Catholic hierarchy internationally had a greater vested interest in preserving authority structures than in inciting politico-religious agitation.
Educated Catholics lacked the organisation to mount an effective and
consistent campaign. Yet Catholic emancipation was seldom off the
Westminster agenda throughout the early decades of the century. It was
part of a crusade led by the Whigs to break, in the names of toleration,
charity and equity, the old Tory–Anglican establishment. This movement
was, in turn, part of a wider radicalism, which attacked every species of
autocracy and sought to dismantle sectarian and class barriers by extending the franchise and opening high office to those hitherto precluded by
law. Many liberals, whether contending for the freeing of slaves, the
lifting of Test and Corporation Acts against Nonconformists, or the rights
of Jews to sit in parliament, based their arguments on Christian teaching.
Arthur Guinness had never faltered in his support for the underprivileged. He campaigned for the inclusion of non-Protestants on the
board of the bank and he was prepared to express his views very strongly
in public.

In the winter of 1812–13 there was a war of petitions. Some prominent
Dubliners, among whom were Arthur, Benjamin and William Lunell
Guinness, urged the government to honour pre-Union pledges to give the
Catholic majority constitutional equality. Arthur personally canvassed for
support in his parish of St Catherine's. The response of Protestant
extremists was to organise their own petition. Some over-zealous bigots
included more than a hundred false names among their supposed
signatories, including that of 'Richard Guinness' of Nicholas Street. A
number of partisans seized on this foolish stratagem to spread the rumour
that the brewing family were really opposed to emancipation. Arthur
immediately enlisted the aid of the press to counter this suggestion. He
was sufficiently angry to offer the considerable sum of £500 to anyone

who would successfully expose the deception and he took the opportunity to re-affirm his support for 'the claims of our Catholic brethren'.

In 1819 Arthur was the principal speaker at a meeting of Protestant
householders summoned to approve yet another petition in favour of
Catholic claims. He spoke with the ardour of an evangelist:

> Our Roman Catholic countrymen and neighbours have expended with us
> their blood and treasures, in bringing to a happy and glorious termination a
> war of unequalled length and devastation, and with us should enjoy the
> undiminished blessings arising from the honourable peace they so eminently
> contributed to obtain. And I feel a conviction that when they are admitted to
> a participation of those blessings which the British Constitution is so well
> fitted to bestow, they will be found as zealous, as steady and as dignified
> supporters of that Constitution as any sect or class of subjects in His Majesty's
> dominions.[7]

Ascendancy boors were not the only people offended by Arthur's independent line. When, on one occasion, the organisers of a Catholic
petition passed a vote of thanks, their more extremist co-religionists
denounced them for fawning on rich and powerful Protestants and urged
a boycott of Guinness beer – a course of action which was the only tactic
on which they and their Protestant enemies were agreed. Such demonstrations made no significant impact on trade but were no less
aggravating for that. The attraction of Guinness-baiting faded after a few
months, though not before the editor of the satirical *Milesian Magazine*
had poked fun at pious Arthur as a brewer of 'Protestant porter' made by
adding Bibles and hymn books to the mash. This unwholesome beverage,
it was alleged, produced in those who drank it an evangelical disposition
to 'singing hymns through the nose'. Incidents such as this influenced
Arthur's decision to avoid national politics. In this way he could hold to
his principles while, as far as possible, avoiding unpleasant repercussions
for himself and his business. By demarcating his life within commercial,
social and charitable boundaries he could and did build a major Irish
industry and at the same time advanced the Catholic cause wherever he
had influence.

4

WHOEVER DESIRES TO UNDERSTAND IRELAND

It was increasingly difficult to maintain a low profile in the post-war years. The Catholic intelligentsia began to organise themselves effectively and every move towards an unprotected franchise threatened the Ascendancy with the prospect of majority rule. The man who was now emerging as the leader of Catholic opinion was Daniel O'Connell, a charismatic Dublin lawyer of violent tongue but essentially moderate policies. The celebrated duel in which he was involved in February 1815 tells us more about the sectarian passions abroad in the city than the personalities of the participants. In one of his less vitriolic outbursts O'Connell had castigated the city council as 'beggarly'. John D'Esterre, an empty-headed braggart who had been an infantry captain and was now a butcher only inches away from bankruptcy, proclaimed himself the champion of the city fathers and the Protestant cause. He taunted O'Connell in private correspondence and open conversation. He boasted that he would horsewhip the 'rebel' through the town and when O'Connell refused to be drawn he wildly trumpeted his cowardice with the object of frightening the lawyer into a grovelling apology. O'Connell was known to abhor physical violence and had recently backed out of another affair of honour. The whole of Dublin was buzzing with news of the argument. Eventually, instead of withdrawing his remarks, O'Connell challenged the bigoted butcher. The meeting took place at a spot twelve miles from the city on 1 February. D'Esterre fired and missed, perhaps deliberately. O'Connell aimed low, intending to avoid his opponent, but so poor a shot was he that his ball lodged in D'Esterre's groin. Hours later the butcher died in agony. The lawyer was devastated but his co-religionists cheered him as a hero who had put one over on the arrogant,

sanctimonious 'Prots'. As for the Guinnesses, D'Esterre was a name they
would hear again.

Raised and dashed hopes characterised the year 1821–2. In August 1821
George IV visited Ireland. This, the first visit by a reigning monarch in
over four centuries, created great excitement in all sections of the population. It suggested that the country's problems were being taken seriously.
Arthur Guinness conducted his majesty on a tour of the bank. Daniel
O'Connell presented him with a crown of laurel. Catholic and Protestant
leaders combined to offer a loyal address. The king was accompanied by
Richard, Lord Wellesley, newly appointed as viceroy. Wellesley was
doubly popular among Catholics and moderate Protestants as the eldest
brother of the hero of Waterloo and a known supporter of Catholic
emancipation. He made his mark immediately, appointing to office men
sympathetic to reform, obtaining greater powers for dealing with
sectarian disturbances and, in particular, curbing the activities of the
Orange Order founded at the end of the eighteenth century and now
spreading rapidly, especially in the North. The Protestant minority were
incensed. When Wellesley prevented triumphalist louts decorating the
statue of William III and organising provocative demonstrations, the
result was a riot which had to be suppressed by the military. Weeks later,
a quart bottle narrowly missed Wellesley as he was attending the theatre.
History does not relate whether the bottle contained Guinness.
Encouraged by the government's willingness to stand up to the Protestant
establishment, O'Connell pressed for Catholic claims to be reconsidered.
But there was no enthusiasm for it in Westminster and an outbreak of
fresh atrocities by extremists of both sides seemed to justify political
stasis.

This was the situation which gave rise to the Catholic Association. It
was formed in 1823 by O'Connell and his supporters to be a more
effective organ of political change and to provide poor Catholics with an
alternative to supporting the men of violence. The association was
organised on a nationwide basis and members were asked to pay a
subscription or 'rent', which could be as little as a farthing a week. The
Catholic Association was an idea whose time had come. It united more
people than any preceding organisation and it secured the blessing of the
Roman Catholic hierarchy. It devised tactics and it had the funds
necessary to carry them into operation. It was an initiative that liberals
like Arthur Guinness could and did support whole-heartedly.

The banker allowed his name to be quoted in campaign speeches and
literature. His colleagues already knew that he was arguing for Catholic
emancipation within the limited sphere of the Bank of Ireland. It was not

the only issue on which the governor was prepared to take an independent line. At the same time he opposed a move on the part of the directors to vote themselves substantial salary increases. The similarities between Arthur I and Arthur II are very striking.

Political manoeuvrings continued against the usual background of sectarian conflict, government procrastination and often ill-tempered outbursts from O'Connell. The turning point came in July 1828. The Tories at Westminster were in disarray. Reform was in the air. The government had just been forced to repeal the Test and Corporation Acts restricting Nonconformists. O'Connell chose this moment to contest a parliamentary by-election in Co. Clare. Amid frenetic excitement throughout the country the Catholic freeholders united behind him and he defeated the government candidate. As a Catholic he was debarred from taking his seat. That would mean widespread anti-government riots. At the next election many more of O'Connell's colleagues would stand and some would be elected. Wellington, the Prime Minister, who took a diametrically opposed view to his brother on emancipation, faced the prospect of civil war in Ireland if he remained obdurate. In April 1829 the Commons passed a Catholic Relief Act and a reluctant king was persuaded to sign it. All offices of state, except those of viceroy and chancellor, were thrown open to Catholics, though the price paid was the abolition of the Catholic Association and the raising of the franchise qualification. Arthur Guinness joined in the wild celebration. Speaking at a meeting in Dublin, he declared:

> I am much joyed at the final adjustment of the 'Catholic Question', as it is wont to be called – but more properly the Irish Question – for hitherto although always a sincere advocate for Catholic freedom, I never could look my Catholic neighbour confidently in the face. I felt that I was placed in an unjust unnatural elevation above him; and I considered how I would have felt if placed in a different position myself. Sorrow was always excited in my mind by such a contemplation, and I longed much to have the cause removed. That consummation, so devoutly to be wished for, is now at hand. My Catholic brother is a freeman. We shall henceforth meet as equals.[1]

Success in Ireland lubricated the wheels of the radical bandwagon. Nationalist-liberal revolts in France and Belgium accelerated its dizzying career and were welcomed by Arthur. A speech of his reported in 1830 reveals how far he had progressed down the road to Radicalism:

> A great change was taking place all over the world. Men were awakening. Reason and intelligence were upon their majestic way, and everywhere the grand principle was beginning to be asserted that Governments were

instituted for the benefit of the people ... the principle of liberty had begun
to be extended, the struggle for popular power had loosened the iron hold of
tyranny, and prostrated the oppression that would seek to build itself on the
oppression of the human race.[2]

The clamour for parliamentary reform in Britain grew to a tumult and
Arthur Guinness was in the ranks of reform. He shared platforms with
progressive speakers and expressed advanced views with an ardour
unusual in the staid banking fraternity. At the general election of 1831,
called after the Tories had attempted to frustrate the passage of a Reform
Bill, he seconded the adoption of a radical candidate. In the rapidly
changing Commons chamber Irish members were already playing a
significant part. Throughout the dramatic events of the next few months
most of them supported the Whigs, who eventually achieved the Reform
Act of 1832.

Moderates everywhere hoped and believed that the concessions fought
for and won would satisfy the advocates of change. They were universally
disappointed. Success merely opened up the possibility of further
triumphs. In Ireland O'Connell repeatedly made his objectives clear to
cheering crowds: 'the repeal of the Union is the only means by which
Irish prosperity and Irish freedom can be secured.' One step towards
achieving this objective was putting an end to the established status of
the Church of Ireland. Catholic MPs worked tirelessly to curtail the
privileges and exactions of the hated Anglican clergy. Throughout the
1830s O'Connell and his colleagues rode a wave of euphoric public
support. When the leader was arrested in 1831 the entire city centre was
packed with enraged protesters. One observer wrote: 'I never witnessed
anything so turbulent and angry as the populace was in Dublin this day.'
The uncompromising demands of the nationalists enabled their enemies
to point out exultantly that they had been right all along: O'Connell and
his rabble were bent on pulling away the constitutional and religious
supports of the Ascendancy. Their friends could only stand back
dismayed.

The parting of the ways for Guinness and O'Connell came around 1835
and it was a bitter separation in which personal conflict coloured political
differences. In 1831 one of the Catholic champion's sons acquired a
brewery almost next door to Guinness's. It was a commercial disaster
which foundered, taking its proprietors with it. Inevitably, there were
those who blamed the failure on unfair competition from the brewery's
more powerful neighbour. Catholic partisans tried to organise a boycott
of Guinness beer and to intimidate Arthur's more impatient customers

into closing their accounts. Ruffians waylaid wagons carrying the brewery's produce and stove in the barrels. O'Connell was at pains to distance himself from such disreputable activities, but he was more open in his opposition to the Bank of Ireland. His conviction that the bank should be placed on the same footing as other financial institutions had a political basis, but was probably strengthened by personal grievance. After a private dispute with the directors he denounced them as 'an Orange confederacy'. Later he threatened to organise a run on the bank's gold reserves and he did block, in parliament, a bill for the extension of the bank's privileges. Arthur Guinness needed no such irritants to conclude that he could not support the overthrow of the existing constitution. Delighted at this parting of the ways, the political establishment tried to persuade Arthur to stand against O'Connell in the 1836 election. This he would not do, but he did cast his own vote against the reformer. O'Connell felt the desertion deeply and denounced Guinness as 'a miserable old apostate'. Ireland was becoming a difficult place for moderates.

Nor was it a thriving home for commercial entrepreneurs. A. B. and W. L. Guinness and Co. (as the company had become after the founder's death) was predominantly an Irish concern and it suffered from the relative stagnation of the Irish economy. The output level of 1815 was not regained until 1833. Initially the business was steered through these difficult years by Arthur, and his brothers Benjamin and William Lunell. Arthur, as we have seen, had other interests, which took up much of his time, and Benjamin died in 1826. The next generation had already been brought into the brewery; Arthur's two available sons, Arthur Lee and Benjamin Lee, became partners in 1820. Their eldest brother, whose baptismal names, Smyth(e) Lee Grattan, record the Guinnesses' proudest dynastic connections, followed the other family tradition of taking holy orders (of Arthur's only three daughters to wed, two married 'into the church').

If the firm was to expand it needed to look to overseas markets. The establishment of more reliable ferry services to Bristol and Liverpool suggested obvious lines of advance. Guinness had long associations with the southern port, where their first agents were G. and S. Lunell. The fact that that name was given to one of Arthur's brothers suggests that the connection extended beyond business. However, it was in partnership with the shipper Samuel Waring that real exploitation of Bristol and its hinterland began in the 1820s. The Irish beer rapidly gained popularity with drinkers in the west of England thanks, in no small measure, to Waring's entrepreneurial skills. Bristol, now the centre of a steadily spreading web of canals, became a sizeable market for the Guinness products – Town Porter, Country Porter, Keeping Beer, Superior Porter and West Indies Porter. Within a decade Waring was regularly supplying the capital. When he found another agent, Sparkes Moline, as thrusting a salesman as himself, to look after the London end of the trade, business there boomed. By 1840 one sixth of the beer supplied to England was drunk in the capital.

Unfortunately, Waring was a little *too* enthusiastic in his desire for rapid expansion. Like many others, he became infected with railway mania and, by 1837, was confronting ruin. The Guinnesses could have let him fail and acquired another agent, but they did not. It was a case of sentiment supported by hard-headed business calculation. Samuel Waring, now in partnership with his son Edward, was a colleague well worth saving. He had served the Guinnesses well and, if he could overcome his current difficulties, was likely to do so in the future. Benjamin Lee was sent over to Bristol to conduct a personal audit. On his recommendation money was advanced to Waring from St James's Gate – on the security of Samuel's fine house at Stoke Bishop. The agency recovered and enjoyed many more years of profitable relationship with the Irish brewers. But matters came within an ace of turning out very differently. The packet conveying the thirty-nine-year-old Benjamin Lee across the Irish Sea was beset by an autumn gale and almost came to grief. Had Arthur's son perished, not only would the family have lost its most illustrious nineteenth-century son, the brewery would almost certainly have been wound up, since Benjamin was the only member of the next generation to take a real interest in it.

The Liverpool agency was a commercial stage upon which Arthur's youngest brother, John Grattan, made a brief appearance. John's childhood and adolescence had passed against the stirring background of the land and sea war with France and he became determined on a military career. As soon as he was old enough a commission was purchased for him in the East India Company's army. He arrived in Madras in 1800 and, with intervals for home leave, remained in the sub-continent for the next twenty-four years. It was while he was serving abroad that he yielded to those importunities of brother Edward that deprived him of his inheritance. When he finally resigned his captaincy in 1824 he returned to Ireland with his health undermined and a wife and four children to support. His East India Company pension was adequate, but would not permit him to live the life of a gentleman and certainly not the life of a Guinness. Not unnaturally, he looked to his brothers for support and guidance, and they found him a place at St James's Gate.

· It did not work out. John was in his forties and was accustomed to giving orders. He knew nothing of brewing or commercial life. He had inherited the family's tendency to affective religion and, when in Dublin, was a worshipper at the York Street Methodist chapel. At St James's Gate his progress was watched and commented on, not only by his brothers, but by employees who knew considerably more than he did about beer-making. It took only a few months for the failure of the experiment to become obvious. Something else must be found for John to do. There seems to have been no suggestion of simply giving him an annuity out of the business. Perhaps Arthur had grown tired of relatives who regarded the family concern as a milch cow. Maybe John was too proud to accept charity. After a quarter of a century away from Dublin (during which time both his parents had died) family feelings had cooled on both sides. John needed a greater degree of independence. It seemed that Liverpool might be the answer.

Regular dealings in that city began in 1821, when a certain Henry Antisell was sent from Dublin to be the Guinness agent there. Antisell dealt also with other Irish breweries and after three years it was decided to set up an exclusive agency. The task was assigned to Messrs Bewley and Nevill, operating from premises in Manesty Lane. They sold porter for the home market and for transhipment to the Indies and the Americas. Within months another company, Guinness, Bewley and Nevill, had been set up. This was an association of John Grattan Guinness with the already established agents, but it appears to have been separate from Bewley and Nevill, and it is not clear what the responsibilities of the new partnership were. In fact, it lasted less than two years because John Grattan Guinness resigned. His commercial ideas – such as they were – either did not work, or clashed with those of his more experienced colleagues. Perhaps he was distracted by his wife's illness, for Susanna died at about the same time.

The distraught widower devoted the next three years to bringing up his teenage children single-handed. Naturally, the 'family banker' assisted. Money was found to help Arthur, the eldest boy, to study medicine and John, the younger boy, was taken into the brewery. The bereaved John Grattan found consolation in his religion and in the friendship of Dublin's Nonconformist Christian community. In that community he met Jane D'Esterre, long-time widow of the Protestant champion who had had a fatal encounter with O'Connell. She was fourteen years his junior and had children of a similar age to his own. They had much in common and mutual needs to be met, and in 1829 they were married. They never 'settled' in the conventional sense; the ex-soldier evidently found this difficult. They lived in a succession of houses in Cheltenham and Bristol, paying occasional protracted visits to Dublin. Over the next decade they produced another family, destined to be the beginning of a truly remarkable line of 'missionary Guinnesses'. In the mid-nineteenth century, as the commercial genius of the clan flowered in the great brewery and the Guinness Mahon bank, the equally strong religious element blossomed in a group of men and women who carried the Christian gospel into many of the earth's darker places – at home and abroad.

The two parts of the family drifted apart. John Grattan had never been very close to his siblings and, after the Liverpool fiasco, his brothers doubtless felt that they had more than generously fulfilled their obligations. Unfortunately, any conviction that their charity was wasted on John Grattan's line was confirmed by the behaviour of his younger son. John had shared the itinerant upbringing of a serving officer's family, had returned to Dublin and the company of very wealthy cousins, had lost his mother at a critical stage of his development, had seen his father remarry and set up a household that may well have seemed oppressively religious. He had much to rebel against – solemn Nonconformity, the social expectations of being a Guinness, the strictures of his uncle and employers at the brewery. He took up with wilder members of the young Dublin set and so far disgraced the family name that, in 1838, he had to be dismissed, not only from the brewery, but also from the city. His for-bearing uncles gave him the opportunity of a new start in Bristol, where they bought him his own brewery. Despite being under the eye of the local Guinness agent, John managed to go bankrupt after only seven years. Thereafter he slipped down the greasy pole to poverty and oblivion, bitterly blaming his wealthy relatives for failing him.

It was not only his more distant kin who saddened the latter years of Arthur Guinness. In 1837, when Irish nationalism was providing the brewery and its owners with many headaches, he lost his second wife. Soon after this the head of the business had to contend with the problems of one of his own sons, Arthur Lee Guinness, who rebelled against the family ethos in several ways. Although he was a partner in the firm and for several years lived in bachelor quarters at St James's Gate, Arthur Lee had little real interest in brewing. He was an aesthete, a voluptuary and, probably, a homosexual. Politically he was an idealist in the Romantic Byronic mould. Like the poet, he was a passionate Graecophile and an upholder of the rights of the oppressed. In Ireland his sympathies lay, uncritically, with the Catholic majority. In the 1830s and 1840s the face of nationalism was changing, thanks largely to Young Ireland, a vigorous, educated Catholic group of men with links to Continental movements. They produced a new philosophy, which moved well beyond the enlightened liberalism of Arthur Guinness and even the political libertarianism of O'Connell. Young Ireland hated England. They exalted every aspect of Irish culture. They despised the political pragmatism which proposed economic justifications for the Union. 'Utilitarianism,' wrote one of their leaders in their organ, the *Nation*, 'which measures prosperity by exchangeable value, measures duty by gain, and limits desire to clothes, food and respectability [has] ... become the very Apostles' Creed of the professions and [threatens] to corrupt the lower classes who are faithful and romantic'.[3] Such were the attitudes, highly uncongenial in the Guinnesses' respectable circles, with which Arthur Lee felt great sympathy.

He was able to pursue his interests and passions discreetly until 1839. Then a scandal broke which occasioned an agonised letter from Arthur Lee to his father:

James's Gate,
13 June 1839

(Forgive such a Note – I *can not now write* letters. ALG)
My dear Father,

I well know it is impossible to justify to you my conduct if you will forgive me, it is much to ask, but I already feel you have and I will ever be sincerely grateful ... I know not what I should say, but do my dear Father believe me I feel deeply ... the extreme and undeserved kindness you have ever, and *now*, *More than ever* shown me.

Believe me above all that 'for worlds' I would not hurt your mind, if I could avoid it – of all the living. Your feelings are most sacred to me, this situation in which I have placed myself, has long caused me the acutest pain and your wishes on the subject must be *religiously* obeyed by me. I *only implore you* to *allow me* to hope and forbear a little longer, I *feel* it but *just* to do so ...

Your dutiful, grateful but distressed son
A.L.G.[4]

The crisis was kept from becoming public currency by the family and the historian can only guess at its nature. Money was involved, since the settlement of the affair was conditional on Arthur Lee's promise to desist from drawing notes on the company. In a letter a few months later Arthur Lee confessed to having enjoyed profits that he had been 'uninstrumental in realising'. This suggests a basic lack of aptitude for and interest in commercial life. The erring son had, it seems, been living off the brewery and using the proceeds to fund a life-style which was an affront to his father's moral rectitude and the good name of the family. The words 'if I could avoid it' suggest that the writer was in the grip of emotions and desires beyond rational control. There could be no financial adjustment and promise to do better. Arthur Lee had to sever his connection with the firm.

The process came close to closing down the Guinness brewery for good. Arthur Lee cashed in his share of the partnership and his younger brother Benjamin Lee (now in effective control of the business) contemplated selling up. The situation was saved by the elder brother leaving some of his capital in the company. He bought an estate at Stillorgan, a few miles south of Dublin on the coast. He refused a more generous settlement from the family on the grounds of preferring 'my present moderate expenditure to an increased one'. However, his humble situation still allowed him to collect paintings and indulge his peccadilloes far from the public gaze. He also devoted himself to the welfare of his tenants. During the appalling potato famine of 1845–51 Arthur Lee Guinness was one of the few landlords who dug deep into his own pocket to bring relief to the starving. For thus identifying himself with ordinary people against the interest of his own class he won considerable popularity. His workers raised a marble monument to him whose awkwardly phrased inscription suggests a sincerity not always found on public memorials:

1847
To Arthur Lee Guinness Esq.
Stilorgan Park
To mark the veneration of his faithful labourers who in
a period of dire distress were protected by his
generous liberality from the prevailing destitution.
This humble testimonial is respectfully dedicated
consisting of home material.
Its colour serves to remind that the memory of benefits
will ever remain green in Irish hearts.

Arthur Lee's extravagances, whether motivated by philanthropy or personal indulgence, brought him back time and again to the St James's Gate well.

The Great Famine is Ireland's holocaust. The dreadful facts and the many legends to which they gave rise have for ever shaped Irish self-perception and, perhaps more importantly, the perception of Irish communities abroad. The 'Hunger' ranks alongside the Cromwellian massacres in the list of proofs of English perfidy and brutality. From 1845 to 1851 between a half-million and a million people died of starvation and famine-related diseases. One and a quarter million fled to other lands, braving the appalling emigrant ships' conditions in the search for a life which could only be better than one-crop subsistence farming. Bands of desperate men ranged the countryside, breaking into the homes of the better off to steal food for their families. Politically the Union was ill-equipped to deal with the results of the potato blight. It was an Irish problem requiring an Irish solution. In Westminster the House of Lords was more sympathetic to the plight of estate owners driven into bankruptcy by the agricultural calamity than the distress of their tenants. The Commons listened to the clamours of their own constituents, who were more interested in feeding the home market than in making cheap grain available for the relief of the Irish poor. Government lacked the experience, administrative machinery and even the will to cope with a disaster of such proportions. It was a couple of years before the nation's leaders had gathered sufficient information to provide a coherent picture of the size and nature of the human tragedy. Relief, when it came, was piecemeal and ill-organised, a hodge-podge of private charity, government work schemes and local hand-outs.

When the full horror of the famine became known in Dublin several leading citizens calling themselves the 'Irish Council' came together to discuss the crisis and ways of dealing with it. The joint secretary of this body was Samuel Ferguson, a thirty-seven-year-old lawyer, journalist and antiquary. Ferguson was a graduate of Trinity and a leading member of the Dublin intelligentsia, who numbered such writers as J. Sheridan Le Fanu among his close friends. He was a not inconsiderable poet – indeed, W. B. Yeats in later years reckoned him among Ireland's great men of literature – and a passionate collector and arranger of old Irish ballads and legends. Patriot he may have been; revolutionary he most decidedly was not. He was too kindly and compassionate a man ever to allow his fervour to degenerate into fanaticism. Yet he was roused to great indignation by the dreadful events of 1847 and the failure of the imperial government to deal with them. The Irish Council made several recommendations to Westminster, which were either rejected or acted upon in a half-hearted, useless way.

This rejection incensed Ferguson and convinced him that the restoration of an Irish parliament was vital, not only to the alleviation of current suffering, but also to proper consideration of all the country's ills. He threw his weight behind the aims of the Protestant Repeal [of the Union] Association and in May 1848 delivered to its members an impassioned speech:

I have felt the utmost indignation at the unworthy manner in which this ancient kingdom – this loyal, great, and peaceable people – have been spoken of by English representatives in the House of Commons – spoken of with ribald insolence, which, if we had been represented by Irish gentlemen of independence, would never have been ventured on, much less permitted, and repeated...

But, whilst they have exhibited this contempt for us, and this hostility towards us, they have also exhibited great ignorance of our affairs, and utter incapacity to make laws salutary for this country. What impresses this on my mind with particular force is, that when, by the occurrence of the calamity that has lately visited us, it became essential that we should make large pro-vision for the support of the poor of this country – when that necessity arose (and here I speak from personal experience) fifteen months ago, parties representing all sections of Irish politicians – representing both creeds and all classes in the community – saw what the difficulty was with which we had to contend, and clearly saw what was the remedy. It was perfectly evident that if, on the first of January 1847, we had had a local Legislature in this country, not only would moneys have been raised adequate for preserving the lives of all her Majesty's subjects ... but that in apportioning taxation ... no one class in the community would have been made to suffer more than another.... We are not a colony of Great Britain – we are an ancient kingdom, an aristocratic people, entitled to our nationality, and resolved on having it.[5]

Two days later Samuel Ferguson approached Robert Rundell Guinness to ask for the hand in marriage of his eldest daughter, Mary. It was not an easy interview. Mary's father had read the speech and thoroughly dis-approved of it. As a land agent and banker he was closer to the problems of rural Ireland than his brewing relatives (see below pp.57–64). Moreover, he doubted whether a struggling barrister could keep his daughter in the style to which she was accustomed. However, he declined to stand in the way of their happiness and the couple were married in August 1848.

Ireland's miseries were unabated and Ferguson, supported by his wife, continued to urge effective relief measures and radical constitutional change. It was difficult to disentangle politics, humanity and national culture and the Fergusons' house at 20 North Great George Street became such a popular and frequent meeting place for many inclined by emotion or intellectual conviction to radicalism that it was popularly known as 'The Ferguson Arms'. A particular favourite of Mary Ferguson's was Charles Duffy, a dangerous friend for any member of the Dublin élite, for he was a leader of Young Ireland and spent a spell in prison in 1848 when the organisation was outlawed by the government. Half a century later, when her country's problems had still not been solved and most of her male relatives were fervent unionists to a man, Mary quoted with approval Duffy's recently published analysis of the Anglo-Irish conflict:

> [Englishmen] see with amazement and dismay a whole people who profess to have no confidence in their equity, who proclaim that they do not expect fair play from them, and who fall into ecstasies of triumph over some disaster abroad or embarrassment at home which endangers or humiliates the empire; and they will not take the obvious means of comprehending this phenomenon. For whoever desires to understand why Ireland is distressed and discontented, while England is prosperous and loyal, must assuredly seek the causes in history: to-day is the child and heir of yesterday ... I am convinced that confusion and disaster will continue to mark the relation between the islands, till Englishmen confront the facts courageously, and with a determination to discover the springhead from which discord flows.[6]

Back in the Famine years Mary's family, at least as far as extant records reveal, were not to the fore in the campaign for the relief of their suffering countrymen. There is no evidence that they took part in the ill-fated Irish Council and it may be that, like many prominent citizens, their charitable instincts were hobbled by their fear of rebellion. Doubtless, through their churches and commercial associations, as well as privately, they contributed to relief funds. But, with the exception of Arthur Lee, they gave at a distance, cocooned in Dublin comfort from the horrors being suffered by their countrymen. The only direct evidence we have suggests that Arthur did not begin to grasp the seriousness of the situation until some time in 1849. He was staying in Torquay and read, in a London newspaper, about conditions in Connemara. He immediately wrote to tell his son that the account presented

> ... a picture of the state of destitution ... exceeding in horror and misery anything we have before observed. May the Lord in His infinite mercy direct our Government and all individuals also possessing means to do so to the use of measures to relieve if possible the sufferings of our wretched poor people. I wish to know any mode in which we might be able to aid in the work. You know my dear Ben that my purse is open to the call.[7]

On his return home he read with frustration reports of the continuing crisis. In another letter to his son he pointed out the lack of well-organised relief schemes devoid of sectarian or political encumbrances. It was the instinctive liberal and practical businessman writing. It was also the wishful thinker; the human disaster did not exist in a vacuum separate from class and religious prejudices.

There have been scores of attempts to analyse and demythologise the Great Hunger and simple judgements have long since been abandoned in academic circles. The famine did not 'cause' Irish depopulation; it accelerated a trend which had been operating for two decades. Rural society was not a two-layer cake of exploited cottagers and wealthy, largely absentee, landlords; there were intervening tiers of larger and smaller farmers many of whom (Catholic as well as Protestant) were less well-disposed to poor tenants than were their masters. Though clearances were a very real and terrible part of the agrarian ' solution', their numbers have been exaggerated. Landowners were not a universally heartless breed of men who set the militia on defaulting families and burned down their dwellings; a substantial minority sustained considerable financial loss in preference to being the cause of still further suffering.

Contemporaries, however, lacked the statistics and the breadth of documentary evidence to reach nicely balanced conclusions. To many of the Guinnesses' friends and neighbours, secure in a social world that might have been in a different continent, the collapse of the rural economy was seen as proof of Catholic peasant fecklessness: those at the bottom of the economic ladder bred like rabbits, were too lazy to farm properly, defaulted on their rents and thus created problems for their lords and masters. From the standpoint of religious bigotry the answer appeared simple in the extreme: 'The two great deficiencies in Ireland are want of capital and want of industry. By destroying small tenancies you would obtain both'.[8] Some Protestant relief schemes were linked with proselytising, 'convert and eat' being their unashamed slogan. On the other side of the argument were the nationalist campaigners who attributed the disaster to a century of exploitation by Protestant landlords. Tithes and rents had been ruthlessly exacted by aliens, who spent no money on improvements.

Arthur did not share the unthinking arrogance of either party. He might have turned his back on O'Connell's radicalism, but he retained a basic respect for the Catholic community and a heart readily touched by human suffering. What he could see was that short-term charity was in itself inadequate. The element of truth in both partisan assessments of agrarian decline was that stagnation was the result of an archaic system of land tenure, which meant that freeholders and tenants lacked the resources and the will to maximise production. That was why he joined the great land grab.

In the aftermath of the famine £20,000,000 worth of Irish estate land changed hands. Its owners, crushed between the upper and nether millstones of falling rents and rising rates (imposed to pay for relief operations), were forced to sell their ancestral holdings. The purchasers were neighbours who possessed or could borrow the necessary funds to take advantage of a falling market, local speculators, upwardly mobile small farmers – and city businessmen who grabbed the never-to-be-repeated opportunity to buy into the landed gentry. Some of the new owners were no better than their predecessors, but there were those who acquired estates in order to demonstrate how reform could be carried out. Arthur Guinness was of their number. He obtained sizeable acreages in Wexford and Wicklow, and instructed his agent (George Weller, a kinsman of his youngest daughter. Rebecca had married Sir Edmund Weller, Bart, the head of an ancient Tipperary family with a considerable stake in the political and economic life of Ireland) to remove unproductive tenants and replace them with selected farmers able to absorb new methods. He had the land scientifically drained and converted from arable to pasture for the raising of beef and dairy herds. Thus, Arthur Guinness played a part in the depopulation of rural Ireland. For a man of business who was a man of God the situation presented a dilemma. He had a responsibility to steward his capital wisely and productively but that could only be achieved by becoming a party to the clearances. The way he resolved the paradox was by being as generous as possible to the departing tenants.

Arthur Guinness outlived all his brothers and all but one of his sisters. When he died in June 1855, the preacher at his funeral in Bethesda Chapel had a problem. The officiant was expected to give voice to that political and religious correctness to which the deceased's relatives subscribed and accordingly he spoke warmly of the prominent citizen's religious zeal and sincere Protestant faith. But there was the difficulty of Arthur's political opinions and, particularly, his frequently expressed attitude towards papists. The minister knew that the word 'liberal', whether applied to theology or politics, was anathema to many of his congregation. He therefore felt it necessary to wipe away the stain of liberalism from the dead man's reputation by exaggerating his 'conversion' in later years. Arthur Guinness, he suggested, developed certain views,

...partly it might have been from his associations, partly from his circumstances, and with a judgement not yet fully enlightened in divine truth, and, therefore, without the perception of their error and evil tendencies ... But more marked still was the decision, the fearless and undaunted resolution, with which, when once convinced of his error, he passed over, and took his stand on the opposite side – on that side which shall ultimately be pronounced true liberality by the voice of God.[9]

'Taking sides' – it was a concept alien to Arthur Guinness, as it had been to his father. Like Grattan and O'Connell, they had been men with a passion for a united Ireland which would be home to men and women of all religious persuasions. If they were partisans, they were reluctant ones. The same was not true of succeeding generations.

5

FRAUGHT WITH DIFFICULTY
AND DANGER

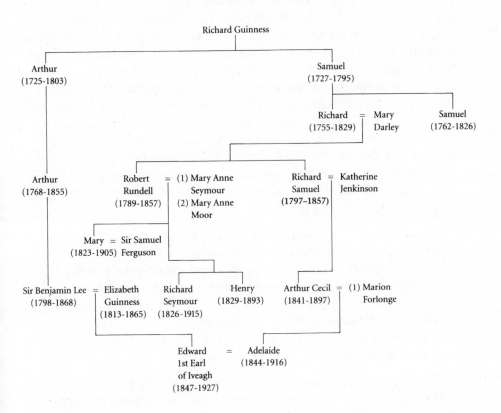

B y the opening years of Victoria's reign the Guinness clan had become Dublin's mercantile and professional leaders. Together with their Darley, Lee and Smyth relatives they dominated a sizeable part of the city's social, cultural, religious and business life. They intermarried. They met constantly in their clubs, societies and offices to do deals and discuss issues of local politics. They had their own pews in church and chapel. They made the rounds of each other's balls, dinner-tables and garden parties. Their womenfolk called at each other's town houses and arranged family visits to their country places close to the city. In short, they were essential vertebrae in the frame of Dublin life.

Some were less than satisfied with this restricted sphere of activity. Arthur's first cousins, Richard (Dick) and Samuel (sons of Samuel the goldbeater), took to the law. After study at the Inns of Court they were called to the Irish bar. Through their profession and through their father's trade they had connections in London, where they aspired to mix in the highest society. Among their friends in the capital were members of the wealthy Rundell family who were silversmiths and jewellers to the royal court. One of them stood godfather to Dick's eldest son Robert. Dick married one of the Darley girls and by her had ten children, of whom two boys and four girls survived infancy. The barrister brothers lived next door to each other in Mercer Street, close by St Stephen's Green, and enjoyed fashionable and profitable practices, in contrast to the Catholic barrister Daniel O'Connell who, because of his religion, was obliged to take on clients of modest means. Ever anxious to improve their situation, they became financially involved with Edward Guinness, the would-be ironfounder, though their knowledge of the law enabled them to extract themselves without suffering too much loss. In the midst of the collapse Samuel wrote to his brother in words that, though forthright, betray a certain anxiety:

> ... if by any act of E[dward] or J[ohn] G[rattan]'s my property is unjustly trenched-upon, their Brother Arthur is my mark for full reparation ... [Edward must] learn that Partners tho' Anonymous are not mere Cyphers, and that he can't bind them by a Lease or Deed, tho' he certainly could by a Bill of Exchange, however improperly, during the existence of their joint firm, tho' thank God, not before or after the existence of said joint firm, as ascertained by the clear Evidence of this Deed, and not by rigmarole talk or foolish ungrammatical construction of a plain instrument.[1]

Their purses and reputations survived their cousin's misfortune.

The experience does not seem to have caused any serious rift between the cousins. Dick was a member of the Dublin Council and when opportunity served or necessity demanded he represented there the interests of his family. Thus when, in 1814, a smear campaign was launched against the city's brewers, who were accused of adulterating their beer with harmful additives, he affirmed, as reported in *Freeman's Journal*, that he 'was connected with a brewer, of whom he may be allowed to say that he had arrived at the top of his profession and realized an affluent fortune by the practice of every virtue that is estimable in a tradesman or a man'.[2] Dick's son Robert Rundell Guinness was Arthur's lawyer, the shrewd patriarch recognising in this distant relative a hard-working and intelligent man, who possessed the necessary skills to look after the legal aspects of his many interests.

Both Robert and his brother Richard Samuel followed the family's law tradition, although Robert appears to have started out in the brewing trade. One family story places the young man, not at St James's Gate, but in the brewery at Stillorgan, south of the city, run by his maternal uncle Henry Darley. Certainly, when it came to business affairs Robert had a better head on his shoulders than did his brother. The two young men could scarcely have been more different. Cautious and dependable Robert married a clergyman's daughter and when she died young he took to wife another child of the cloth. Richard's ambitions were on an altogether larger scale. In the 1820s the younger brother wanted to found a bank and land agency. He persuaded Robert to put in some start-up capital. Robert was to discover that commercial success was no more guaranteed to R. Guinness and Co. than it had been to the enterprise set up by cousin Edward, but recently returned from years of skulking in the Isle of Man. All went reasonably well until 1833 when Richard married.

Intent on social climbing and determined to join the political élite, he allied himself with one of England's leading families. Robert Banks Jenkinson, eighth baronet, Baron Hawkesbury and second Earl of Liverpool was, with one brief intermission, Prime Minister of the United Kingdom from 1812 to 1827. He was one of a high Tory family long active in politics. His ancestors for most of the preceding century had sat in parliament and his father had been a member of Lord North's administration. It fell to Liverpool to oversee the concluding stages of the Napoleonic Wars and the ensuing peace. He was, throughout his time in office, a firm opponent of Catholic emancipation in Ireland and was committed to the preservation of 'a Protestant ascendancy, a Protestant parliament, a Protestant council and Protestant judges'. In 1827 a stroke removed him from public life and the following year he died. He was succeeded in the earldom by his half-brother who was currently MP for East Grinstead and Under-Secretary of State for War and the Colonies. He was very close to court circles and Princess Victoria often visited him at his estates in Sussex and Shropshire. After the queen's accession he became Lord Steward of the Household and a privy councillor. Ill health forced him to resign all his offices in 1846 and he died five years later. As he had no direct heir the earldom became extinct, but the baronetcy devolved upon his cousin, Charles Jenkinson, MP for Dover. It was Katherine, the twenty-five-year-old daughter of this Charles Jenkinson whom Richard Guinness, then thirty-six, married in 1833.

It is hardly surprising that his exalted new connections should have gone to his head. He had always been a self-seeking snob, but now his arrogance, encouraged by his wife, assumed the nature of mild megalomania. In the family he was something of a figure of fun. He affected high collars, which forced his head back and gave him an even more haughty appearance. Behind his back his relatives called him 'Old Pelican' or 'Old Pel', an allusion to his protruding, up-turned nose. It was scarcely conceivable that Dublin could be a fitting setting for such a couple as the Richard Samuel Guinnesses. They spent much of their time in their London town house, and visiting Katherine's exalted friends and relatives. Inevitably R. Guinness and Co. suffered from its managing director's lack of application to day-to-day business. Robert Rundell remonstrated with his brother. He was spending the business's profits and unwisely extending credit to 'fashionable' clients. Richard did not mend his ways and, in 1836, the growing rift between them widened into a chasm when the elder Guinness removed his capital from the firm. R. Guinness and Co. survived for several years, but eventually went under in the land crisis brought on by the Great Hunger. Richard had accumulated estates and, like many proprietors, found himself unable to collect rents from an impoverished tenantry. The collapse of land values hit the agency side of his business and the need of customers for ready cash created a run on gold. R. Guinness and Co. went bust in 1849, leaving its founder bankrupt.

For the previous couple of years Old Pel had been paying even less attention than usual to business. Ambitious to join his parliamentary in-laws and to endear himself to the Tory establishment he contested and won a Kinsale seat in the 1847 general election. This necessitated an almost permanent removal to London and delivered Mrs Guinness from the tedium of Dublin society. Unfortunately, Richard did not long enjoy his success. In their anxiety to win, he and his agent were guilty of certain electoral irregularities, which culminated in the result being declared void a few months later. This, followed by the collapse of the business, led to total humiliation for the Richard Guinnesses. Few people had a good word to say for him, especially as he had obtained sureties from some of his friends and now absconded, leaving them to settle his debts. But in distant London he and his wife did their best to ignore their difficulties.

Richard strove mightily to keep in with his Tory relatives and friends at the Carlton Club. Although he cannot have been considered much of an asset, party leaders were prepared to cultivate him. The Conservatives were in utter disarray, split into liberal and reactionary groupings, and divided on the major contemporary issues – parliamentary reform, industrial legislation, the Crimean War and Ireland. Their Whig opponents fared little better. As a result government was in pawn to the political deal-makers. In the twenty years after 1846 eight administrations came and went, and most of them enjoyed no parliamentary majority. In this situation Irish members began to emerge as a distinct pressure group. Although they were, in 1850, almost equally divided between Whigs and Tories, they were capable in the prevailing volatile party situations of uniting behind matters of common concern and effectively flexing their lobby muscles.

But it was not as an Irish MP that Richard Guinness commended himself at the Carlton Club. The events of 1847 had damaged his reputation too much for him to contest successfully another seat in his own country. His in-laws and their associates, the supporters of Lord Derby, who had declared himself determined 'to stem the tide of democracy', searched around for an electorate who could be bribed to support the Irish lawyer. In 1854 he was put forward as a candidate for the Devon constituency of Barnstaple, referred to during the subsequent legal proceedings as 'the most notoriously corrupt borough that infests the country'.[3] He and his colleague, a Mr Laurie, were successful and duly took their seats in the House in December. But Old Pel was not to be allowed to enjoy his new dignity free of controversy. He spent the next year defending himself against various charges of malpractice and dishonesty.

The defeated candidates mustered a corps of lawyers in their attempt to overturn the hustings verdict and they had the support of the local newspaper which, in reference to Richard Guinness, gloated, 'the real position and antecedents of that gentleman will be exposed'.[4] The protesters presented a petition to parliament claiming that some of the electors who had been 'bought' by the Tories were ineligible to vote and that the once-bankrupted Guinness had falsely declared his income from Irish rents and lacked the necessary property qualification required of MPs. A Commons committee was set up to consider the complaint and in due course it exonerated the new member. Predictably, this did not satisfy the critics, who complained that the adjudicating body was packed with 'Tories of the first water' and that Guinness had summoned to his aid all those who had colluded in the bribery of voters and a whole regiment of 'taffy-men' (sycophantic party followers). It was an age when corruption in parliamentary elections was more the rule than the exception. Nothing had changed in the conduct of voting procedures since Dickens had lampooned it in the fictitious Eatanswill campaign twenty years earlier. Nothing would change until the introduction of the secret ballot eighteen years hence. Bearing in mind Richard's earlier record, his ardent desire for a parliamentary seat, his financial difficulties and the no less urgent concern of the reactionaries to increase their support, it can scarcely be doubted that the new member and his friends had used every stratagem available to make certain of success.

The committee's verdict did not end Old Pel's troubles and what followed tends to confirm the judgement of Richard Guinness as an unprincipled and shallow self-seeker. His own agent proceeded against him in the Court of Common Pleas for non payment of fees and expenses. On 29 May 1855 judgement was given for the plaintiff. Guinness immediately appealed and the litigation dragged on for several months, before the decision of the lower court was substantially upheld.

Meanwhile the member for Barnstaple had taken his place on the opposition benches. Lord Palmerston had just assumed office as Prime Minister and one of the earliest issues to be laid before him was the continuing plight of poor tenants in Ireland. He received a deputation asking for security of tenure and protection against the ruthless activities of 'improving' landlords. Richard Guinness was among the first to get to his feet in the chamber and castigate what he called a 'disgraceful and disgusting' delegation. This brought an angry response from his enemies. The *North Devon Journal*, accusing Guinness of toadying to the Tory leader, Lord Derby, poured forth its vitriol upon the unpopular member:

> The Journal asks: Whether there is anything 'disgraceful and disgusting' in a man abusing the confidence of his friends who had become his sureties for £9,000 or £10,000 and by default leaving them to pay the money. 2 Whether it is 'disgraceful and disgusting' for a man to offer himself as a candidate for parliamentary honours who has nothing but a sham qualification, to charge his agent with the election expenses – even for the dinner he eats at a first class hotel – and then to cheat him out of the amount by raising a technical objection to payment necessitating an article at law to recover the same. 3 Whether there is anything 'disgusting' in such a one denominating the crime of bribery as a mere 'compliment' paid to the bribed voters. 4 Whether there is anything 'disgraceful' in promising a subscription to a local charity and not paying the money. 5 Whether it is not both 'disgraceful and disgusting' for a man to get into parliament simply because he hopes by his vote to get 'plenty of money'. 6 Whether he knows any Irishman sitting for an Irish borough whose conduct has been thus 'disgraceful and disgusting'.[5]

The newspaper may well have been quoting an overheard remark of Old Pel's when it referred to his ambition to benefit financially from membership of the Commons, or it may have been inferring the MP's attitude from his unprincipled conduct. There is no doubting the desperate straits that Richard found himself in. He had failed in business. His legal practice had not furnished the income to keep him in the style to which he aspired. He had been found guilty of political chicanery once and only just escaped a second charge. His reckless career had left in its wake bruised friendships and a fractured relationship with his brother. He had brought shame on his wife and her family. He was pursued by impatient creditors. The only accomplishment he could set against all this was that he had, by fair means or foul, got himself into parliament and now enjoyed the reasonable prospect of being able to use his influence to set all to rights. But luck refused to smile on poor Old Pel – or perhaps it was simply a case of a scoundrel receiving his just deserts.

In March 1857, when Richard had been an MP for less than fifteen months, he lost his seat. Palmerston, banking on his widespread personal popularity, called a snap election. There was no question of Guinness being advanced by his party to defend the Barnstaple seat. The man was a positive liability to the Tories and his old backers deserted him. He had come to the end of the road. At the age of sixty, bankrupt and with no trade or profession, he could not provide for his wife and children. There were still three unmarried daughters who would need dowries if they were to be suitably married off and three boys to be equipped for adult life. Richard was reduced to begging aid from his Guinness and Jenkinson relatives. The humiliation and sense of failure were more than he could bear. His life came to an end on 27 August. There are no details of what brought him to the grave, but the fact that he was not buried in consecrated ground suggests suicide. Even in death, Richard Guinness was dogged by misfortune. He was interred in a plot of ground near Kildare Street, Dublin. A few years later the land was required for building. When his family refused to allow Richard's remains to be removed a parish hall was built over them and the ex-barrister/MP's tomb was located in a dark corner underneath a staircase.

Richard's brother, Robert Rundell, predeceased him by less than six months. Since the parting of the ways their lives could scarcely have been more different. Robert was content to live and work in Dublin. He applied himself patiently to business, had no social ambitions and was the successful founder of an important merchant bank. Although the famine years and their aftermath were difficult ones for the landed interest, the middle decades of the century were boom years for the mercantile economy and the financial institutions which resourced it. The increased importation of foodstuffs to feed the victims of the Great Hunger, followed by Ireland's railway boom, created a greatly increased demand for cash and credit. The Bank of Ireland opened several local branches and found itself in competition with a new clutch of joint-stock banks.

This was the situation in which Guinness Mahon and Co. was founded.

When, in 1836, Robert Rundell liberated his capital from R. Guinness and Co. it was with the intention of redeploying it in another enterprise. From his brother's firm he head-hunted a young man with impressive financial flair and useful family connections. John Ross Mahon came from a long line of Galway landowners. To the new company he brought his own capital and several customers who were anxious to develop their estates more profitably. Guinness and Mahon began as a land agency, but it was inevitable that the firm would soon extend its range of financial services. The business began operating from elegant premises at 26 South Frederick Street, half a mile from the city centre. Robert, whose first wife died in the summer of 1837, threw himself into the new venture with enthusiasm partly, it may be supposed, as a therapy to assuage his grief. He was soon involved in a wide range of activities from travelling the country by coach and jaunting car collecting rent to negotiating financial transfers with the Bank of Ceylon. He was closely involved in the halting development of Ireland's infrastructure. Having come from the Dublin mercantile community and being related to men of trade in various lines of enterprise, he was enthusiastic for the growth of the country's modest commercial base, something which was inextricably linked in his mind with political imperatives. Writing in 1844 to commend to a client shares in the Dublin-to-Cork railway company, he observed, 'It will, I believe, assist in tranquillising Ireland'.[6]

Few wealthy Dubliners knew better than Robert Rundell just how un-tranquil parts of rural Ireland were. He and his staff were in regular contact with tenants unable to pay their way and landlords impatient with the 'prevarications' of their peasantry. As middle men they suffered abuse, and sometimes worse, from both sides. When the Great Famine broke, Robert Rundell may have disagreed with his son-in-law about the political solution of the crisis, but he agreed with Ferguson about the need to do something about the suffering and the violence to which it gave rise. Tragedies like that of the unfortunate Major Mahon brought home to him the people's desperation. Mahon (no relative of Robert Rundell's partner) was a client with an estate in Co. Roscommon. In the midst of the disaster Mahon offered to help some of his tenants 'escape' to America. He chartered a ship at his own charge and embarked scores of peasant families upon it. Time passed and no word of the emigrants reached their anxious relatives at home. When the conviction spread that the vessel had foundered with all hands a group of Mahon's half-crazed tenants waylaid his carriage, dragged him out and battered him to death. Days later news of the ship's safe arrival reached Roscommon.

Guinness and Mahon could not but be on the side of the landlords from whom came their bread and butter. The threat to law and order had to be resisted at all costs. Violence must be countered by vigorous policing. However, Robert Rundell acknowledged that proprietors and their agents could do something to ease tensions. He encouraged rent moratoriums, the distribution of food and the inauguration of work schemes to provide the destitute with wages in cash or kind. From his own pocket he supported many programmes for the alleviation of distress.

Yet Robert Rundell believed that his principal means of helping his country lay in building up its economy. He always described himself as a reluctant banker. By this he probably meant that he did not enjoy the nuts and bolts of keeping ledgers and balancing accounts. In the broader spectrum of encouraging commercial and industrial enterprise he was very interested. He was a director of several companies, including two pioneering railway ventures. Gradually the emphasis of the firm shifted more and more towards banking, although land agency work gave Guinness Mahon a secure financial basis. It was this that enabled the firm to survive when others were failing. A spate of joint-stock banks had come into existence since the 1820s, but there simply was not enough commercial activity in Ireland to sustain them all. By the middle years of the century most of them had crashed or merged. By 1885 only two remained and Guinness Mahon was one of them – or rather Guinness Mahon and Co., as it had become in 1851.

The new partners were Robert Rundell's two sons, Richard Seymour and Henry, who had already been working in the office for some years. They brought new interests and developed new contacts. Guinness Mahon and Co. branched out into insurance and assurance. They also did a growing amount of business through London. The company's increased stature was marked in 1854 by a move into more prominent and commodious premises on College Green, in the very heart of Dublin and opposite the Bank of Ireland. Robert Rundell died in the spring of 1857 and, since John Ross Mahon spent most of his time supervising land agency business from Strokestown, Co. Roscommon, his sons effectively ran the business in the capital.

So matters remained until 1873. Overseas business had grown so much, especially after Guinness Mahon had come to an arrangement with the Bank of Ireland for discounting bills, that the brothers decided to open a London office. This was a major development for the bank. From this moment it operated in two cities from which its financial tentacles spread the world over. It had finally shed its image as funder of landowners, cornchandlers and railway builders essentially operating within Ireland. The move was a major one for the elder brother. Richard Seymour Guinness uprooted himself, his cousin-wife Elizabeth Darley and their nine children (one more, Herbert, was born in 1876) to a modest house in St George's Square, Pimlico. Every day he travelled into the City and did his business at the City Carlton Club in St Swithin's Lane, close by the Bank of England. For the first few years he had no premises, kept no clerk and wrote up no ledgers. Conscious, no doubt, of the impressive and ancient financial institutions all around him he kept his own counsels and acquired the reputation of being a very 'private' banker. He was his father's son, content to grow carefully and slowly, and reporting by daily correspondence to his brother in Dublin. Only after six years did he take a small office in St Clement's Lane. At about the same time he moved his home address to the more affluent Rutland Gate, Knightsbridge. His brewing cousins, when they set up London establishments, lived in considerably greater splendour.

While his relatives made and lost fortunes and reputations it was the head of the 'brewing line' who ruled as the unchallenged king of Dublin's mercantile world. Benjamin Lee Guinness was named after his maternal grandfather, Benjamin Lee of Merrion, Co. Dublin. By the time of his father's death in 1855 he was fifty-seven and had been *de facto* head of the family business for sixteen years. Yet through all those years he lived in the shadow of the great patriarch. Although far from being a man devoid of character he was almost completely overawed by the force of Arthur's private and public virtue. It is no easy matter to be the son of a man of strong opinions, great integrity and popular acclaim. Benjamin's eldest brother had inherited Arthur's religious devotion and taken holy orders. The next had found that piety too oppressive and, not without expressions of shame and anguish, had gone his own way. Other family members involved in the business from time to time had died, or been found wanting. Patiently, Benjamin shouldered the responsibility and was content to remain under his father's watchful eye. He consulted his parent on all major policy matters and usually deferred to his judgement. Arthur even influenced his choice of a bride. Bessie, daughter of the unfortunate Edward, was the old man's favourite niece. She often visited Beaumont and shared her uncle's enthusiasm for the style of worship at Bethesda Chapel. Benjamin had little time or inclination to look for a wife with a suitable fortune. It was almost with a sigh of relief that he allowed the family to arrange his union with Bessie. In personal matters Benjamin bowed to his father's wishes even when well into middle age.

It was in 1851 that he was strongly pressed to accept the nomination for a safe Tory seat in Dublin. He asked papa's advice and the forthright Arthur did not hesitate to give it: '... the office of sitting in Parliament for a great city and especially such a city as Dublin where party and sectarian strife so signally abound and more especially if filled by one engaged in our line of business, is fraught with difficulty and danger.' Benjamin declined the offer and the old man lifted hands of thanksgiving to God 'for the measure of his Grace which has led you to this happy decision'.[7] As long as his father lived, Benjamin Lee shunned ostentation. He had a small estate at Clontarf, two miles from the city, and a modest house in a Dublin terrace. He presided over a steady, unspectacular expansion of brewery sales and in 1855 the St James's Gate establishment looked much as it had done at the beginning of the century.

The changes that occurred in the life of Benjamin Guinness and the brewery in the thirteen years between his father's death and his own merit the description 'revolutionary'. He moved as one in a desperate hurry, anxious to make up for lost time. He trebled the acreage covered by the brewery and made it the largest porter manufactory in the world. He became the richest man in Ireland, owning substantial country estates, a town mansion in fashionable St Stephen's Green and a house in London's Park Lane. He now became a member of parliament (see below pp.71–2). His public works were prodigious and brought him a baronetcy. And within a few years of his death a statue had been erected to his memory in the shadow of St Patrick's Cathedral. Benjamin's qualities had long been recognised in the mercantile community. He took on the city council the place that had become the Guinnesses' almost by right and when, in 1851, he was elected Lord Mayor the event was marked with a lavish inaugural banquet, a foretaste of things to come. By the time he took over as un-disputed master at St James's Gate and inherited his father's fortune he was every inch the thrusting Victorian industrialist – diligent in accumulating wealth, jealous of his position in society, conscious of his many responsi-bilities, an affectionate if stern paterfamilias, an established churchman of conventional piety and a conservative-minded upholder of the *status quo*. If he transformed Guinness into Ireland's leading manufacturing enter-prise it was partly because he was able to ride the stream of events. The Great Exhibition of 1851 was the flamboyant signal which proclaimed an era of unprecedented commercial expansion. Railways, modernised banking, new overseas markets, steam-powered ships and a continuum of ingenious technical innovations enabled manufacturers and entre-preneurs to finance, produce and market their wares as never before. Ireland remained the most backward part of the United Kingdom, but it still took a share of the new prosperity.

The Great Famine made Guinness and Co. A moderately successful local brewery that a few years before the tragedy had come close to closure burgeoned quite spectacularly in its aftermath. This is not to suggest that there was anything sinisterly exploitative about the firm's marketing strategy; simply that it responded cleverly to dramatically changed conditions. The famine acted like a drastic economic medicine. Death and emigration left a reduced population, which could extract a more viable living from the land. Agrarian improvement was slow and piecemeal, but where it occurred it increased productivity. Railways and the importation of cheap manufactured goods from England helped small-scale commerce. Villages grew into small towns, new shops were opened, the agrarian middle class expanded. Poverty remained a serious problem, but more people than ever before had spare money. Some of it was spent on porter.

Benjamin Lee Guinness was aware of this economic sea change in a way that his father never had been and immediately set about exploiting it. Whenever opportunity arose he bought up properties neighbouring the brewery, erected new malting houses and bottling plants, and installed the latest vats, furnaces and mashing engines. He appointed Guinness agents in several urban centres. By staying several steps ahead of the competition Benjamin Lee ensured that his company absorbed most of the new demand. He also followed the time-honoured business principle, 'keep it simple'. While other breweries invested in tied public houses Guinness restricted its labours to what it did best – making beer.

One initiative that Benjamin developed *had* been his father's. In 1849 Arthur had set up two of his nephews in their own business. Edward and John Burke were the sons of his sister Mary and her husband the Reverend John Burke, who lived in Co. Galway. He had earlier taken them into the brewery and this had proved to be one of the more successful attempts to provide his relatives with careers. At a time when so many enterprising young men were seeking their fortunes by venturing into developing lands across the seas the brothers came to their uncle with a proposition: they wanted to set up a bottling plant in North America in order to sell Irish beer in the boom towns across the Atlantic. The experiment was so successful so quickly that, by 1860, the Burkes had opened agencies in South Africa and Australia as well. In fact, their expansion was *too* rapid and on more than one occasion Benjamin, and later his son Edward Cecil, had to bail the company out. Finally, in 1874, Burkes' sole agency was rescinded, but by then Guinness was well established in important overseas markets and other bottlers were eager to sell the Dublin brew. These distant sales represented only a small part of the brewery's annual turnover, but they were important in establishing the Guinness marque internationally.

By the time of his death Benjamin Lee had overseen a fourfold increase in sales of his beers in rural Ireland and made Guinness the most popular beverage throughout the country. Although sales in Dublin, Britain and overseas had risen, it was the Irish market which provided the bedrock of the brewery's remarkable success. This was acknowledged in 1862 when Benjamin Lee registered a new trade mark, the famous harp, which has since then appeared on the label of every Guinness product. This may be considered the first in a long series of brilliant advertising initiatives, although sixty-five years were to pass before the launch of the series of posters which would make Guinness a household name.

At Trinity College, Dublin, an ancient musical instrument is displayed known in popular legend as 'Brian Boroimhe's harp'. It has as much connection with the tenth-century hero-king who delivered Ireland from the Danes as Drake's drum has with the mariner who trounced the Spaniards, but as an emblem of national identity and pride it serves a similar purpose – or did so in the last decades of the nineteenth century. Both were relics which helped to keep alive nationalist myths. Brian Boroimhe (anglicised to 'Boru'), a hardy warrior and ruthless clan chieftain, was lauded by later romantics as 'he that released the men of Erin and its women from the bondage and inequity of the foreigners'. It was this legend, deliberately exploited and turned against England by nationalists of every stripe such as O'Connell, Young Ireland, the Fenians, and the Gaelic League that the strongly unionist Benjamin Lee Guinness permanently associated with his product. It was the kind of paradox that could only flourish in Ireland, one the Guinnesses have come increasingly to rely on.

This harnessing of legendary 'Irishness' to its product gave a boost to the Guinness brewery in other markets. By the mid-1860s it had come to dominate the Dublin trade. It effectively controlled the pricing structure for beer in the city's public houses, bars, hotels and clubs. Other producers either matched Guinness prices or went out of business. Irish emigration gave a boost to Guinness sales abroad. In Britain the Dublin brewery's products had to compete with those of hundreds of local manufacturers, but Irishmen who crossed the sea to work on the railways, roads and building sites of booming Britain acted as evangelists for their favourite drink. This goes a long way to explaining the discrepancies in sales to Liverpool, Bristol and London during the third quarter of the century. In 1855 exports to the three centres were virtually equal. By 1875 trade to Bristol and London had more than doubled, but that to Liverpool had quadrupled. The northern port, of course, had a large and growing Irish population. It was also the principal port of embarkation for the New World, where thousands of Irish families sought a better life.

Benjamin Lee was one of the great Victorian industrialists and, like most others who fell into that category, he felt the need to make public demonstration of his wealth and status. He invested in land in the west of Ireland acquiring a shooting estate at Ashford on the shore of Lough Corrib, which became the family's favourite retreat. But it was in Dublin that he made his most extravagant statement. Not content with 80 St Stephen's Green, he took the opportunity to buy the neighbouring property cheaply from its bankrupt owner and turned the whole into one of the city's most imposing residences. He then annexed several adjoining acres to make private pleasure grounds appropriate to his thirty-bedroomed mansion (they were later given to the university as the Coburgh Gardens). Here he and Bessie lavishly entertained leading members of the Ascendancy, as well as important visitors from London.

In an era when private enterprise and public benevolence were both articles of the successful businessman's creed, Benjamin Lee could not be seen to be expending his fortune entirely on his own comfort. Just as prominent to Dubliners as the renovations in St Stephen's Green was the work he carried out on St Patrick's Cathedral. It was this that brought him acclaim in those circles he cared about and for which he was created a baronet. The cathedral, a stone's throw from St James's Gate across the area once beyond the city wall known as the Liberties, symbolised the Church of Ireland: it was ostentatious and it was falling to pieces. This monolithic Norman structure, long the spiritual home of the Protestant Ascendancy, was in decay because the religious minority in Ireland could not or would not support it. Parliament, which ultimately controlled the destiny of the established church, was not disposed to come to its aid, so Benjamin Lee Guinness stepped into the breach, devoting £150,000 to the restoration and becoming solely responsible for its completion.

His benevolence cannot be explained entirely in terms of ostentatious charity and religious commitment. It was a sacramental statement; an outward and visible sign of his political, social and spiritual convictions.

The Protestant legislature of the empire maintains in the possession of the church property of Ireland the ministers of a creed professed by one-ninth of its population, regarded with partial favour by scarcely another ninth, and disowned by the remaining seven [ninths]. And not only does this anomaly meet us full in view, but we have also to consider and digest the fact, that the maintenance of this church for near three centuries in Ireland has been contemporaneous with a system of partial and abusive government, varying in degree of culpability, but rarely ... to be exempted ... from the reproach of gross inattention (to say the least) to the interests of a noble but neglected people.[8]

When William Gladstone spoke thus in parliament in 1838 the Church of Ireland had, in fact, begun to put its house in order. Spurred on by the growth of evangelicalism and by Catholic emancipation, Anglican clergy were, on the whole, taking their pastoral and evangelistic responsibilities more seriously. It was too little, too late. In an atmosphere of constitutional reform and the assertion of minority rights the immense privileges enjoyed by one branch of Ireland's Protestant population seemed increasingly untenable. Irish members constantly pointed this out, while agitators at home stirred up anti-tithe riots. Parliament responded in a piecemeal fashion. First, they shifted the tithe burden from householders to landowners, then they replaced state-aided Protestant schools with a system of national, non-denominational education. Smaller concessions accelerated the demand for greater. Nor was it only Irish radicals who were clamouring for change. Aroused by their own religious revival and by the proselytising zeal of their Protestant rivals, the Roman Catholic hierarchy now found a new dynamism and a new unity. Under the leadership of their parish clergy more and more Irishmen were raising the cry of disestablishment. It was against this trend that Benjamin Lee and his close relatives resolutely set their faces. They did not follow Arthur's liberal and tolerant attitudes towards the social and political aspirations of the Catholic majority. For the next half-century the Guinnesses would be staunch advocates of Protestant Unionism.

6

THE CLOSING DAYS OF THE
THIRD GREAT DISPENSATION

The Great Famine diverted attention from constitutional issues of church and state, but from the mid-1850s Nationalism and Unionism asserted themselves with renewed vigour, and the established church was one of the bones over which the hounds of conflict fought. 'Fenianism' was a term which covered a disparate movement involving a clutch of societies with innocent-sounding names such as the Emmet Monument Association, but which belonged to the secret Irish Republican Brotherhood and were supported by funds from the Fenian Brotherhood, based in America. It was a largely bourgeois, romantic, semi-intellectual movement, drawing its inspiration from the mythical past (the name 'Fenian' referred to the army of the ancient saga hero Fion Mac Cumhail). More specific in its objectives was the National Association of Ireland. This alliance of Catholics and Nonconformists directly targeted the Church of Ireland. They wanted it disendowed and the liberated revenues used for largely educational purposes. The NAI mounted a well-organised campaign in concert with English and Welsh Nonconformists, who were also tilting against the Anglican establishment. Although these were the main contenders in the field, there were several other groups – cultural, literary, political and religious – seeking and asserting an idealised Irishness freed from influences from across the water.

'The Ferguson Arms' continued to be open house to people of varying political and religious opinions. Sam and Mary – who, to their great sadness, were childless – took great delight in entertaining their friends and relatives. Whatever their parties may have lacked of the splendour of Guinness hospitality they more than made up for in the enthusiasm of home-made entertainments. They arranged plays, poetry readings, musical soirées, children's games (greatly enjoyed by their Guinness nephews and nieces), picnics, dances and zoo visits, as well as dinner parties where more serious matters of current concern were discussed. In 1867 Samuel was able to give up the law and devote himself entirely to the study of Ireland's heritage, when he became deputy keeper of the public records. Despite the work of William Bethan a generation earlier, much remained to be done in the way of organising the Dublin Castle archive and for his endeavours Samuel Ferguson was knighted in 1878.

Samuel's politico-cultural activities provide an indication of how ill advised it is to simplify Nationalist aspirations or, for that matter, Anglo-Irish sentiments. Unionism was not as rainbow-hued as Republicanism, but it contained the potentially violent Orange Order, as well as spokes-men who roundly attacked the British government over such policies as Irish church reform. Politics in the fifties and sixties tended to be a matter of issues rather than principles, of prejudices rather than strategies. Alliances, like jerry-built houses, could be quickly constructed and as rapidly crumble.

Benjamin Lee could identify with the Gaelic revival, while being completely committed to the British connection. The use of the harp trade mark was proof of the former; his rescue operation on St Patrick's Cathedral gives evidence of the latter. He could not allow the greatest symbol of Protestant supremacy to fall into decay. That would have sent out entirely the wrong signal to a country experiencing a major Catholic revival. Under the leadership of Archbishop Paul Cullen (1852–78), who became Ireland's first cardinal in 1866, the number of Roman Catholic clergy doubled and they were galvanised into more vigorous activity. Many of them belonged to the temperance movement and in their sermons perpetuated the myth that alcohol production was part of a Protestant conspiracy to soften the brains and weaken the wills of good Catholics. With religious opponents on the Protestant side also urging disestablishment and a government disposed to listen to their demands (Palmerston returned to power in 1859 with Gladstone as his Chancellor and leader in the Commons) someone had to make a stand that was both practical and symbolic. Benjamin Lee personally supervised the total overhaul of St Patrick's between 1860 and 1865.

In the latter year Dublin's most prominent citizen yielded to the pressure to offer himself as a Conservative candidate for the city in the general election. It took him several years to go against the wishes of his late parent in this matter, but during those years much had changed. Arthur had considered overt political involvement bad for business because one would inevitably upset some of one's customers and thus risk driving them into the arms of rival brewers. By 1865 Guinness and Co. were so firmly established as market leaders that such considerations could be safely ignored. The position of the established church was now under very serious threat from a Liberal government being hard pressed by well-organised interest groups and that church mattered more to Benjamin than it had to his father. He lacked the convinced evangelicalism that Arthur had supported at Bethesda Chapel. He belonged to what was, in reality, an ecclesiastical family; one of his two brothers and all but one of his brothers-in-law were clergymen. He was lauded as the saviour of St Patrick's and, indeed, as Ireland's leading Anglican layman. As a respectable and respected member of the establishment he felt he had to do whatever lay in his power to maintain the established church. If, by 1865, he needed encouragement into a new arena of public debate, that was provided by the formation of the National Association of Ireland (see above). Now that the fiasco of Richard Samuel's parliamentary career was well in the past his cousin could safely expose himself upon the hustings.

There was never any doubt of Benjamin Guinness's election and he spent the greater part of his remaining three years in London faithfully supporting Derby and Disraeli who, having forced a crucial vote on parliamentary reform in June 1866, came into power though having a technical minority in the Commons. The two dominant issues were franchise extension and the Irish church. Disraeli carried a new Reform Act in 1867 and hoped that the multitude of new voters would massively confirm the Conservatives in office and, among other things, enable him to strengthen the Union and kill the aspirations of the disestablishment lobby.

The Tories hoped to profit from the Fenian scare. The end of the American Civil War in 1865 released on to the mercenary market a posse of Irish-American soldiers with no taste for civilian life, who returned to the 'old country' to fight for its independence. They took a solemn oath 'in the presence of God, to renounce all allegiance to the Queen of England, and to take arms and fight at a moment's warning to make Ireland an independent democratic republic'. Activists toured Ireland and England forming 'secret' branches, delivering inflammatory speeches, disseminating pamphlets, and using every opportunity to gain publicity and provoke debate. The Fenians were never a serious military or political threat. Their abortive raid on the arsenal at Chester Castle in February 1867 was easily dealt with. Attacks on Irish police stations were demonstrations rather than proofs of real power. A terrorist outrage in

Clerkenwell, which killed twelve people and wounded a hundred and twenty others, was recognised by the leadership as a tactical blunder.

What Fenianism did achieve was to keep the Nationalist issue on the agenda. By alarming opponents, enthusing supporters and troubling the consciences of fair-minded men of goodwill it prevented what was coming to be known as the 'Irish Question' being pigeonholed. It contributed to a growing distinctiveness between the parties at Westminster. Disraeli's government suspended *habeas corpus* in Ireland and promoted a vigorous response. Gladstone urged serious consideration of Irish grievances as the best way of defusing the situation. Like all politicians, the two great combatants looked to the popularity or otherwise of their proposed policies. It was Gladstone who judged that the Fenian outrages had 'produced that attitude of attention and preparedness on the part of the whole population of this country which qualified them to embrace, in a manner foreign to their habit in other times, the vast importance of the Irish controversy'.[1]

Benjamin Lee represented a very different constituency and responded differently to the new expressions of Irish nationalism. A written address to his own employees revealed that he had mastered the political techniques of overstatement, universalisation and appeal to xenophobia. The Fenians, he asserted, were

> wicked and worthless adventurers who would not only deprive our country of the advantages which, as a part of the British Empire, we enjoy, but who would overturn all the social arrangements of society – would break the ties which bind man to man, and, by a reckless destruction of property and of human life, would deluge our country in bloodshed and reduce the industrial classes to want and misery, and take from others the ability of advancing the onward progress lately so evident in our beloved country.

True Irishmen were not taken in by these American terrorists; they recognised that the foreigners were wicked men

> who hope by deception and by pillage to grasp from its owners their property, and during the proposed panic to escape with their plunder to whence they came – thus avoiding the just vengeance of society, and to leave to their wretched dupes the sad and direful consequences of the crimes to which they had incited them....[2]

For such outspoken advocacy of the Tory position, as well as for his public benevolence, the Derby administration created him a baronet in April 1867.

Sir Benjamin enjoyed his new dignity for little more than a year. He died in May 1868 and his last months were clouded by dark events and darker forebodings. By the end of 1867 the Fenian insurrection had collapsed. Most Irishmen had no taste for violent revolt and the Catholic hierarchy firmly opposed it. However, the prevailing mood in the House of Commons was for change in Anglo-Irish relations. On 16 March 1868 Gladstone opened his campaign by boldly declaring that the alliance of church and state in Ireland must come to an end. A few days later he proposed a resolution to this effect, which was carried by a majority of sixty votes. The result was cheered in the chamber and when the Liberal leader made his way home to Carlton House Terrace he was followed by an applauding crowd. 'This is a day of excitement, almost of exultation,' he wrote to a friend. 'We have made a step, nay a stride ... on the pathway of justice, and of peace, and of national honour and renown'.[3]

Sir Benjamin was not exulting. He and his Tory friends were downcast. Disraeli announced his intention of calling a dissolution at the earliest convenient moment. It took place in November and Guinness did not live to witness the humiliation of his party (the Liberal majority was 112). Neither did he see the earlier rejection of Gladstone's disestablishment bill by the House of Lords, but he knew that peers and bishops could not resist indefinitely the severing of the ecclesiastical link. The Irish Church Act passed into law on 1 July 1869.

In February 1858, when the finishing touches were being put to Benjamin Lee's fine Dublin mansion, a very different Guinness arrived in town. The Reverend Henry Grattan was little more than a third of his first cousin's age, but he had already packed a great deal into his young life and was destined to be as prominent in his own world as Dublin's first citizen was in his. He was one of the Guinness poor relations: the elder son of the ex-soldier John Grattan Guinness and his second wife, nephew of the failed Edward, who had wasted his father's patrimony as well as his own, and half-brother of the John who had gone bankrupt in Bristol. Those of his closest relatives who had made anything of their lives lived modestly in clerical or medical households and were not dependent on brewery money. Arthur did offer the teenage Henry an opening at St James's Gate, but the boy turned it down. Nor did the settled life of a doctor or minister of religion appeal to him. He had inherited something of his father's restlessness and this would never allow him to walk in the paths of conventionalism.

Although the family was based in Cheltenham during most of Henry's childhood they moved house fairly often. Captain John, well into his fifties when Henry was born, could rarely settle at home for long, but

must be always visiting Dublin, Bristol, or some other town to see relatives, friends or business contacts. When he did spend time with his
young second family, sitting with them in the nursery or taking them on
walks in the park, he had many stories to tell them – of voyages over wild
oceans, military feats and 'heathen lands afar'. Little wonder, then, that
Henry and also his younger brother Robert Wyndham craved an
adventurous life. Both boys left home to go to sea. Thereafter, their stories
followed a pattern highly popular in nineteenth-century evangelical
literature. They entered fully into the hard life of crewmen on tall ships
racing through cruel seas to make profits for owners secure in the comfort
of their home ports. They swiftly learned about hauling on sheets with
frozen fingers and unfurling sails from giddily swaying yardarms. They
experienced the angry lash of a master's tongue and the heavier stroke of
a mate's fist. They made one with hard-swearing older mariners in the
fo'c'sle and went with them to spend their pay in harbour taverns and
brothels. They were, in the words of religious tract writers, 'engrained
sinners'. Then came dramatic conversion.

Henry Grattan and Robert Wyndham had been brought up in a devout
dissenting home. Through family prayers, Sunday services and frequent
midweek meetings they had received a firm biblical grounding. Their
mother was an evangelistic dynamo, who worked among Cheltenham's
poor, particularly the women of the streets, and was ever ready to make
public testimony of her faith. It was almost inevitable that the boys
would rebel against the restrictive piety of their upbringing and also that,
given the right circumstances, evangelical Christianity would later reclaim them. It was the younger boy, always known as Wyndham, who
was converted first. He fell under the influence of one Peek, the godly first
mate of the *Francis Ridley*. The man was ridiculed for his faith below-decks
– until a storm of unprecedented ferocity threatened to destroy the ship
and all aboard her. When all the arts of seamanship had been applied
without avail and the frightened crew members were clinging to masts
and deckrails in immediate fear of being swept into the water, Peek knelt
on the bucking deck and raised his voice in supplication to God. Soon the
rage of wind and wave abated. The seventeen-year-old Wyndham was
among the several sailors who were now prepared to respond to Peek's
exhortation to seek the salvation of their souls from the God who had so
dramatically delivered their bodies from certain death. At the end of the
voyage Wyndham returned home to recount his experience to his
brother.

Henry's conversion was immediate, but it was many months before he
discovered his destiny, the task to which he believed God was calling him.

In the spring of 1855 he retired to a small farm in Tipperary. He had in mind the possibility of taking up agriculture with the aid of a £400 legacy from his uncle Arthur, but he was also searching for the peace to pray, think and study the Bible. The truth when it came was transparent and absolute: 'The gates of glory and immortality opened to my mental vision and there shone before me an eternal vista of pure and perfect existence in the life to come. It was the marriage of the soul; the union of the creature in appropriating and self-yielding love with him who is un-created, eternal love'.[4] This classic mystic experience was accompanied by a compulsion to proclaim the truth. He wasted no time and within days was out and about in the fields and rutted village streets preaching from the Bible to a rural populace 'enslaved' by Rome. He had found his vocation as an itinerant preacher.

There followed a couple of years during which his 'zeal for souls' struggled with the formalities of the religious establishment. He attended a theological college, but left when the constraints placed on his preaching activities proved irksome. At the same time, the twenty-one-year-old zealot with the strong voice, compelling gaze and shoulder-length dark hair made an enormous impact in the open places and the dissenting chapels where he spoke. He was regarded as a phenomenon. At Moorfield Tabernacle, from which George Whitefield had launched the Great Awakening in Britain over a century before, the elders recognised in young Henry Guinness a man worthy to occupy the pulpit of the legendary revivalist. They invited him to become their resident minister but he declined, feeling himself unable to be restricted to one location. Consciously or unconsciously, he was following the precedent of Whitefield himself who, in 1749, had appointed others to look after the chapel so that he might continue with his field preaching. The parallel seems not to have been lost on the Moorfield leaders. Having further prayed over the matter, they ordained Henry Grattan to a travelling ministry. He immediately set off for preaching tours in Wales, Scotland and the Continent. Thus, he became one of the prime movers of the Second Great Awakening.

Revivalism is not the same thing as evangelicalism. The latter is the mark of a doctrinal constituency within Anglican and Nonconformist churches issuing in certain social and religious imperatives including pro-clamation, pastoral care, charity and the reform of manners. Revivalism is concerned with the spontaneous, dramatic transformation of large numbers of individuals, often accompanied by spectacular demonstrations of ecstasy and issuing in commitment to strict personal holiness regimens. Revival is the volcanic eruption of spirituality. Evangelicalism is the core of molten lava from which it bursts. Evangelicalism had had its ups and downs in the early nineteenth century but had essentially remained strong in British church life since the days of Wesley and Whitefield. The revival which exploded sporadically in parts of these islands for two decades after 1859 was a phenomenon which had profound consequences. That the time was right for religious renewal is demonstrated by the contemporaneous reinvigoration of Roman Catholicism and of ritualism within the Church of England.

Great movements result when remarkable individuals are added to singular events in the test-tube of history. In the years preceding the nineteenth-century revival there had been a rediscovery of open-air preaching and this provided an acceptable medium for the Gospel. Primitive Methodist and Baptist chapels were eagerly training and sponsoring men for this type of ministry. In addition, American preachers had taken to organising British campaigns and some of them claimed to have reduced (a particularly apt word) revival to a science. Thus, by the mid-1850s, many fresh green buds were to be observed in the dusty hedgerows of British religious life. What brought the summer sheen of revival out in brilliant show was the preaching of a handful of bold and talented proclaimers. Three such men in particular stand out; three exact contemporaries who were in the full flush of youthful zeal and vigour. Charles Haddon Spurgeon, Dwight Lyman Moody and Henry Grattan Guinness were born within about two and a half years of each other. Between them they would be responsible for hundreds of thousands of conversions. The fame of Spurgeon and Moody may have suffered less erosion over the years, but it could well be argued that in terms of worldwide Christianity Guinness was the most influential of the three.

Henry Grattan arrived in Dublin in the first cold weeks of 1858 to a fanfare of press acclaim. The young preacher was the talk of the town for two reasons. His ascent to the hortatory heavens had been as swift and spectacular as a rocket. Reports told how, over the past six months, he had followed a punishing regime, speaking at hundreds of meetings, often to crowds of more than a thousand people. Added to this, of course, was the fact that he was a Guinness. Everyone who was anyone wanted to see him and hear him.

... Few preachers have ever addressed congregations more select. They consisted of the élite of all denominations, including a considerable number of the Established Clergy. The wealth, the respectability, the cultivated intellect, as well as the evangelical piety of the city, have been represented in a measure unprecedented, we believe, on such an occasion in this country. Judges, members of Parliament, distinguished orators, Fellows of College, the lights of the various professions, and, to a considerable extent, the rank and fashion of this gay metropolis, have been drawn out to a dissenting chapel which was thronged, even on weekdays, by this new attraction. On Wednesday morning the Lord Lieutenant was present, with the gentlemen of his Excellency's household; and yesterday morning we observed among the audience the Lord Chancellor, the Lord Justice of Appeal, and Baron Pennefather ...[5]

What one would love to know and what is unrecorded is what passed between the Guinness cousins at their meeting. It is inconceivable that Benjamin Lee did not open his house to his suddenly famous relative. Had he not done so the local newshounds would certainly have scented a family rift. But the two men can have found little in common. They represented two elements – religious zeal and commercial flair – which had long jostled together in uncomfortable harness and which had now separated. Henry disdained money; Benjamin was well on his way to becoming a millionaire. The Dublin Guinness drew his wealth from beer; Henry was an advocate of temperance. The evangelist believed in the imminent return of Christ and the establishment of a new order; his cousin had made himself exceedingly comfortable in this world; Henry was the advocate of intense, personal faith; Benjamin represented a religious establishment which his Nonconformist relative could only regard as spiritually moribund.

Whatever impact he made in Dublin, it was Henry's onslaught of the northern counties that was to go down in the history books. He spent most of the next eighteen months on a tour of Ireland and was greeted by scenes of mounting excitement. Commentators agree that he used no oratorical tricks aimed at provoking mass hysteria. As with Billy Graham a century later, those who attended his meetings expecting emotional firework displays were disappointed. Yet the results of his preaching were dramatic indeed. Men, no less than women, gave way to prolonged weeping, they cried out, they fell to the ground ('slain by the Holy Spirit'), they poured out their hearts in unintelligible glossolalia. Nothing on this scale had been seen since the days of Wesley. Yet it was in Ulster that Guinness's mission made its greatest impact, particularly when the preacher returned for his second visit in the autumn of 1859.

Belfast was Ireland's only real industrial city. The rapid development of linen mills and shipbuilding yards had brought with it all the ills experienced in the urban sprawls of Britain's North and Midlands – over-population, insanitary housing, bad working conditions, poverty and class tensions. Add to that rampant Orangeism and acute religious confrontation (the city was already dividing itself into Protestant and Catholic ghettos) and the result was a society where angry, unhappy and frustrated people were looking – usually in vain – for hope, purpose and peace. That, by itself, does not explain the success of Henry Grattan's campaign. Other factors were the preacher's conviction and his understanding of the situation. He refused to adopt a sectarian stance, pointing out to all his hearers, whether they called themselves Catholic or Protestant, their need of a Saviour. This put his message above politics and made it easier for all parts of the community to attend his meetings. And attend they did. Halls and churches were packed to overflowing. People swarmed up trees and on to roofs to see him in the open air. Penitents in their multitudes professed conversion.

The work begun by Henry was taken up by others. Membership of Ulster's Protestant churches alone increased by 100,000 between 1859 and 1862. From northern Ireland the spiritual epidemic spread to Scotland, Wales and parts of England. The Second Great Awakening was no flash in the pan. When Moody and Sankey visited Ireland in 1874–5 observers remarked that their meetings attracted people from both sides of the sectarian divide. At the closing 'Christian Convention for Ireland' in Dublin, clergy of all churches sat on the stage behind the evangelists. 'It was the first time that all these ministers had met on a platform broader than their churches,' one reporter wrote. So far had the mood changed in the city that when a pair of music-hall comedians made the Americans the butt of some of their jokes their ribaldry was drowned out by the audience lustily singing one of Sankey's hymns.

By this time Henry Grattan's leading role in the revival had come to an end. It was not that he ceased to believe the Gospel, nor that he stopped working tirelessly for its propagation. What happened, put very simply, was that he became suspect in evangelical circles. In 1860 he married Fanny Fitzgerald, a woman a few years his senior. The couple had much in common. Like Henry, Fanny was a poor relation of one of Ireland's great Ascendancy families. Her father had also been a soldier but, despite a distinguished military career, had been disowned by his relatives for marrying a Catholic. When she was still a child Major Fitzgerald had, in a fit of depression, leaped from the deck of a cross-channel packet. Since then, Fanny had been brought up by a devout Quaker couple living, latterly, in Bath. There, her foster-father had suffered a stroke and, unable to cope with physical and mental restrictions, he too had taken his own life. In recent years Fanny had come under the influence of one of Victorian Britain's numerous Nonconformist splinter groups, the Brethren (or Plymouth Brethren). It was the influence of this sect that was to change Henry Grattan's direction.

The Brethren began to find followers in the 1820s in Dublin among Christians – Catholic and Protestant – dissatisfied with their own churches. One of the leading figures was an ex-Church of Ireland clergyman, John Darby, a man who came to reject the teachings of the established religion, while craving the status and authority conferred by ordination. As is the nature of breakaway religious movements, the Brethren fragmented into sub-sects gathered round forthright leaders and nice variations of doctrine. They were exclusivist, preoccupied with apocalyptic and (particularly that section of the movement which followed Darby) rigidly authoritarian. Rival preachers and pamphleteers ardently anathematised each other over their interpretations of end-time chronology.

Henry Grattan fell under the influence of some of these little men with big ideas and even bigger self-regard. It was now that his earlier rejection of theological training exacted its toll. He lacked that understanding of the broad avenue of religious life and its millennial culs-de-sac that would have enabled him to see Brethren speculations in perspective. From this time on he directed much of his mental energies into abstruse calculations about the Second Coming and later wrote books timetabling future events in mind-numbing detail. It is worthwhile to quote a snatch of Henry Grattan's millenarian observations to show how a man so devoted to practical evangelism and, later, missionary endeavour could, at the same time, be obsessed by theological abstractions:

In the adjoined plate the millenaries measuring the course of human history are divided into Messianic cycles, and may be compared with the months and days of the Levitical calendar sketched in the centre.

A thousand years equal 29 3/4 Messianic cycles (analogous with the 29 3/4d. lunar month); *thirty* Messianic cycles (analogous with the 30d. calendar month of the Prophetic Times) equal exactly 1007 solar years and 7 lunations; and 180 Messianic cycles (half 360) equal 6045 solar years, 5 months.

According to the Hebrew chronology ... we have now about reached the termination of the first six thousand years of human history; and history as well as prophecy abundantly confirm the view this fact suggests, that we are now living in the last or closing days of the third great dispensation, and on the verge of another and a better age. *Half a vast year of Messianic cycles, measured from the creation of man, is now expiring*; and as it expires, there dawns upon the world the light which immediately precedes the sun-rising; there arise around us the solemn yet joyful evidences of the nearness of the glorious kingdom of our God ...[6]

It says something for the fervour and intellectual stamina of Victorian Christians that *The Approaching End of the Age*, from which the above extract is quoted, went through a dozen printings in the ten years after its publication in 1878.

Henry always resisted any denominational affiliation, but he soon found himself tarred with the Darbyite brush. Churches that had once welcomed him began to regard him with suspicion. But his new friends did him an even greater disservice: they admonished him (on 'the authority of the Holy Spirit') to beware of vanity in his preaching. This, according to a recent biographer, deprived him of the open-hearted directness which had up till now marked his public speaking.[7] Although he continued his preaching tours he became subject to worried self-examination and prepared his sermons with a care that robbed them of their immediacy. The next five years were hard. The couple, to whose itinerant household three babies were added in this period, struggled with a steadily declining income. In 1865 they returned to Dublin. On this occasion there was no excited flurry of newspaper articles. Henry and Fanny, with young Harry, Mary and Lucy, rented a run-down eighteenth-century terraced house in a district which had long since ceased to be fashionable. They worshipped in the nearby Brethren assembly at Merrion Hall and it was there that they met and virtually adopted a recent convert of bubbling and infectious enthusiasm by the name of Thomas John Barnardo. The following year the young man left to start medical training in London. But the Guinnesses had not heard the last of him.

7

A CIVILISED BODY

KELVIL You cannot deny that the House of Commons has always shown great sympathy with the sufferings of the poor.

LORD ILLINGWORTH That is its special vice. That is the special vice of the age. One should sympathise with the joy, the beauty, the colour of life. The less said about life's sores the better, Mr Kelvil ...

KELVIL May I ask, Lord Illingworth, if you regard the House of Lords as a better institution than the House of Commons?

LORD ILLINGWORTH A much better institution, of course. We in the House of Lords are never in touch with public opinion. That makes us a civilised body.

Oscar Wilde, *A Woman of No Importance*

England's most famous Irishman hugely enjoyed pointing out the discrepancies between rich and poor in the High Victorian age. The stage upon which the cynical aesthete sauntered was London, the world's centre, a city that embraced sordid dockside slums, as well as the elegant terraces and gay pleasure palaces of the West End. It was to this metropolis that the Guinness story now moved its centre – or, rather, its centres. While the family's businessmen and playboys paraded in their carriages along the Mall and left their calling cards in Mayfair and St James's, their Grattan Guinness relatives were living and working among the squalid tenements of Stepney.

By the time the queen's reign reached its glorious apogee the brewing Guinnesses had made the vital transition from the busy necessities of trade to the leisured graciousness of the Ascendancy. They had the wealth, the titles, the connections, the influence, the estates, the accoutrements of fashion to prove it – and the politics. For now that they belonged to the Anglo-Irish élite they devoted no small part of their energies to working for the Unionist cause, which alone could preserve their privileged life-style. They were able to shrug off the bourgeois values of the first two Arthurs and dissociate themselves from the embarrassingly emotional religion of their evangelical relatives, though not the ardent anti-Catholicism which in most cases accompanied it. Their lives were punctuated by calendarian fixed points – the London season, the Dublin season, the hunting and shooting season, reciprocal country house parties, Ascot, Henley and, increasingly, court events. St James's Gate still had to be supervised, but the family had excellent managers in place and, in an age of unprecedented commercial expansion, annual profits in-creased with a momentum that seemed unstoppable.

Benjamin Lee was in his fifties before he became a father and did not live to see all his children well settled in life. He did, however, make an excellent marriage for Anne, his only daughter. A 'somewhat romantic' girl, she was described by a friend as 'light, gay, cheerful and very attractive in looks and manner', but as one who also had a very serious side to her nature and 'never wearied in service for the poor and sick and unhappy'.[1] There was no doubting the depth of her religious conviction. Her own Bible was thick with annotations and underlinings, and she kept notebooks for her own reflections on spiritual themes. Nor was hers a private Christianity. While her father's faith displayed itself in commitment to the institution and buildings of the Irish church, Anne was more concerned for the material and spiritual well-being of its people. She was scarcely out of her teens before she began to give practical expression to her concerns. To Anne it was an unacceptable irony that the area around the cathedral, being painstakingly restored to its former splendour by her father, housed some of Dublin's worst slums. Appalled by the moral degradation she witnessed in the crowded, insanitary streets, she formed a small committee to fund and support the work of a 'Bible-woman', an evangelist-cum-social worker. This did little more than bring to light the true scale of the suffering and, within a couple of years, a district nurse was also provided. Anne Guinness's intrepid ladies worked tirelessly, providing free medicines, advice on hygiene, clothing and spiritual counsel to the Protestant poor, though if complaints from local priests are to be believed, their proselytising zeal sometimes took them into the homes of their clients' Catholic neighbours. In fact, the little enterprise grew and grew in response to the size of the problem and, in 1876, a pioneer institution was founded, staffed by dozens of practising and trainee nurses committed to working in the community. St Patrick's Nursing Home was the first of its kind in Britain and was not inhibited in its work by sectarian considerations.

Long before Anne Guinness's compassionate enterprise had blossomed in this way she had changed her name. In 1863 she became the wife of William Conyngham Plunket, a young man being groomed for high positions in both church and state. William had grown up in the shadow of his grandfather, after whom he was named. The first William Conyngham was a great patriot, politician and orator in the tradition of Henry Grattan. Indeed, he was one of the foremost of those upon whom Grattan's mantle fell. As a member of the Dublin parliament he resisted the Union of 1800 and for the next quarter of a century he was the foremost of those Protestant politicians who laboured ardently for Catholic emancipation. In Commons debate he was forthright, but also elegant and witty, and the victory of 1829 owed more than a little to his eloquence. He was raised to the peerage as Baron Plunket and served for several years as Lord Chancellor of Ireland. As well as being one of the wealthiest of Dublin's citizens he was also one of the most widely respected.

His grandson was an ordained minister of the Church of Ireland and acted as secretary and chaplain to his childless uncle, the Bishop of Tuam and second Lord Plunket. Barring any act of God he was destined, in the fullness of time, to inherit the family title. The younger William Conyngham was a serious and earnest churchman of decidedly strong Protestant views. As an active member of the Irish Church Missions Society, he was committed to succouring small Protestant communities throughout the land and forwarding the work of converting Roman Catholics. Plunket had the care of some of the wilder, more remote parishes of Co. Galway, and knew at first hand the hostility that Protestant clergy and their parishioners not infrequently experienced from the Catholic majority and their priests. Attending the funeral of a lay evangelist he observed the following incident:

> ... just as the remains of that poor man, attended by his many friends and by his poor, weeping, frantic widow, were being carried past the gates of that monastery where the priest in company with the monks of the place resides...
>
> A number of ragged boys, collected together, it would seem, by the monks for the occasion, were stationed in the school-house, while behind these boys some of the monks themselves tried, as well they might, to screen themselves from observation. Such preparations having been made, a poor man ... who was evidently put forward by others for the purpose, advanced towards the

roadside as the solemn procession approached, and addressing one of the Scripture readers, in a tone of cruel triumph exclaimed, 'The priest has laid that man low; which of you can raise him up?' And upon some of the mourners remonstrating against this indecent outrage, the boys, who had stood within the school-house grinning and chuckling at the awful speech, joined in with a strange, unseemly ribaldry, which was continued until the train had passed away from sight.[2]

As a well-connected young man with excellent prospects and one deeply committed to the Church of Ireland, Plunket readily commended himself to Benjamin Lee Guinness and also to his more devout wife Bessie. The marriage of Anne and William may or may not have been made in heaven; it was certainly made in the drawing-rooms of Ireland's Barchester. Within months of the nuptials Benjamin engineered his son-in-law's appointment to the treasurership of St Patrick's and when the cathedral precentorship fell vacant in 1869 Plunket was the obvious candidate. He was now firmly ensconced in the ecclesiastical hierarchy and two years later the ranks of the peerage opened to him when he succeeded his father as Baron Plunket of Newtown, Co. Cork.

Despite bearing her husband six children (or, perhaps, because of so doing) Annie Plunket enjoyed indifferent health, necessitating frequent stays at Continental spas and resorts. Her devoted husband raised no complaint about the interruptions to his work occasioned by travels outside Ireland. 'It is with Annie here', he wrote to his mother from Nassau, 'as it has been everywhere else, a case of "here we go up, up, uppy, and here we go down, down, downy"!'[3] These enforced intervals little affected his preferment. He took the opportunity when on the Continent of conferring with foreign ecclesiastics and visiting reformed congregations in Catholic lands with whom he felt much sympathy. In Ireland and England he campaigned energetically against disestablishment, that 'monstrous injustice which Mr Gladstone and his party propose to inflict on the Churches of Ireland'.[4] His prominence in ecclesiastical life and his excellent connections secured for Plunket the bishopric of Meath in 1876 and the archbishopric of Dublin eight years later.

When not abroad on convalescence Lady Plunket was able to enjoy the company of family and friends in Dublin. She and her husband divided their time between their residence in the city and their country home, Old Connaught, at Bray, a few miles down the coast. Annie continued her interest in St Patrick's Nursing Home and other charitable institutions such as the Clergy Daughters' School. She actively supported evangelistic enterprises and was warmly appreciated as a friend to young clergymen and their families. Lady Plunket died in 1889 at the age of fifty. The tributes to the wife of such a prominent man were, of course, numerous, but the fact that over 5000 people attended her funeral gives a truer indication of how widely she was loved.

Anne Guinness was not the only one of Benjamin Lee's children to marry into the peerage. Two of her brothers (Arthur and Benjamin) took earls' daughters to wife, while Arthur and Edward were eventually ennobled in their own right. Such iridescent futures could only be guessed at during their father's last days, but Benjamin Lee certainly had the further aggrandisement of his family in mind. He intended that his sons should build upon his social and political success, and that they should also continue the expansion of the brewery that provided the wherewithal to maintain their status. He was well aware that the boys might well find it difficult to follow his example of holding together a public and a commercial career, and he made it clear to them that the brewery was no milch cow, existing solely to nourish extravagant life-styles. If his heirs ever failed to be involved closely in the family firm, or to understand its workings, they would be destined to watch its profits dwindle or fall into alien hands, he warned.

Benjamin sent his eldest son to Eton and Trinity College, Dublin. Arthur, as his heir, must be equipped to live the life of a gentleman. Benjamin Lee – always known as 'Lee' – the next in line, opted for a military career. He was another wastrel Guinness, unable to cope with wealth without responsibility. He incurred heavy gambling debts and frequently had to be bailed out by his father. In due course, a commission was secured for him in the Royal Horse Guards. Eventually, in his father's will he was left £20,000 to purchase promotion, or land, or a business opening. He opted for a modest estate, subsequently married a wealthy heiress and settled to the life of a country gentleman. That left Edward. It would, therefore, have to be the youngest boy who was initiated into the mysteries of brewing beer. Edward's schooling ended at fifteen and he began work at St James's Gate. When he decided that he wanted a better education he had to be content with a part-time course at Trinity, which he could attend outside business hours. It was hard on the baby of the family, but it was probably the making of him. He spent the next few years living on a relatively modest allowance and learning from men of humble station who were, nevertheless, his masters in the art of beer-making. By the time his father died, Edward had been five years in the business and was well on the way to being able to take control at St James's Gate. Meanwhile, Arthur enjoyed a larger income and the cultured life of Dublin society. It is hardly surprising that relations between the brothers were not easy. If the younger resented the elder's freedom, the elder smarted at the younger's tendency to make unilateral decisions about the family business. The alienation had deeper foundations. With seven years between them, Arthur and Edward had never been close. Throughout most of the younger's childhood his brother had been away at school in England. When Arthur began to take his place in society Edward was scarcely into his teens. Yet, despite the advantages of age and the material benefits provided by generous parents, Arthur was never able to keep his little brother in his place. Edward was charming, clever and easily made friends. Somehow, he always seemed to be a rival.

In his will, Benjamin Lee took cognisance of this state of affairs. He left the bulk of his estate to his two Dublin-based sons. Arthur was to have the rural properties at Ashford and St Anne's, while his brother was given the town mansion. However, Benjamin's main concern was to preserve the brewery – by making it difficult for capital to be alienated from it – and to this end he entrusted St James's Gate to both young men to 'belong to and be held by them as co-partners in trade'. His testament then continued in words revealing his underlying anxiety: 'and I direct and earnestly hope that my said sons ... shall continue to carry on the said brewery and the business thereof which has been heretofore carried on by their ancestors for so many years'.[5] He laid down specific instructions designed to bind Arthur and Edward together with strong financial chains. The bulk of the business's capital was to be kept intact. In the event of either brother wishing to dissolve the partnership the departing sibling was to take with him only £30,000 plus half the value of stock-in-hand, such money to be paid over eight years. Since Sir Benjamin's assets (of which the brewery formed by far the greater part) were valued for probate at £1.1 million this represented a virtual pittance for a partner who decided to defect. Furthermore, should either son run himself into bankruptcy his interest in the brewery was to cease immediately, so that the business should not be encumbered with his debts. During his seventy years Benjamin had seen several of his relatives squander their patrimony by extravagant self-indulgence or incompetent business management. He had devoted most of his own life to Guinness and Co. and, in 1839, played a major part in preventing it being sold off. He was determined to obstruct its possible future liquidation – even from beyond the grave.

Thus, when their father died in the summer of 1868, two young men in their twenties inherited between them the bulk of Ireland's greatest fortune and the reputation of Ireland's most popular countryman. A contemporary photograph of the three young Guinnesses presents them as a trio of very self-assured young dandies (see Plate 5). Dublin society courted them, fêted them and watched to see how they would fare. Arthur was immediately involved in the political arena. The crucial campaign in the long-running church disestablishment war was about to begin. The elder Guinness was unopposed when he presented himself to the Dublin electorate as his father's successor. However, he barely had time to acquaint himself with Commons procedure before Disraeli called a general election. In December Gladstone came to power with a majority of 112, made up of radicals, whigs and reformers, who were soon known as the Liberal party. There immediately began that relationship of hostility between the Ascendancy and the Gladstonians, which was to develop into mutual loathing. The Conservatives needed every member they could muster if they were to make any show of resisting a government whose Irish policy, according to Disraeli, 'legalised confiscation, consecrated sacrilege and condoned high treason'. Sir Arthur Guinness was among those who took his seat on the opposition benches. But not for long.

The 1868 election was one of the last to be conducted under the old regulations and was open to those corrupt practices which had become part of the system. Arthur and his supporters should have had every confidence of success without having recourse to dishonest methods. For some reason Arthur's agents did not. Anxious, perhaps, that their candidate's youth and inexperience would adversely affect the outcome, they laid out a substantial amount of Guinness money in bribes. The result was swiftly challenged in the courts and Sir Arthur's election was voided. Although he was personally exonerated his humiliation was considerable. Political antagonists with long memories were not slow to remind Dubliners of the scandals surrounding Richard Guinness in the 1850s. Worse was to come. Arthur's supporters now turned to his brother to fight the by-election. Edward accepted the nomination, but a few weeks later changed his mind. We can only guess at what may have passed between the young men in the interim. Arthur had been publicly dishonoured and here was Edward, only a few months into his majority, deliberately trying to upstage him. It must have been intolerable. The young men had no parents or older relatives, save possibly their sister, to knock their heads together. Somehow, they resolved their differences but the events of January–February 1869 were not quickly forgotten.

The impetus Sir Benjamin had given to the business quickened dramatically under Edward's management. Output doubled between 1868 and 1876. To keep up with demand the company had to acquire adjacent property whenever opportunity arose. Over the years houses, workshops, whole streets were levelled to make room for brewing plant, offices and staff accommodation. It may be a cliché but St James's Gate brewery in these years really was a gold mine.

To present a black-and-white image of the two brothers would be to distort by over-simplification. Edward did not spend every day at his desk, poring over sales figures, and Arthur did not fritter away his hours in the pursuits of the idle rich. Both of them were young men with a great deal of money and no stern parent to exercise a restraining hand. For all his business diligence Edward knew how to delegate and was as enthusiastic as his brother about enjoying himself. Both were prominent at the leading events of the Dublin social calendar – the Kildare hunt's spring race meeting at Punchestown, the August horse show and the numerous balls, dinners and house parties clustered round these events at which the Ascendancy celebrated their superiority and exclusivity. Under Edward's genial supervision, 80–81 St Stephen's Green became the venue for Dublin's most sumptuous and extravagant parties. With their absentee and part-absentee friends they enjoyed the London season and both of them maintained West End establishments. Increasingly, Arthur inclined to the rural life, but this did not keep him from what he saw as his duty. His interest in politics was genuine and, in 1874, he returned to parliament. Now that the Guinnesses had risen above the mercantile class, membership of the city council was no longer appropriate, but they were able to serve their fellow citizens in other ways. Arthur continued to support work on the cathedral fabric and was able to complete his father's rebuilding of the neighbouring Archbishop Marsh Library. Both brothers helped to finance the Irish Exhibition of 1872, one of the more positive products of Nationalism, which aimed to make a proud demonstration to the world of all that was good in Irish economic and cultural life. It was a measure of the prominence Edward had achieved in a short space of time that he became Dublin's youngest Deputy Lieutenant in the following year. In fact, beside his industriousness there ran a certain intuitiveness and impetuosity. He was lively and athletic, an expert driver of a four-in-hand, and given to sudden decisions and spontaneous acts of generosity.

Amid all this activity Arthur and Edward found time to go courting. In 1871 Arthur's marriage to the twenty-one-year-old Olivia Hedges-White was the wedding of the year. Olivia was one of the daughters of the Earl of Bantry, a substantial landowner in Co. Cork. The Whites ('Hedges' was a recent addition) had been in Ireland as long as the Guinnesses and had been ennobled in 1797 for repulsing Wolfe Tone's French allies, who had attempted an ineffective but none the less alarming landing on Bantry Bay the previous Christmas. Subsequent holders of the title had served in the House of Lords, but had otherwise been singularly undistinguished. On the death of Olivia's only brother without issue in 1891 the earldom lapsed. There is a certain irony about the Guinness peerage connections at this time. Of the three brothers both Arthur and Benjamin married into earldoms on the verge of extinction, while Edward founded an earldom. But that was in the unknown future. What mattered in 1871 was that the head of the Guinness family was marrying into the nobility.

Edward, by contrast, chose as his bride his own second cousin once removed. Adelaide, known to intimates as 'Dodo', was the daughter of Old Pel, one of the family's more spectacular failures. After her husband's death Katherine (née Jenkinson – see above p.61) took her younger children to live in Paris, where her sister was married to the Duc de Montebello. Katherine always insisted that she was 'grindingly' poor, but the generosity of her French and Irish relatives, who genuinely took pity on her family, enabled her to live in reasonable style. In France she had access to the court of Napoleon II and Eugenie, and she maintained a London establishment, as well as the family home at Deepwell, Dublin. Her seven offspring were a very mixed bunch. Most of them were still young when their father died in 1857 and Katherine was faced with the task, not only of starting them out in life, but also of fulfilling her own exalted ambitions for each of them. She managed to see her daughters properly 'finished', one son provided with an infantry commission and another taking a degree at Oxford. Yet, despite her best endeavours, she did not live to see her children achieve greatness. Of her three elder daughters one remained unwed and the others married two brothers of mere gentry stock. Arthur Cope made something of a splash in London, having gone to Australia and married money, but he proved unable to hang on to his fortune (see below p.248). Reginald, by contrast, was a successful businessman and Claude left university with a first class degree – so there was hope there for a proud mother. That left the youngest girl, the demure and diminutive Adelaide, who had learned in France the manners and social graces that would fit her for an aristocratic husband. When Sir Benjamin and Elizabeth took an interest in the younger children Katherine adopted the attitude that beggars could not be choosers, though she found it insufferable to be patronised by 'tradesmen', however wealthy. What was her mortification, then, when Edward Guinness proposed marriage to her Dodo? Her humiliation was made complete later when her two younger boys were employed in the brewery.

Adelaide was almost three years older than Edward and brought to the match an element of stability that her groom had hitherto lacked. There is no doubt that the couple were in love. Had Edward's parents still been alive they, like Katherine, might have tried to steer him towards a more 'suitable' union. As it was, he and Dodo enjoyed forty-three years of happy and devoted married life.

That life began in May 1873 in a simple ceremony at Ascot parish church, where the bride's brother-in-law, the Reverend Beauchamp Kerr-Pearce, was rector. The couple set off immediately for a two-month Continental honeymoon, much of which was spent with Adelaide's elegant French relatives. The experience was something of an eye-opener for Edward. The Montebellos, as well as being at the centre of Parisian society, owned a château and champagne vineyard on the Marne. Edward had long been accustomed to the life of Dublin's *haut monde*, but now he was brought into an ambience more sophisticated and refined than anything the Ascendancy could provide. This way of life, which Adelaide took for granted, was a revelation to her husband. He was largely ignorant of the delights of fine music, literature and art, and his horizons were dramatically and rapidly widened. He set himself methodically to learn those things which a cultured European gentleman should know. It was the beginning of a process of self-creation. Edward's desire to achieve truly gracious living would conflict increasingly with the reality of his home country.

Mounting stress and more frequent outbreaks of violence were tearing Ireland apart.

> I have showed your letter to my brother & Plunket and I have first to thank you from my Brother and myself for the kind feeling it expresses towards us relative to his candidature for the City. He has resolved not to contest Dublin but I must say, as you have alluded to a rumour that there was a chance of his adopting what are commonly called National views and opinion such was not the case for, while none can feel more strongly a truly National desire for the advancement of Ireland materially and intellectually, we do not and cannot think this is to be achieved by Repeal [of the Act of Union] or by any half measure of Repeal but by the determination of the Irish nation to oblige their representatives to enforce irrespective of party the rights of those they represent which they now almost entirely neglect ...[6]

So ran a letter of 25 May 1870 from Sir Arthur Guinness to Isaac Butt. In and between its lines it testifies to those incompatible political views which were to prevent a solution to Ireland's problems being found within the framework of the United Kingdom. One of the most popular items of bedroom furniture in Ascendancy households of the 1870s and 1880s was a chamber pot with William Ewart Gladstone's face portrayed in its centre. The administration over which this earnest idealist presided from

1868 to 1874 was among the great reforming administrations of modern parliamentary history. Therefore, it made so many powerful enemies among British and Irish vested interests as to ensure its downfall. Gladstone took an almost perverse pleasure in confronting establishments and there was scarcely a single powerful lobby that he did not offend. The Irish Church Act and the Universities Tests Act upset the religious establishment. Cardwell's army reforms and the modernisation of the civil service put an end to the domination of those professions by men who had the wealth or influence to secure top jobs irrespective of merit. A Licensing Act began to tackle the problem of alcoholism and alienated the entire brewing industry. The Ballot Act, by introducing secret voting, freed tenants and employees from the political pressure of those who controlled their livelihoods. And the first Irish Land Act, by guaranteeing certain rights to those at the bottom end of the rural economy, was inevitably regarded as government interference in landlord–tenant relations. Gladstone had surrounded the castle of inherited privilege and opened up a barrage from several directions. Small wonder that its wealthy defenders hated him.

As every schoolboy knows, or used to know, Gladstone came to power in 1868 with a 'mission' to 'pacify Ireland'. He believed that, by a series of bold measures, he could right the wrongs of centuries. The first salvo of his Irish bombardment was the disestablishment of the church (1869) and he followed this immediately with a Land Act (1870) which, although not putting an end to evictions (which, in any case, had dwindled in number), did oblige landlords to compensate the dispossessed for any improvements they had made and facilitated the purchase of holdings by sitting tenants. In practice, the Act applied only to a small percentage of landholders. What infuriated the estate owners was that the government had received representations from petitioners who, in the view of their 'betters', were covert Fenians and had tacitly accepted that tenants had moral rights. This measure had just passed through all its parliamentary stages when Arthur Guinness wrote his letter to Butt. It is not difficult to see what he had in mind when he accused the government of neglecting the rights of Irish electors.

Isaac Butt, the addressee, was a veteran politician, an accomplished Dublin lawyer and an ex-professor of Trinity College. He was a close contemporary and friend of Samuel Ferguson, and shared the archivist's brand of nationalism. In politics he had always been very far to the right, but in recent years had come to believe that Nationalist aspirations could only be assuaged and the sting of Fenianism drawn by some degree of constitutional accommodation. What he had in mind was a form of federalism. What he called it was Home Rule. The idea was a half-way house between Unionism and repeal. There would be a devolved parliament in Dublin for determining Irish affairs, but the nation would remain loyal to the crown. This appealed to a wide constituency including Protestants, who feared Fenianism and despised Gladstone. In 1870 Butt founded a party to commend his programme to the people and canvassed prominent Irishmen to contest the next election on a Home Rule ticket. Among those he wished to win to his cause was the charismatic and popular Edward Guinness. He approached Arthur, as head of the family, and Arthur discussed it with Edward and their brother-in-law. The resulting letter of 25 May made very clear that the Guinness entourage stood firmly behind unadulterated Unionism.

Sam and Mary Ferguson continued to preside, a few streets away, over a more open-minded court. 'It has been observed', wrote Mary, 'by an eminent classical scholar familiar with the habits and modes of thought of the ancient Greeks, that a dinner-party in Dublin resembles the *deipnon* of the Athenians more nearly than a similar social function elsewhere. The resemblance consists chiefly in the animated interchange of ideas, quick and versatile wit and humour being characteristic of both races'.[7] The antiquarian's table was renowned for its intelligent and good-natured conversation. Politics did not divide the couple from Mary's family. She and Sam retained the closest links with the Rundell Guinnesses and were particularly fond of their young nieces, to whom Sam enjoyed writing teasing–flattering verses:

> The sponsors at the font, dear Annabel,
> With hopeful prescience named the infant well.
> Infant and child that presage you're approved,
> Now grown a damsel, lovely and beloved,
> Accept this 'Book of Flowers' an offering meek
> For such a Flower, fresh-blooming, pure and sweet.[8]

His heart was wide enough to embrace Arthur Guinness, a reactionary with whom he had little in common. Learning that Arthur had been taken ill abroad, he immediately sent for further news and wrote to his wife, 'Heaven grant that the poor fellow may not be cut off from his career of honourable usefulness!'[9]

This is the point to add an ironical footnote. In the very year of Benjamin Lee's death and Gladstone's electoral triumph, when the Guinness brothers were beginning to emerge as Unionist combatants, a distant cousin – distant both genealogically and geographically – was making a name for himself as a champion of Irish Nationalism. Arthur Robert Guinness was the son of that restless Francis Guinness who had left Britain in the 1840s. He was born in Calcutta, but grew up first in Australia, then in New Zealand. He studied law and became a barrister in 1867. The following year he was engaged as junior defence counsel in a very high-profile case. Some Fenian agitators had killed a policeman and duly paid the price for their crime. But afterwards sympathisers engaged in demonstrations on behalf of the dead men and their cause. They were arrested and put on trial for sedition. It was Arthur Robert's 'brilliant and persistent advocacy' which secured their acquittal and laid the foundation of his own reputation in law and politics.

Arthur Robert was a founder member of the New Zealand Liberal party. He was elected to parliament in 1884 in the days before radical, anti-Westminster elements had coalesced into a coherent political force. In the last decades of the nineteenth century the growing colony was impatient to develop the institutions of nationhood free from Colonial Office interference. A new country with no upper class accustomed to wielding political power, New Zealand made rapid constitutional strides once the reformers assumed office in 1891. Guinness's eloquence had by then marked him out as an effective debater and he played a prominent part in carrying through a series of measures which were well in advance of anything achieved in Britain. The government introduced old age pensions in 1898 (a reform Guinness urged with particular passion), brought in workers' protection legislation and encouraged the formation of trade unions, restricted the powers of the governor and the unelected legislative council, established a graduated income tax and enforced the repurchase of large estates to prevent the growth of a land-based aristocracy. New Zealand made history in 1893 when, having already introduced adult male suffrage (the expression 'one man, one vote' was coined there in the 1870s), it extended the vote to women. Guinness supported all these progressive measures at a time when similar proposals by Gladstone, Asquith and Lloyd George were being ardently attacked by his relatives in the 'Mother of Parliaments'. In 1903 Arthur Robert received the ultimate accolade his colleagues could bestow when he was elected Speaker of the House of Representatives. He occupied that office until his death in 1913 and was, thus, a major participant in the ceremonies associated with New Zealand's achievement of dominion status in 1907. A well-deserved knighthood for his many services had to wait until 1911.

8

THE FLAME OF DIVISION
AND STRIFE

In Gladstone's monumental first term as premier a legislative programme was carried through which would have taxed the resources
of the most able cabinet. In addition the government had to cope
with highly flammable situations in foreign policy. The Franco-Prussian
War seriously upset the balance of power in Europe. Russian pan-
Slavism under the guise of Christian indignation confronted Turkey's
corrupt Islamic regime in the Balkans and threatened to embroil the
Continent in a second Crimean War. Diplomatic relations with post-
Civil War America were delicate. As early as the spring of 1872 Disraeli
was able to turn the administration's achievements to his own advantage when, in a famous speech, he likened the government front bench
to 'a range of exhausted volcanoes. Not a flame flickers upon a single
pallid crest. But the situation is still dangerous. There are occasional
earthquakes, and ever and anon the dark rumblings of the sea'.[1] As
Gladstone's popularity waned with various sections of the community
he became increasingly vulnerable. He experienced his first Irish policy
defeat over a bill to set up a Roman Catholic university linked with
Trinity College, Dublin. By enforced toleration in academic circles the
Prime Minister hoped to weaken further the ramparts of religious
prejudice. Predictably, the scheme infuriated Trinity's past and present
alumni, and failed to find favour with the Catholic bishops. At the
beginning of 1874 Gladstone, in an attempt to silence his critics,
submitted himself to the electorate. The Conservatives won a Commons
majority of forty-eight. Among the new faces on the government
benches was that of Sir Arthur Guinness.

The most important result of the 1874 election had nothing to do with the fortunes of the two main parties. There sprang into the arena a third combatant, maverick and eloquent. Butt's Home Rule Association had returned forty-six members and another thirteen MPs declared their support for his principles. For the first time Irish voters had their own, independent party; moreover, the secret ballot had, at a stroke, deprived the landowners of political power – at least as far as the lower house was concerned. However, Butt's principles were soon discarded by the organisation he had brought into being. From 1877 the dominant figure in the Home Rule Association was Charles Stewart Parnell and what he meant by 'home rule' was independence.

What swelled the flood waters of Anglophobia was another agrarian crisis. Since the end of the Great Famine there had been occasional years of poor, even disastrous, harvests, but none of them was as bad as the run of low-yield years 1877–9. When tenant farmers and poor leaseholders struck hard times they looked to their landlords for relief and it was the response of the magnates that largely influenced popular perceptions of the Ascendancy both at home and abroad. Several individual estate owners dealt generously with their suffering tenantry and were locally blessed for it, but it was their more arrogant and unfeeling colleagues who by ousting rent defaulters branded the whole class as the worst kind of feudal baronage. Nationalist extremists now had not only a powerful voice in parliament, but a cause with which even many of their opponents could sympathise.

On 2 April 1878 a band of IRB assassins waylaid the Earl of Leitrim's carriage on a quiet coastal road in Donegal. Leitrim was an irascible tyrant who treated his 'underlings' with total disdain, quarrelled with his neighbours and had few friends in the upper ranks of Irish society. The IRB men shot the peer, his secretary and his driver, before making their get-away by boat. Other members of the Ascendancy were not surprised. Some were not even outraged. 'The wretched old man has been practically working for his own destruction for many years,' one landowner observed.[2] The Donegal atrocity provoked more indignation in Westminster than in Dublin's clubland. To Britain's comfortable, prosperous legislators acts of terrorism were associated with foreign fanatics and excitable 'Continentals'; they were bizarrely out of place in the open society upon which the Victorians prided themselves and in which both Napoleon III and the supreme advocate of class war, Karl Marx, alike had found sanctuary. The assassination provoked a heated debate in the Commons chamber and when Parnell would not denounce the culprits he was accused of condoning murder. Such, however, was the upper-class complacency on both sides of the water that few identified

Lord Leitrim's murder as the precursor of another period of agrarian unrest.

Life for land agents was never easy and often dangerous in these years. John Ross Mahon took care of most of the estate management work of Guinness Mahon and Co. from his office in Strokestown, but younger Guinnesses coming into the business were sent to him to begin their apprenticeship. It was a means of anchoring them in a reality to which their upbringing in affluent London and Dublin homes had not exposed them. As long as a substantial part of the firm's income derived from Ireland's rural economy it was right and proper that initiates should understand the problems of landowners and tenants. Therefore, all six Guinness sons of the next generation who came into the business saw something of its 'sharp end'.

In Dublin Henry and his wife Emelina, who came from city merchant stock, brought up twelve children. Of their five sons the eldest, Henry Seymour, eventually inherited the family estate at Burton Hall, Stillorgan, and lived the life of a country gentleman. He is of interest in the Guinness story in that he was the family historian. He devoted years to patient archive research and correspondence with relatives to establish an accurate family tree. It was Henry Seymour who critically examined the by now widely accepted claim to descent from the ancient and noble clan Magennis. He rejected this version of family origins in favour of a rival theory, which connected his ancestors with the Cornish bloodline of Gennys. This version of Guinness kindred had been held to in Henry Seymour's family since the days of his great-grandfather, well before Hosea had stamped heraldic authenticity on the Magennis story by obtaining a grant of arms. Henry Seymour willingly conceded that there was no cast-iron evidence for his preferred version; the Guinness line simply could not be traced back convincingly beyond Richard of Celbridge. That situation pertains to the present day and modern Guinnesses (or those who are interested) tend to accept whichever theory most appeals to them.

Of Henry Seymour's brothers one decided on an army career and another took no interest in the family business. The youngest, (Richard) Noel born in 1870, eventually chose the legal profession. This left only the third son, Howard Rundell, to take his place in the family business. He joined at the age of sixteen at the height of the Land War. It was a baptism of fire. Not only was the land agency caught up in the rural unrest, the bank also was under pressure from commercial clients in difficulty. There was a record number of business failures in the 1880s.

Howard's father was in his fifties and the remaining founder, John Ross Mahon, perhaps because of the increasing stress caused by the changes, went into part-retirement. Within a few years he died without heir. He left his interest in the business to a nephew, but after a short trial this young man decided to cash up his share and take off to foreign parts. The burdens were too heavy for Howard's young shoulders and he was joined by two of his cousins. Robert Darley Guinness, Richard Seymour's eldest son, came over from London, married a girl from Westmeath and, apart from a few years spent in London qualifying as a barrister, settled in Dublin until the crisis years had passed. His brother, Gerald Seymour, worked in the Castle Green office while reading for his degree at Trinity. Meanwhile Richard Seymour continued to run the Clement's Lane office, still regarded as the 'London agency' of the main business, in his idiosyncratic way.

The Land War took the Ascendancy by surprise. It began when hard-pressed tenants asked for rent reductions or for more time to pay. There was nothing new about that; landlords were quite used to hard-luck stories, both genuine and feigned. They responded in a variety of ways. Absentees, who delegated hard decisions to their agents, owners whose estate finances were already squeezed dry by mortgage pressures and those who treated their lands as milch cows for the nourishment of a high life-style used the latest hardships as means of replacing defaulting tenants. Their richer or more charitable neighbours took a lenient view, agreeing to rent reductions or, in some cases, forgoing payment altogether. There are stories of Ascendancy wives meeting tenants as they arrived on rent days and surreptitiously slipping them the necessary cash to pay their dues to their less sympathetic husbands. What was new in 1879 was the extent of the problem and the determination of the IRB and the Parnellites to make political capital out of it. At a Dublin meeting in October the Irish Land League came into being, headed by Parnell and covertly supported by some elements of the Fenian movement. Its declared objectives were to enforce lower rents and to engineer the transfer of freeholds to tenants. Land League activists regarded these merely as the first steps towards driving out the Anglo-Irish ruling class and achieving legislative independence.

In its initial impact the campaign was alarmingly successful and, by its influence on Gladstone, it came close to realising its long-term objective. Secure in the support of the League, hundreds of tenants withheld rent. Landlords who responded with eviction were 'boycotted', a word added to the dictionary by the unfortunate experiences of Captain Charles Boycott, who managed an estate bordering Lough Mask, which belonged to Earl

Erne, whose principal residence was in Fermanagh. When the dearth struck he announced a ten per cent reduction in rents, but this was not enough for the hard-pressed tenants and the IRB, who were strong in the area, threatened Boycott: he could bring the exactions down a full twenty-five per cent or share Lord Leitrim's fate. The agent refused to yield to terrorist pressure and began proceedings against defaulters. It was then that he discovered that he was no longer dealing with timorous, forelock-tugging individuals; the whole local community was organised against him. In a recent speech delivered seventy miles away at Ennis, Parnell had urged his supporters to solidarity. Any neighbour co-operating with the enemy was to be purdahed behind a wall of contempt: 'you must shun him in the streets of the town, you must shun him at the shop-counter, you must shun him in the fair and market-place, and even in the house of worship ... and you may depend upon it, if the population of a county in Ireland carry out this doctrine, that there will be no man so full of avarice, so lost to shame and to dare the public opinion of all right-thinking men within the county.' This challenge to the very socio-economic fabric was, in the short term, effective and Boycott was the first to feel the brunt of it. His labourers deserted; tradesmen would have no dealings with him; countrymen shouted insults as he rode past; even in Dublin he could find no hotel which would give him a room. For weeks he was completely isolated.

The only person who came to his aid at this time was Arthur Guinness, whose simplistic commitment to the *status quo* was outraged by this challenge. The owner of Ashford Castle maintained a steamer on Lough Corrib for the benefit of villagers around its shores. Arthur used this to send provisions and horses to the northern end of the lake and thence, under the escort of some of his heftier estate workers, to the house of the beleaguered agent. Such examples of defiance drove further stakes into the fence separating rulers and ruled. Demonstrators obstructed shooting parties and disrupted hunts. In 1882 Punchestown races were abandoned. Police and army units had to be dispersed widely to maintain the normal pattern of rural life. Landed families, deprived of indoor and outdoor servants, experienced unprecedented hardship. They had to perform their own household and farmyard chores. 'Poor Willy's back and neck were quite doubled over ... and my arms were weak with milking ... we can neither of us sit down in a low chair without groans over our poor legs,' complained one Ascendancy lady experiencing the novelty of hard work. Her only balm, she averred, would be to see Mr Gladstone hung in chains.[3] For others, the Land War marked the end of the road; it drove them into bankruptcy. But though the Land League mounted an overall, effective Nationalist campaign, its impact was never universal. Where landlords enjoyed the respect, even affection, of their tenantry revolutionary agents fought a losing battle.

Arthur and Olivia Guinness, meanwhile, were busy extending Ashford Castle, throwing up wings and courtyards in a bewildering medley of styles. Foreign travel had bestowed upon them a certain architectural eclecticism. They rebuilt St Anne's Clontarf in the Italianate taste and at Ashford steep French Renaissance roofs joined Gothic crenellated turrets and a fanciful Tuscan campanile. Fountains plumed in the midst of silken lawns. Gravelled walks provided for genteel exercise. Shaded arbours offered spectacular views across the lough upon which Arthur's steam yacht sailed, providing his guests with excursions and waterborne picnics. Arthur also carried out extensive afforestation and made Ashford into one of Ireland's finest shooting estates.

Looking after it and its farms involved hundreds of servants and tenants, and there was considerable interest in how this outspoken Unionist would fare during the troubles. His support for Boycott marked him out as a prime target for the Land League and they tried to spur his tenantry into combining against him. Their organisation was very strong in Galway; the level of serious and violent disturbance between 1879 and 1882 was higher there than in any other county except Kerry. It was there, in September 1880, that another member of the Ascendancy, Viscount Mountmorres, was gunned down close to his home and one of his own tenants refused to allow the body into his cottage for medical examination.

Arthur determined to stand up to the terrorists. It was a classic confrontation: *ancien régime* versus the forces of revolution; a popular and generous landlord versus the enemies of his class; paternalism versus idealism; the security of old ties versus the vision of new freedoms. And we have to add another element: the Guinness name. The bottle with the harp on the label was well-known throughout the land; its contents enjoyed in every town and country bar. Guinness stout was the nation's most famous product; its most popular export. It was rapidly becoming a part of what it meant to be Irish. Already established in the collective unconscious was the impression that to show disrespect to a Guinness was akin to treason. It was, perhaps, this consideration above all others that threw a defensive wall about Ashford during the crucial months of the Land War. Local people hated the policies Arthur openly paraded and they had grievances with his agents, but they would not vent their spleen on him. As for Arthur, he faced the crisis with sang-froid and blinkered paternalism. He brushed aside an offer of police protection. 'I have a little force of my own,' he observed, 'consisting of my gamekeepers, who are loyal men and true, and I prefer to trust them. Besides, my tenants are all on good terms with me, even though they may be frightened by those who are about them ... Whatever danger landlords are in is owing to the agitation which goes on around us'.[4] His understanding of the situation was simple: Irishmen were good fellows whose interests were well looked after by the establishment. The only people who wanted to change things were Parnellite revolutionaries, foreign agitators and wishy-washy English Liberals who buckled at the first sign of Nationalist hostility.

Arthur may have been as much out of touch with the aspirations of ordinary people as was Wilde's fictional Lord Illingworth, but according to his lights he was greatly concerned about the men and women of Ireland. In October 1876 he withdrew completely from any involvement in the brewery. He had never had much interest in St James's Gate and what interest he did have dwindled after his marriage and his election to parliament. As we have seen, he took his politics very seriously, and he and his young wife found that their social life in London, Dublin and Ashford engaged most of their time and energies. The expiry of the existing partnership agreement in 1876 provided the opportunity for the brothers to consider seriously the future of the family business. It was a repeat of the situation that had occurred in the previous generation. Then Arthur Lee Guinness had resigned his interests in favour of his younger brother, Benjamin, in order to enjoy his own life-style. Now it was Benjamin's heir who left the brewery for essentially the same reason. Lord and Lady Ardilaun were, so far, childless (and were destined to remain so). By contrast, Adelaide had just given birth to her second son. Everything pointed to the advisability of the business becoming the preserve of the family's cadet branch. But Arthur was not prepared to yield on the terms outlined in their father's will, which had been devised to prevent the decapitalisation of the brewery, not to allow a retiring partner to establish a considerable personal fortune. Since 1868 the value of the plant and goodwill had multiplied considerably. The brothers eventually agreed that Arthur was to receive £680,000 on relinquishing his interest. This meant that, with his properties and investments, he was already a wealthier man than his father had been at the time of his death a mere eight years earlier.

He laid out a not inconsiderable portion of his riches in public benefactions. In Arthur Guinness compassion and duty were inextricably entwined. He was one of a breed of Victorian philanthropists whose Christian conscience made a clear connection between the possession of wealth and the doing of good. At the same time it cannot be denied that he had a political point to make: Ireland was better off under a system which permitted Protestant gentlemen to derive profit from their local interests and plough back some of that profit into the community.

He followed the family's long tradition of support for St Patrick's Cathedral. As well as continuing Sir Benjamin's building work he helped to maintain the choir school and contributed handsomely to the central coffers of the disestablished Church of Ireland. Dublin had other reasons to be grateful to him. He was a pioneer of slum clearance and the building of new homes for the city's working class. Many of the once-fine streets and terraces built in his great-grandfather's time had slipped down the social scale. Houses had been sub-divided, with the resultant over-crowding and squalor. In addition, the expanding capital had known its share of jerry-builders in the earlier years of the century. By the 1880s urban redevelopment was an urgent necessity, as it was in most of Britain's major cities.

Arthur's concern must be seen in the context of the social and political realities of the last decades of the century. Rich and poor lived cheek-by-jowl in the ever-sprawling metropolises of the world's leading industrial nation and the contrast was impossible to ignore. A miscellany of publicists and campaigners laboured to ensure that it was not ignored. Frederick Engels's *The Condition of the Working Class in England* was a blueprint for the waging of class war. Henry Mayhew, one of the founder editors of *Punch* magazine, was no revolutionary but his vivid sketches of the metropolitan sub-culture, *London Labour and the London Poor* (1851–62) brought home to many comfortable citizens the realities of urban life. Anarchists played on misery and resentment. One advocated dynamite as cure-all for social ills: 'place in the immediate vicinity of a lot of rich loafers who live by the sweat of other people's brows, and light the fuse. A most cheerful and gratifying result will follow.' Such extremism was rare, but politics was never far below the surface in any discussion of urban renewal. Trade unionism and working-class parties were new shades in the political spectrum. Many poor town dwellers now had the vote and their needs could not be ignored. Middle-class Christians like Thomas Barnardo, William Booth and Henry Grattan Guinness felt compelled to identify with the sufferings of the lower orders (see below p.136). Others published scientific surveys designed to bring home the realities of urban poverty – e.g. G. R. Sims's *The Bitter Cry of Outcast London*; Charles Booth's *Pauperism*; William Booth's *In Darkest England* and Seebohm Rowntree's *Poverty: A Study of Town Life*. Governments responded with royal commissions and piecemeal legislation.

In the Commons Arthur's vote helped to bring in such radical municipal reform measures as the great Public Health Act and the Artisans' Dwelling Act. These established new standards for the building industry and gave corporations widespread powers of purchase and re-development. The way was open for councils, companies and individuals to share in the rejuvenation of city centres. Pioneers like Joseph Chamberlain (in Birmingham) led the way. Arthur Guinness was among those who followed only a few paces behind. He helped set up and became president of the Artisans' Dwellings' Company, the first such body to be inaugurated in Dublin. The citizenry also benefited from another Guinness benefaction. Arthur approached his wealthy neigh-bours on St Stephen's Green (the Ardilauns' town residence was Number 42) and purchased from them twenty-two acres of the elegant grounds, which residents enjoyed exclusively for their own recreation. He then presented the land to the corporation to be used as a public park. In its midst the grateful city fathers raised a bronze statue to Lord Ardilaun – an honour only bestowed posthumously on his father. Well might Dubliners show their appreciation of the man who in one way or another returned almost half his fortune to the city and the country that had helped to create it. Among his other benefactions were the rebuilding of Coombe maternity hospital in 1877, a gesture which may have had something to do with the fact that he and his wife had no babies of their own. Nor was Arthur's generosity confined to the capital. In distant Co. Kerry he bought the Muckross estate around the beautiful lakes of Kilarney specifically to prevent it falling into the hands of a syndicate of English developers. For such public-spiritedness even committed Nationalists were prepared to forgive Arthur Guinness his extreme opinions.

Those opinions became even more right-wing and more passionately held as the political situation worsened. Gladstone inherited, in 1880, an Ireland almost out of control. The Conservatives' only answer to the growing number of outrages (236 in 1877 rising to 4439 by 1881) had been 'tough measures'. They provided more military support for the land-owners and encouraged the eviction of rent defaulters (the annual tally of dispossessed topped 10,000 in ˙1880). Such measures exacerbated class conflict and were useless against an enemy who could strike anywhere at will and find shelter among a population grown desperate by suffering. Gladstone had a clear majority in the new House of Commons, but his party was far from being united over Ireland and the Parnellites, with sixty-five seats, were strategically placed. While their colleagues across the water created mayhem by maiming cattle, firing barns and intimidating farming families, the Nationalists in Westminster disrupted the work of the chamber with filibustering speeches and procedural blocking measures.

Gladstone's first attempt to draw the sting of civil conflict was frustrated by the House of Lords. They defeated a new Land Bill by 282 votes to 51, but the government were determined to balance firm policing with attendance to genuine grievance and within months they had brought in a still more far-reaching piece of legislation.

The 1881 Land Act was the beginning of the end for the Protestant Ascendancy. The laws which eased the suffering of thousands of tenants drove hundreds of landlords into bankruptcy and forced sales. Of more lasting significance was the intense bitterness and sense of betrayal it provoked among those who held on to their estates. Together with their friends among the English ruling class, they waged war on Gladstone's attempts to secure Home Rule for Ireland and, for thirty years, continued to oppose the principle of self-determination. If any single-interest group can be held responsible for prolonging intermittent bloodshed on both sides of the Irish Sea for a further century it is the bigoted Unionists of 1885–1915, many of whom were, like the Guinnesses, absentee landlords, who frustrated the creation of a peaceful federated or independent Ireland. The feelings which the Guinnesses shared with the majority of their Ascendancy friends were those of any élite colonial minority, an amalgam of anger, fear, cultural–religious intolerance and a sense of social superiority.

Their apprehensions were certainly not ill-founded. Irish Nationalism was fragmented into several parts, some of which were totally committed to violence. One such group of thugs, calling themselves the 'Invincibles', perpetrated what, though not the worst outrage of the time, was certainly the one which most stunned and horrified people of goodwill on both sides of the Irish Sea. On the evening of 6 May 1882 four assassins armed with surgical knives waited in Phoenix Park for their quarry, the hated Under-Secretary for Ireland, T. H. Burke, to emerge from the Viceregal Lodge. James Carey, their accomplice, was to give them the signal from his vantage point beside the polo ground. When Burke appeared he was accompanied by another unrecognised man. It made no difference to the terrorists: committed as they were to their ghastly enterprise, they hacked down both of the Englishmen. Only afterwards did they learn that their unknown victim was the new Irish Secretary, Lord Frederick Cavendish, a moderate and popular politician who had arrived that day to negotiate with Nationalist leaders. Samuel Ferguson, who understood the feelings of both sides in the endless conflict, was moved to write a poem, 'At the Polo Ground', in which he tried to put himself inside the mind of Carey:

... Here I am
Beside the hurdles fencing off the ground
They've taken from us who have the right to it,
For these select young gentry and their sport.
Curse them! I would they all might break their necks!
Young fops and lordlings of the garrison
Kept up by England here to keep us down:
All rich young fellows not content to own
Their chargers, hacks, and hunters for the field,
But also special ponies for their game;
And doubtless, as they dash along, regard
Us who stand outside as a beggarly crew....[5]

It was, for Ferguson, a departure of both style and subject matter from his usual verses and was an indication of his inner tensions.

The Tories managed to dislodge Gladstone for a few months in 1885–6, but he returned, committed to Home Rule and dependent on Parnellite votes. On 8 April he entered the Commons through shouting and placard-waving crowds to introduce his proposals for a Dublin parliament with wide-ranging powers. The policy alienated several of his colleagues, even though they were equally appalled by Salisbury's comparison of the Irish people to uncivilised Hottentots who after a further twenty years of English rule *might* be in a position gratefully to receive concessions from a benign Westminster government. Members of the extended Guinness family expressed their views on public platform or printed page.

To Henry Grattan Guinness the religious implications were clear:

If 'home rule' could be obtained for Ireland, it becomes at once a Papal kingdom and a perpetual menace to England ... The chief result of home rule is *the extirpation of Protestantism in Ireland* ...

The question before our country now is, whether we are willing to make a further and most decisive advance on the road in which we have already travelled too far, and to grant to an alien and antagonistic political power a most real practical supremacy over five millions of the queen's subjects in Ireland, including a million of loyal Protestants in that land.'[6]

The Nonconformist preacher was supported by his kinsman, the Archbishop of Dublin, in a speech to the Church of Ireland General Synod:

I contemplate with terror the thought of the possible fratricidal strife that the introduction of such a Bill might cause ... it fills me, as I am sure it does all of you, with pain and indignation to think that just at this moment there should come among us a statesman, whom I can only describe as a political incendiary with this Bill in his hand to light up the flame of division and strife in our native land! ... I appeal to the Almighty God of Justice, who reigneth though the people be never so unquiet. We have heard with our ears, and our fathers have declared unto us, the noble works that Thou hast done in their day and in the old time before them. O Lord, arise, help us and deliver us for Thy name's sake – and for Thine honour too![7]

On another occasion Plunket spoke prophetically of the Protestant majority in Ulster seceding and 'throwing to the wolves' their co-religionists in the rest of Ireland.

The most poignant response came from the pen of Samuel Ferguson, who had always gone against the Guinness grain in his understanding of and sympathy with the aspirations of campaigners for self-determination. A few months before his death he explained to a friend,

I sympathised with the Young Ireland poets and patriots while their aims were directed to a restoration of Grattan's Parliament in which all the estates of the realm should have their old places. But I have quite ceased to sympathise with their successors who have converted their high aspirations to a sordid social war of classes carried on by the vilest methods ...[8]

Yet still he could not see how the cold war could resolve itself without some form of Home Rule and still he inclined to the constitution that had pertained before the Act of Union: 'The Irish of our day will not give attention to any other political project save that of Home Rule. I think that the safest form of Home Rule – if we are to have it – that can be adopted is that of a restoration of the Parliament of 1799'.[9] He died in August 1886 and his widow reflected,

... the close of his long life of patriotic endeavour to raise and elevate his countrymen was saddened by their evil-doings. 'There have been men', wrote a distinguished author, 'who have felt in their country's humiliation and loss a far sharper pang than in any personal suffering.' These words express Ferguson's feelings. All his correspondence at this time evidences the grief and pain which filled his heart. To 'wait and pray', to hope and trust that the virtues of 'truth and manliness' would reassert themselves – these were his consolations.[10]

9

PUBLIC COMPANY –
PRIVATE MAN

After 1876 Edward Guinness was entirely his own man. He had a wife and two infant sons. He had newly acquired a country mansion just outside Dublin. Farmleigh, the centre of a sixty-acre estate on the banks of the Liffey, was a recently built house, but Edward spared no expense in turning it into the finest gentleman's seat in the city environs, with the possible exception of the viceregal residence in neighbouring Phoenix Park. And, of course, he was sole master of the business, to the continued development of which he applied himself with such vigour that annual profits doubled in the decade following the dissolution of the partnership. One of the attractions Farmleigh held for the brewery chairman was that it was a short and agreeable ride from St James's Gate. In 1876, also, came the first public recognition: he was appointed High Sheriff of Dublin city. He had already added considerable lustre to the most important family name in Ireland. He was one of the leaders of Dublin society and had begun to make his mark in London. All this was before he reached his thirtieth birthday. Edward Guinness was a young man who had everything and might well have been content.

Yet he was not. He wanted more – greater wealth, increased public recognition, a higher social profile, impressive titles and honours. Ambition drove him on relentlessly. Yet, paradoxically, this young man in a hurry was essentially taciturn and reserved. The twin goads that prodded him forward were a desire to achieve the refinement of his mother-in-law's relatives (for Katherine, we may be sure, lost few opportunities to point out the innate superiority of blue blood) and his brother's social and political pre-eminence. In both Dublin and London

Edward felt himself to be in Arthur's shadow. In their home town Arthur had naturally and easily slipped into his father's role as first citizen. Hailed as a great philanthropist, honoured with a public statue, Sir Benjamin's heir enjoyed a prominence for which he had never had to do a day's serious work. On his departure from the Commons Arthur's Tory friends rewarded his service with the barony of Ardilaun. That fact alone would have been galling for Edward, but what made the situation even more intolerable was the attitude of the Ardilauns. They lived up to their position and distanced themselves from their 'tradesmen' relatives. Their grandiloquence was a standing – if sometimes bitter – joke in the family. When a member committed some social gaffe the cry would go up, 'Whatever would Lady Ardilaun say?'[1] In London, too, Arthur cut a dash. He was a member of parliament from 1874 to 1880 and intimate with all the grandees of the Tory party.

The rivalry between the two brothers was intensified by marriage, for Olivia and Adelaide inevitably became competing hostesses. They were leaders in both the London and Dublin seasons and, like other *grandes dames*, it became a matter of intense, anxiety-provoking pride to outdo each other in the sophistication and lavishness of their entertainments. Their social contests were described, blow by blow, in the drooling gossip columns of the national and provincial press. Reporting from London on 7 July 1879, the *Irish Times* trumpeted:

> Lady Olive Guinness gave a ball here last week which cost £4000 ... The decorations of the ballroom and mansion are still talked of with admiration in Mayfair. The choicest and costliest blooms and blossoms were used with magnificent profusion, and every arrangement was in keeping. Lady Guinness is said to have achieved the success of the season, though it is shared with her sister-in-law, Mrs Guinness, who had an equally brilliant reception a few nights before.[2]

As far as Dublin was concerned, whoever occupied the castle, it was the Guinness brothers and their wives who were the kings and queens of Ascendancy society. By the granting or withholding of favour they could make or break reputations.

> ... Mrs Guinness's ball has been for three weeks the one, the universal, the absorbing, the all-important topic. It has murdered sleep for many an aspirant to fashion, for not to be invited was social damnation. As the day drew near the excitement increased. Stories filtered through the clubs of great names rejected; the flying column of Irish aristocracy, who at this season wing their flight through Dublin to the brighter spheres of London society, were amazed

to find that the mere announcement of their names at Maple's or Morison's was not sufficient to ensure a card; but Mrs Guinness can command her company and does not need such reinforcements.[3]

With the eye of the *haut monde* upon him Edward used the 1880s to metamorphose his own life and that of the dynasty. His campaign was fought on three parallel fronts: he manipulated the business in order to unlock its vast capital resources; he created for himself a variety of magnificent settings, and he utilised his wealth and political contacts to achieve an ardently coveted peerage.

It may well have been Arthur's ennoblement in the spring of 1880 which finally spurred Edward into action. It was insufferable to see Lord and Lady Ardilaun enjoying the congratulations of the Castle set and boasting of their favour with the queen and Disraeli. At the same time Arthur's exit from the Commons did provide an opening for his brother. Edward's closest friend at this time was David Plunket, brother of his brother-in-law, the Archbishop of Dublin, and Plunket was something of a political fixer. He became Edward's champion in the selection of a candidate to contest one of the two Dublin County seats on the retirement of Colonel Taylor, the incumbent MP. Public speaking and the obligations of political office held no attraction whatsoever for Edward, but the cachet of belonging to the 'most exclusive club in London' was considerable.

Even more influential was money. Edward set about laying his hands on large amounts of it and employing it prudently. From 1880 he began taking immense sums out of the business. In 1879, when the brewery's annual profits stood at £363,000, he had been content with £30,000 for his personal needs. The following year, when St James's Gate profits actually fell to £319,000, Edward helped himself to £159,000. This rose to £326,000 in 1881 and £440,000 in 1882 (which was actually more than the brewery profits for the year). He also held discreet conversations with Nathanial Rothschild about the possibility of floating the family business as a public company and releasing a substantial portion of the assets tied up in it. Some of his capital was reinvested and some went into 'buying art' (see below) but appreciable sums were laid out in donations to Conservative party funds. Nor was Edward averse to buying himself friends in the Liberal government. He advanced £17,000 to the directors of Aston Hall colliery and clayworks, Clwyd, taking a mortgage on the plant as security. This was very close to the Prime Minister's country home of Hawarden and his son, Herbert Gladstone, was in fact the managing director.

With greater funds at his disposal Edward could now 'put himself about' socially with increased bravura. In 1880 he took a three-year lease on a Scottish grouse moor, so that he could not only enjoy the exclusive sport of royalty and nobility, but also offer splendid hospitality to the men who might help him up the social ladder. Two years later he took up a still more élitist sport. Yachting was a favourite pastime of the Prince of Wales and therefore became all the rage among those who could afford the enormous expense involved in keeping a handsome craft and crew. Edward bought the schooner *Cetonia* from the Earl of Gosford, an intimate of the prince (subsequently Lord of the Bedchamber to the Prince of Wales and Vice Chamberlain of the Household to Queen Alexandra) and joined the racing–cruising set. In 1883 he was elected to the Royal Yacht Squadron and bought a house in Cowes as another venue for his by now legendary hospitality.

Meanwhile Edward's political plans had suffered a set-back. Early in 1883 Colonel Taylor was obliged for reasons of health to resign his seat. However, the Tory leaders, instead of honouring their virtual pledge to Mr Guinness, asked him to step aside in favour of another candidate. Edward did so with a good grace and even contributed £1500 to electoral funds. However, he was determined that his services to the party should not go unrecognised – or unrewarded. He and Plunket made representations to the Carlton Club grandees, hinting as strongly as they could with any delicacy that some title or honour would be appropriate. Months of not very subtle intrigue drew forth nothing more tangible than effulgent expressions of the party's gratitude and an offer of nomination for one of the Dublin city seats in the next election. This put Edward in something of a dilemma. He did not want to jeopardise his standing in the party by declining the offer, but he really did not want to stand for a city seat. A rural constituency was one thing; it carried status encumbered with little responsibility. On the other hand, to be MP for a populous conurbation would make him available to clamouring constituents and their tiresome problems. At the same time his relationship with Herbert Gladstone had turned sour. The Aston Hall colliery failed and Edward was obliged to threaten legal action. After an exchange of cool letters an out-of-court settlement was agreed.

The spring of 1885 saw Edward brought to prominence in another capacity. His acquaintance with the Prince of Wales had grown into respectful friendship. He was recognised as a member of the Marlborough House set, the 'courtiers' Prince Edward gathered round him in his deter-mination to make the royal family more accessible to the people. It was decided that a visit to Dublin by the heir to the throne might be a sound political move and go some way towards reconciling the warring factions. This was planned for April 1885 and Edward Guinness, probably on the prince's recommendation, was appointed High Sheriff of Co. Dublin in order to oversee the arrangements.

This involved him very closely with Dublin Castle and he was stunned by the change of policy being promoted by Lord Carnarvon and his staff. It was not just Liberals who opposed the uncompromising stance against the Nationalists; the Tory leadership now appeared to be pulling out the rug from beneath their Irish supporters. In Dublin, popular feeling was very divided about the royal progress. Many people were excited by it, but Nationalists were affronted and city authorities were anxious for the prince's safety. Edward had to put all his energies into creating a positive attitude towards the visit; the success of the whole event and his own reputation depended on it. Alarmed to discover that the Dublin Chamber of Commerce were not taking a lead in making the necessary preparations, he summoned several prominent citizens to a meeting and told them:

> At any time and under all circumstances we should desire that our Royal guests should be met with the hospitality which our People is wont to claim for itself as a characteristic quality, and those who are now coming amongst us have long ago earned for themselves the right to a special welcome …
>
> But we feel also that their visit on this occasion is not merely one of Pomp and Pleasure but that their coming is a courageous and sagacious act of Public Service and we, on our side, are determined that such conduct shall be met in the spirit and with the enthusiasm which it deserves.[4]

The speech was well publicised in the loyal press, where it put heart into the leaders of society and drew attention to Edward's devotion to the royal family. When the prince's entourage arrived he was in close attendance. Edward escorted the royal party on tours of prominent attractions, helped to host the grand citizens' ball and was seldom far from the prince's side throughout the five days of the royal progress. He made the most of every opportunity to commend himself and tangible reward was not long in following. Two weeks after the visit Gladstone, on behalf of the queen, wrote to offer Mr Guinness a baronetcy, 'in recognition not only of your high position in Ireland but especially of your marked services rendered by you on the important occasion of the visit recently paid to that country by the Prince and Princess of Wales'.[5]

It was a start but, as far as Edward was concerned, only a start. That summer he took by storm the 'quality' assembled for Cowes Week by arriving in a floating palace, the 106-ton SS *Ceto* which became *the* coveted venue for party-goers, including members of the royal suite. There was still the issue of the forthcoming election to be resolved. After a further discussion over tactics Plunket went right to the top. He urged on Lord Salisbury, the Tory leader, Guinness's many services to the party and the personal sacrifice he was contemplating in making himself available for a city seat. Suggesting that a peerage should be promised, Plunket came close to blackmail: 'St Stephen's Green Division of Dublin is, as you know, the only Irish Constituency outside Ulster (except Dublin University) where there will be any chance of returning a Conservative and it will be difficult to win even with Guinness as our candidate and without him there will be no use in attempting it.' Salisbury would not be pushed:

Private   Hatfield House
                                                            Hatfield, Herts
                                                            August 17, 1885

My dear Plunket,

  You ask me with respect to Sir Edward Guinness. I earnestly hope he may be induced to stand for Dublin. He is a man whose reputation is an ornament to Dublin – and indeed to Ireland. He has already done most valuable service to the Conservative Party, and I hope he will add yet this to his claim upon our gratitude. It is of the greatest importance that the Loyal party should be as strong as possible in the next Parliament.

  Yours very truly
    Salisbury

Thus ran the letter Plunket was authorised to show to his friend. A covering note was more explicit.

Very Confidential   Hatfield House
                                                            Hatfield, Herts
                                                            Aug. 16, 1885

My dear Plunket,

  I have marked the enclosed 'Private' but of course you may show it, if you think fit, to Guinness. But it is fair that I should say to you that I am not in a condition to promise that 'gratitude' means a Peerage – at all events as yet.

  Yours very truly
    Salisbury.[6]

With this Edward had to be content. He donated another £10,000 to Tory coffers and he contested the election in December, though with no very great enthusiasm. Certainly he was not altogether dismayed when he lost to a Nationalist by almost 2000 votes.

During the run-up to polling day Plunket advised his protégé that, in order not to forfeit the goodwill of the Dublin electorate, 'it *may be necessary* to keep all whisper of parting with the Brewery out of the newspapers'.[7] Plunket was one of very few people who was party to the secret Edward had kept closely guarded for five years: the disposal of the family business. In 1881 Edward had brought his wife's youngest brother Claude on to the board as trainee managing director. This had proved wholly successful; as well as possessing a first-class brain, Claude was a considerable athlete. Fit, energetic and clever, he was soon in a position to take over the running of the St James's Gate brewery. He was provided out of brewery funds with yet another prestigious Dublin residence, Knockmaroon House, so that he might uphold the Guinness presence. Three years later Edward offered Claude's brother, Reginald, a directorship. This, too, worked out very satisfactorily. Reginald was already a successful Dublin businessman and for a few years he and Claude worked well together. Not only that, they maintained the Guinness traditions of hospitality and involvement in the life of the city. They were prominent in municipal affairs, generous supporters of local charities and were to be seen at all the important social events. Reginald was, in fact, knighted for his services to the community in 1897.

The motives underlying the transfer of day-to-day control of the brewery to his in-laws must be sought in Edward's own divided inner counsels. On the one hand lay his loyalty to the 130-year-old family business and, on the other, his ambition for himself and his descendants. He wanted Guinnesses to control the activities of St James's Gate and plan future policy, but he wanted his sons (all of whom were educated at Eton) to take their places in the ranks of the English aristocracy. Adelaide's brothers seemed to hold the perfect answer to the problem. Ever since the death of their unfortunate father the Lee Guinnesses had helped to support them and their siblings. As well as being Adelaide's brothers, Reginald and Claude were close friends of Edward Cecil and he felt that he could trust them. He was right. The results, as far as the business was concerned, were highly gratifying: they were natural businessmen, who brought devoted industry and real talent to the brewery.

All was now in readiness for Edward to throw off the shackles and associations of business. On 20 October 1886 he wrote to the senior staff at St James's Gate:

Owing to the constant and rapid increase of the Brewery, and its probable further development I have for some time felt that I should not long be able to support the evergrowing strain upon my health which the conduct of so large a business and its many anxieties of necessity entail – I have therefore sought to share these labours and responsibilities with others and have concluded an arrangement by which in the future St James Gate will be worked as a Company by a Board of Directors. At the same time I have felt extremely reluctant entirely to sever my connection with the Brewery and to surrender my interest in the welfare of those with whom I have been so long associated. I have accordingly arranged that I shall be Chairman of the Company retaining a substantial interest in the undertaking. I hope and believe that the business will be conducted on the same principles in every respect as heretofore, and I trust that you and all my friends at St James Gate will continue to favour me with that assistance which you have always so ably given me in the past.[8]

This was the first intimation anyone outside Sir Edward's small circle of confidants received of the decision that had been six years in the maturing. Nothing had come of his initial negotiations with Rothschilds; instead, Edward eventually closed a deal with their rival, Barings. The plan was for two thirds of the company's share capital (valued at £6,000,000) to be floated and for Edward to keep the rest. This was by some way the largest commercial stock issue which had ever been handled in the City. For a point of comparison we might consider the British government's purchase of a controlling interest in the Suez Canal Company in 1869. Then, the financial world had caught its breath at Rothschilds' raising £8,000,000 in a few days. The offer of Britain's largest brewing concern to the public created similar excitement – and not a little anger.

The reason the deal received a bad press was that the bankers skimmed the cream for themselves but it also has much to do with Edward Guinness's natural reserve and his casual 'gentleman's club' attitude towards matters of high finance. In all his dealings he operated on a strictly 'need to know' basis. Thus Sir Edward arranged the deal personally with Edward Baring (who became Baron Revelstoke in 1885), the head of his family's bank, whose interests were largely confined to his own professional and social circle. Neither man was much concerned with modest English investors and even less with modest Irish investors, who did not receive prospectuses until the day of the launch. Thus, the details of the most stupendous financial transaction of the decade were decided by the two Edwards in what they would have considered a highly civilised fashion. To Guinness's enquiry whether Barings would want seats on the board Lord Revelstoke responded with a reassuring negative: 'The more Guinnesses the better; all Guinnesses if you can manage it'.[9] Sir Edward, of course, could not manage it. The only family members involved in the business were his brothers-in-law Claude and Reginald, and there was no question of bringing in either of the Rundell brothers. When Sir Edward explained this Baring recommended one of his banking friends, Herman Hoskier, to be a London director, assuring his client that with Hoskier's expert help 'you should not have to work so hard as chairman'.[10]

That throwaway remark exposes Sir Edward's primary motivation. His claim to the brewery staff that he was concerned for his health was certainly ingenuous. He was still a vigorous man in his thirties when he set in motion the process of turning Guinness into a limited company. Although he subsequently relinquished the chairmanship for a few years, he resumed it in his fifties and was from then to the end of his long life very active in brewery affairs. The truth lay in his ambition for social position, titles, honours, an impressive life-style, which in turn required a large disposable income and the leisure to employ it advantageously. His business sense told him that with the brewery showing enormous profit growth now was the right time to go public. The City concurred and *The Economist* gauged its mood well when it commented, 'Considering what has been the experience lately of the pressure of hard times, and the curtailment of trade profits, the enormous increase is simply astounding ... with what envy must those be filled who are engaged in other branches of business'.[11]

It was this envy – and greed – which resulted in the first Guinness scandal. Lord Revelstoke undervalued the company, then he and a favoured circle of associates took up the lion's share of the issue. Barings the bank and leading members of the Baring family received well over a million pounds' worth of shares. Other banks and City institutions accounted for another £1.2 million. By comparison, members of the family closely connected with the brewery and senior staff were granted very modest holdings – Lord Ardilaun, £15,000; Claude, £3010; Reginald, £2000. John Tertius Purser, the sheet anchor of the brewery who had worked for sixty-two years, most of them as head brewer and virtual manager at St James's Gate, turned down an offer of £5000 worth of shares (less than the £6010 awarded to the new director, Herman Hoskier), considering it an inadequate return for faithful service to three generations of the Guinness family.

What was left for the general public was stock to the value of a mere £1.7 million. And they clamoured for it. A crowd of frenzied potential investors mobbed Barings' office in Bishopsgate, breaking through a police cordon and smashing a door as they scrambled for the crumbs from the rich men's table. Of course, the share value soared and the rich men became even richer. Sir Edward himself entered the market and by 1888 had acquired a controlling interest in his own family business.

Disappointed applicants and press commentators now raised the universal shout of 'Foul!'. The committee of the Stock Exchange and the board of the Inland Revenue intervened and, although accusations of fraud were dismissed, Barings were reprimanded for technical mismanagement. To put this short-lived scandal in historical perspective we must re-emphasise that the Guinness flotation was a pioneering venture. Merchant banks were not used to handling the incorporation of large private concerns and the associated legislation only existed in rudimentary form. Putting the world's biggest brewery up for public ownership would have created enormous interest and, probably, some criticism however it had been handled. It began a new era in the development of joint-stock companies. Whitbread, Allsopp, Bass and scores of other rival concerns hastened to follow Guinness's example and in August 1888 the Stock Exchange for the first time listed brewing companies as a separate category.

To mark the transformation from private to public ownership Edward distributed £60,000 among the St James's Gate employees. The gesture was well received, but recipients might have reflected that it was a benefaction one of the richest men in Britain easily could afford. There is no record of brother Arthur's reaction. Ten years after agreeing to the dissolution of the partnership and accepting £680,000 for his acquiescence he saw Edward pocket several million, while retaining virtual sole control. Edward's decision to buy back shares at a higher price than their flotation value can only be explained by his ambivalence towards the family business. Over the years since 1880 he had considered various options from selling up completely to maintaining financial control of a public company. In the event, he had pocketed as much of the sale proceeds as possible, consonant with keeping the business in the family. Belatedly he realised that he had gone too far. Without a majority shareholding the business could easily slip from the family's grasp. When the chips were down he found that he could not divorce himself completely from brewery affairs. For a few years he enjoyed the best of both worlds: he was titular head of the company and the final authority on policy matters, but these responsibilities did not take up much space on his social calendar and St James's Gate was in the capable hands of his in-laws.

As soon as Edward found himself, in 1887, with what must have seemed limitless funds he went on a spending spree. His first requirement was for suitably splendid settings. His quest for an English country seat was beset with problems (see below pp.130ff), but in London he acquired Numbers 4 and 5 Grosvenor Place, and converted them into what was more a town palace than a mansion, containing a ballroom, a suite of spacious reception chambers and accommodation for dozens of guests. These impressive spaces needed to be filled and, as one of his close associates observed, 'he began to purchase things of beauty, here a piece of tapestry, there a piece of sculpture or old furniture, an occasional picture or engraving, a jewel, a piece of old embroidery, a fine carpet. He built extensively, and under sound advice as far as the outside of his houses were concerned, but he dealt with the interiors from his own knowledge and taste'.[12] The closing decades of the nineteenth century were one of those times when new wealth was aggressively taking over from old. Agricultural depression had led to the break-up of several ancient estates in Britain and on the Continent. Men with ready cash – most of them American – were putting together great collections and Edward Guinness joined the besieging army.

In fact, he had been an active collector ever since his marriage. Always at the back of his mind was the unselfconscious grace of the Montebellos, whose cultured lives were nurtured by roots deep sunk in a noble ancestry. As Lady Ottoline Morell observed, this was a quality which set the *ancien régime* apart from the *nouveau riche*:

Coming of a long line of men and women who have enjoyed inherited wealth and so have been free to move about in the world – to travel hither and thither – and who have sunned themselves in the sunshine of art and culture and who, too, have taken part in weaving the tangle of history, have become conscious of what civilization and subtlety of thought and quickness of action mean, must influence one and make one more complex, more mature, and richer in comprehension, and must lay a foundation of quick perception and understanding.[13]

This was the one commodity Edward's wealth was inadequate to purchase and his abhorrence of appearing *arriviste* lent urgency to his accumulation of the trappings of high taste.

On his honeymoon he had taken in several of the art centres of Europe and over ensuing years he returned to do business with leading dealers, usually in the company of experts whose task was to protect him from the predators who prowled the jungles of the international art market. In one year – 1877 – he was to be found in Florence in the spring, buying statuary and antique furniture; in Madrid in the autumn to purchase Spanish school paintings; and in the London sale rooms at the end of the year, snapping up yet more pictures and marbles.

This determined, if desultory, accumulation continued until 1887, when Edward embarked on an almost frenetic bout of spending. His new houses and his extensions to other residences provided him with literally acres of floor and wall space to be filled. He furnished whole rooms with matching period items – panelling, hangings, furniture, carpets, porcelain, plate and pictures. What he was creating was the ambience of a cultured English gentleman.

His buying was a mixture of impulse and calculation. The story has often been related of how he amassed a treasury of old masters in an impatient four years. One early June afternoon in 1887 he walked into a Bond Street gallery and asked to see some top-quality paintings. The proprietors were at lunch and the assistant was too nervous to deal with the request himself. Edward Guinness was not used to anyone saying 'No' to him and marched out angrily. Minutes later he marched into Agnew's and there repeated his request. This time a more enterprising salesman proffered a variety of canvases, several of which Edward bought. The sequel was that thereafter he dealt exclusively with Agnew's, acquiring through them over the next four years two hundred and forty paintings and drawings by over ninety European masters, including Rembrandt, Veronese, Rubens, Gainsborough, Canaletto, Reynolds, Van Dyck, Watteau, Vermeer and more modern artists such as Millais and Landseer. Between 1887 and 1901 Edward spent over half a million pounds with Agnew's alone. All transactions were carried out with characteristic secrecy and the principal's identity was masked with code names, but *habitués* of the art market were not deceived and it is small wonder that rival collectors complained that it was useless venturing into the sale rooms if Sir Edward were in a buying mood.

The items Edward Cecil Guinness chose to buy (a few of which have been kept together for public display at Kenwood (see below, pp.195ff) tell us a great deal about his character. The collection is that of a gentleman of quality and not of an aesthete. The largest single group of paintings (about a hundred) were executed by the society portraitists of the eighteenth century. In these radiant masterpieces by Gainsborough, Romney (a particular favourite), Reynolds, Raeburn, Lawrence, Hoppner and Kauffman, proprietorial landowners stand with contrived non-chalance among their rural acres, and porcelain-cheeked women and children pose in silks and velvets in idealised landscapes or elegant interiors. These are the icons of the Augustan age of English country house culture. Edward bought several landscapes, seascapes and genre pieces – but not a single religious work nor any item betraying a Catholic, transalpine provenance. Englishness, patriotism and Protestantism were essential features of Edward Guinness's self-concept. He created the illusion – for himself and his guests – of an English gentleman born of several generations of English gentlemen. His affectation of reserved aloofness may have been a deliberate aping of the attitude he perceived among 'top' families. Equally, it could have been a defensive rampart thrown up by a man who was never completely secure in the role he had elected to play. For one senses that all the philanthropy, prodigious display, competitive entertainment and courting of the right people were part of a deliberate act. Edward's sons, who shared the playing fields of Eton and the battlefields of Africa and Europe with a new generation of the English élite, were much more relaxed.

By 1888 Sir Edward Guinness was reputed (perhaps exaggeratedly) to be the second-richest man in England. Accepted in court circles, an arbiter of fashion and a leading contributor to Tory party funds (he donated at least £30,000 during the decade and possibly very much more), he was still denied the longed-for peerage. In the spring of that year a by-election was called in Dublin city and the Lord-Lieutenant, the Marquess of Londonderry, pressed Guinness to make himself available. What he was in reality asking for was political self-immolation, since no Unionist candidate would stand a chance of success. Edward was not prepared to expose himself now without a firm promise from the party leaders and once more attempted to use this call on his services as a lever. Londonderry, it seems, was prepared to give Edward the desired under-taking but David Plunket, now an MP and in daily contact with the party hierarchy, pointed out that Edward must be careful not to find himself outmanoeuvred by more skilful operators:

Confidential   House of Commons
                                                                April 23, 1888

My dear Ned …

I should be very careful in talking or writing to anyone, and especially to that slippery fellow Ashbourne [Lord Ashbourne, Chancellor of Ireland], not to take any other tone except that nothing but the strongest pressure from the Government would induce you in the present circumstances to stand.

For instance suppose S.[alisbury] answers L.[ord] L.[ondonderry] to this effect:

'By all means get G to stand if that is the only way to save us from a catastrophe with Sexton as our candidate, but I cannot give him the promise you ask for.'

I'm afraid that would leave you in rather a hole …

Of course if S. sanctions your standing on the terms suggested by L. L. that would suit you very well, but I can hardly realise that as probable.

Of course the true solution in a political sense is that we should not let
Sexton or any other bad man stand and Ashbourne holding the view he does
about such folly ought to put his foot down on it and crush it, but I should
say he'll see the whole Unionist movement d-d first!! ...

I have not heard anything more from Balfour or A. Douglas or anyone else
and I'll not approach them in the present state of affairs for the reasons I gave
Dunbar. Please keep me posted up.

Yrs always affectly

D. Plunket.[14]

Edward took the warning to heart and with the withdrawal of his name
from the list of possible candidates his active involvement in politics –
such as it had ever been – came to an end.

If we raise our sights from the narrow ambitions of one man to the wider
political prospect we can immediately see why the Unionist bosses were
prepared to employ any stratagem, short of enlisting the peerage-creating
prerogative of the crown, to gain every possible seat. The period from
June 1885 to July 1886 has been called 'the most dramatic thirteen
months in modern English party history' (R. C. K. Ensor, *England
1870–1914*, Oxford, 1936, p.99) and Ireland was the main player in the
tragi-comedy. The two evenly matched principal power blocks were
forced to negotiate with Charles Parnell, the kingmaker. This involved
Salisbury in making secret concessions to the Nationalists, which would
be hard to sell to the right wing of his party. In the election of
November–December 1885 these manoeuvrings failed. Gladstone
returned to the dispatch box and within months had drafted his first
Home Rule Bill. The breadth of the measure provoked near panic among
those whose comfortable incomes derived from Ireland. How would
established businesses fare in an independent nation? Already hundreds
of estate owners had been 'despoiled' of their rights by a British
government seemingly in league with the men of violence. Matters would
become incalculably worse if the country were handed over to the
Nationalists. In an atmosphere of wild rumour and speculation it was
only too easy to believe that Irish politicians, let off the Westminster
leash, would gather with greedy eyes and slavering jaws around Ireland's
most profitable industries. At the very least life could be made difficult for
a family business whose proprietors were heartily and openly opposed to
Nationalist aspirations. In parliament the Bill provoked stronger feelings
than any measure in living memory. Sixteen days of passionate debate
were expended on the constitutional issue and at one point members

actually came to blows on the floor of the chamber. At the end of this marathon class loyalties proved stronger than party ones. Refusing to waver on a point of principle and reach an accommodation with unhappy members on his own benches, Gladstone saw ninety-three colleagues go into the opposition lobby.

The spectre of Home Rule had been exorcised on the floor of the Commons and the Tories who had effectively wielded bell, book and candle returned to power. Their Irish friends congratulated themselves, offered up pious thanksgivings and resumed the even tenor of their ways. But the ghost had not been laid permanently. Ireland remained the most contentious issue in British politics. Advocates and opponents of constitutional change alike used violence and dirty tricks in pursuance of their objectives. There continued to be sporadic outrages on both sides of the water. On 13 November 1887 a detachment of Life Guards rode down Socialist and Irish Nationalist demonstrators in Trafalgar Square – the first 'Bloody Sunday' in the chronicle of Anglo-Irish relations. In February 1890 a long-running judicial enquiry into the publication of letters by Parnell ostensibly supporting the Phoenix Park murders came to a head when the documents in question were exposed as forgeries. (The perpetrator of this piece of Unionist chicanery subsequently shot himself.) Such events kept alive sympathy for the Home Rule cause. Even Parnell's public disgrace when his long-standing affair with Mrs O'Shea was revealed in 1890 and his sudden death the following year did not irreparably blight the Nationalist cause. Agitation continued within Ireland, while in Westminster Liberal dependence on Hibernian support ensured that Home Rule remained a wide plank in the party's platform. Gladstone tried again in 1893, only to be frustrated by the Lords. It fell to Salisbury and the Conservatives to demonstrate that they could pacify Britain's closest imperial possession. Arthur Balfour ('Bloody Balfour' to the Nationalists), as Chief Secretary for Ireland, coupled rigidly enforced coercion laws with measures of reform and economic improvement. Most important as far as estate owners were concerned were the measures of 1887, 1891 and 1903 (Wyndham's Land Act) which provided large sums of Treasury money to facilitate land purchase on a much wider scale than before. This complete reversal of the colonisation schemes of the past nine centuries transferred most of Ireland's productive acreage back into Irish hands and eroded the territorial cement of rural society. Many members of the Ascendancy welcomed the development. Some saw it as the only route back to financial solvency. Some, among whose number was Edward Guinness, believed that it would smother in its cot the squealing brat of Home Rule.

Sir Edward's preoccupations were, as usual, elsewhere. With the 1880s drawing to a close and no foot upon the golden ladder of nobility he had to cast around for fresh ways to commend himself to the bestowers of favour. His first action was a monumental public display of charity. He collaborated with three friends who were also parliamentarians: David Plunket; Charles Ritchie, MP for the St George's division of Tower Hamlets, President of the Local Government Board and a member of the cabinet; and Baron Rowton, man-about-town, a senior member of the Tory hierarchy and a close friend of the queen. In the spring of 1889 this weighty junta formed the Guinness Trust for the Housing of the Poor and Sir Edward provided its massive capital base of £250,000. He instructed that four-fifths of the money was to be directed towards clearing slums and building tenements in London's East End, where the population was growing by around 15,000 a year, the influx coming largely from Ireland and pogrom-ravaged eastern Europe. Only £50,000 was available for Dublin. Guinness Buildings erected in the imperial capital were a much better personal advertisement than similar structures across the water.

To say that Edward's motives were mixed is not to deny him genuine compassion. The squalor of London's back streets had been worsening for decades and only the wilfully ignorant were unaware of it. Even in the pulpit of fashionable St Margaret's Westminster, where he and his wife worshipped, occasional discomforting references were made to Dives and Lazarus, and if they wanted eyewitness accounts Edward and Dodo only had to talk with Henry Grattan Guinness and his family, with whom they maintained a desultory contact (see below pp.136ff). Edward was no stranger to the construction of working-class dwellings, nor to the amelioration of living conditions for the lower orders of urban society. At the brewery he had inherited a tradition of care for employees. It was widely recognised that Guinness workers were better paid and looked after than those of most other comparable concerns in the whole of the British Isles. The business provided free medical treatment and what we would now call a social services department for all staff, and maintained several residential properties close to the brewery. Edward had a social conscience and he also knew that worker welfare was an example of enlightened self-interest. It was not easy to find fit and healthy potential employees. Reporting to the Royal Commission on the Poor Laws in 1908, the brewery's directors stated 'few town-bred men satisfy the Company as regards physique'. Of 329 job applicants in the previous year 225 had had to be rejected on health grounds. Now, as a genuinely concerned man of substance who also fully subscribed to the theory of

Tory free enterprise, Edward sought to demonstrate that creating a series of urban tenements would address a social problem and also provide a viable investment. That said, it must be noted that Edward was not an innovator in this area of reform. By 1891 it had become a socially acceptable vehicle by means of which scores of upper-class benefactors displayed their generosity – very publicly. Lord Ardilaun, as we have seen, had already climbed aboard this particular charity bandwagon, as had several of his wealthy friends. When, in front of cheering crowds, Edward arrived in his monogrammed carriage to open the latest block of Guinness Buildings in Walworth or Deptford, or to conduct the Prince of Wales on a tour of inspection, he was performing a ceremony that was becoming familiar in the poorer parts of the capital.

However, Edward's munificence dwarfed the contribution to solving the problem made by any other benefactor. Even Lord Rothschild's Four Per Cent Industrial Dwellings Society (1884) was not so well funded. He could, of course, well afford it. In a personal memorandum drawn up in 1887 he estimated that, after allowing for personal expenses of £100,000 p.a., he would be left with a residue for reinvestment that over the next seventeen years would amount to between £7 million and £15 million.

Contemporary commentators were by no means united in their applause of such 'ugly offspring of a reluctant paternalism'. 'These are not HOMES,' one wrote of a similar development, 'They entirely rob the beautiful English word of its wonderful charm.' Rather, they were hasty solutions to a pressing problem. Two-, three- or four-roomed flats with their shared facilities were a definite improvement on the conditions from which their occupants moved, but they were destined to become a new generation of slums before many years had passed.[15]

However, it is difficult to associate such criticisms with some of Edward Cecil's projects. For example this was how he proposed to tackle the renovation of the notorious area to the north of St Patrick's Cathedral:

As soon as the ground is cleared I am binding myself to cover the whole of it, excepting only some pieces to be given to the Corporation for street widenings, with two classes of buildings:

(1)   Workmen's Dwellings on the lines of the Guinness Trust houses, and a Lodging House for men on the model of your own admirable houses.

(2)   A block, or blocks, to contain a Concert Hall, a room suitable for Loan Exhibition of Pictures, etc., a couple of Reading Rooms, Lecture or Class Rooms for music, etc., a Gymnasium, and a Swimming Bath.

The Bill provides that the buildings Class 1 shall be let on the same principle as the Guinness Trust buildings (though not in these words), and that the Rental receivable therefrom, after all expenses and a Depreciation Fund are deducted, shall be placed in the hands of Trustees as an endowment for what I may call the non-remunerative buildings in Class 2.

The special object of this endowment is to enable the Trustees to open the buildings to the public for the purposes specified, and to provide concerts and other entertainments at prices within the power of the poor inhabitants of the district to pay, perhaps at times or in part gratuitously. The use of the buildings to be on non-sectarian or political lines.

I propose to place an organ in the Concert Room and provide all the necessary instruments, music, etc., for an Orchestra, with the intention that the organist shall be specially engaged to teach, and train – at no expense to the pupils – an Orchestra and Choir, from the boys and men, and possibly girls of the district.[16]

At the same time as Edward was drawing up his plans for the Guinness Trust he was arranging to distance himself still further from the brewery. He relinquished the chairmanship in favour of Reginald. His first intention had been to elevate Claude to the top position, with his brother in the support role of vice-chairman, but Claude held back in favour of his older brother.

It was totally in keeping with Edward's secretive nature that he did not discuss his decision with Reginald, who was completely *bouleversé* by the news:

St James's Gate, Dublin.
17 July 1890

My dear Edward

As you may imagine the news contained in your letter and Claude's received this morning has caused me the most profound astonishment. It is not only that your retirement from the Chairmanship has taken me so completely by surprise, but the changes involved therein which you are so very good as to contemplate, and which so materially affect me personally, have come upon me so unexpectedly that I can scarcely yet realise the position of affairs.

It is more than good of you my dear Edward to think of such an advancement for me, and it is very generous of dear old Claude to put me forward and keep himself in the background, and I appreciate his goodness most heartily but I confess to a feeling of great diffidence when I think of myself as *Chairman*, and I fear, should the arrangement be carried out, that I shall prove a very poor successor to you. I know too how much better a Chairman C. would make but I try to comfort myself with the feeling that while I should be a bad Chairman I should probably be a worse Managing Director! With his practical knowledge and experience he is of course much better fitted for the work of Managing Director, and if you and he really think me in any way fit for the position of Chairman, I shall be only too delighted to do my utmost to fill the post satisfactorily.

Ever my dear Edward

Yours affectionately

Reginald Guinness.[17]

At the time this must have seemed the best possible arrangement both for Edward and the brewery. He had finally thrown off the stigma of 'trade', he had maintained financial control and he had transferred day-to-day operations to another branch of the family, which might, in its turn, yield a dynasty of productive entrepreneurs. Yet, if one could identify any single point at which the family business reached its summit of success and began to descend towards mediocrity and lost dynamism the transfer of the chairmanship to Reginald would be that point. This was not because he or his brother were ineffective; the reverse was true. It was fate and Edward Guinness's indomitable will that set the company on a gentle but steepening downward slope. Fate decreed that there would not be a second strain of Guinnesses born to the management of the brewery. Neither Reginald nor Claude had a son. Then, in March 1895, the talented Claude, after a quarter of a century of excellent service at St James's Gate, was afflicted with a sudden and distressing illness. He suffered a complete mental and physical collapse, and died within weeks. Edward, meanwhile, continued in effective control of the business, while persuading the world and himself that he was detached from it. Reginald was no mere paper chairman, but he took no major decision without reference to his brother-in-law. Where Edward miscalculated was in the application of this Janus policy to his posterity. Wanting his children to take their places at the top of British society, he abandoned the family tradition of putting at least one son through a rigorous training at the brewery. In fact, his second boy, Ernest, did devote himself to the business (see below p.152), but though he had a real flair for technical innovation he was something of a stick-in-the-mud when it came to developing a vision for the future. In any case he, too, had no male heirs to continue the brewing dynasty. When Reginald resigned the chairmanship in 1902 there was no one else in the family to take it on and Edward was obliged to resume the reins into his own hands. By then the process had begun of distancing the Guinnesses from the manufacture of the product that bore their name.

The Edward Cecil Guinness who entered the last decade of the century at the age of forty-three was a complex character. He had few close friends and he was difficult to get to know because he seldom revealed his feelings. 'Secrecy', 'privacy', 'certainty', 'self-control', 'discipline' – these are the qualitative nouns used of him by people who knew the mature Edward Cecil Guinness. We can see all these attributes in the tight-lipped, stiffly posed portraits of his middle and later years which present an almost caricature version of the self-made Victorian peer. Through letters and the reminiscences of others we gain glimpses of him: conducting family prayers every morning in the library, all the staff, including liveried footmen and crisp-aproned maids, arranged in rows according to rank; standing proprietorially before Landseer's *Stag at Bay* in his study; slipping away from his guests via concealed doors and staircases installed for that very purpose. From his children he obtained obedience, which in later years turned to respect, but affection was something he found as difficult to receive as to give. Edward was a stickler for the observation of proprieties. One of his grandchildren, who was genuinely fond of him, recalled how during his schooldays he used to exchange letters with the old man. On one occasion, because he would be seeing his grandfather in a few days, he neglected to reply to one of them. On the next visit he was severely reproached for his lack of manners. 'You're not the nice little boy you used to be,' Edward Cecil told him, as he rushed crying from the room.[18]

Edward Cecil was a man locked inside himself. Some years later, when he was a Suffolk landowner, he caught the vicar who served his country estate villages peering in through a ground-floor window of his mansion. Not content with reproving the man, he had a new vicarage built farther away so that neither the clergyman nor any of his successors would have any cause to approach his house unless summoned. In 1886 the editor of the Dublin *Farmers' Gazette* asked permission to write a history of the Guinness brewery for a forthcoming symposium of Irish industry. In refusing, Edward wrote: 'It is quite contrary to our usual course to bring our establishment in any prominent manner before the public'.[19] He could, and doubtless would, have said exactly the same about himself.

Towards no one did he exert sterner discipline than himself. He laid down clear objectives and he devoted all his energies to their accomplishment. As a result he gained those rewards that he so single-mindedly sought. In the New Year's Honours List for 1890 he was elevated to the peerage as Baron Iveagh of Iveagh.

10

CORONETS AND KIND HEARTS

rthur Guinness, Lord Ardilaun, entered his sixties and the twentieth century with the fixed conviction that the country was going to the dogs. Whatever chagrin he may have felt at his youngest brother's stupendous rise to fame and fortune was as nothing compared with his anger and frustration with politicians – of all hues. Nationalists, of course, were quite beyond the pale of civilised society – aiders and abettors of murder and pillage. Gladstone's crew of scoundrels were their co-conspirators. But now even the Conservatives, by the Land Acts, were dismantling the time-honoured social order of 'the rich man in his castle, the poor man at his gate'. So strongly did he feel that the landlords had been betrayed by their Tory friends that in 1900 he declined to receive the Lord-Lieutenancy of Co. Dublin at the hands of Earl Cadogan who, as well as being the government's man in Dublin Castle, was also a member of the cabinet. Arthur was determined to do all in his power to preserve the tried and tested Ascendancy system. To advance this endangered polity he resolved to become a press baron.

This was the era of the newspaper tycoon. Wealthy entrepreneurs like William Waldorf Astor and the Harmsworth brothers, seeking profit, prestige and power, were buying up journals and using them as mouthpieces for their own opinions. Around the turn of the century readership was increasing. Educational improvements and the proliferation of working men's clubs and public libraries gave more people than ever before access to the written word. Arthur realised the importance of propaganda. It was not sufficient for the Ascendancy moguls to congregate in their clubs and smoking rooms to deplore the activities of 'revolutionaries' and the government's capitulations over land law. The gospel of 'true Irishness' had to be taken to the people. Home Rulers and Land Leaguers were winning the argument in towns and villages by diffusing a sense of Irish identity independent of and hostile to Britain. With the formation of associations such as the Gaelic League (1893) culture, religion, heritage and history were being vigorously utilised to buttress the politico-economic struggle. There was a desperate need for counter-intelligence. As president of the Royal Dublin Society from 1897 Lord Ardilaun organised the publication of that body's history. It would show how, for more than a century and a half, the leaders of Anglo-Irish society had laboured for the nation's welfare, reviving native culture as well as encouraging commerce, urging urban renewal, sponsoring agricultural improvement and facilitating the development of canals, roads and railways. But the message had to reach beyond the intelligentsia and to this end, in 1900, Arthur acquired the Dublin *Daily Express* group which also controlled the *Morning Mail, Evening Mail* and *Weekly Warden.*

In July 1901 Arthur, now fully fired with the crusading spirit, was sworn to the House of Lords. Britain had a new sovereign and a new prime minister, but Arthur was determined that the nation should not turn its back on old values. In the upper chamber he spoke solely on Irish rural concerns. He attacked Wyndham's Land Bill, upbraiding the government for abandoning the class that had 'stood by them in the days of stress and trouble and who were only now reaping the benefit of their industry and courage'.[1] He urged non-interference with the landlords' rights to evict and relocate tenants in the interests of estate improvement. He asked for tougher laws against fish poachers. When the new Act came into effect Lord Ardilaun declined to obey it – or so, at least, some of his Kilarney tenants claimed. Their MP complained in the Commons that although his deer were spoiling the crops of leaseholders the landlord refused either to let them buy their holdings or to fence the land properly. In a very short space of time he was marked as an arch-reactionary and became a prime target for both radicals and moderates. In January 1902 he was attacked in the Commons for fomenting strife by obliging his editors to exaggerate the significance of minor disturbances. All this trouble, claimed Mr T. Healy MP,

is due to the newspaper of one discontented Peer – not only discontented, as I am told now, but also a pro Boer in disguise – Lord Ardilaun, because he does not get his step in the peerage, a Star or a Garter … It was his newspapers in Ireland that have served up the whole thing. If Lord Ardilaun had not existed … there would not have been one single word about these arrests.[2]

His lordship went on his blustering way careless of all criticism. He clung as closely as he could to tradition, defying new men and a new century to do their worst. As far as the life-style of Arthur and Olivia was concerned, the Ascendancy lived on. They resided splendidly at 11 Carlton House Terrace, St Anne's and Ashford, where they were privileged to be among the last subjects to offer private hospitality to the old queen.

The title Edward chose for his barony rested upon the researches carried out by Hosea almost a century before. According to the cleric the family was descended from the Arthur Magennis who was created Viscount of Iveagh, Co. Down, by James I. Edward Cecil elected to underline this claim to ancient noble ancestry by taking the same title. The honorific might be Irish, but when Lord Iveagh set about the quest for a country seat suitable for his new dignity he looked for something very English. The search had, in fact, begun in 1888. The Prince of Wales had remarked to him on one occasion, 'You ought to buy some shooting in Norfolk' and Edward had set his agent to find something suitable. What he found was Elveden, an Anglo-Indian mansion which had housed Duleep Singh, the last ruler of the independent Punjab, brought to England when his territory was annexed to live as a pensioner of the crown. Singh had replicated in East Anglia the wantonly luxurious style of an oriental prince. There were no tigers to hunt in this northern latitude; the nearest he could get to the shikar was the pursuit of game birds with gun and dog. To indulge this sport he acquired the Suffolk estate on the edge of Thetford Chase and set about transforming the house into a little bit of India. The state rooms of Elveden Hall were decorated in Mogul Empire style, glittering with mirrors, gilding and primary colours, sumptuous with patterned marble and velvet drapes. But eventually its occupant tired of it and took himself off to live in Paris. The Elveden trustees were instructed to sell. They were eager to discharge their responsibilities and when Sir Edward, through intermediaries, made an offer they accepted. Guinness was just as keen as the vendors and considered the matter settled. They had all reckoned without the prince. Duleep Singh demanded a higher price and when Edward agreed to pay it, he began negotiations with a third party in order to raise the stakes still further. After several frustrating months the 'Sovereign of the Sikhs', as he signed himself, broke off the discussions. Edward next tried to buy the Savernake estate in Wiltshire from the Marquess of Aylesbury. Once again, all went well for a time. Then, in 1892, the marquess's heirs sought an injunction to prevent him alienating the land. The case spiralled through various courts all the way up to the House of Lords, who finally gave judgement for the plaintiffs. By now Sir Edward Guinness was Lord Iveagh and even more in need of an impressive rural seat. However, kindly death had, in 1891, removed Duleep Singh from the property market. The Elveden trustees came back to Edward and, in April 1894, he acquired the Breckland estate for the bargain price of £160,000.

If the prince's treatment of Elveden was spectacular, the baron's was grandiose. He extended the estate to 23,000 acres, resited the village and banished the plough from productive areas in order to enlarge the coverts. As for the house, he made of it an oriental extravaganza, twinning the existing mansion, creating, in effect, two wings for a new central domed structure, the Marble Hall. This vast reception area glowed with smooth, variegated stone, carved and pierced in the Mogul style, fashionable ever since Victoria had been proclaimed Empress of India. Elveden was equipped with all the latest enhancements to civilised living, including modern plumbing and electric light. It was among the half a dozen most sumptuous houses in England, described by one visitor as 'almost appallingly luxurious'.

This was the last great age of conspicuous; unselfconscious consumption, before the advent of graduated income tax, death duties and legislation aimed at social levelling. There were virtually no government restrictions on the acquisition and enjoyment of wealth, nor any sense of guilt attaching to lavish expenditure. The very rich vied with each other in the accommodation they offered their guests and limitations of neither wealth nor taste inhibited them. Ferdinand de Rothschild had built a French Renaissance palace at Waddesdon. William Waldorf Astor had created a mock-Tudor village at Hever. Anyone who wished to be considered 'top drawer' simply had to enter the 'country house stakes', which meant building without restraint and filling guest books with exalted names. Lord Iveagh welcomed to his estate most members of the royal family, the nation's political leaders, diplomats, visiting foreign royals and many of the lords and ladies whose pedigrees were to be found, with his own, in the pages of Burke.

Opinions varied about the delights of Elveden. Some found the Marble or Indian Hall both impressive and comfortable when the fires were lit and a large party of guests assembled to hear singers and instrumentalists brought from London for their entertainment. Other visitors were less enthusiastic:

If Killeen was the coldest house in Ireland, the marble Hall at Elveden must have been the coldest room in England. We used to assemble there for tea after a shoot and we sat there in the evening. There was only one large fireplace, and during the King's visits [Edward VII came every year both as prince and king], when etiquette and courtesy had to be observed, a good many of us froze. My maid remembers looking down from the gallery above and seeing King Edward, 'a big fat man shaking with laughter'. I was sitting beside him, so perhaps I had succeeded in making him laugh with one of my Irish stories, although as a rule they did not appeal to him. I never found it easy to amuse him, although he was always very nice to me. 'Jolly little lady,' he used to say, 'jolly little lady,' when he found my name on a list submitted to him for a party to meet him, and he never scratched me out....

I usually had the same room when I stayed at Elveden. It was next door to the King's suite and there was a double door between the rooms, which was concealed on his side by a large bookcase. I often heard conversations in the next room, however hard I tried not to. I heard some State secrets in this way, which I will not betray, and once I said to Arthur Balfour: 'You must be careful. I can hear everything you are saying to the King.' ... It was a world of its own and a life now gone for ever.[3]

Elveden did, indeed, represent a way of life on the verge of extinction. Lord Iveagh believed that he was buying into something that had deep roots, permanence and stability. In fact, he was able to enjoy the gilded environment he had created for himself and his family for only a few years. In 1902, on reaching the age of sixty, Sir Reginald resigned as chairman of Arthur Guinness, Son and Co. Ltd. Since there was no family member to take his place, Lord Iveagh resumed his position as head of the brewery. Business decisions and concerns once more pressed in upon him, but that was not all that took the bloom off the peach. For rather less than two decades Edward and Adelaide had enjoyed being leaders of English society, keeping great state in London and Suffolk, holidaying aboard their steam yacht, enjoying the friendship of the royal family, always being prominent at Cowes, Ascot and other obligatory events on the calendar. In 1895 the Iveaghs were among those invited to travel to St Petersburg for the coronation of the tsar. How could they even begin to guess that Nicholas would be the last of the Romanovs? Only slowly did they become aware that the stucco of their world was flaking and the structure beneath revealed as flawed. They were disappointed to discover that their three sons had no taste for the baroque extravaganza they had created. They were indignant when egalitarian breezes began to blow through government and the oaks of privilege were obliged to bend before 'punitive' taxes and 'interfering' legislation. The days were not far distant when the great balls and parties would cease and the garnered treasures would sleep beneath dust covers.

Meanwhile, charity among the élite was no less lavish and conspicuous. Edward continued to be generous with his growing income – generous but not careless. Two principles governed most of his benefactions: he distributed them between London and Dublin, and he supported with major donations only those causes in which he had a personal interest. The establishment of the Iveagh Benefaction is an excellent example because it illumines several aspects of the donor's character. In February 1896 Jim Jackson, a senior member of the Elveden outdoor staff, was bitten by his own dog. There was at the time considerable concern in the medical profession about the spread of rabies and the doctor who treated Jackson referred the incident to Lord Iveagh with the recommendation that the employee should receive a course of inoculation. Edward agreed to send Jackson off to London for treatment, to discover that such treatment was available only at the Pasteur Institute in Paris. Thither the worker was despatched to enjoy a French holiday while the antitoxin took effect. The reason why medical pioneering work was lagging behind in Britain was public opposition to research. The British Institute of Preventive Medicine was desperately trying to raise funds for a new laboratory and treatment centre, and being frustrated by anti-vivisectionists and local people who believed they would be vulnerable to germs emanating from the establishment. Lord Iveagh had already decided that he wished to make another spectacular gift to some London-based charity and wondered whether the British Institute might be the appropriate recipient. His enquiries were both secretive and thorough. He personally inspected the Paris laboratories and sent his eldest son to talk with staff of the British Institute. Rupert, at the age of twenty-two, was already fascinated by medical science and was able to report back informatively. These overtures, during which the nature of Lord Iveagh's interest was never so much as hinted at, were followed by a meeting between his lordship and Joseph Lister, the veteran medical pioneer and chairman of the institute, who had just been ennobled as Baron Lister of Lyme Regis and received the Order of Merit. Lister endured such a grilling from Lord Iveagh that he entertained no hope of a donation. It was by now the autumn of 1898. Just before Christmas Lord Iveagh's office issued a press release announcing a gift of £500,000, half to be bestowed on the relief of the Dublin poor and the other half – the Iveagh Benefaction – to be invested on behalf of what was to be called the Lister Institute of Tropical Medicine. The conditions the donor imposed included the right of himself and his heirs to nominate three trustees. He held one of these positions himself and the family has always been represented on the governing body.

The money Edward gave Dublin was used for slum clearance, and the creation of parks and recreation facilities. In 1903, on the occasion of Edward VII's first visit as king, Lord Iveagh presented a cheque for £5000 to the city's hospitals. Significantly, when he welcomed the arrival of George V in 1911 with a similar gesture, the donation had risen to £50,000. Among several benefactions to his old university he provided new research laboratories. A grateful Trinity College elected him as Chancellor in 1908. By this time Baron Iveagh had become Viscount Iveagh, an honour recommended by Lord Salisbury's nephew and successor as Tory Prime Minister, A. J. Balfour. On his resumption of the chairmanship of Arthur Guinness, Son and Co. Ltd he began to take a closer interest in Dublin once more. In 1909 the corporation presented him with an illuminated address in recognition of his generosity and civic patriotism. He accepted with pride. When, however, he was approached with the offer of the lord mayoralty he declined. Strong as his associations with Dublin were, his home was now in London and he was unprepared to forgo its pleasures for a whole year.

The banking Guinnesses had not bought into the brewery on its incorporation. Although Dublin's leading private bank handled much of the family's financial affairs in Ireland, its partners apparently did not belong to the charmed circle whose members had received privileged information about the deal. The London end of the business was still very low key. Before the end of the century Robert Darley had returned from Dublin to help his father in the City where a younger brother, Arthur Eustace, was also in partnership. However, Richard Seymour, who entered his seventies in 1896, was still very much in charge, running the business in his own individualistic way, keeping no books, corresponding regularly with Henry in Dublin and relying on personal contacts. Such behaviour was not bizarre by the standards of the time. There was still a very strong tradition in financial circles that banking was a suitable occupation – hobby almost – for wealthy gentlemen of leisure. If Richard kept written records to a minimum it was because the word of a client was sufficient guarantee and because discretion was the undergirding of all his dealings. His only concession to business expansion was moving into a two-roomed office in St Swithin's Lane in the mid-1880s.

His sons did not see things entirely in the same way. Robert Darley, although he managed to combine Guinness Mahon business with the work of a barrister and the running of a Warwickshire estate, was a very active banker. He travelled frequently to Dublin and kept a suite of rooms above the bank's premises in College Green. He was conscious of living in a changing world. No longer were all important deals transacted by cabals of well-connected gentlemen in the clubs and withdrawing rooms of London, Paris and Vienna. The twentieth century's *homme d'affaires* would be a professional, communicating with clients by telegraph and telephone. He would go in search of business, taking advantage of trans-continental express trains and luxury liners. Guinness Mahon's growing reputation in the acceptance credit business involved them in an increasing number of international transactions. Robert Darley paid several visits to the USA, as well as Continental Europe. It was a way of life that obviously appealed to him. In the winter of 1902 he reported home from a frozen St Petersburg whither he had gone to sort out a cotton deal between Russian and American principals: 'The Neva is frozen and tramcars run across it. The snow is on the streets and one goes every-where on small sleighs. The distances are very great from point to point. The city is enormous, built on a colossal scale. We enjoy it very much'.[4]

Inevitably, the time came when the past relinquished its grip on the firm. Henry died in Dublin in 1893 and, on the eve of the new century, his brother retired. Almost immediately the partners acquired spacious premises at 80–81 Lombard Street, took on more staff and began to organise the business in a 'modern' way.

Life, however, was not without anxieties for the counting-house Guinnesses. Henry's last days were troubled by the activities of his wayward youngest daughter Lucy. It was a constant fear within the family that their girls would fall prey to gold diggers. That happened – or so it seemed – to Lucy. In 1892 she had been sent to a finishing school in Munich, where, despite the vigilance of chaperones, she met and fell for a highly 'unsuitable' young man. Philip Alexius László de Lombos was, at twenty-three, only a few months older than Lucy, but their upbringings could scarcely have been more different. Philip had been born of poor parents in Budapest and had turned his back on a 'sensible', 'secure' job in order to become an artist. Paying for tuition fees by scene painting and tinting photographs, he studied at first in his home city and was subsequently taken into the Munich atelier of the fashionable portraitist Franz von Lenbach, who numbered among his clients Bismarck, members of the German imperial family, Wagner, Liszt and W. E. Gladstone. When Lucy's father and brother learned that she had received the attentions of an impoverished painter, leading a bohemian life and supporting himself by drawing likenesses of people he met in cafés and bars, they were horrified. A member of the family was immediately despatched to bring Lucy home and thus put an end to the infatuation.

However, the stratagem did not succeed. Although Philip and Lucy were kept apart and did not, in fact, see each other for almost seven years, they maintained their love through a regular interchange of letters. During this period Philip's fortunes altered dramatically. Spurred on, at least partially, by the desire to be reunited with the woman he loved, he became his master's professional heir. Through Lenbach he gained access to the world of German and Austro-Hungarian high society and, in 1893, executed his first royal portrait (Prince Ferdinand of Bulgaria). De László's career rocketed: commissions poured in from Europe's élite and his peers acknowledged him by awarding him the Paris Salon's Gold Medal in both 1899 and 1900. In the latter year he travelled to Dublin to claim his Lucy. Her brothers no longer had any reasonable grounds to refuse the match. Financially de László was not in their league, but he could certainly support a wife in comfort and, anyway, Lucy could no longer be regarded as a headstrong girl. The couple were married in 1900 and, after a couple of years in London, where Philip began to attract the attention of English society (though not, apparently, of Lord Iveagh. When he wished to commission romantic studies of his sons no artist would do but James Sant RA, official portrait painter to the queen), they moved to Vienna, an agreeable base from which they visited the royal courts and *soigné* resorts of *haut monde* Europe and America, where Philip's work was now in spectacular demand. Theirs was a vivid, whirling dream world of success and acclamation. Sadly, it could not last.

Back in Dublin these were busy years for Lucy's brothers. Wyndham's Act fanned the land agency side of Guinness Mahon's business into a final blaze of activity. Millions of pounds' worth of estate land changed hands as tenants and proprietors clamoured with equal alacrity to arrange transfers. Howard and Gerald Seymour and their staff were kept fully occupied with three-way negotiations. Values had to be agreed between buyers and sellers. Government had to approve the twelve per cent to be added to the purchase price out of treasury funds. Machinery had to be set up for new owners to pay by instalments and for vendors to be remunerated with government stock. The completion of Ireland's territorial revolution generated an enormous amount of paperwork and income.

While his distant cousins were accumulating titles and fortunes that very different Guinness, Henry Grattan, was acquiring an equally remarkable celebrity within the religious world. In 1872, he had set up home in London with his wife and seven children, ranging in age from three to eleven. Their house was about four miles as the crow flies from the residences of their wealthy relatives, but the distance between their life-styles was galactic. Henry and Fanny had no servants to make their beds and lay out their clothes. Their palates were never at the risk of becoming jaded by an abundance of rich foods. Their children did not live a separate life marshalled by nannies and governesses. Their home was habitually filled with visitors and friends, but they were not statesmen, princesses and bishops. They were, for the most part, trainee missionaries.

When Thomas Barnardo left Dublin in 1866 it was to study medicine in London with the objective of joining the China Inland Mission. In his spare time he became involved in the social and evangelistic work of a Brethren assembly in the East End. The experience changed his plans completely. He had been quite unprepared for the degree of squalor and human degradation which now confronted him – men taking refuge from misery in drink; women forced into prostitution to provide food for their families; people dying on the street of disease and starvation; children begging for coppers, their faces pinched with malnutrition, their health already broken by brutality or manual labour. It was the children who touched him most. Like Mayhew, he saw 'rough-headed urchins, running with their feet bare through the puddles, and bonnetless girls, huddled in shawls, lolling against the door-posts'.[5] Barnardo started a ragged school to get some of these children off the streets and provide them with the rudiments of an education, but he had to turn away far more than he could accommodate. Passionately he sought more effective ways of making an impact on the problem and approached men of wealth for the funds to support them. In 1870 he opened, in Stepney, his first home for destitute boys with the backing of the veteran philanthropist and social reformer, Lord Shaftesbury. Like Barnardo, the earl was a zealous evangelical who believed that the most effective way of changing society was to change men's hearts. The 'passion for souls' was something which created an evangelical consensus of Christians from the established and nonconformist churches, as well as the separatist tradition represented in the last decades of the century by such movements as the Salvation Army and the Brethren. This was the age of the mission halls – 'tin tabernacles' or converted secular buildings dedicated by Christian enthusiasts to the preaching of the Gospel. When Barnardo appealed for funds to buy and transform a local music hall, the Edinburgh Castle, into a centre for Christian outreach he found ready support from Lord Shaftesbury and his circle.

The ebullient, twenty-five-year-old medical student kept in close contact with Henry and Fanny, the friends who had helped to nurture his infant faith, and it was partly his urging of the work that needed doing in the capital that enticed the Guinnesses to London in the closing days of 1872. However, Henry Grattan's vision was not for social work among the urban poor. H. M. Stanley returned from East Africa in 1872 and published an account of his travels – *How I Found Livingstone*. This instant best-seller caught the imagination of the general public and provided a fresh surge to a tide already running strongly in evangelical circles. Converts to biblical Christianity took very seriously the Gospel injunction to 'make disciples of all nations'. Now that distant lands as diverse as China, Japan, Central Africa and Thailand were being opened up by explorers, diplomats and guns, a wholly new opportunity existed to make world-wide conversion to Christ a reality. Hundreds of earnest young men and women, encouraged and supported by their own church members, felt the call to the mission field. The problem for many of them was training. The established, denominational societies had their own colleges, where those destined for the field could study theology, languages and practical skills. Little provision existed for the preparation of independent missionaries. It was this gap that Henry Grattan Guinness believed God was now calling him to fill.

He set up the Stepney Institute, a short walk from Barnardo's mission church, and his friend was the first living-in supervisor. The Guinnesses took a house in euphemistically named Stepney Green, which, although it had its own garden, was surrounded by smoke-exuding factories and down-at-heel terraces. The institute was a faith project; the Guinnesses relied on donations from congregations and individuals to cover the students' tutorial and living expenses. Income was limited, but if living conditions were spartan this was not entirely due to the college's modest funding. Gospel pioneers who were planning to spend years in 'heathen lands afar' would have to resign themselves to doing without the comforts of civilisation. They would also, in many cases, be encountering extreme poverty and the diseases associated with inadequate diet, poor housing and lack of medical treatment. This was one reason for choosing to locate the institute in London's East End. As part of their training, students were regularly involved in open-air preaching and relief work among the city's destitute. Despite the rugged conditions the first year's course was soon oversubscribed. It is a testimony both to Henry Grattan's reputation and to the zeal of Protestantism's evangelical fringe that the institute catered for thirty-two students in the first year and then had to expand into additional premises at Harley House, Bow. The college, now called the East London Institute for Home and Foreign Missions, also increased its scope. Although Henry and Fanny remained primarily interested in overseas work it had become obvious that the separatist churches they served needed a place where lay people could be trained for inner-city evangelism.

During the very years that the Guinnesses were establishing their college the religious temperature in Britain rose to its highest point since the heyday of Wesley and Whitefield. Much of this was to do with the arrival of a thirty-five-year-old, bearded, Connecticut-born evangelist. Dwight L. Moody made his first transatlantic voyage in 1867. He spent several weeks of what was, basically, a trip for the sake of his wife's health visiting East End Brethren and Baptist circles, meeting among others Thomas Barnardo and Charles Spurgeon. Moody learned much from his English friends that was valuable in his work in the Chicago slums. In 1872 he was invited back to speak at a few Christian conferences and conventions. His warm, homely style made an immediate impact and when he spoke in his hosts' churches and tabernacles he enjoyed a response such as he had never known in his own land: hearers in their scores and hundreds came forward to profess conversion. Now the English evangelical community urged him to return for a full-scale preaching tour and excitedly he went home to Chicago to prepare for it. 'I want to dream great things for God,' he told a supporting congregation. 'To get back to Great Britain and win ten thousand souls'.[6] Thus began the remarkable revivalist campaign of 1873–5. With his singing companion, Ira D. Sankey, Moody visited city after city, addressing packed halls and churches. Whether or not he reached his target is not recorded, but certainly thousands of people were converted, or had their faith deepened. The impact on the British Christian community was galvanic. At services and meetings and informal parlour groups around the piano people sang with gusto from Sankey's *Songs and Solos*, an instant best-seller. New activists and new enthusiasm enlivened churches, missions and Christian organisations. Speaking in 1875 of Moody's and Sankey's influence in London, Lord Shaftesbury said, 'I have been conversant for many years with the people of this metropolis, and I may tell you that wherever I go I find traces of these men, of the feeling they have produced, of the stamp that, I hope, will be indelible to many'.[7] One indelible mark was the impulse to lay activity. No longer content to be passive recipients of an essentially clerical religion, the men and women of the pews sought divine guidance and took initiatives. Hundreds offered themselves for 'full-time work' at home or overseas and many applied to Harley House.

The Guinnesses and their circle were at the centre of this revivalist activity. They entertained the evangelists, who shared a keen interest in their work. Sankey was staying with Barnardo when he wrote the music to one of the more enduring new hymns, 'Beneath the cross of Jesus I fain would take my stand'. The presence of scores of eager missionary trainees looking for practical experience was a spur to all kinds of activity. A number of mission churches were started from Harley House. Fanny ran a flourishing Sunday school. A ship, christened *Evangelist*, was commissioned to take the Gospel to the crews of vessels moored in the docks. To meet the demand for institute places more houses had to be acquired as dormitories for the students. Then, in 1875, a wealthy Midlands Christian bequeathed to the institute his modest Derbyshire mansion, Cliff House, Calver, on the banks of the Derwent. This, too, was soon filled with eager young men and women, as well as groups of Barnardo's boys brought into the country in order to see a world very different from their own 'mean streets'. Three years later Harley College, a purpose-built structure, was opened on land adjacent to Harley House.

Running the institute could have been a full-time occupation for Henry and Fanny, but their activities were much more extensive than that. They collaborated on books (most of them dealing with apocalyptic) and, from 1878, published a monthly missionary magazine, *The Regions Beyond*. Henry continued to undertake preaching tours, urging his hearers to embrace the Gospel and to consider committing themselves professionally to its service. Not content with preparing students for the mission field, the Guinnesses helped to organise new societies as fresh areas were added to the map of the known world. In 1874 H. M. Stanley rekindled the imagination of two continents when he returned to Central Africa to continue Livingstone's work of exploration. He sent frequent despatches to his newspaper and one of them, from Uganda, reported that its leader, Kabaka Mutesa, had asked for Christian teachers to be sent to his land. Stanley went on to complete a nightmare transit of the continent. Trekking through the Congo forest he lost all his white companions and experienced many kinds of earthly hell. Further reports, augmented after his return by another blockbuster, *Through the Dark Continent*, helped to maintain the high profile of evangelical Christianity. To be involved in the spread of the Gospel, whether at home or abroad, was to take part in an exciting adventure. Like the advance of Britain's colonial regiments, it had about it an aura of danger and glamour. Not without reason did William Booth rename his evangelistic society the 'Salvation Army' in 1878. In that same year the Guinnesses began to direct missionaries towards what would soon become the Congo Free State by establishing the Livingstone Inland Mission. This was followed by the Congo and Balolo Mission and organisations for evangelising Argentina and Peru. Before the end of the century all this activity was brought under one umbrella organisation, The Regions Beyond Missionary Union. A hundred years later this society still supports around two hundred missionaries throughout the Third World.

If Henry and Fanny did not spare themselves it was not simply because of their own religious zeal. They read the signs of the times and had no doubt about how to interpret them. The surge of Christianity into regions hitherto quarantined by geography, politics or religion could only mean one thing. Writing of the 'dark continent', Fanny observed, 'Why has God in these last days permitted the covering veil to be removed from this immense, unevangelised division of our world? ... The end of all things is at hand, and the Gospel must first be preached among all nations before the end come!'[8] Since Christ's return was so obviously imminent it behoved his servants to keep their lamps filled and their wicks trimmed.

The personal cost of their dedication was great for the Guinnesses. Inevitably they lost friends and colleagues in tragic circumstances. Letters from around the world occasionally brought news of the deaths of former students from disease or persecution. Two of their own children were carried off by diphtheria contracted in the East End slums. When two others felt the call to the mission field their parents were proud, but also saddened by the inevitable separation. Long hours, frequent travels and multiple anxieties wrought upon their own health. Henry, sometimes accompanied by his wife, was constantly on the move – speaking, preaching, visiting some of the more accessible mission stations. Being separated from most of her children and, for long periods of time, her husband, keeping up with the office work and the growing volume of correspondence, and frequently having to appeal for funds all took their toll of Fanny's constitution. Then, in 1885, an attack of Bell's palsy left her cruelly facially disfigured and added to her sense of isolation. Seven years later she suffered a stroke, which left her permanently invalided for the remaining six years of her life.

Fanny's affliction was not allowed to stand in the way of her husband's work. Famous world-wide through his books, lectures, sermons and his connections with prominent figures in the international network of evangelical Christians, Henry was much in demand. After 1885 he travelled ever more extensively, judging his responsibility to the Gospel to be more important than ministering daily to his wife's needs. His elder son, Harry, took over the supervision of the Guinness headquarters and this left Henry free to respond to those who were clamouring for his services. In 1889 he spent several months in America where, among other things, he saw the beginnings of missionary schools in Boston and Minneapolis, based on the Harley College model. Most of the years 1896–7 were spent on an Asian tour taking in India, Burma, China and Japan. Henry Guinness never possessed a fraction of the personal wealth enjoyed by his brewing and banking relatives, but he travelled more widely and had a more detailed knowledge of the world than any of them.

The sharing of a family name was as much an embarrassment to the Grattan Guinnesses as it was to their Lee and Rundell cousins. Henry, a passionate teetotaller, wanted nothing to do with money that came from beer and had scant respect for those who devoted their financial resources to frivolities and personal aggrandisement. The children of Benjamin, Robert and Richard had lifted themselves well above the level of ordinary people. Such religious sentiments as they possessed were channelled into formalised, respectable worship. It was hard for them to understand the emotionalism that possessed other Guinnesses to share public platforms with vulgar American evangelists, to live in the slums and to pour out their lives in the service of foreign savages.

Yet those who shared the same blood and who, for different reasons, were constantly in the public eye, could not ignore each other. The press certainly never tired of pointing out the family connection when reporting Henry Grattan's preaching engagements or Lord Iveagh's latest act of benevolence. There was, also, a common inheritance passed on through the physical or moral genes; a mix of religious conviction and social concern which, though it expressed itself in different ways in men like Edward and Henry, nevertheless sprang from a common stock. There must also have been cross-fertilisation. When Arthur and Edward embarked on schemes of urban renewal they were very aware that their famous cousin had already been involved for some years in various projects to help the people of the slums. Henry Grattan was responsible for modest undertakings – setting up orphanages and schools, providing food and clothing for the destitute. His millionaire relatives could not match the religious passion that lay behind these initiatives, but they could give what their Stepney cousins could not – money.

There is little evidence of close personal contact between the London-based Guinnesses. Henry Grattan, it seems, never approached his relatives for donations, even in the early days of Harley House, when family and college finances were often almost unbearably stretched. The basis of his work was faith in a faithful God. Had not Jesus said 'Do not worry, saying, "What shall we eat?" or "What shall we drink?" or "What shall we wear?" Seek first God's kingdom and his righteousness and all these things will be given to you as well' (Matthew 6, 31–3)? If Henry Grattan thought at all about the West End Guinnesses, with their palatial residences and monogrammed carriages, it was probably to reflect on the fatal lure of Mammon. Invitations to the grand houses were sometimes received and Fanny then had to dress the children in their best clothes and parade them for inspection by Adelaide or Olivia. In their teen years there was a more relaxed relationship between the Grattan Guinness youngsters and the sons and daughters of the London banker Richard Seymour Guinness. Apart from such contacts the families were divided by a common name.

We can, however, recognise one important example of cross-fertilisation. Edward and Adelaide's eldest son, Rupert, was born at their London residence (then in Berkeley Square) in 1874 when Henry and Fanny were just getting used to Harley House, Bow. He was in his late teens when his father began the series of princely donations to housing associations and medical institutions. In other words, he was at the age of rebellion. He could not share the detached paternalism of Lord Iveagh or Baron Ardilaun, whereas the commitment of his distant relatives in Stepney had a distinctly romantic appeal. Whether in the slums or in foreign lands, they and their friends lived among the people they worked to serve. It was a lesson he took to heart when he sought to represent a poor London constituency in parliament. The Iveagh's youngest son, Walter, grew up with a passion to see the 'untamed' parts of the world and developed a wild bravado that scoffed at danger. He, too, had more than a sneaking admiration for his pioneer missionary relatives.

It is certain that none of the London-based Guinnesses would have approved of Oscar Wilde, though they would have had different reasons for disregarding the cynical voluptuary. Yet Wilde, in more reflective mood, could have had them in mind when he wrote:

> O well for him who lives at ease
>   With garnered gold in white domain,
> Nor heeds the splashing of the rain,
>   The crashing down of forest trees.
>
> O well for him who ne'er hath known
>   The travail of the hungry years,
> A father grey with grief and tears,
>   A mother weeping all alone.
>
> But well for him whose foot hath trod
>   The weary road of toil and strife,
> Yet from the sorrows of his life
>   Builds ladders to be nearer God.

11

FOREIGN ADVENTURES

O'Driscoll drove with a song
The wild duck and the drake
From the tall and tufted reeds
Of the drear Hart Lake.

And he saw how the reeds grew dark
At the coming of night-tide,
And dreamed of the long dim hair
Of Bridget his bride.

He heard while he sang and dreamed
A piper piping away,
And never was piping so sad
And never was piping so gay ...
W. B. Yeats, 'The Host of the Air' (1899)

The ambivalence felt by Ireland's greatest poet at the transition from
Victorian certainty to the exciting and drear possibilities of a new age was
widely shared. No one, at the turn of the twentieth century, could fail to
sense a shift in the order of things. Fun-loving Teddy had taken the place
of a queen who had never been able to drag herself out of mourning for
a consort dead forty years since. The electric theatre, the horseless
carriage, the replication of sound through the phonograph, the achievement of manned flight offered a myriad suggestions for the improvement
of life-quality. But to make way for the arrival of a new train an old one
had to leave the platform, taking with it its freight of political, religious
and imperial certainties. The Boers had been trounced, but only at the
cost of British blood and reputation. The Boxers had been taught to

accept European commercial and military supremacy, but not to respect them. The Sudan had been reconquered, but not before foreign anxieties over Britain's colonial ambitions had been fanned into flame. Europe was at peace, but only because power-block alliances constituted temporary deterrents. Ireland was, as it had been for centuries, British-controlled, but not British. Such were the instabilities upon which Edwardian life rested, but no subject of the new king would have anticipated the rapidity with which that fragile society would crumble.

> A wedding of considerable interest to Nonconformists took place on Tuesday at the Robertson Street Congregational Church, the contracting parties being Miss Grace Russell Hurditch, daughter of Mr Russell Hurditch (founder and director of the Evangelical Mission, London), and the Rev. Grattan Guinness D.D. (founder of the East London Training Institute, Harley St, Bow).[1]

What the local newspaper discreetly omitted to report in its brief account of this ceremony was that the groom was sixty-seven and the bride twenty-six. Fanny Guinness's last illness-hampered years had been a trial to her and scarcely less so to her husband. All their married life they had worked as a team. They had shared the hazards and excitements of evangelistic tours. They had laboured together over books and magazine production. They had cared for hundreds of students and kept in touch with them when they dispersed to distant mission fields. They had agonised together in prayer during times of economic hardship and personal grief. Never had they entertained the slightest doubt about the task God had united them to fulfil. When Fanny became a disfigured invalid Henry experienced not only personal loss, but disruption of the work. In a real sense he had lost his helpmeet well before she died. In fact, her death brought him a new freedom. Little more than a year later he was praying for a replacement, someone who would once more complete his life and restore his effectiveness as a servant of the Gospel. It was another three years before his supplication was answered.

Charles Hurditch was a close contemporary of Henry Grattan and a spiritually internal man in the same mould. After his conversion in 1858 he became a prominent member of the Brethren, lived in London and was committed to Christian outreach among the underprivileged. He was a leader of the YMCA, actively involved in running soup kitchens, providing coal and food tickets, and helping destitute young men to find employment. But these activities by no means exhausted his energies, as his daughter later recalled:

He published in succession five magazines, changing their character and style according to the needs of the day. Thirteen million Gospel papers and tracts, of which he was the editor, had been issued from his office in sixteen years. He compiled two hymn books – and was himself the composer of thirty of the hymns – which reached a circulation of over half a million. Then there were his constant preaching tours throughout England, Ireland, Scotland and Wales.[2]

Grace was the youngest of Hurditch's seven children. She trained as a nurse but spent much of her time helping with her father's religious enterprises. She and Henry met in June 1903, when Henry paid a visit to the Christian guest-house Hurditch had recently opened in St Leonard's-on-Sea. They were married within four weeks.

Henry Grattan Guinness still had a very impressive presence – slim, erect and with a mane of waved white hair. Grace was what contemporaries would have called 'a fine figure of a woman'. For more than a dozen years Henry had been denied a partner to share bed, board and bureau. Now that deficiency had been made good – and by a woman who was young, gay and beautiful to boot. A post-Freudian psychologist might affirm that Grace, for her part, was unconsciously seeking a father figure, someone as similar as possible to her own beloved parent. Whatever the inner compulsions of Henry's and Grace's whirlwind romance, it was successful in launching them upon a happy, if brief, married life, which lasted a little under seven years. During that time Henry twice more became a father. His widow survived him by fifty-seven years and never remarried.

Henry's children by his first wife were all considerably older than their stepmother and had made lives of their own in distant Christian outposts. In 1897 the youngest, Dr Gershom, travelled to China to join his sister Geraldine and brother-in-law Howard Taylor (son of the missionary pioneer J. Hudson Taylor). They were working in Sheqizhen, a remote riverside town in the shadow of the Fu-niu Shan mountain range of Honan province, over five hundred miles inland from Shanghai as the crow (or its Chinese equivalent) flies and twice as far by tortuous roads. The arrival of another doctor enabled the overworked resident missionaries to take a holiday in Australia. Thus, Geraldine and Howard escaped the tumult of the Boxer uprising. Gershom was not so fortunate.

Between 1842 and 1860 the Chinese government had been bombarded with treaties – almost literally since western fire power had played a major part in the 'diplomacy' of those years. The closed empire had been opened up to outside commerce and cultural influences, which added a third destabilising element – foreigners – to the already tense relationship between the imperial court and regional governors, all of whom were actual or potential warlords. For the mandarin class and all traditionalists the most resented intrusion was Christianity. Missionaries fanned out across the interior, spreading ideas that undermined the Confucianism which supported the religious, moral, social and political beliefs of the people. By the end of the century hundreds of missionaries from many lands and representing most colours of the Christian spectrum were operating within the empire. Protestant missions alone had baptised 80,000 converts and licensed 5000 Chinese co-workers. These people were protected by law and welcomed by many among whom they laboured for their medical and other skills rather than their revolutionary teaching, but the foreigners had many clashes, sometimes fatal, with officials and nationalists. The devastating outbreak of opposition which began in 1898 had its origins in Shansi and Shandong provinces to the north of Gershom Guinness's Honan base, but rapidly spread over a wider area. The Empress-Dowager Tz'u-hsi vacillated until she was convinced of the power of the 'Righteous and Harmonious Fists' – the Boxers – then placed government support behind the insurgents. On 18 June 1900 she sanctioned the summary execution of all foreigners. Some regional officials declined to put the imperial decree into effect, but that simply added to the chaos and confusion. Over the following summer weeks bands of zealots scoured the country seeking out the representatives of alien culture. The tally of butchered Protestant missionaries stands at 189. Almost as many Catholics also suffered, as did thousands of Chinese converts and supporters.

The awful news reached Sheqizhen in early July only hours ahead of the first attack on the mission stations. Gershom and his colleagues hid in a neighbour's attic, while a mob searched, plundered and bayed for blood. For two and a half weeks they moved from hiding place to hiding place, menaced as much by the insanitary nature of their cramped, stifling conditions as by the visitations of suspicious Boxers. This ordeal was followed by a ten-day voyage down river in a cramped fishing boat to Hankow, where several European trading posts had been established at the confluence of the Han and Yangtze rivers. Days later the party travelled on, under escort, to Shanghai, where they learned that an international expeditionary force had lifted the Boxer siege of the foreign legation in Peking, inflicting a severe humiliation (ultimately fatal) upon the imperial dynasty. The terrible experiences of 1900 prompted the recall of many missionaries, but Gershom stayed on, devoting several years to spreading the Christian gospel in China.

Meanwhile, Harry Guinness, Henry Grattan's eldest son, was the only member of the missionary family to become involved in politics. He had continued to administer the various enterprises begun by his parents, visiting Harley College graduates in the field and generally supporting missionary endeavour. In the years when rival European powers were scrambling, not only for Africa, but for every scrap of undeveloped continent or island which might have economic potential or strategic importance, the Christian churches had their information networks which were often more efficient than diplomatic channels. When it came to reporting on conditions in areas remote from western civilisation, missionaries were certainly more candid and objective than colonial or commercial agents. Thus it was that Harry Guinness was able to gather and co-ordinate intelligence about appalling conditions in the Congo Free State.

In May 1885 an Act was signed in Brussels under the terms of which the President of the International Association of the Congo made over all the association's treaty rights to Leopold II, King of the Belgians. This legal instrument was not widely publicised for the very good reason that the President of the International Association of the Congo (a trading and development company) and Leopold II were one and the same person. The king thus obtained a personal fiefdom of a million square kilometres which was still in the process of expansion as his representatives (including H. M. Stanley) penetrated the forest and the upper reaches of the Congo, urged on towards the great lakes by their distant master. In this domain Leopold was subject to no constitutional restraints, a situation he exploited to the full. The costs of opening up this vast, inhospitable region were immense. In order to recoup his capital and show a profit Leopold sold rights to approved companies and appointed governors to develop the regions retained as *domaine privé*. All the white men sent out to exploit the Congo's natural resources were under intense pressure to maximise the colony's potential and since few squeamish people were around to tell tales they soon made the CFS a byword for brutality.

However, there were protest voices. Several missionary societies were operating in the region and, though some were deterred from speaking out for fear of losing their licences to operate in the CFS, others reported back a catalogue of horrors to their headquarters. They told tales of villages burned, babies killed so that their mothers would not be hampered in their work of collecting latex from rubber trees, hostages taken and only released on payment in crude rubber or animals, men whipped into carrying heavy loads of ivory, rubber or supplies over long distances, and having ears or hands cut off as punishment when they stumbled from sheer fatigue. The entry of Europeans into Central Africa had been hailed as a sure means of ending the slave trade, but the new masters exploited the native population just as badly as their Arab predecessors had done.

As we have noted, the Guinnesses founded the Congo and Balolo Mission which, from 1889, established stations along the middle reaches of the mighty river. Harry Guinness visited the area in 1890 and saw at first hand the barbarism in which Africans and the supposedly civilised CFS representatives shared. In London he reported to the Aborigines Protection Society, who in turn made representations through diplomatic and political channels. They received assurances that the agents of the CFS and the companies would be kept on a tighter leash, but reports continuing to arrive at Harley House proved these to be empty promises. In 1896 Guinness travelled to Brussels to present his case personally to Leopold II. The king sympathised and set up a committee of missionaries from various societies, the Commission for the Protection of the Natives, but this was no more than another palliative gesture. Harry continued, terrier like, to worry political leaders and the international press, but the years passed and thousands more Congolese perished at the hands of their white masters.

It took the appointment of Roger Casement as British Consul to the Congo Free State in 1901 and the widely syndicated exposés of the journalist E. D. Morell to shame European governments into taking decisive action. Casement, an Ulster Protestant, was a man with a passion for justice. He was moved to fiery anger by his experiences of colonial practice in Africa (he had previously served in Mozambique and Angola) and, subsequently, in South America. His indictment of CFS atrocities in 1903 turned him into a public hero. It was his tragedy that, ten years later, he became equally incensed about English attitudes towards Nationalist aspirations in Ireland (see below p.172). At last, events obfuscated by distance, expediency and prejudice were thrust into the full view of public awareness. Governmental and diplomatic blind eyes could no longer be turned. In 1904 the Congo Reform Association was set up to gather more detailed information and make recommendations for action. Harry Guinness was appointed to the committee. Now, with the backing of an official body and with powerful friends, he redoubled his efforts on behalf of the thousands who had no voice of their own in the assemblies of the powerful. He toured the country with first-hand accounts of the Congo evils and heart-rending magic-lantern slides to back them up. He lobbied ministers and MPs. He visited the USA and laid the CRA's case before President Roosevelt. Again he confronted King Leopold. Guinness was not now a lone voice in the wilderness, but he was one of the most insistent. On 18 October 1908 he had the pleasure of seeing the result of his labours: the Belgian government, accountable to the Belgian people and answerable for its actions in the court of international opinion, took over the administration of what became the Belgian Congo; no longer was it a feudal kingdom.

The difficulty of raising public concern over events in Central Africa was an indication of changing times. The generation that had thrilled to the exploits of Livingstone and Stanley and been outraged at the fate of Gordon in Khartoum had been replaced by another, which had lost fathers and brothers in the South African wars and seen international tension raised over far-away places with unpronounceable names. Christian revival had been on the wane long before the death of the old queen. Free-thinking was encouraged by the spread of education and the challenging of religious, social, moral and political dogma associated with such names as Marx, Huxley, Darwin, Annie Besant and Shaw. One casualty of the changing mores was the support for overseas missions. Harley College and its ancillary activities fell upon hard times after the turn of the century. Training, publication, administration of the missions still expanding into new areas, preaching tours and deputation work swallowed money. As old supporters died off they were not replaced in sufficient numbers to guarantee the continuation of the work. In 1903 Cliff House was sold to the Methodist Church for use as a training college. In 1911 Harley College, too, had to be relinquished. For a few years Harry and his wife continued to teach a depleted band of students in their own home, but the outbreak of war brought even this activity to an end. Ten months later Harry Guinness died at the age of fifty-three. Even more than the death of his father in 1910, Harry's passing marked the close of an age.

All except one of Henry Grattan's children accepted the religious ideology of their upbringing or, as the patriarch might have expressed it, grew up 'to know, love and serve the Lord', as missionaries, missionary wives and clergymen. No such prominent markers were laid down for the three sons of the first Lord Iveagh, Rupert, Arthur Ernest (always known by his second name – perhaps because Uncle Arthur was never popular in Edward Cecil's family) and Walter. Brought up to experience and to expect the best that money and influence could provide, they naturally absorbed many of the attitudes of their class; they were, for example, all Unionists. However, one of the advantages of inherited wealth (perhaps its only real advantage in moral terms) is the freedom it provides to develop individual interests and enthusiasms. The sons of the house of Iveagh took the same initial steps, but their pathways soon divided.

They were sent to those schools where attendance had become *de rigueur* for the sons of the ruling élite. At St George's, Ascot, Rupert had for a classmate a certain Churchill, W. S., but their paths diverged when Winston went to Harrow and it was Walter who later developed a close friendship with the politician. From their early years there were some qualities the brothers shared. The first was mutual affection. Brought up together by governesses in the nursery and emotionally distanced from their stern father (with the possible exception of Walter who was probably Edward Cecil's favourite), they found real comfort and pleasure in each other's company. Perhaps because Elveden and Grosvenor Place were associated in their earliest experience with an austere domestic regimen, none of the boys cared very much for their grandiose surroundings. What they did enjoy were the summer holidays aboard their father's steam yacht and all of them developed a love affair with boats and boating. This showed itself very strikingly at Eton. The three brothers were naturally athletic and readily took to rowing. Rupert was a member of the Eton eight, which won the Ladies Plate at Henley in 1893, and he went on to win the Diamond Sculls twice. By the age of twenty-one he was recognised as Britain's leading oarsman. Not to be outdone, Ernest shared his elder sibling's prowess, winning the Silver Goblet at Henley. In 1895 they tossed up to see who should contest the Diamond Sculls; they would not compete against each other. Walter, going through the Eton regime four years later, had a family reputation to live up to. Although he did not reach the same heights of athleticism, he was a member of the school eight three years in succession and became captain of boats.

Rupert went up to Trinity, Cambridge, to continue rowing, but left after a year when a question mark was raised over his health. If his academic prizes did not match his sporting laurels it was not entirely his fault. He suffered from what we now call dyslexia and what was often dismissed in his schooldays as idleness. In areas of study not dependent on reading and writing he showed great enthusiasm and when he was given a microscope it became his favourite toy. Ernest was the brainy one of the trio. He followed Rupert to Trinity and emerged with a good engineering degree. Gadgets and things mechanical always fascinated him. He was one of the first young men of his generation to own a motor car and he took up flying when it was very much in its infancy. His British pilot's licence was, in fact, the second to be issued. In 1923, when the first autogyro was manufactured, he acquired one and kept it in his garage.

Where Rupert was solid, dependable, serious and Ernest studious and slightly eccentric, Walter was extrovert, unconventional and totally without fear. He was a charismatic personality at school and a natural leader with a lively, imaginative and enquiring mind. He had widespread interests and a mental capacity capable of storing the information amassed by his enthusiasms. He would probably have gone on to Oxford to pursue a degree course in biology had the outbreak of the Boer War not offered rather more exciting prospects.

Whatever he may have felt about the way he and Arthur had been brought up, Lord Iveagh repeated the pattern with his own sons. Rupert was trained in all the attributes of a gentleman, a landowner and a leader of society. Ernest, the second son, was despatched to St James's Gate, to train as a brewer, becoming assistant managing director in 1902 and vice-chairman in 1913. In effect, he fulfilled the role in the family business that his father declined to occupy. And he loved it. He was as fully involved in the life and work of the brewery as his grandfather had been and for even longer. Ernest was destined to be the last direct descendant of the first Arthur whose life was devoted to family concerns. His special interest was in machinery and he was always exploring ways of improving efficiency by technical innovation.

When the Boer War broke out there was no question of Ernest being spared to serve, but both his brothers were keen to do their bit. Lord Iveagh was far from enthusiastic about his heir risking life and limb on the veld and in any case there was the problem of Rupert's suspect health (a non-existent problem as it turned out). In the event, father and son found a compromise. As his contribution to the war effort Lord Iveagh raised a medical contingent in Ireland. His friend, Frederick Lord Roberts VC, currently commander of the British army in Ireland, was appointed to take over from General Buller at the Cape at the end of 1899. Iveagh offered to supply the iatric needs of his train. He secured the services of the country's most eminent surgeon, William Thomson, President of the Royal College of Surgeons in Ireland and Irish representative on the General Medical Council, who had recently been knighted for his services to public health. As well as being pre-eminent in his field, Thomson was an enthusiast and a campaigner on behalf of causes such as the reform of the poor law, about which he felt passionately. This activity brought him frequently before the public eye, as did his marriage to Margaret, sister of Sir William Stoker, Bart and the novelist Bram Stoker. Thomson eagerly responded to Lord Iveagh's desire to provide a fully staffed and equipped field hospital and accepted the condition that Rupert Guinness should accompany the expedition as Thomson's ADC.

The application of up-to-date surgical practice and hospital care were still something of a novelty to an army that had learned precious little since the days when Florence Nightingale had had to fight vigorously against closed minds in the Crimea. During the siege of Ladysmith the officer commanding a hospital where shell-torn men were obliged to lie cheek-by-jowl with comrades suffering from dysentery was subjected to an inspection from the principal medical officer, who angrily demanded to know why the soldiers' clothes were not neatly folded and their boots tidily placed beneath their beds. War correspondents reported on inadequate provisions, poor sanitary arrangements, which facilitated the spread of typhoid and dysentery, and the disagreements between medical experts and headquarters staff. Thomson and his ADC were determined that their unit should not attract such criticisms. For several months they enjoyed the luxury of not having to work under field conditions and arouse the attentions of an enemy who ignored international conventions by firing on lines under the 'protection' of the red cross. They were stationed in Cape Town caring for the wounded arriving by trainload from the front. Most of the patients were officers; at one time, Rupert noted, all the beds were occupied by Old Etonians. For him the war often resembled an educational tour more than any thing graver. He took the opportunity to visit mines and a leper colony. Wealthy settlers welcomed Rupert to their homes and farmsteads. He experienced at first hand the assumed superiority of the master race over the majority population, but the similarity to Ireland probably did not occur to him. However, the procession of maimed and dying was a continuous reminder of the reality of war, which intensified when the hospital moved up country to maintain closer contact with the reinforced British army when, at the turn of the century, it went on to the offensive. Thomson's unit accompanied Lord Roberts on the victorious northward march, which relieved Afrikaner-menaced townships and reached Pretoria in June. There he set up a 600-bed hospital in the Palace of Justice where, despite the interference of Lady Roberts and her unqualified gaggle of 'nurses', he maintained standards and organisation which served as a model of all that a military hospital should be.

At the end of 1900 Roberts was replaced as C.-in-C. by Lord Kitchener and his entourage returned home with him. In Dublin Thomson and his staff, including Rupert Guinness, were welcomed at a public banquet given by the Royal College of Surgeons. More permanent honours followed: Sir William received the Queen's Medal with three clasps and Rupert was appointed a Companion of the Order of St Michael and St George. But what was more important to the younger man was the privilege of having worked with the remarkable surgeon. He had learned at first hand about the practicalities of hospital administration and the technicalities of health care. He knew how the Pretoria hospital had avoided being a breeding ground for those germs that had turned other medical centres into death traps. He had absorbed Thomson's enthusiasm for health reform and listened to him expatiate on the principles he had enunciated in his seminal report of Ireland's poor law medical services in 1891. Rupert became a ready convert and devoted much of his energy in later years to the furtherance of Thomson's ideas.

Walter, meanwhile, had an amateur soldier's war. In December 1899 the War Office reached the astounding conclusion that conventional infantry and massed cavalry were no match for small, highly-mobile bands of Boer horsemen armed with rapid-fire mausers. They announced the creation of the Imperial Yeomanry, a force of 5000 young men drawn from the 'hunting and shooting' community of the shires. The Secretary for War believed that, by consulting local 'men of affairs [and] masters of fox-hounds ... in touch with the young riding farmers and horse-masters of this country' it would be possible to find sufficient patriotic adventurers eager to 'do their bit' for the empire.[3] Walter Guinness immediately signed on with the City of London Volunteers, a unit of the IY raised by the Lord Mayor of London, and went out to the Cape at about the same time as his brother. The Imperial Yeomanry were the counterpart of Boer commandos and, though their devil-may-care ethos and distaste for military discipline created problems for the officers to whose command they were assigned, they had many uses: they made lightning raids on Afrikaner positions; they skirmished ahead of advancing columns; they rounded up fleeing stragglers; they fired undefended homesteads to deny their use to the enemy.

Walter revelled in the excitement and danger of pitting himself against settler marksmen for whom he had more respect than for British regulars and their field officers. He was not even deterred when a bullet furrowed his cheek and almost deprived him of the sight of one eye. His greatest moment of glory occurred during Roberts's northwards march. As the column approached Johannesburg the general divided it in two. The main force circuited the city to the east, while a more mobile contingent headed westwards to sever communications between Johannesburg and the townships of Krugersdorp, Florida and Maraisburg. Major-General Hamilton, leading the latter, launched an attack on a Boer position at Doornkop on the last day of May. In what was one of the few set-piece battles of the war the Volunteers and the Gordon Highlanders carried the ridge in a frontal assault that was as heroic as it was foolhardy. Walter survived the volleys of Afrikaner fire, only to sustain his wound hours later in a mopping-up operation at Witpoortjie. His courageous action won him a mention in despatches and the Queen's Medal with four clasps. In October 1900 the CIV went home. Their march through London was a triumphal procession applauded by crowds who needed something to cheer about. Walter and his comrades-in-arms, many of them scions of prominent houses, had had 'a good war' – brief and glorious. In 1914 some of them, with their younger brothers, would embark for another front, expecting the same thrilling and easy victory, but not even that experience would deprive Walter of his craving for adventure. Something else the Boer War gave him was a love for Africa.

For the next few years, while Ernest applied himself to the brewery, the lives of his brothers ran on remarkably parallel lines. Both were married in 1903 and both decided on careers of public service. In this they were following a family tradition, but with a difference. Not for them the remote paternalism of their father and grandfather, who gave incredibly generously to charitable causes and sat on committees. Inspired, perhaps, by men like Henry Grattan Guinness and William Thomson, they espoused a more 'hands-on' philanthropy. Rupert was elected to the London County Council and Walter followed him in 1907. Both had set their minds on parliamentary careers and Walter stole a march over his brother by reaching the House of Commons a few months before him in 1907. Among the impulses which impelled the two men into the political hurly-burly were the state of the Conservative party, the continuing problems of Ireland and their friendship with the Onslow family.

12

THE ARENA OF INTERESTS*

When Arthur Balfour took over the premiership from his uncle in July 1902 he inherited what was, on paper, a very healthy Tory majority. But in reality his party was split on imperial and Irish policy, and vulnerable in the volatile field of foreign affairs. The issue of free trade versus imperial preference raised emotions out of all proportion to its economic importance. The nation had just emerged from a colonial war in which contingents from British possessions round the world had helped secure victory. It seemed to the advocates of protective tariffs, led by Joseph Chamberlain, that the mother country had a moral responsibility to hedge around the developing territories with trade barriers. Their opponents, looking over their shoulders at Germany and the USA emerging from commercial adolescence into aggressively thrusting manhood, were equally convinced that it would be folly to abandon the principles of free trade on which British success had rested. These matters had diplomatic implications in a world where rival empires were 'defending their interests' with defiant alliances and increased expenditure on armaments.

No attempt to improve the situation in Ireland could now avoid aggravating one or other of the parties concerned. Lord Ardilaun was not alone in distrusting the Viceroy (until 1902), Lord Cadogan; *The Times* also took up the charge of 'timidity' alleged in Arthur's newspapers, but the government stuck to a policy of spiking Nationalist guns by progressive economic measures. The Irish Secretary, George Wyndham, and his Under-Secretary, the Irish Roman Catholic Sir Antony Macdonnell, were

---

*'I have never regarded politics as the arena of morals. It is the arena of interests' – Aneurin Bevan

responsible for the Land Act of 1903 which, as we have seen; by making available a larger government subsidy than ever before, eased the transfer of large tracts of land from estate owners to tenants. This was a short-term boon to hundreds of hard-pressed members of the Ascendancy, who reduced their acreages or sold up altogether, but it irrevocably altered the socio-political make-up of the country. Small and moderate-sized holdings accounted for an increasing amount of the landscape. It was inevitable that their proprietors would demand a commensurate share in Ireland's affairs. Elective local government had been established in 1858 and could only be a precursor to some kind of national assembly. Wyndham and Macdonnell began to hold secret exploratory discussions on the subject. When news of these talks leaked out Unionists howled their outrage. Balfour, in a vain attempt to preserve the illusion of party unity, threw Wyndham overboard in February 1905. This was a major blow to the Prime Minister's own reputation and his resignation followed ten months later.

William Hillier, fourth Earl of Onslow, was a member of a highly political clan who could trace their ancestry back to an Elizabethan Speaker of the House of Commons (two other Onslows subsequently held this position) and had an almost unbroken record of service in both chambers from the mid-seventeenth century. William had served a term as Governor of New Zealand before returning in 1892 to become Under-Secretary of State for India and, subsequently, for the colonies. In May 1903 he joined the cabinet as President of the Board of Agriculture. His elder son was already in the diplomatic service and his younger daughter would marry the man who would become Earl of Halifax, Foreign Secretary and one of the principal actors in the Tory party crisis of the late 1930s. As well as his involvement in the national assembly Lord Onslow had been an alderman of the London County Council in the closing years of the old century. The life of his family and that of the Guinnesses, therefore, touched at several points and connections were strengthened through grouse-moor and ballroom gatherings. It was thus that Rupert met Gwendolin Onslow, the earl's elder daughter, a serious-minded young lady, every bit as politically committed as her male relatives. She was very concerned about social reform and, as she confided to her diary, 'impressed by the great gulf between the rich and the poor and the misery and squalor of the slums'.[1] Rupert was already a member of the Guinness Trust and helping to administer his father's tenement building schemes. The events of 1903 showed just how deep his commitment was. That was the year he married Gwendolin, was accepted as Conservative candidate for the Haggerston division of Shoreditch, joined the LCC (because he was advised that local government was the best political nursery), began service on the London School Board *and* bought for his town residence, not an elegant house in St James's, but 266 Kingsland Road, in the middle of the constituency he now began to cultivate.

It was not a very propitious time to seek a parliamentary seat, especially for someone well on the right of the Tory party. Following Balfour's resignation there was a general election in January 1906, which resulted in the celebrated Liberal landslide. The Conservative–Unionist block held on to just 157 seats, while Campbell-Bannerman's party took 377. Even more significant were the results of the smaller parties. Fifty-three 'Labour' candidates were returned – working-class members put up by the unions and the Labour Representation Committee. And the Irish Nationalists had put their troubles behind them to elect eighty-three MPs under the leadership of the ardent but pragmatic John Redmond. In the depressed area of Haggerston the Hon. Rupert Guinness stood no chance of stemming the anti-government tide. Walter, now also married (to Hilda Erskine, daughter of the Earl of Buchan) and resident at Hardwick House near Bury St Edmunds, fared no better when he offered himself to the electors of Stowmarket. However, in another intriguing parallel, by-elections set both brothers' feet on the parliamentary ladder. Walter had no difficulty in winning Bury St Edmunds in 1907. He and his father were leaders of local society and major employers. The following year, when the death of the Liberal member caused a vacancy in Haggerston, five years' hard work on the part of Rupert and Gwendolin paid off. Aided by a small turn-out and the intervention of a Labour candidate, Walter's brother joined him on the opposition benches.

Thus the two Guinnesses were in their places in time for what was to be one of the most tumultuous epochs in British constitutional and political history. It saw the emergence of Lloyd George, the Liberal social reforms of the Asquith government, the struggle with the House of Lords, the re-emergence of the Home Rule issue, female suffrage, the conduct of the First World War and the partition of Ireland. Walter and Rupert were party men through and through – staunch Unionists, upholders of the privileges of the Tory-dominated upper house, imperialists and tariff supporters, and always ready to attack Liberal reform measures. Chancellor Lloyd George's budget of 1909 gave them and their colleagues plenty to get their teeth into. It was a monumental piece of social engineering. Labour exchanges, road improvements, children's allowances and other novelties were to be paid for by taxation increases, which would impact most on the wealthier members of society. No amount of Tory protest could impede the Finance Bill's progress through the

Commons, but the opposition could safely rely on their friends in 'another place' to defeat it, as they had defeated a number of recent government bills. Asquith immediately challenged the Lords' power of veto and called an election. This time the Conservatives made up some ground, denying the government its overall majority. However, in the Haggerston division of Shoreditch the sitting member lost his seat. It is a measure of Walter's popularity that he was returned unopposed and would continue to be so until he left the Commons in 1931.

Rupert and Gwendolin spent the next year touring Canada and the USA. They made speeches about the situation in Britain, the importance of imperial ties and Irish Home Rule as the thin edge of a wedge that would rive the empire. Lady Gwendolin, a more instinctively political animal than her husband, discovered during this trip that platform speaking was her *métier* and in future years she campaigned often more energetically than Rupert. The main purpose of the Guinnesses' visit to Canada, however, was not propaganda, but to see for themselves the successes and failures of immigration from Britain. Settling families on virgin territory in the open spaces of the colonies and dominions was an aspect of imperial policy that Rupert was particularly interested in. It was the most efficient methodology for achieving cultural cohesion, providing for Britain's dispossessed and unemployed, and establishing a bulwark against the expansionism of other powers. Did he, one wonders, ever ask himself why English settlement had not worked in Ireland, or did he believe that, despite centuries of conflict, it had?

During his absence Britain reached an unprecedented pitch of political excitement and bitterness. In the Westminster menagerie peers and commoners roared and screeched their demands for and opposition to constitutional change, and journalists translated the caterwauling for an intrigued populace. Nor was parliamentary procedure the only morsel over which the legislative predators fought; Home Rule had once more been thrown into the cage. The demography of the Commons chamber was similar to that of the 1880s: a Liberal government dependent on the votes of Irish members. Unionists now had no alternative but to oppose with all the energy and vehemence at their command the dishonourable deal they conceived Asquith and Redmond to have struck. If the Liberals got through a Parliament Bill which would strip the upper house of its power of veto and then introduced a Home Rule Bill the war they had waged for a quarter of a century finally would be lost. Their last hope of salvation was the second election the Prime Minister called in 1910. When that resulted in a 'no-change' situation the fur began to fly in earnest.

Walter Guinness threw himself into the thick of the fray. From 1911 he became one of the most frequent of speakers in the House and one whose contributions were eagerly awaited, as much for their hyperbole and passion as for their clarity of thought. He harried the Parliament Bill through all its stages. Attacking its introduction in February 1911, he lashed out at the Socialists and Irish Nationalists as anti-democratic power-seekers. Then he embarked on a history lesson about 'Communist tyranny'. The Long Parliament of the 1640s, he suggested,

> Having abolished the House of Lords ... proceeded first of all to set up a new court without any system of jury, from which the only appeal for mercy was to this House. ... That is liberty under a Single-Chamber system. They proceeded to muzzle the Press; they interfered with the rights of popular election; they threw the Lord Mayor of London into prison; they banished 30,000 men from London without any sort of trial; they confiscated quite arbitrarily the estates of their enemies; and finally they so neglected the Navy that Van Tromp was able to land a raiding party on the coast of Kent to sweep the Channel.[2]

Having made a case for the upper chamber not as a bastion of upper-class privilege but as an arsenal for the defence of common liberties, Walter conceded that the hereditary principal might, perhaps should, be jettisoned. One wonders what his father or, more pertinently, his Uncle Arthur made of that.

That was about as far as he was prepared to go in departure from the *status quo*. In a speech the previous summer on the Parliamentary Franchise (Women) Bill he had lambasted both the objectives and methods of the suffragettes. In the process he drew another parallel as unlikely as that between Herbert Asquith and the seventeenth-century regicides. He managed to link Mrs Pankhurst's demonstrations with outbreaks of unrest in Irish history and drew the following moral: 'seeing the disastrous results of always buying off violence by legislative bribes ... ought to be a warning to this House not to repeat this performance in the case of woman suffrage'.[3] He opposed state intervention to reduce unemployment on the grounds that industry and business, if left to their own devices, would create wealth and generate job opportunities.

The determination to oppose everything that the Liberals attempted to carry became even stronger after the passing of the Parliament Act in August 1911, which was followed rapidly by a Home Rule Bill. For Walter the political confrontation was no less a war than the struggle against the Boers had been. It was even more desperate because the Unionists' backs were to the wall. A whole culture was at stake and in the name of survival no quarter could be given and no stratagem rejected. It was now that the Ulster issue moved to centre stage. The Protestants of the North, led by the Orange Order, determined that if they could not be big fish in a large pool they would be big fish in a smaller pool. If Home Rule could not be prevented at least they would, by force of arms if necessary, prevent it becoming a reality in Ulster. Edward Carson, the new leader of Irish Unionism, launched Ulster's 'Solemn League and Covenant' at a crowded meeting in Belfast in September 1912. It affirmed:

> Being convinced in our consciences that Home Rule would be disastrous to the material well-being of Ulster as well as of the whole of Ireland, subversive of our civil and religious freedom, destructive of our citizenship and perilous to the unity of the Empire, we, whose names are under-written, men of Ulster, loyal subjects of His Gracious Majesty King George V, humbly relying on the God whom our fathers in days of stress and trial confidently trusted, do hereby pledge ourselves in solemn Covenant throughout this our time of threatened calamity to stand by one another in defending for ourselves and our children our cherished position of equal citizenship in the United Kingdom and in using all means which may be found necessary to defeat the present conspiracy to set up a Home Rule Parliament in Ireland. And in the event of such a Parliament being forced upon us we further solemnly and mutually pledge ourselves to refuse to recognise its authority.

This document had the full support of the Guinnesses. Challenged in parliament to say why non-resident Irishmen should lend their weight to such seditious sentiment, Walter replied:

> ... every Irish Protestant will recognise that, under the present conditions, it is the duty of Ulster members to take the opportunity of trying to secure for their constituents freedom from this iniquitous measure. I believe that Unionists living outside Ulster would blame their allies in this House if they opposed this exemption. It would be merely a dog-in-the-manger policy for us who live outside Ulster to grudge relief to our co-religionists merely because we could not share it.[4]

Later, in a heated exchange across the floor of the Commons Walter, who could be vituperative, though never uncontrollably so, in debate referred to the Home Rule Bill contemptuously as 'this garbage which you are forcing down their throats'.

In the spring of 1912 Rupert Guinness returned to the parliamentary battlefield. He had been selected as candidate for the safe seat of South-East Essex and on the retirement of the sitting member he took his place without a contest (on the subsequent division of the constituency he became the MP for Southend). He was not the orator that Walter was, nor did he have the same passion – at least, not for the political causes his brother so vigorously defended. But he was a 'steady' party man. When he made his acceptance speech in November 1911 his party, as has always been the wont of disillusioned and disappointed Tories, had just scapegoated their Commons leader of twenty years' standing. It may not, therefore, have been altogether tactful for Guinness to refer to Balfour as 'one of the most wonderful men history will be able to record', but it did display loyalty to a leader he had come to know and respect. It was as the direct result of a meeting with Balfour, who suffered from respiratory disorders, that he set up the Wright-Fleming Institute of Microbiology where, under the aegis of two of the age's leading men of medicine, vital pioneer work was done on the treatment of allergies. For the rest he dutifully denounced Lloyd George's National Insurance Bill as a measure 'being shamefully rushed through as the result of a deal with Redmond' and he declared that Irish Protestants and the British exchequer would bear the brunt of Home Rule 'just to please the Irish people'.[5] However, once elected, he never raised his order paper to speak on the major issues of the day.

Rupert Guinness was essentially a practical man. He saw parliament, not as a platform for campaigning bombast, but as a power centre from which to get things done. The debates to which he did contribute and the parliamentary questions he raised were for the most part concerned with the care of the physically and mentally handicapped, urban housing, the state of hospitals and the operations of the poor law. More of his energies went into using his resources in private schemes which would make a positive contribution to the causes he believed in. On his return from Canada he resolved to do something which would better equip young men setting out to farm in an unknown land. On an estate bought from his father-in-law at Pyrford, Surrey, Rupert set up the Emigration Training Farm to initiate would-be emigrants into the realities of life in the dominion. *Country Life* commended Mr Guinness's pioneer enterprise:

> His method of doing it is as original as the idea itself. He refuses to have the scheme described as being philanthropic in character, but at the same time he is not seeking to make any profit. His return comes in the shape of additional interest added to life and in the gratification of being able to give a much better start to the young men under his charge than they would otherwise have been able to secure; and these after all are no slight rewards, especially if taken with the consideration that his work is of high Imperial value.[6]

Coupling the work at Pyrford with the Public Schools Emigration League ensured that the 'right sort' of young men went out to the colonies.

Although Asquith was Prime Minister it was Lloyd George who was the real *bête noire* of the opposition benches. He was brash, clever, popular in the country and particularly adept at wrong-footing his opponents in debate. Therefore he was the prime target of Conservative vendetta. Walter went after him with gusto whenever he had the opportunity. When the Balkans exploded in war in 1912 the major powers were intent on not allowing themselves to be damaged by flying sparks. In Moscow, Berlin, Vienna, Paris and London governments considered their responses to a complex situation in the light of their own foreign policy requirements. Asquith's cabinet, and particularly Lloyd George, came down on the side of Greece and her allies against the crumbling power of Turkey. Walter Guinness promptly went off to the Mediterranean to conduct his own maverick researches on the ground and came to opposite conclusions: a despairing Turkey, he believed, would be certain to grasp at any alliance which offered a restoration of her European possessions or a guarantee of protection against future aggression. He urged this argument in vigorous debate against the government. Time proved him right. In 1914 the Ottoman Empire was sucked into military support for the Central European powers and became a strategic barrier protecting the eastern flank of Germany and Austria–Hungary.

So determined was Walter to train every possible piece of artillery against his political enemies that he acquired a weekly magazine, *Outlook*, to popularise his views and snipe regularly at the government and particularly at the Chancellor. During the summer of 1912, while its proprietor was on a hunting safari in South Africa, *Outlook*'s financial correspondent, Wilfred Lawson, in the course of his usual exposés of Liberal economic policy, lit on the 'Marconi affair'. The Postmaster-General had accepted, subject to parliament's ratification, the tender of the Marconi Company for the establishment of an imperial wireless system. Lawson objected to the way the business was handled. The publicity started various rumours, including suspicions that government ministers, profiting from inside knowledge, had speculated in Marconi shares. Among the 'culprits' was Lloyd George and *Outlook*, together with other Tory press organs, pursued him with relish. The whole thing was a storm in a teacup and a parliamentary committee exonerated the members concerned. What turned it into a *cause célèbre*, which came close to toppling the Chancellor, was the government's inept handling of the affair and the Conservatives' terrier-like determination to cling on until the last moment in the hope of inflicting serious damage on their opponents. The persistent rumours rumbled on for almost a year and they were by no means all one-way. On the floor of the House Lloyd George accused the member for Bury St Edmunds of making unsubstantiated accusations of corruption and Walter was suspected, inside and outside parliament, of playing a dirty game. It was on 18 June 1913 that the accused members made statements to the House which were then debated. Walter took the opportunity to offer a personal explanation. His magazine, he insisted, had charged government ministers with inefficiency, not corruption. It was not a very convincing performance. Whatever words *Outlook* had used, the political intent behind them was quite clear and, when pressed, Walter had to acknowledge that the magazine had spread the unwholesome rumours, once started. All in all the Marconi Affair was a sordid business from which no one emerged with any credit.

In reality, it was a clamorous and distracting side-show to the main political event of the pre-war years – Home Rule. The twin parliamentary demons which whipped Ireland towards the precipice of bloodshed and partition were Liberal pragmatism and Conservative viciousness. Neither side had the interests of Ireland at heart and Redmond's group of comfortable, middle-aged MPs did not speak for a younger generation of virulent Nationalists hostile to the very suggestion of compromise. Compromise – or, rather, seeming-compromise – was something projected by Lloyd George as early as 1911. He took seriously Ulster's determination not to be part of an independent nation and suggested a temporary opt-out (the period varied between three and six years during subsequent debate) from the provisions of the Act by any county whose people voted for it. His subtle mind reasoned that at the end of the trial period Unionists would be unable to engineer a sufficient majority for continued exclusion. By the time this tactic became part of official government policy the moment when it might have succeeded had vanished. The Home Rule Bill yo-yoed back and forth between Commons and Lords, Unionists in both places raising wrecking and delaying amendments to a measure that they knew must eventually pass into law in some form.

The dominant characteristics of Conservative parties in the wilderness are confusion and rage. Long association with the ruling élites of commerce and county has conditioned them to regard power as a birthright and the regaining of power an end legitimising any means. The opposition front bench, mistrustful of the government's motives and furious at the way the House of Peers' teeth had been drawn, resorted to extra-parliamentary tactics to make Home Rule unworkable in the event of its introduction. Bonar Law, the Tory leader, refused co-operation with

Asquith in the search for a solution. He encouraged the formation of the Ulster Volunteer Force and urged army units to disobey any orders to enforce a new constitutional settlement. He was supported by top brass in the army and judiciary (including Lord Roberts and Sir Henry Wilson, Director of Military Operations at the War Office). Their overt and covert support for violence led directly to the smuggling of a large quantity of arms into Belfast and culminated in the Curragh 'mutiny' of March 1914, when fifty-eight senior army officers announced that they would resign rather than 'coerce' Ulster. Such activity stimulated similar responses on the Nationalist side: the Irish Republican Brotherhood was revivified and Sinn Fein began to emerge from the confused ranks of the extremists. Ireland was being delivered into the hands of the men of violence.

In the House of Commons Walter Guinness frequently displayed the intransigence of his party, although there was often an individualistic element in his rhetoric. He came perilously close to supporting the Curragh 'mutineers' when he asserted the right of British soldiers not to fight in Ulster if this was against their conscience. On several occasions he pointed out what he conceived to be the lessons of history: 'Unionists ... believe that in the past a Protestant ascendancy has worked appalling injury to Irish interests, and they believe also that now that this Protestant ascendancy has at last been swept away for ever it would be disastrous to set up in its place a Roman Catholic ascendancy.' Many of those for whom Walter claimed to speak would have put a different value on Ireland's Protestant inheritance and would have been uncomfortable to be identified as playground bullies who, finding themselves up against more powerful adversaries, had experienced a spectacular conversion to pacifism. They would, however, have been happy with their colleague's rejection of separate development and his call for a general election:

> [Division] will put back the cause of conciliation in Ireland for centuries ... As an Irishman who, whatever happens about Home Rule, must live in one of the three southern provinces, I do trust, even now, that the question will not be decided merely by compromise between parties in this House, but that it will be decided by the ballot box.[7]

Walter's self-identification as someone who 'must live' in Ireland had about it a certain artlessness. Although he was on the Guinness board, he had no involvement in the running of the brewery and kept no establishment in the land of his fathers. His Suffolk estate and his house in Grosvenor Place (this street facing the gardens of Buckingham Palace had become something of a Guinness enclave; as well as Lord Iveagh's mansion at Number 5 there was Walter's town house at Number 11 and

Ernest's at Number 17) were quite sufficient for his domestic needs, but even in England he was not truly at home. He was a rover, a citizen of the world. What Irishness there was in Walter Guinness showed itself in a romantic wanderlust. The passion for boating developed in childhood never left him – as it never left Rupert or Ernest – and he liked nothing better than boarding his steam yacht *Roussalka* with a few carefully chosen companions and sailing for the Caribbean, the Levant or the Far East. 'For the last twenty-five years,' he wrote in 1936, 'every holiday that I could snatch has been spent in distant travel on all the non-arctic continents and oceans of the world ... My own instinct has always been to get away from the great ports and centres of modern life and to visit human races, birds and beasts, rivers, mountains and forests where they still remain untouched by Western development'.[8] He was not alone among the wealthy young men of his generation who rebelled against the effulgent luxury and studied ease of their Victorian sires by escaping to the 'real' world of primitive peoples and untamed landscapes. When on safari in Africa, Walter frequently made hunting expeditions with only local people for company.

It is a measure of the man's breadth of mind that, as an amateur scientist–explorer, he could accumulate information, gather specimens for museums and write reports on a range of observed phenomena in the intervals between being one of the best-informed and most active of parliamentarians (see below pp.224ff). By contrast Ernest, who *did* have to live in Ireland, at least part of the time, adopted a more cautious attitude to his responsibilities. He took over the small estate of Glenmaroon, near Dublin, which had been acquired for Claude Guinness when he was managing director. Ireland's relationship with Britain and the rest of the world was of considerable importance to the success of the brewery, which was one reason why, in the early years of the century, the board toyed with the idea of establishing a subsidiary plant in Manchester. It was Edward Cecil's maxim that a business either goes forward or backward. Going forward for Guinness meant opening new markets.

This was no easy matter in the changed economic climate of 1900–14, when Britain's long-held economic supremacy was being challenged by Continental and overseas powers, many of whom were protecting their home industries with tariff walls. The company's attitude had hitherto been the rather complacent one that its excellent product sold itself – 'good ale needs no bush'. Aggressive marketing and 'showy' advertising were alien to the Guinness ethos. 'It is our general rule to advertise in no way. We never do so in England or Ireland.' This was Lord Iveagh's position in 1909.[9] He was prepared to allow overseas agents to promote Guinness beer, but only if it was clear that advertisements did not emanate from the company.

It is almost of the essence of family businesses that tradition puts up a strong resistance to change and so it proved with Arthur Guinness, Son and Co. Ltd, as the board dithered over expansion into Europe. At Lord Iveagh's urging, in 1908, the directors reluctantly sent a Mr Haines to explore the current state of the Continental market. Their appointee was somewhat hampered by a total ignorance of foreign languages, but he provided his employers with a cogent report and urged them to assign a sales representative for Europe. The board agreed – and did nothing about it for two years. Then they engaged the services of a French ex-cavalry officer, M. Rodier. He survived less than two years before being dismissed as 'too proud'. His replacement was a man 'of higher social standing' (but presumably not tarnished with hubris) capable of dealing with 'a higher class of establishment'. This excellent gentleman appears not to have survived even his trial period. By this time the First World War was only months away, when European trade came to a standstill. This was only one example of how the directors, meeting in London or Dublin, found it difficult to accept the advice of agents who had a better understanding of local situations.

With the arrival of the late summer of 1914 other priorities forced themselves upon the attention of the Guinnesses and the nation.

13

A HOUSE SHAKEN

Sir Hugh Lane was a noted connoisseur and patron of modern art. Born in Co. Cork, he established himself while still in his twenties as a leading London dealer. In 1909 he returned to his homeland to become founder-director of Dublin's gallery of contemporary painting, to which he proposed to bequeath his own collection. When an appeal was launched to create suitable accommodation for an expanding cultural treasure house, one prominent citizen made a grudging contribution accompanied by a letter indicating that more largess might be forthcoming once the project was safely off the ground. What may seem a prudent attitude drew forth a rebuke from Yeats:

'To a Wealthy Man who Promised a Second Subscription to the Dublin Municipal Gallery if it were Proved the People Wanted Pictures'

> You gave, but will not give again
> Until enough of Paudeen's pence
> By Biddy's halfpennies have lain
> To be 'some sort of evidence',
> Before you'll put your guineas down,
> That things it were a pride to give
> Are what the blind and ignorant town
> Imagines best to make it thrive.
> What cared Duke Ercole, that bid
> His mummers to the market-place,
> What th'onion-sellers thought or did
> So that his Plautus set the pace
> For the Italian comedies? ...

The 'Wealthy Man' whom Yeats urged to emulate the Estes and other Renaissance Maecenases was Arthur, Lord Ardilaun.

The irascible master of Ashford, St Anne's Clontarf, Muckross and other extensive acres throughout Ireland was never the aesthetic patron the poet would have liked him to be, for all his presidency of the Royal Dublin Society and his accumulation of fine furniture and paintings to equip his many houses. It was his wife, Lady Olivia, who, despite political convictions which she held just as fiercely as her husband, supported and encouraged poets, playwrights and artists of every hue from strident green to blazing orange, either because she was indulgent of their views or failed to understand them. She was a patroness of the Abbey Theatre, where Yeats and his friends were experimenting with dramas based on Gaelic legend and where J. M. Synge's *The Playboy of the Western World* was booed from the stage in 1907. She held a salon at her Dublin home when she and Arthur were there for the season and there is something very eighteenth-century about one such gathering which was, doubtless, not atypical. Olivia's favourite living poet had been engaged to entertain her fashionable friends.

> 'I'll speak now.' Yeats, still standing in the doorway, paused while everybody hurriedly sat down. He then looked past everybody, as though he had seen a vision.
>
> 'I speak of the moon.'
>
> And he spoke of the moon at length, in a slow, chanting voice. Nobody could understand a word.
>
> When he had stopped, as abruptly as he had started, Lady Ardilaun asked him to recite *Innisfree*. He ignored her request.
>
> 'A verse to the moon.'
>
> It only consisted of four lines, half spoken, half sung. Yeats then bowed, told Lady Ardilaun that he would not be staying to tea, and hurried away.
>
> 'Quite batty I suppose, poor fellow.'
>
> The officer who put forward this supposition did so in tones redolent of the hunting field. There followed the rumble of an old and deaf peer.
>
> 'Couldn't catch it all, but there's no moon tonight.'[1]

The Ardilauns were passionately Anglo-Irish, more so than any of their relatives, and in this they overlapped with Yeats's romanticised Hibernianism. The Guinnesses and their ilk might lack the spirituality to appreciate modern artistic trends but they, and the dullard bourgeoisie, were the traditional sustainers of the creative element in society. The poet's ideal Ireland was peopled by hard-riding Protestant aristos and Catholic peasants steeped in Gaelic lore. While Arthur was prophesying to the House of Lords the imminent collapse of progressive farming through the forced sale of land to men 'who had failed everywhere else, either through their own fault or through the fault of those agitators who had urged them on to their own ruin',[2] Yeats was penning the lament 'Upon a House Shaken by the Land Agitation':

> How should the world be luckier if this house,
> Where passion and provision have been one
> Time out of mind, became too ruinous
> To breed the lidless eye that loves the sun? ...

To Yeats there was something reassuring about the life-style of Lady Ardilaun who, when travelling to London, had her ferry cabin decked with flowers from her own garden, was conveyed on the Holyhead–Euston train in a private compartment and was met at the terminus by her own carriage and pair, which had been sent on ahead. That way of life was already disappearing rapidly when Britain lurched into war in August 1914. No one had the slightest inkling of how violent the forthcoming tremors would be, how furiously they would shake the very foundations of society, or how civil war would be brought to the streets of Dublin.

Arthur Guinness did not live to see it. He died in the first weeks of 1915, inveighing to the last against a weak government intent on selling out Ireland's ruling class. Because his own marriage was childless, the barony came to an end, but the Guinness baronetcy devolved upon brother Benjamin's eldest son, Algernon. The prospect can scarcely have pleased the aged peer; his nephew was a wild young man with a passion for fast cars and its associated partying. He had spent his own inheritance before he even received it on coming of age in 1906 and attempts to redeem the situation drove him into the hands of moneylenders. There was no longer any question of the head of the family bailing him out, as would have happened in the days of the second Arthur. When Algernon appeared in the bankruptcy court in 1911 he was on his own and only the sale of his Irish estates could save him.

His other uncle, the multimillionaire Lord Iveagh, was too busy doing whatever he could to safeguard his own fortune to spare much thought for improvident Algernon. Having resumed chairmanship of the brewery in 1903 he retained firm control until the end of his days. His three sons were brought on to the board, Rupert was appointed vice-chairman alongside Ernest but none of the brothers was permitted much say in matters of policy. Just as his grandfather had kept Benjamin Lee firmly under his thumb, so Edward now restricted his heir's involvement in the family business. Family capital tied up in Ireland was a major cause of anxiety throughout the elasticated Home Rule debate. The profits from beer rose almost unfalteringly year on year, but they were not immune from the effects of political change. For several years the directors toyed with the idea of moving the brewing operation, or at least setting up a subsidiary production line and, in 1912, they acquired a site beside the Manchester Ship Canal. Plans were drawn up and building began, only to be halted by the war. Guinness wealth needed protecting from what Lord Iveagh regarded as the rapacity of a Liberal government, as well as the possible acquisitiveness of a future Nationalist administration in Ireland. Lloyd George had increased death duties and there was every reason to suspect that his successors might levy further imposts on inherited wealth, forcing family members to sell shares. Iveagh therefore invested his capital prodigally in anything which was likely to appreciate in value or bring in a steady income – a 500-acre estate in Suffolk, old master paintings, property in London's Earls Court. One unpublicised reason for Rupert's visit to Canada in 1910–11 was to explore the possibility of buying cheap farmland in the dominion and several million pounds subsequently found their way across the Atlantic. All these capital assets were then tied up in trust funds, where the taxman could not reach them.

In 1915 Lord Iveagh's wealth and responsibilities were boosted by the death of his brother. Arthur had decided to keep the bulk of his fortune in the family. After leaving his wife the Clontarf estate, the houses in St Stephen's Green and Carlton House Terrace, and half a million in spending money, he bequeathed the rest of his landed estates to his brother. Lord Iveagh had now reached the Everest of personal wealth. He was among the richest half-dozen men in England and was determined that generations to come should benefit from his wise provision. As the expected 'brief' war lengthened into an unspeakable and seemingly unending nightmare, and violence of a new order beset Ireland, the head of the Guinness family could reflect that whatever happened he had secured the future. Then, in 1916, his beloved Adelaide died and his own future looked suddenly empty.

Walter was home in uniform in time for his mother's funeral. He had enlisted immediately on the outbreak of hostilities as a major in the Suffolk Yeomanry (the Duke of York's Own Loyal Suffolk Hussars). The War Office recognised his expertise in Middle East affairs and despatched him to staff headquarters in Egypt. In the spring of 1915 it was decided to break through the barrier the Central Powers had thrown up in south-east Europe. Successive waves of British and Imperial troops battered the coast of Gallipoli, to be halted by effective Turkish fire from the heights above. Walter had himself transferred to the war zone and fought alongside soldiers from Australia and New Zealand in one of the more ill-conceived and poorly executed campaigns of a war rich in military blunders. The only part of the operation which was successful was the withdrawal of the army from the area at the end of the year.

Walter returned home and immediately used his recent experience to attack in the Commons political and military mismanagement. He was instrumental in forcing the coalition government to set up a committee of inquiry into the Gallipoli fiasco. He also had a great deal to say about the Irish situation.

War precipitated the final crisis. Ireland had been exempt from conscription so as not to exacerbate Nationalist feeling. Ulstermen responded by signing on in droves to prove their loyalty. In the South the majority held aloof from 'England's war'. Redmond and the Westminster men urged their followers not to make capital out of the European conflict, but a tiny majority of extremists planned to do just that. They now had in their counsels that champion of the oppressed and enemy of imperialism Sir Roger Casement. He travelled to Berlin to extract promises of practical assistance for an Irish rebellion, while IRB and Irish Volunteer leaders armed their supporters for the fray. In the event, Germany supplied only arms and encouragement; the fatherland was no more ready to provide realistic support for Casement than revolutionary France had been to equip Wolfe Tone with adequate manpower. The result in 1916 was similar to that of 1796. Casement was arrested on landing from a German submarine and before he had time to abort the planned Easter Rising. Confusion, poor communication and do-or-die fanaticism led a force of some 1600 rebels to seize key buildings in Dublin. Most citizens were opposed to and appalled by this demonstration. They were to be deeply shocked by what happened next. The government, which had negotiated with the equally rebellious Curragh mutineers, instantly deployed infantry and artillery against Nationalist positions. Much of central Dublin was reduced to rubble, 450 insurgents, 116 soldiers and 16 policemen were killed and 2614 people were wounded. More importantly, a new myth was created. Freedom fighters had taken over from legislators, as Yeats pointed out:

> How could you dream they'd listen
> That have an ear alone
> For those new comrades they have found,
> Lord Edward and Wolfe Tone,
> Or meddle with our give and take
> That convene bone to bone?
> ('Sixteen Dead Men')

Walter Guinness was among those Unionists who harried the govern-ment, demanding tough measures against agitators, condemning examples of apparent indecisiveness, exposing inconsistencies of policy: a fracas near Shannon Bridge had been the work of men 'of military age', who clearly should have been in the trenches; three civil servants arrested for Sinn Fein activity had been reinstated. The appearance of the first elected Sinn Feiners in the House roused his particular ire; how dare a member of this assembly openly sport a revolutionary favour, he demanded. The fire was not all in one direction; Walter was a favourite target of the Irish members, not least because of his protracted leave. Stung by a taunt that he was afraid to rejoin his regiment, Major Guinness responded, 'Had the honourable Member for East Limerick served with me in Anzac, or if I felt that there was the slightest chance of meeting in the near future that honourable Member ... in the trenches of France, I should attach very much more importance to his criticism'.[3] Modesty doubtless prevented him pointing out that he had been posted back to Egypt, but had requested a transfer to the western front. In August he went to France, first of all as commander of the Tenth Battalion of the London Regiment, then as second-in-command of the Eleventh Cheshires.

Bryan, his elder son, then aged ten, saw his father ride off to war on his horse Butterfly, an upright figure in gleaming boots, sword hanging at his side, for all the world like a shining knight errant from one of his nursery picture books. Something of the same romantic identification entered into Walter's self-image. He possessed that fiery patriotism and disregard of danger that impelled him deliberately into the thick of battle. He really did believe *dulce et decorum est pro patria mori*, but his was no empty-headed braggadocio. The young man who had thought it a lark to canter across the veld under accurate Boer fire had matured into a husband and father, who went not irresponsibly to war, but fought out of conviction and a strong sense that it was the duty of the privileged class to face the hazards and horrors of 'the feast of vultures and the waste of life' and not shelter behind the massed ranks of the lower orders. He was vitriolic about the statesmen who commissioned carnage and the generals who delivered it. But he would do his duty. He did it so impressively that he returned, after nineteen months, with the rank of lieutenant-colonel and also with the DSO and bar. One wonders whether he ever knew that two of his distant Antipodean cousins were among those who had fallen not far from where he was fighting. Two sons of the New Zealand politician Sir Arthur Robert Guinness died in the Great War – Francis Benjamin at Gallipoli and Arthur Grattan at Passchendaele.

Walter's return in the early days of 1918 coincided with a major change in the conduct of the war. Lloyd George, who had become Prime Minister in December 1916, had spent his first year in office circling the ring with the Chief of the Imperial General Staff Sir William Robertson. He was appalled at the macabre stalemate in the trenches, had no confidence in the strategy of the generals and wanted to take strategic decisions out of their hands. His announcement, in February 1918, of Robertson's removal brought howls of protest from all sides of the House, divided the cabinet, dragged the king into the political arena and forced Lloyd George to produce the ultimate bluff of threatened resignation. On the day after the demotion of the CIGS Walter Guinness was among those who leaped to his feet in the chamber to accuse the Prime Minister of political manoeuvring and personal vendetta. Sacking Robertson would, he prophesied, demoralise the army and prove to be a disaster in every way. Walter was wrong. Fresh strategic thinking, the arrival of American troops, the introduction of tanks, the mediation of President Wilson, British success in the Middle East and a generous portion of luck combined to bring about the defeat of Germany within nine months – something which had seemed impossible to all the military experts.

Rupert's war was less exciting and he put to good use his knowledge of matters nautical. In 1903 he had built his own yawl, the *Leander*, with which he subsequently won several races including the coveted King's Cup at Cowes. All this activity brought him into contact with hundreds of fellow enthusiasts, both wealthy boat owners like himself and the crew members they engaged to handle their magnificent craft. There, Rupert realised, was a reservoir of amateur sailors who could be of immense value if Britain ever had to go to war upon the high seas. King Edward and Kaiser Wilhelm both loved showing off their fleets and also scoring off each other in yacht races. Rupert was among those who enjoyed intimacy with the royal family and the creation of the Royal Naval Volunteer Reserve is believed to have been the result of a conversation between him and the king. He brought the support force into being, and devoted much time to recruiting and training over the next few years.

On the outbreak of war he was commander of the London division of the RNVR and daily expected that he and his men would be deployed throughout the fleet. In the event there was no naval conflict. The rival fleets spent the greater part of the war in harbour or on uninterrupted patrols and the battle of Jutland was little more than a skirmish. The RNVR was restricted to onshore duties. In July 1916 Rupert, desperate to be useful like Walter, was appointed acting captain and a naval ADC to the king. In this capacity he toured the country recruiting the men who

were needed in ever greater numbers for the trenches and in the following year he returned to Canada to stir the hearts of overseas subjects to
come to the aid of the motherland. The Guinnesses' London home in St
James's Square became the headquarters of the National Prisoners of War
Fund and Gwendolin Guinness devoted much of her time to this organisation, which distributed food and clothing to captured combatants, and
gathered information for their anxious families.

However, Rupert's major contribution to the war effort was in the
initiatives emanating from his East Anglian estate at Pyrford. His real
interest lay in agricultural reform and in this field he was a pioneer.
Someone who worked closely with him described him as a man who had
'the ability, the courage and the means to venture along an unknown path
and open up new ways of doing things previously thought impracticable'.[4]
His concern for public health, his interest in scientific research and his
practical experience of farming all met at this point. Before the war a few
younger, serious-minded men with wide acres, deep pockets and broad
minds had begun to act out a quiet rebellion against the traditional ways
of the countryside. There was Wilfred Buckley, a dairy farmer who had
studied advanced techniques in America and who held a senior position
in the Ministry of Food from 1915. There was Waldorf Astor (later
Viscount Astor), wartime PPS to Lloyd George, who campaigned successfully for the creation of a Ministry of Health. There was Sir John Russell,
Director of the Rothamsted Institute for Agricultural Research. And there
was Rupert Guinness, the wealthy and interested amateur. He financed
Rothamsted experiments in the biochemistry of farmyard manure and
provided land at Pyrford for field tests. The result was the elimination of
enormous waste and the discovery of the most effective storage methods.
From this the researchers went on to explore ways of breaking down straw
and other vegetable refuse in order to create plant fertiliser. They perfected
a substance which they called 'Adco' and, with Guinness money, set up
the Agricultural Development Company to market it. Rupert's concern
with public health and hygiene, first stimulated in the fever-stalked
military hospitals of South Africa, was stimulated by watching the milking
process on his farms. The work was carried out in dirty barns, by labourers
with unwashed hands using unsterilised equipment. It was the traditional
way of doing things: busy workers and cost-conscious farmers alike were
uninterested in the investment of time and money in more sanitary
methods. Not surprisingly, milk thus produced rapidly went off in warm
weather and, more important, it was a medium for the spread of disease,
particularly tuberculosis. Rupert applied his mind to the problem and
carried out personal experiments over several years. He designed and

installed sterilising equipment; he urged on his labourers the need for cleanliness; and he sought ways of testing his herds to eradicate tuberculosis.

The coming of war focused more attention on public health and food production. The Earl of Selborne, who was President of the Board of Agriculture, recognised Guinness's valuable pioneering work. He had come to know Rupert earlier during his years as First Lord of the Admiralty and soon reached the conclusion that he would be of more service to the country out of uniform. Rupert received government encouragement and resources for his various experiments in the interests of enabling farmers to increase the yield and wholesomeness of their produce. With Wilfred Buckley providing civil service back-up and Waldorf Astor securing the support of the Prime Minister, government schemes were instituted to provide better milk. Farms were inspected by ministry agents. Those where improved milking methods and tuberculin testing were in operation were licensed to sell 'Grade A' or 'certified' milk for a higher price. It was one early step in the advance to government standardisation of agricultural production. Many farmers resented it and only a few with the necessary capital and enthusiasm took advantage of it. But such is the fate of most pioneering ideas, and the gospel of Rupert Guinness and his fellow missionaries spread by degrees in ensuing years both by improving production methods and by ensuring that the public was better informed.

Lord Elveden's interests naturally brought him into contact with most of the advanced thinkers who were bridging the gap between pure laboratory science and the messy world of byre and furrow. One institution that was rapidly making its mark in agricultural research was the University College of Reading, founded in 1892. In 1912 the governing body set up a specialist unit to serve the dairy industry. Despite its shoestring budget it made important contributions in several areas of study and by 1920 was in urgent need of expansion. What was necessary was a farm where experiments could be tested under realistic conditions. These were the days before sizeable Westminster subventions and corporate donations. It was Guinness, Astor and other influential 'better food' standard bearers who put forward a joint scheme. Rupert supplied half the purchase price and, over the next thirteen years, half the necessary development funds, and the Ministry of Agriculture contributed the rest.

It was during the war that Rupert became closely acquainted with another place destined to commend the family name to posterity. In 1751 the Earl of Bute, later to become Prime Minister, had restored Kenwood, an impressive villa he had inherited five miles outside London. The house occupied a site on the heights between Hampstead and Highgate, from which 'the whole city within 16 miles of the River' could be seen.[5] A hundred-and-sixty-four years later the elevated position of the house which had so pleased Bute and subsequent owners appealed to the Ministry of War for another reason. In 1915 they located there the Royal Naval Anti-Aircraft Mobile Brigade, manned by the RNVR. As London commander, Rupert frequently visited the unit to inspect the mounted cannon and searchlights which were there to defend the capital from German planes and airships. The new style of warfare, which for the first time carried devastation to civilian centres far from the battlefields, caused considerable alarm among Londoners and did, in fact, account for over a thousand non-combatant deaths. Lord Iveagh had provided himself with a haven at Heath House, Hampstead, and this was a useful base for Rupert when he was visiting his men – and dining with Kenwood's tenants.

War frequently has its bizarre elements and Kenwood provides a good example. Between 1910 and 1917 it was rented by Grand Duke Michael of Russia, second cousin of the reigning tsar and a close friend of George V. The grand duke entertained generously and it would be surprising indeed if his Guinness neighbours were not included on the Kenwood guest list. So we may legitimately imagine Rupert dining well at a table gleaming with imperial silver and cut crystal, then going out to the stable block to keep watch with his men and warm himself with cheap tea from an enamel mug.

No member of the British Guinness family was among the three-quarters of a million men killed on First World War battlefields, but they could not be other than profoundly affected by the conflict. War had taken away hundreds of indoor and outdoor servants, many never to return. Young friends who had come to shoot over the well-stocked Guinness acres had fallen to hostile fire. Of the six hundred men who joined up from St James's Gate – their jobs kept open, their wives and mothers regularly provided by the brewery with half-wages – a hundred did not come back. In order to minimise disruption caused by the war-time dislocation of maritime freight services Arthur Guinness, Son and Co. Ltd acquired its own ships to operate between Dublin, Liverpool and Bristol. One of these was sunk by a torpedo in 1917 with further loss of life. The hesitant plans for a Manchester brewery were finally shelved in the same year. By the outbreak of hostilities the company had got as far as building a wharf alongside the canal. This was now commandeered by the government. Lord Iveagh also suffered from Whitehall intrusion. Part of the Elveden estate was taken over by the War Office as a proving

The 'Second' Arthur Guinness (1768–1855) was a banker as well as a brewer, a man whose heart was as warm as his head was cool.

From him and his first wife Anne (née Lee 1774–1817), shown here with their youngest child, Rebecca, sprang the Lee Guinness line – the brewing Guinnesses.

Arthur Lee Guinness
left the family business
under a cloud and retired
to his estate to live the
life of an aesthete.

Richard Samuel, known
as 'Old Pell', having failed
as a banker and estate agent,
chose a political career and
was involved in various
electoral scandals.

Three elegant young men about town. Arthur Edward, Benjamin Lee and Edward Cecil were in their twenties when they inherited their father's vast fortune. Two of them became the first Guinness peers.

BELOW RIGHT
Arthur, Baron Ardinlaun

BELOW LEFT
Edward, Viscount Iveagh

Fashion and favour. Members of the royal family were regular visitors to Elveden.
A 1901 shooting party: the future George V is at the driving seat of the car on the left.

Arthur Eustace (1865–1955)

At this time Philip de Lázlo, husband
of Lucy Guinness, was making a name
for himself as a society portrait painter.
He was well patronised by the banking
Guinnesses.

The artist's wife's sister, Eva (b. 1868).

Henry Grattan Guinness, the great non-conformist preacher, spent most of his life working in London's East End.

At the age of 67 he married as his second wife the lovely 26 year-old Grace Hurditch.

March 15, 1912. THE SOUTHEND AND WESTCLIFF GRAPHIC. CARTOON OF THE WEEK.

DISCRETION IS THE BETTER PART OF VALOUR.
"I shan't play. You're much too strong for me—so was the other fellow."
(The Hon. Rupert Guinness will be returned unopposed as the Conservative member for South-East Essex.)

Rupert, eldest son of Lord Iveagh, also started his married life in the East End where he served on the LCC and stood for parliament. He eventually gained the Commons seat of East Essex in 1912. The by-election victories of two Tories on the same day discomfited Lloyd George.

Walter, the adventurer of the family. James Sant RA, Queen Victoria's official portrait painter, seems to have captured Walter's wild, romantic nature at a very early age.

Later, in the intervals of a busy political life, Walter found time to explore some of the world's remoter regions such as New Guinea.

Walter's steam yacht, the converted ferry *Rosaura*.

Kenwood. The Guinnesses first made the acquaintance of Kenwood, on Hampstead Heath, during the First World War when Rupert commanded an RNVR anti-aircraft brigade stationed there.

In 1925 his father, Lord Iveagh, bought the house and presented it to the nation along with part of his magnificent collection of paintings, including such famous masterpieces as Self-Portrait (1663) by Rembrandt.

If he can say as you can
Guinness is good for you
How grand to be a Toucan
Just think what Toucan do

In 1935 the first really famous Guinness poster hit the hoardings with a text provided by one of S. H. Benson's talented copywriters – Dorothy L. Sayers.

Over the next half-century Arthur Guinness Son and Co. Ltd became a national institution. The last member of the family to preside over it was Benjamin, 3rd Lord Iveagh (1937–1992).

ground for its latest secret weapon – the tank. Lord Iveagh's sacred coverts were spared, but heavy machines trundled over acres near where royal shooting parties had once enjoyed their sport, turning them into a fair imitation of the squelching fields of Flanders.

A more serious potential threat to the Guinnesses and all their dependants was posed by moves to clamp down on the beer trade. There was genuine (though probably exaggerated) concern about loss of efficiency in the armed forces and the munitions factories caused by excessive consumption of alcohol. Campaigners urged that poor people should be given every encouragement to spend money on wholesome comestibles rather than beer, and that grain and spirits should be used to maintain the food and munitions industries instead of breweries and distilleries. Responding to this concern, Lloyd George set up the Central Liquor Board and, no less alarming to the Guinnesses and their trade rivals, George V took the king's pledge for the duration of the war and urged his subjects to follow his lead. All manner of rumours spread around the drinks trade about action that the government was supposedly contemplating, ranging from reduction of the gravity of beers to nationalisation and prohibition.

All the leading manufacturers combined their efforts to deflect government from draconian policies and for the first time it became apparent just how powerful the brewing lobby was. Its members assailed frontbench leaders on both sides of the Commons. The Guinnesses even found an unlikely champion in the Nationalist leader, John Redmond, who opposed large rises in duty on St James's Gate heavier gravity beers, which accounted for four-fifths of all Ireland's brewing output. Primed by company spokesmen, he told the government that it would be impossible for the Dublin brewers 'to manufacture light beers which would have any of the characteristics of Irish stout ... therefore so far as the brewing trade in Ireland is concerned your proposal would practically put an end to it. Guinness's lightest porter at the moment has a gravity of 1057; therefore the full 36s. super-tax would fall on every single barrel brewed by this firm'.[6] Lloyd George did raise the duty on alcoholic beverages quite severely and he also imposed restrictions on public house opening hours but, under pressure from the manufacturers, he resisted the demands for more extreme measures.[7] Sales fell off during the war; overseas trade was disrupted; material and other costs increased, and duty went up by more than 450 per cent. Despite all this, brewery profits rose from £1.25 million p.a. to £2.14 million p.a. This was due to price rises and reduction of the gravity of some beers.

The brewery could not avoid being involved in the brief but bloody

Irish rebellion of 1916, even though there was no attack on the St James's Gate premises. As soon as the fighting started it rapidly became evident that neither side had adequate medical facilities. Guinness's company doctor responded by organising first-aid posts and an ambulance service, which were at the disposal of all injured combatants on both sides.

The war almost put an end to the London branch of the Guinness Mahon bank. The dislocation of international commerce imposed a strain on all financial institutions, but this does not seem to have been the fundamental reason why the shutters went up in Lombard Street. The truth was that Richard Seymour's banking sons had tired of business. In contrast to their three brothers (see below), Robert Darley, Gerald Seymour and Arthur Eustace had stepped into an already flourishing concern. They had worked at it and, after their father's retirement, re-organised it. But now they were simply too rich to bother with it. The London office was still technically an offshoot of the parent bank, which was being run very successfully by their cousin. They were middle-aged and wanted to enjoy to the full the fruits of their labours. By the turn of the century they had become fully fledged members of the country house set. They enjoyed the social life of England's heartland shires. Robert was squire of Wootton Hall, Wootton Wawen, near Stratford-on-Avon. Gerald and Eustace were very close and their love of fashionable country pursuits took them to the hunting country of Oxfordshire and Northamptonshire. Both brothers married into the local gentry in the summer of 1897. Ernest acquired Greens Norton Hall, near Towcester, and Gerald lived in Jacobean splendour at Dorton House, in the Vale of Aylesbury, widely known as 'Rothschildshire' after the family which dominated the social scene from their mansions at Mentmore, Tring, Waddesdon, Halton and Aston Clinton. The Guinnesses' most influential friends were the de Capell-Brookes, an Anglo-Irish family of great antiquity, whose two and a half thousand acre estate was centred at Great Oakley, near Kettering. Ernest, who was for a time master of the Grafton Hunt, rode to hounds with Sir Arthur de Capell-Brooke, fifth baronet, and Gerald married Sir Arthur's first cousin Grace.

The banking Guinnesses were not as wealthy as their brewing relatives but, like Lord Iveagh, they aspired to the social life, shorn of the tiresome distractions of business. The only barrier to their disengagement from the City was their father. As he entered his ninth decade Richard Seymour was in full possession of his faculties and in no mood to contemplate the winding up of a financial institution he had started more than half a century before. None of his sons dared broach the possibility to him. Not until the old man breathed his last in December 1915 were they able to realise their ambition. Then they wasted no time; they announced their intention to retire and to transfer all the London office's business to Dublin.

Howard Rundell, therefore, was left with total responsibility for an Anglo-Irish bank on the eve of the Easter Rising. Life was hard for Guinness Mahon and their clients. To help Howard cope with the problems created by war and severe deterioration of relations with England his solicitor brother Noel came into partnership. Like some of his brewing cousins, Noel shared the current fashion for yachting. He kept his own craft in Dublin Bay, and his house on the Hill of Howth commanded a fine view of the harbour and the open sea beyond. He may well have felt that he, too, would like to have indulged in the luxury of devoting more time to his private life, but he dutifully shouldered the burden laid down by the London partners.

While their elder brothers were enjoying membership of the hunting, fishing and shooting fraternity, Richard Seymour's two younger sons carved out individual careers in the world of international finance. Benjamin was by nature an adventurer. The bank held no appeal for him and at the age of fourteen he elected to embark on a naval career. In his case the adage about travel broadening the mind was certainly borne out. By the time he retired from active service in 1891 he had visited several countries and acquired a much clearer understanding of the way the world worked than was possible from the city of London, blinkered by its own success. The years 1865 to 1914 were the years of the United States' economic revolution. Population more than doubled; home demand soared; the nation benefited from transport and factory technology developed in Europe, and added the innovations of native genius such as electric light, the telephone and mass production; coal, oil and agricultural produce existed in abundance to feed new industries, and financial institutions rapidly developed to service the greatest economic expansion the world had ever seen. There was, of course, bust as well as boom; America could not avoid the laws of cyclicality; fortunes were lost as well as made; but there was no halting the free enterprise machine which transformed the USA into the world's leading industrial exporter by 1910, and which created the first multimillion-dollar trust companies and hugely powerful monopolies. In the closing years of the nineteenth century Benjamin Guinness was one of a small number of European businessmen who fully understood what was happening.

He took up a partnership in Guinness Mahon and after a couple of years moved to New York to look after the firm's interests there. And also to trade on his own account. He became a major player on the Wall Street market and built up large holdings of railway, steel and manufacturing equities. He was soon powerful enough to take his seat on the boards of several major corporations. By the turn of the century he was an Anglo-US business tycoon – one of the first of the breed – shuttling between his Long Island and Surrey homes. At the age of thirty-four he took time out to get married. Like Gerald, he chose a bride from an ancient titled family. Sir Richard Williams-Bulkeley, whose daughter Bridget he married, was the eleventh in a line of Welsh baronets first honoured by Cromwell. Equipped with an elegant hostess, Benjamin entered, with a vengeance, high society on both sides of the Atlantic. In America he raced motor cars and threw wild parties. Entertainment at his Ascot home was rather more sedate and his town house proved inadequate to receive the kind of company he was now keeping. He rectified this in 1915. After the death of Lord Ardilaun his widow had no need of an impressive London residence. She was happy to receive an offer from Benjamin Guinness for 11–12 Carlton House Terrace. There is real symbolism in this transfer of one of the family's grandest metropolitan houses from Arthur, the conservative landed magnate, to Benjamin, the financial whiz-kid. Soon Benjamin and Bridget were throwing dinners and balls for the cream of international society, which rivalled anything offered by their Grosvenor Place cousins.

It was, indeed, the Seymour Guinnesses who were taking up the social running from the Lee Guinnesses. Lord Iveagh's family still had the wealth and the connections. When occasion demanded they could and did put on a show. But the excitement of unlimited resources had faded. They had nothing to prove by ostentation and guest-list competition. Not so the bankers and financiers. Whether in London or the shires, Richard Seymour's sons were very self-conscious of the impression they were creating. Richard Sidney, the youngest son, made his fortune in insurance and stock-market speculation. At the age of twenty-two he married Emilie Weimar, whose father was a serving officer in the Kaiser's Imperial Guard. The German connection was no embarrassment during Victoria's reign, but over the ensuing decade, as relations between Eddy's and Willy's governments deteriorated, Richard's wife became a social drag. The couple were divorced in 1912 and Richard then espoused Beatrice Jungmann, flamboyant and eccentric widow of a society painter.

With Guinness money, artistic flair and her own bizarre personality, Beatrice became one of the most celebrated hostesses of the age. The house in Great Cumberland Place where she held court was a mecca for the stars of the artistic, theatrical and literary sub-cultures. They flocked to the table of this large woman, who served unconventional meals and presided over them with fearsome authority. They listened to her out-rageous comments on mutual. friends delivered in a voice half-way between a boom and a growl. They made fun of 'Gloomy Beatrice', her tent-like gowns and festoons of beads – but they kept on coming. Social excesses were considerably played down between 1914 and 1918, but even war could not subdue Beatrice Guinness.

Life was far less glamorous and agreeable for another Guinness lady living in London. In 1906 Philip and Lucy de László had returned from Vienna because – or so Philip claimed with a fair degree of accuracy – the artist had painted most of the leading members of Continental society and needed a new challenge. The move was entirely successful. Within months Philip had had an exhibition at the Fine Arts Society, which had been visited by the king and queen, who immediately commissioned a study of their daughter, Princess Victoria. Inevitably, where royalty led high society followed. Aristocrats and political leaders beat a path to de László's door and his popularity even eclipsed that of John Singer Sargeant, who abandoned portraiture in 1910.

All went well until 1916. Then the fashionable world dropped de László as rapidly as it had taken him up. The reason was the war. Philip became a British citizen in 1914, but that did not protect him from the fervid xenophobia of those whose sons were being killed fighting Germany and her allies. De László was marked out as one who had strong links with the Habsburgs, whose patronage had launched his career. By the middle of the war Allied politicians had 'discovered' that they were fighting for the dismemberment of the Habsburg empire and the self-determination of 'subject' peoples. There was, of course, no logic in transferring to an artist the opprobrium people felt for the Austro-Hungarian system. Philip associated himself very publicly with various wartime charities and offered his services, very cheaply, to families who wanted portraits of their young men just going off to war. But propaganda has little connec-tion with logic, and Philip and Lucy found themselves widely shunned. Galleries refused to show the artist's pictures and embarrassed art societies demanded his resignation. Lord Northcliffe, the press baron whose portrait de László had executed in 1911, used his newspapers to mount frequent attacks on the painter. Worse was to follow: in 1917 Philip was interned as a spy and sent to Holloway prison, where he suffered a nervous breakdown. Transferred to a nursing home, he slowly recovered, but never shook off the bitterness he felt at being deserted by so many former patrons and friends.

Lucy stood loyally by her husband in his humiliation and illness. So, to their credit, did several members of her family. When, after the war,

Philip was rebuilding his confidence and his career, various relatives came forward with commissions. Richard Seymour's son Eustace, and Henry's grandson Henry Samuel, were among Philip's sitters in 1919, and the artist painted many more Guinness men, women and children in the ensuing years. The head of the Lee Guinness clan, however, remained consistent in ignoring this distant relation in favour of more socially acceptable artists. When Lord Iveagh decided to sit for a portrait after the war it was to the highly acclaimed fellow Dubliner Sir William Orpen that he turned. While de László had been incarcerated for suspected unpatriotic activities, Orpen had enjoyed celebrity as an official war artist and was knighted for this in 1918. Philip had to fight his way back to favour. A fickle and shameless society insouciantly opened its doors to him once more in the 1920s and soon the artist was producing works more prolifically than ever. In 1930 he was elected President of the Royal Society of British Artists. Once again, Lucy was able to hold her head high in London society and entertain in her Hampstead home, though her guests were not those who graced the salons of Great Cumberland Place or Carlton House Terrace.

14

THE CEREMONY OF INNOCENCE IS DROWNED

As the commercial disruption of the years 1914–18 and the period of reconstruction that followed made no permanent inroads into brewery profits it might have seemed that there was nothing to stop the Guinnesses simply picking up where they had left off before the beginning of hostilities. There is, indeed, an element of continuity about their activities. Lord Iveagh pursued his charitable work with unmitigated vigour and, in 1919, was raised to the rank of earl. Rupert devoted more and more of his time to farming. Gwendolin helped him with his party and constituency work, and her prominence was signalled by her election as vice-chairman of the women's branch of the National Unionist Association six months after the end of the war. In the intervals occasioned by military service Walter pursued his political career more energetically, his advancement being made possible by the fact that his party was a partner in the wartime coalition government, which continued until October 1922 and enjoyed power in its own right from then until December 1923.

Yet beneath the seamless outer covering there were profound changes of attitude and circumstance. The fine houses in town and country were no longer the settings for lavish balls and extravagant entertainments. It was not only the absence of the hostess of Elveden, Grosvenor Place, Farmleigh and St Stephen's Green that rendered inappropriate the grandiose hospitality of a former era. The self-confidence, the national pride and the belief in a permanent social order which the pre-war life-style had displayed had been exposed as fashionable and precious trappings hanging limply on the shrunken frame of a discredited élitism. The younger generation of Guinnesses certainly did not see all this in the clear yet dazzling light of Damascene vision. They were confused; tenaciously holding on to old thought patterns, while recognising the need for change. They feared the emergence of a political party of the working class and the 'Bolshevism' they saw lurking behind it, while at the same time recognising the need to incorporate Labour members into the parliamentary system.

Walter's response of 12 February 1919 in the debate on the king's speech indicates a certain knee-jerk conservatism over major issues of the moment. He insisted that Germany should be made to pay to the uttermost for her war crimes and criticised the Versailles conference for not making speedy progress towards decisions which, to his mind, were clear-cut and inevitable. He was particularly scathing of the mediating efforts of and high moral tone adopted by the American leader. 'Since the days of Mahomet no prophet has been listened to with more superstitious respect than has President Wilson,' he insisted and his colleagues responded with gleeful laughter to the man who had emerged as one of the most effective Commons debaters. Walter went on to urge the administration to have no truck with the revolutionary junta in Moscow. 'The complete indifference with which the Government and the Press received the news of the murder of the Imperial Family and of their loyal friends in Russia was', he insisted, 'a disgrace to this country'.[1] Lloyd George, responding, assured the member for Bury St Edmunds that he, too, had no love for Comrade Lenin and Co., but pointed out that if Britain were not prepared to go to war with them she would have to learn to live with them. The following day the announcement of Walter's membership of the Coalition Group on Foreign Affairs indicated a more pragmatic attitude towards the complex situation left behind in the wake of war. The new back-bench body was drawn from all parties and set up 'to exchange views with prominent Allied politicians and to make a close and continuous study of questions of foreign policy in the House of Commons'. Sir Simon Hoare was its first chairman and Lieutenant-Colonel Guinness its secretary.[2]

It was Ireland which, as ever, most exercised the minds and hearts of the Guinnesses. In the aftermath of the Easter Rising the ideological citadels of Nationalism and Unionism loomed large and gaunt over the political landscape and determined Irishmen streamed steadily into the haven of their defiant, unforgiving walls. Caught as ever between the Scylla and Charybdis of coercion and constitutional reform, the government alienated thousands of people who had not hitherto been committed to either camp. Three thousand nationalists were rounded up, held for months without charge and subsequently released. Ringleaders were shot or hanged (the treatment of Casement being particularly sordid), their names swelling the roll of martyrs. A nation claiming to fight in Europe for the rights of small states to self-determination appeared morally bankrupt in its dealings with its own reluctant subjects. Throughout the South support drifted steadily towards Sinn Fein. In 1917 the House of Commons held sixty-eight Nationalist MPs, eighteen Unionists and seven Sinn Fein. In the December 1918 election the balance changed dramatically: the numbers, now, were seventy-three Sinn Fein, six Nationalists and twenty-six Unionists.

Even Lloyd George, enjoying immense popularity and almost dicta-torial power during the second half of the war, could not achieve a settlement. Rather, his subtle manoeuvrings made the situation worse. In July 1917 he authorised a meeting of all the interested parties in Dublin, the Irish Convention, on the principle of letting Irishmen solve their own problems. It was a last attempt to retain a united Ireland in which moderate counsels prevailed, but the Sinn Fein representatives simply boycotted the gathering and the Ulster Unionists refused to discuss any solution which did not involve partition. Even more ominously the name IRA began to be heard in the land. Lord Iveagh experienced the northerners' arrogance at first hand. On the eve of the convention he gave a dinner party at 80 St Stephen's Green for eleven southern Unionist delegates. While they were still sitting at table his guests were summoned to a meeting with their Ulster counterparts. Hastily clambering into cabs, they arrived at the appointed rendezvous, only to be kept waiting another hour before the northerners deigned to see them. When they were admitted to the discussion table it was to be informed that a united Ireland was ruled out. Despite this snub the Ascendancy 'rump' con-tinued to work for a constitution that would satisfy the Nationalists and provide safeguards for minorities. This was now the best that political realists could hope for and the Guinnesses were obliged by their immense commercial and landed interests to be realists. Unfortunately, the onward march of extremism trampled all moderation and compromise into the dust.

As the war dragged on the Guinnesses found themselves in a world where the old clear-cut political divisions had disappeared. They could no longer attack a Liberal government for weak policies and alliance with the Nationalists, since the cabinet coalition included Unionists and the Nationalists no longer counted as a political force. It was, in fact, Lloyd George's yielding to Tory back-bench pressure which threw the final log on to the fire of incipient revolt. The Guinnesses and their colleagues clamoured with mounting vociferousness for conscription to be extended to Ireland. They were supported by the military high command, particularly by Sir Henry Wilson, the new CIGS, who was an Ulster Unionist and had been a supporter of the Curragh malcontents. Their opponents warned that nothing would be better calculated to unite all shades of Anglophobe feeling than drafting Irish sons and husbands to the Flanders killing fields. In the spring of 1918 the Prime Minister thought he saw a way of using compulsory enlistment as a political lever: he would introduce it, but only activate the policy after the acceptance of Home Rule. The stratagem failed; Catholic leaders, moderate nationalists and ordinary, good men who loathed the very idea of civil war threw their weight behind Sinn Fein and its leader, Eamon De Valera. In January 1919 the newly elected MPs set up their own, Republican, parliament rather than attend the 'enemy's' assembly in Westminster, then set about stamping their authority on the nation by boycotting all British institutions and sanctioning violent attacks on the police.

Ireland was now effectively out of control. The government went through the motions, which could only be yet more variations on the old theme of coercion and concession. The Government of Ireland Act (December 1920) provided Home Rule under the Crown for two distinct provinces centred on Dublin and Belfast. Now it was the turn of southerners to reject the principle and Unionists to accept it. But not *all* Unionists: 'As an Irishman I could not bring myself to vote in a single division on the Irish question. I did not believe in the policy. I do not yet. I hope I am wrong. I want to see quickly – as soon as possible – a proper Government, a peaceful Government – in my native country'.[3] That was how Rupert Guinness (created Lord Elveden) explained his Commons abstentions to a constituency meeting. There was now clear water between his attitude and his brother's. Walter had reluctantly gone into the government lobby for all the significant votes.

The other side of Lloyd George's policy was the disastrous tactic of recruiting volunteer soldiers to augment the police and restore order. The notorious Black and Tans and Auxiliaries were made up largely of violent and vengeful men.

> If … a policeman is shot, five Sinn Feiners will be shot. It is not coercion, it is an eye for an eye … Are we to lie down while our comrades are shot by the cornerboys and raggamuffins of Ireland? We say – 'Never!' and all the inquiries in the world will not stop our desire for revenge. Stop the shooting of the police, or we will lay low every house that smells Sinn Fein.[4]

The reign of terror throughout 1920 and 1921 destroyed over 700 lives on each side and laid waste scores of buildings.

Lady Ardilaun was among those who suffered serious loss – at the hands of both parties. Her family home, Macroom Castle, Co. Cork was commandeered as a base by the Black and Tans, attacked by a Republican force and seriously damaged by fire. What made the outrage doubly outrageous in her ladyship's mind was the fact that the perpetrators were led by an Englishman. Erskine Childers, chiefly now remembered as the author of the adventure story, *The Riddle of the Sands*, was related to Olivia's friends, the Bartons of Co. Kildare and in happier days had visited Ashford on shooting parties but his sympathies had become engaged by the Nationalist cause, and he joined Casement's group of agitators and conspirators. He was elected to parliament for Co. Wicklow in 1918, was among those who set up a rebel assembly in Dublin and then became an insurgency organiser. He was executed in 1922 for illegally bearing arms (later, his son became one of only three members of the Dáil to come from an Ascendancy background).

Lady Ardilaun, who persistently and defiantly lived the life of a beneficent *grande dame* to the end of her days, felt even more bitterly about Britain than she did about her fellow Irishmen fighting for their independence. Bequeathing to a relative the presentation to All Saints Clontarf, she stipulated, 'under no circumstances is an Englishman to be appointed' and she left a fund for the education of Protestant sons of the Irish gentry 'in reduced circumstances owing to the loss of income from their Irish landed estates'.[5] Lady Ardilaun, who died in December 1925, spent her last years, according to a friend, 'a lonely figure in her wealth, childless and feeling the old life shattered around her'. Her conversation was all of the good old days, of visits from *the* queen, dinners at Buckingham Palace and 'those nice young officers who used to write their names in our book'.[6]

When Nationalists were divided among themselves, Anglo-Irish ladies inveighed against perfidious Albion, Ascendancy sons fought in the Republican cause and Unionist brothers were uncertain whether or how to cast their votes on Irish issues, anguished uncertainty might be said to reign; that and weary disillusionment felt not only by those who lamented the passing of the old order, but also by many who had pinned their hopes on the new.

> Turning and turning in the widening gyre
> The falcon cannot hear the falconer;
> Things fall apart; the centre cannot hold;
> Mere anarchy is loosed upon the world,
> The blood-dimmed tide is loosed, and everywhere

> The ceremony of innocence is drowned;
> The best lack all conviction, while the worst
> Are full of passionate intensity.
>
> W. B. Yeats, 'The Second Coming' (1921)

Further horrors were yet to come.

Negotiations between Dublin and Westminster led to the conclusion of a treaty in December 1921, but only at the cost of widening the faction split within Irish nationalism. De Valera resigned the presidency and walked out of the Dáil to form the Republican Party, which was immediately joined by a section of the IRA. A fresh epidemic of violence now broke out between those who were content with autonomy within the Empire and those who demanded total independence. The next fifteen months were the most ghastly in the history of a country that had witnessed many horrific episodes. This was true civil war, Irishman against Irishman. No longer was there a common enemy to be the object of national spleen. No longer were rivals shooting at each other across a cultural–religious divide. The armed parties were not even contending over an issue of substantial political power, for there was virtually no area of Irish life over which the Dublin parliament was not sovereign. The combatants were slaughtering, burning and rabble-rousing over ideology and, as in all such contests, slogans were more persuasive than reasoned arguments. In the blood-letting Sir Henry Wilson was gunned down on the steps of his London home; Michael Collins, the first leader of the IRA, was ambushed and assassinated by the Republican faction. The Four Courts building in Dublin was blown up, taking with it most of the country's records. And under cover of the smoke of battle, malcontents took the opportunity to settle old scores against members of the Ascendancy.

Republican gangs ranged the country displaying contempt for estate owners and their families. They demanded money; they billeted their men in the elegant rooms where titled guests had slept; they drove off cattle; they commandeered some of the more solidly built mansions as command posts; they stole motor cars; they held Ascendancy ladies to ransom; they summarily 'executed' those they deemed to be enemies of the people – and they burned. As the Republicans were driven back by government forces they destroyed hundreds of fine houses, partly to deny their use to the enemy and partly out of sheer vindictiveness. The attitude of the vandals is well illustrated by the fate of Desart Court, a beautiful Palladian mansion in Co. Kilkenny. It was gutted in February 1923, but the servants managed to save some of the furniture. This was subsequently packed on to a van for removal to a place of safety. The vehicle was waylaid by rifle-brandishing Republicans and set on fire. When eventually the new Irish Free State government restored order an irreplaceable part of the nation's heritage had gone up in smoke. Stalwart landowners prepared to rebuild, discovered that their new masters lacked the funds to pay adequate compensation for war damage and that they could only sell their estates at severely reduced values. Some soldiered on, but the majority left for England or the colonies.

In the luxurious security of their London and rural mansions the Guinnesses received letters and telegrams from friends, relatives, servants and tenants bearing distressing news. They felt helpless and anxious about the future of their Irish interests, but in fact, the brewery and the bank were both safe. The new rulers needed them. The product of St James's Gate was so popular and its continuance so vital to the Irish economy that it never came under threat. Detachment from the struggle could lead to quite bizarre incidents. Ernest frequently gave brewery staff short trips on his magnificent barque *Fantôme*. One such guest recalled a Sunday morning, sailing down the Liffey:

> ... he sat in a deck chair, being offered drinks by Ernest's valet when shooting broke out between the buildings on the bank and he could see men firing at each other with great danger to life and limb, which did not affect the life on board though there was a separation of no more than 400 yards.[7]

Guinness Mahon was also a necessity for the new administration. Dublin was not well endowed with sophisticated and experienced financial institutions and the Free State needed access to money markets. When the government floated its first national loan in November 1923, Guinness Mahon was nominated as one of the agents – an important milestone in the firm's emergence as a fully fledged merchant bank. Howard and Noel were committing themselves professionally to the new regime and, in so doing, taking a not inconsiderable risk. The civil war was only just over, but out-and-out Republicanism was far from dead and no one in Dublin would have offered short odds on an enduring peace. This was one reason why the brothers took the prudent step of reactivating the London bank. It would have been foolish to keep all their eggs in the Irish basket, and direct access to a more active financial centre would enable them to serve their corporate and private clients better.

There were also personal reasons for reopening a British bank. Howard Rundell had spent most of his sixty years in Dublin and witnessed in his beloved country greater changes than he could possibly have imagined when he first came into the business. The country was divided; the greater part of it had been delivered into the hands of the Nationalists, who were now squabbling among themselves; the Ascendancy had disappeared. For four decades he had borne the heat of battle, trying to ease the pain for the once-great families of the disintegration of their ancestral holdings. Now he had had enough. The new Ireland was not his Ireland. The time had come to emulate his cousins, who were spending their last years as respected members of the upper class in civilised, secure, Protestant England. Thus, while Noel, aided by his son, Henry Eustace, soldiered on in Dublin, Howard Rundell migrated to London with his three elder boys. They opened a new office at 20 Bishopsgate and Howard acquired a country estate in Surrey. Within a very short space of time the traditional roles of the two banks were reversed. Guinness *and* Mahon, as the Dublin office was now called, played second fiddle to Guinness Mahon in London, whose rise among the ranks of merchant banks in the capital was steady through the 1920s.

In comparison with many family friends, even those, like themselves, who were absentee landlords, the Guinnesses lost little during the 'troubles'. Yet they felt keenly the collapse of the Union and the disappearance of a way of life, even one from which they had distanced themselves for more than forty years. Speaking in the debate on the Irish Free State Bill (which ratified the constitution proposed by Dublin) Walter declared that he would vote for it reluctantly, preferring 'a slippery slope to a precipice'. He was very sceptical about the ability of the new government in Ireland to restore order and rule constructively, and prophesied that when a Tory administration no longer 'palsied by indecision' came to power it would find itself in the position of having to restore firm government throughout the island. He was cheered when he complained of the way Ulster was being treated in the boundary negotiations; promises were being broken to appease the Nationalists, he asserted. Yet, like all his colleagues, for whom Unionism had been their political *raison d'être*, he could do nothing but bluster while accepting change.[8] In the event he would not go as far as his more bellicose colleagues who were making noisy, unrealistic demands for military intervention.

If Walter was moderating his Commons rhetoric it was, in part, because he was keeping a wary eye on the Westminster weather vane. As the basic political issues changed with the growth of a Labour party which eroded the Liberal vote and frightened Tories with the prospect of social disintegration, the wind indicator swung erratically. Walter was forty-two and a leading back-bencher who wanted a share of political power and had assiduously commended himself to the Conservative grandees. Now the excited talk in committee rooms and corridors was of his party's possible return to government after an interval of seventeen years. Lloyd George had alienated so many erstwhile supporters that Tory electoral success was a possibility – if they could unite behind a suitable leader.

The issue which, somewhat surprisingly, brought down the Coalition government was one on which Walter felt qualified to voice a strong opinion. In the summer of 1922 the old rivalry between Turk and Greek flared up again. A renascent Turkey under the leadership of Kemal Atatürk marched against her old enemy and regained territory lost in their previous encounter. When the invader assaulted the coastal fortress of Chanak (Cassakkale), thus threatening shipping passing through the Dardanelles, defying an international peace settlement and confronting a small British garrison located there to keep the peace, Lloyd George felt honour bound to act. Not to do so, he insisted, would involve 'the greatest loss of prestige which could possibly be inflicted on the British Empire'. Not for the first time Walter Guinness challenged the Premier's pro-Greek policy. He had a profound respect for the Turks, which had only been reinforced by his experiences in Gallipoli, and believed that they had been treated shabbily after the war. He said as much in the Commons and in the Coalition Group on Foreign Affairs. Fortified by his arguments, the party leaders detected an issue on which they could mount an effective challenge. The country was in no mood for another war and Andrew Bonar Law, who now emerged from semi-retirement to lead the Conservatives, repudiated the policy of Britain acting as the sole 'policeman of the world'. He withdrew his party from the Coalition. In the resulting election the Tories won a handsome victory over a still-emerging Labour party and divided, disillusioned Liberals.

The Times noted that the new Prime Minister deliberately encouraged fresh talent and was gathering around him 'younger Tories who have proved their parliamentary ability in criticism, not necessarily hostile, of various aspects of Coalition policy'. Walter Guinness's reward was his appointment as Under-Secretary of State for War. His boss at the War Office was Lord Derby, a genial man, and a close friend both of his father and of King George V. Perhaps more significant was the fact that the outgoing Liberal minister, who had made a deep impression on his Whitehall staff, was Winston Churchill.

The period from 1918 to 1932 that Walter spent in the House of Commons was one of party political turmoil during which six general elections were fought and eight administrations went in and out of office. Labour and Tory activists swarmed over former Liberal territory like greedy legatees unable to wait for the demise of a wealthy relative before grasping their inheritance. Neither party was able to sustain a convincing

parliamentary majority long enough to carry through a manifesto programme. Lord Elveden's fluctuating fortunes at the hustings illustrate well
the ebb and flow of support for the Tories. In 1918 he had a comfortable
9000-vote lead over his Liberal rival. Three years later he was facing down
an opponent who gleefully informed the electorate that out of 1269
divisions during the life of the parliament, Rupert had been absent from
913 and that, although he had bought a house in Southend, he was
seldom to be seen there. Clearly, the elder Guinness had not developed
an enthusiasm for political life. It may be, therefore, that we should take
with a pinch of salt his explanation of his failure to vote on the Irish
question. His declared distaste for the manoeuvres and bargaining of the
government and the Nationalists may simply have been a cover for the
fact that much of the time he was absent. Despite the criticisms, however,
he easily held onto his seat with a majority of just under 7000 in the
election which carried Bonar Law into Downing Street. Matters were very
different a mere fourteen months later when the issue of the day was the
protectionist stance of the new Tory PM Stanley Baldwin. The prospect of
higher duties on imported foreign goods lost the Conservatives over
ninety seats. Rupert's campaign organisers in Southend were very
worried. Their meetings were going badly and their candidate pleaded
illness when his presence was required on the hustings. On 6 December
the ever-popular Walter spoke in support of his brother at what the local
press described as 'the liveliest Conservative meeting that has taken place
in Southend for many years'. The speaker's words were drowned in a
cacophony of boos and catcalls, and at one point he had to sit down.
When he resumed it was to exchange insults and ribaldry with his
hecklers. He accused the supporters of the Liberal candidate of being
dangerous radicals in league with the Socialists, confronting voters with
scare stories about increased taxes; deceiving them with 'sob-stuff'.[9]
When the votes in this once-safe Tory seat were counted Lord Elveden
was found to have scraped home by a mere 113.

It was soon after this that Rupert's father made his most spectacular
public benefaction. In 1920 the owner of Kenwood decided to sell *en bloc*
the house and its contents. It proved to be no easy matter; no one in the
post-war era wanted a magnificent out-of-town residence and the life-
style it represented. Months passed and it seemed that the splendid
building was doomed, like many other deserted stately homes at this
time, to be demolished to make way for a sprawl of suburban streets.
Well-wishers set up a committee to try to find some way of protecting this
architectural treasure. In vain they approached the government. They
launched an appeal, which was only moderately successful, but which did

allow much of the estate to be bought and turned into a public recreation area. By 1925 Lord Bute's magnificent villa was still under threat. Then, enter Lord Iveagh.

15

GOOD FOR YOU

L ord Iveagh's beneficence continued until the end of his life. Like all wealthy men he experienced frequent calls upon his charity. He bestowed his wealth shrewdly and usually after careful investigations of the merits of his petitioners, as did most businessmen. He could, however, act impulsively. His interest in agricultural research was in part the result of his sons' enthusiasm, but he was spurred into action by a personal experience. He had acquired his country estates in order to pursue the field sports which were an essential part of a gentleman's life. The farms in England and Ireland were supervised by agents and he did not involve himself overmuch in the minutiae of food production. The story goes that he happened to be touring one of his farms with his secretary when he came upon a labourer and his team ploughing the poor Breckland soil. He noticed that one of the horses had a leg bound with old sacking and, on enquiry, discovered that this filthy 'bandage' covered an open wound. He was shocked to learn that such traditional 'treatments' signified the extent of most farmworkers' understanding of animal welfare. He immediately discussed with his aide the possible ways of dispelling such ignorance. The result was the Chadacre Institute, established at Hartest, between Bury St Edmunds and Sudbury. Its object was to provide the sons of farm labourers, smallholders and small farmers in Suffolk and adjoining counties with a grounding in theoretical and practical husbandry.[1]

Yet, the enterprise which has most preserved Lord Iveagh's name – certainly in the minds of art lovers – is the saving of Kenwood. By the spring of 1925 the Kenwood Preservation Committee had raised sufficient money, with the aid of the London County Council, to acquire the bulk of the estate, but they had not been able to prevent the fine furnishings and pictures being sold off by auction in 1922, and the house itself now stood empty and doomed. If only a buyer could be found he could acquire the fine building and a sizeable curtilage for less than £108,000. Quite how Edward Guinness decided on the course of action which resulted in the Iveagh Bequest is not known, but we can speculate about some of his motives. He was well past the biblical span of three score years and ten, and may well have reflected upon how he would be remembered after his death. Tenement blocks in Dublin and London bore his name, but they would not stand indefinitely, nor did they record anything about him other than his generosity. Most of his benefactions had been carried out quietly and their details were not known beyond the small circles concerned with their administration. If he wanted to leave something more personal, something of himself for future generations to reflect upon, it would have to take the form of an exhibition of objects that he loved and which represented his taste. Thus, the idea grew of acquiring Kenwood for the nation and using it as a setting for paintings, drawings, books and furniture he had bought for his London mansion. The magnificent donation would also lessen the death duties burden on his family.

Today's visitor to Kenwood is aware that he is gazing at one of the most stunning private collections of European paintings assembled during the last hundred years. Here he will see such oft-reproduced masterpieces as Rembrandt's *Self Portrait c.1663*, Vermeer's *Guitar Player*, Romney's *Lady Hamilton at the Spinning Wheel* and Gainsborough's *Mary, Countess Howe*, as well as prime pieces by Hals, Van Dyck, Reynolds, Boucher, Cuyp, Ostade, the Van de Veldes and other leading artists of the seventeenth and eighteenth centuries. Lord Iveagh's bequest was, by his instructions, to come into effect in 1935, or on his death, whichever was the sooner. In the event, he died two and a half years after buying Kenwood. He was chairman of what was by far the world's largest brewery and his taxable estate, exclusive of trust funds and public benefactions, was £11,000,000. The death duties levied by the Exchequer on the possessions of this one man made a significant addition to the government's income for 1925–6.

Edward Cecil's last years were dogged by uncertainty in the land from which he derived the greater part of his income. The Free State government was established and successfully asserted its authority but De Valera's quasi-constitutional Fianna Fáil party, rejecting what slender British connections remained, demanding the formation of a republic and an end to partition, would not take its place in the Dublin assembly. The IRA emerged as a violent sub-culture sanctifying with political cant their love of murder and destruction. Those who watched from England saw the men in power, a Catholic bourgeoisie, defining Ireland as culturally and politically distinct from Britain and holding at bay – but for how long? – those who were hostile to Britain. The brewery's directors still debated from time to time the advisability of building on an English site, but as long as the running of St James's Gate suffered no interference they always came down in favour of the *status quo*.

In 1925 one of the directors succinctly summarised the prevailing attitude of the board: 'we should be slow to change as long as we are successful'.[2] The only trouble with that analysis was that success was slipping. High profits and healthy dividends masked a deteriorating trading situation. After a brief period of post-war surge, sales began to decline in the early twenties. Instability in Ireland, prohibition in the USA and a general trade sluggishness affected the whole brewing industry. Guinness was not alone in experiencing this downturn, but in addition their position in relation to leading rival breweries was faltering. For this there is only one major explanation – complacency. To the suggestion, in 1925, that drastic measures should be considered to reduce costs and boost sales, Lord Iveagh responded, 'I am not in favour of passing on any of our profits to our customers. [I do] not at all like the idea of increasing our capital by distributing our reserve, and as to [resuming our plans for] Manchester, I feel we shall have to be in a very serious plight before we can contemplate that move'.[3] The board refused to go in for price-cutting because they believed their product was superior to anything else on the market and that knocking a few shillings off per hogshead would spoil its image. Furthermore, since the company owned no retail outlets they had no way of ensuring that any reduction would be passed on to the end consumer. Unfortunately, the quality card could no longer be played with conviction because rival brewers were seriously contending for the public taste. Year on year, the shareholders were provided with optimistic forecasts based on no serious market research and adverse figures were blamed on external factors such as the General Strike (1926). It was not until the last days of Edward Cecil's chairmanship that his colleagues began an objective trade analysis and it was his successor who was charged with augmenting new policies.

There was some surprise at St James's Gate when Lord Iveagh insisted that that person should be Rupert, a man who already had many other calls upon his time and energies, before the Iveagh title brought still more. Ernest, the brother who knew the business intimately and had a lifetime commitment to it, was passed over in favour of the new head of the family. Perhaps Lord Iveagh considered his second son too staid.

Certainly Ernest, for all his belief in technical advance, was very conservative in matters of policy. Perhaps the problem was a dynastic one; Ernest
and Chloe had three daughters and no sons. In fact, Edward Cecil made
it impossible for any of his sons to exercise the degree of control that he
had achieved. He divided his shareholding equally between Rupert,
Ernest and Walter, which made for company–family solidarity, but not for
dynamic leadership.

Rupert was intelligent and, in those areas in which he was knowledgeable, innovative, but these did not include the brewery. He had grown
accustomed to deferring to his father, his brother and the Dublin management, and he now developed a 'hands-off' style of chairmanship. The
question must, therefore, be asked to what extent the second Lord Iveagh
was responsible for inaugurating that policy change which, above anything else, was to make 'Guinness' a household name throughout the
world – the seventy years of brilliant advertising campaigns which are
part of the folklore of the PR industry.

The first Lord Iveagh was by nature reserved and regarded publicity as
tasteless. Furthermore, he believed that such a self-evidently superior
product as Guinness stout needed no promotion. However, he conceded
that there might be a case for advertising in foreign markets. In 1924 a
newly appointed travelling representative toured Australia, India, Burma,
Malaya, Java, Egypt, the USA and Canada, and returned to recommend
greater expenditure on advertising. As a result, the company set aside
£10,000 p.a. for overseas promotion. In the last months of his life and in
response to the fall in sales Lord Iveagh was seriously contemplating
changing the attitudes of a lifetime. In 1926 he debated with the board the
possibility of a full page advertisement in *The Times*, but decided that it
was not worth the £750 demanded by the newspaper. Nevertheless, it was
resolved to do some market research. This was followed by typically
lengthy debate on the board, during which Walter declared himself in
favour of the initiative and Ernest opposed it. It was January 1928 before
a modest trial campaign was mounted in Scotland and another year before
space was taken in a national newspaper to promote Guinness stout.

It was a very wordy, very dignified prototype treating readers to a potted
history of the company, a lesson in brewing techniques and a dissertation
on the restorative properties of the beverage. The punch line 'Guinness is
Good for You' was recommended by the advertising agency, S. H. Benson,
but the directors were almost shocked by the slogan's naïveté. Of course
Guinness was good for you – everyone knew that! Thus they bolstered
their promotion by listing the beneficial properties of the brew. They even
did a survey of 28,000 doctors to obtain testimonials. Bensons, of course,

were proved right. By the mid-1930s they had come up with a series of simple legends that were to provide the themes for numerous variations over ensuing decades – 'Guinness is Good for You', 'My Goodness, My Guinness', 'Guinness for Strength'. In 1935 the first members of the Guinness menagerie appeared; a sea lion and, more memorably, a toucan with two full glasses and copy written by a certain Benson employee, Dorothy L. Sayers;

> If he can say as you can
> Guinness is good for you
> How grand to be a Toucan
> Just think what Toucan do.

The ostrich, the tortoise and other creatures followed in rapid succession.

The humour, the puns, the clever manipulations of established ideas rapidly caught the public imagination. The advertisements became part of the nation's life, bringing a smile to countless lips during the drear days of economic depression. Nothing indicates this more than the extent to which they were parodied by artists for other causes. In May 1936 the Guinness sea lion appeared in advertisements for a betting firm, a university rag appeal – and even a temperance society.[4] Yet, in the short term, all this creative energy, coupled with serious attempts to revive overseas trade, failed to produce the desired result. Annual profits declined from £3,209,000 in 1927 to £2,495,000 in 1939. On the eve of the Second World War Arthur Guinness, Son and Co. Ltd was only generating twice as much income as it had at the beginning of the First World War. Behind the bold and appealing front projected from advertising hoardings was a management that official historians of the company, writing thirty years later, castigated as 'palpably inadequate',[5] a family business muddling through with occasional flashes of genius.

Part of the company's troubles in the thirties was due to the Depression, which began with the Wall Street Crash of October 1929. National un-employment and declining export markets severely reduced the demand for beer and had it not been for energetic advertising, which enabled Guinness to increase their market share, the loss of business would have been alarming. But in 1932 a potentially worse disaster struck. In February Eamon De Valera and his Fianna Fáil were victorious in the Irish general election. 'Eire', as southern Ireland now called itself, became to all intents and purposes a foreign nation, although it was not until 1937 that a fresh constitution embodied the changed status. The new Prime Minister immediately set about severing the imperial connections guaranteed in the 1921 treaty. In Britain the Unionist rump railed against the perfidy of the Irish and the naïveté of ministers who had trusted them, but in truth, for most people outside Ulster the 'Irish Question' had now entered the realm of 'old, unhappy, far-off things, and battles long ago'. The Westminster government had to go through the motions of protest and one measure of retaliation against Dublin's refusal to honour its financial obligations under the treaty was the imposition of a twenty per cent tariff on Irish imports.

This hit Arthur Guinness, Son and Co. Ltd very hard. Not only was it a further blow against company profits, it created a highly sensitive diplomatic situation. The immediate economic problem could be dealt with by setting in hand the reserve plans for building an English brewery. But what would the long-term result of that be? The spring and summer of

1932 passed in an atmosphere of wild rumour and frenzied attempts by all parties to discover what the others were planning. The Dublin *Evening Mail* told its readers that Guinness were all set to move production to Manchester. But at St James's Gate the directors were juggling several balls and had certainly not made up their minds: how expensive would the move be? How long would it take to recoup the capital outlay? How would the Dublin government react? Would an English plant make for greater long-term efficiency? Would it enable Guinness to play a more prominent part in the counsels of the English brewers? Irrational fears, boardroom disagreements and the complexity of the situation produced an initial paralysis. The MD even advocated traditional Guinness indecisiveness in a memo to Lord Iveagh: 'we have two or three months still during which we can work as hard as possible but not make up our minds'.[6]

Looked at in an historical context the crisis of 1932 is important only because it pushed the company into making a decision which, in the light of subsequent world events, was absolutely vital. The anxieties generated in the process in fact proved groundless. The company were driven to cloak-and-dagger intrigues by fears that an administration which was refusing to pay the remaining compensation due under the Land Purchase Acts on the grounds that the properties in question had been stolen by the English in the first place might well confiscate the plant at St James's Gate using the same argument – that it belonged to the Irish people and not to foreign shareholders. The reality was that there were no punitive measures the Dublin government could take which would not rebound upon themselves. Guinness produced four-fifths of the beer drunk in Ireland and it was the largest contributor to the exchequer. Interference with its successful operation could only have had a crippling effect on the Irish economy. After all the arguments had been rehearsed to the point of exhaustion and, particularly, after Ernest's conservative opposition had been overcome, the momentous decision was taken.

What Lord Iveagh and his boardroom colleagues then achieved was a quite amazing clandestine operation. Once they moved they moved quickly and set in hand negotiations for the purchase of a site, not in Manchester, but in London, the company's largest market. They considered various options in their quest for a location with a plentiful supply of high-quality water and adequate sewage facilities for the factory's effluent, but were hampered by their own self-imposed anonymity: 'we spent some hours explaining to the Twickenham Urban District Council how fortunate they would be to have us … without, however, being able to disclose to them who we were'. Another promising site had to be discounted because the owner was a crusading teetotaller.[7] The lightning evaluation of potential sites ended eventually on the city's outer fringe. Park Royal (so named because it had briefly been the site of the Royal Agricultural Society's annual show) lay beyond the north-western boundary of the metropolis; a place of fields and ramshackle barns earmarked for industrial and residential development. Guinness bought land there through intermediaries and began construction within six months. Amazingly, they were able to keep secret the purpose of the complex of offices, and production and bottling plant. Local people believed that the hush-hush nature of the enterprise had something to do with the government's covert rearmament programme. It was even rumoured that the military were proposing to make poison gas at Park Royal. For two years the cloak-and-dagger operation went on. Under the auspices of 'Agricultural Processes Ltd' contractors and sub-contractors were engaged; key staff were brought over from Dublin and worked under assumed names; plans were discussed behind locked doors and curtained windows; code words were devised for the various buildings and installations. No inkling of what was happening at Park Royal leaked out despite the widening circle of operatives and consultants who had to be in the know. Only in August 1934 were the wraps taken off, when Lord Iveagh revealed to the AGM that production would be divided between the two breweries. 'We still regard Dublin as the home of Guinness,' he declared, 'and ... we still hope to brew stout for as much of our English trade as may be possible in Dublin'.[8] The board waited nervously for the reaction from across the water. Even then, it seemed that the fates were in on the conspiracy: the story failed to 'break' dramatically in Dublin because it arrived in the middle of a prolonged newspaper strike.

In February 1936 the first mash was set in operation. It was a combination of old and new, for it took place in the most up-to-date equipment and was supervised by experts brought over from Ireland. Beer began to flow on to the market early the following year, although building work did not come to an end until shortly before the outbreak of war. The most important development since the first Arthur's acquisition of the St James's Gate brewery a hundred and eighty years before thus passed off remarkably quietly. One reason why the move to Park Royal failed to become a *cause célèbre* was that in the mid-to-late 1930s Britain was preoccupied with more momentous events.

Rupert's first love remained scientific farming and as soon as he inherited Elveden he set about bringing it into the 1920s. Despite its less frequent use in recent years it had been maintained by the first Lord Iveagh as essentially a sporting estate, supporting the dignity of an English peer and certainly not run with profit in mind. It was evident to Rupert, the agricultural moderniser, that this no longer made economic sense, nor did it square with the changed mores of the post-war years. The new owner gradually reduced the acreage devoted to the rearing of game birds and let the shooting rights on part of the estate to a syndicate. Farming profitability was improved by the introduction of cost-effective crops such as sugar beet and lucerne, and the provision of pasture for ever-growing herds of tuberculin-tested dairy cows. Mechanisation in the arable fields and the milking parlours increased efficiency, but the reverse of the coin was a reduced workforce, something Lord Iveagh was very reluctant to sanction at a time of rising national unemployment. The problem was largely avoided by bringing more and more land into effective production.

Walter Guinness's first experience of government office was brief. After Ramsay MacDonald's electoral victory in December 1923 he returned to his familiar seat on the other side of the chamber. But not for long. For the first time in its history Britain had a Labour government – ostensibly a government of the working class for the working class. The old pattern was now erased, of patrician parties divided into reactionary and reformist camps, but united in their belief that it was their right to legislate for the masses. The class-based discontents that had rumbled since the war, growing steadily in volume, were for the first time represented at the despatch box. A government, buttressed by TUC funds, was pledged to solve the country's ills – unemployment, industrial disputes, agricultural decline and social deprivation – by dismantling the capitalist system which was perceived to lie at the root of all these problems. Shudders of fear and revulsion shook the *ancien régime*. Socialists and their big brothers, Bolsheviks, had their hands on the levers of power and would ruin all. Winston Churchill, newly returned to the Tory fold, urged Liberals and Conservatives, between whom, he insisted, there were no serious ideological differences, to unite against the common menace. He lambasted MacDonald's pro-Soviet, anti-imperialist policies.

> Our bread for the Bolshevik serpent; our aid for the foreigner of every country; our favours for the Socialists all over the world who have no country; but for our own daughter states across the oceans, on whom the future of the British island and nation depends, only the cold stones of indifference, aversion and neglect.[9]

'The existing capitalist system', Churchill insisted, 'is the foundation of civilisation and the only means by which the great modern population can be supplied with vital necessities'.[10] This was the man for whom, a few weeks later, Walter Guinness would be working.

Anti-Socialist panic, fanned by hustings oratory, dubious opposition tactics and the failure of Labour to usher in an immediate workers' paradise, brought about another general election in October 1924 and a Tory landslide. Prime Minister Baldwin offered Churchill the Chancellorship of the Exchequer and Churchill chose Walter as his financial secretary. Walter, a man of sundry enthusiasms, threw himself with a will into everything he did. He had to be occupied and could not bear wasting time. When, for example, travelling to distant places in his yacht he could not regard such voyages as simple holidays; he had to be fact-finding or specimen-collecting. His new master certainly indulged his appetite for action. Churchill was a man whose mind brimmed with ideas, all of which he was impatient to carry out. Within days the new minister had hammered out with Walter and his staff a programme of financial and economic reforms, which were the most far-reaching since those of Lloyd George in 1903–9. Their aims, he insisted, were 'the appeasement of class bitterness, the promotion of a spirit of co-operation, the stabilisation of our national economy, the building of the financial and social plans upon a three or four year basis'.[11] His 'Liberal' budget set up a more comprehensive national insurance scheme, extended the payment of old age pensions, placed new taxes on luxury goods, reduced direct taxation on lower wage earners, but declined to give any help to the idle rich and the owners of large estates because the process of 'squatting on old wealth' was of little value to the nation. To underpin these measures with international confidence and to demonstrate that Britain had virtually recovered from the war he announced a return to the gold standard, which the country had been forced to abandon in 1919.

The man charged with introducing the Gold Standard Bill to the Commons was Walter Guinness. On 4 May 1925 he rose to present the government's arguments to a packed house. It was an historic moment, a heady one for the financial secretary. For the first time in his life he had the eyes of the nation upon him as he delivered a message of patriotic pride and hope for the future. His speech was received with cheers and acclamation, and even with muttered approval from the other side of the chamber. Those who raised doubts were prophets crying in the wilderness and, like the prophets, they were proved to be right.

Walter became as effective a defender of government policy as he had earlier been a denouncer of it. His political rise was now rapid. For the best part of two decades his ambition had been thwarted by war and the decline of Tory fortunes. Now he made up for lost time. After a year at the

Treasury he achieved full cabinet rank. His friend and relative by marriage, E. F. L. Wood (later Earl of Halifax) was raised to the peerage as Baron Irwin in preparation for his appointment as Indian Viceroy. This left a gap at the Ministry of Agriculture and Fisheries to which post Walter was appointed in November 1925.

It was no sinecure. Native farmers had to compete with cheap imports of meat and grain, and Baldwin's abandonment of tariffs and protectionism had removed their last hope of government assistance, leaving them at the mercy of harsh free-market winds. Hundreds of smallholdings, some of them operated by returning servicemen after the war to a 'land fit for heroes', had gone bankrupt. Labourers were laid off by economising landowners and lost their tied cottages as well as their wages. With the prices of produce fluctuating and frequently inadequate, farmers had neither the resources nor the incentive to modernise. Much of British agriculture was, therefore, caught in a downward spiral. Walter was not as involved as his brother in the application of science to work on the land, but he was knowledgeable about and took an interest in the farms on his Suffolk estate. In particular, he encouraged sugar production. During the war tillers of the heavy soil of central Suffolk had been persuaded to grow sugar beet in order to reduce the nation's dependence on imported cane sugar. Walter's tenants joined the scheme in the early twenties, relieved to find a paying crop (by 1931 there was less land under wheat than at any time since the eighteenth century). At about the time that he took over the ministry Walter brought together a consortium of Suffolk farmers. They planted five thousand acres with the crop and negotiated with a Hungarian company to build a sugar processing plant in Bury St Edmunds. The growth of this section of the industry was one of the few sunlit areas in an otherwise drear economic landscape.

Walter's relationship with Churchill steadily developed into friendship. They were alike in being adventurous, unorthodox and determined to get things done. Winston was the dominant personality in Baldwin's administration, as Lloyd George had been in Asquith's. His parliamentary friends admired him enormously and spoke openly of their hope that he would eventually move from 11 Downing Street to the house next door. But his friends were not the majority in the party. Most Conservatives viewed this maverick with suspicion. He was a Liberal in sheep's clothing; a man lacking sound judgement. Walter, now that the Unionism issue was, for good or ill, settled, became less and less of a party man. Like Churchill, he was impatient with dogma when it was used as a short cut bypassing informed, rational thought. The new Minister of 'Ag and Fish' was a member of that intimate circle invited for informal weekends at

Chartwell and private-room dinners at the Savoy. The Chancellor used such events to explore ideas. One such was de-rating.

It was obvious that something must be done to revive Britain's flagging industry and agriculture. Protection, which would raise costs to the consumer, was out of the question. The solution Churchill found was a roundabout way of subsidising producers: they would be de-rated and central government would make good the loss of income to local authorities by means of new indirect taxes. Walter saw the immediate benefit of the scheme for farmers and, along with most members of the cabinet, welcomed it warmly. The only one who sounded a strong note of caution was Neville Chamberlain. The confusion of personalities and policies which would soon drive the Chancellor into the wilderness was already manifesting itself. Churchill was indisputably the finest parliamentary performer of the day. His ideas were bold and he had the panache to carry them against all opposition. He was the Cyrano de Bergerac of the Commons chamber and, like the rumbustious French free-thinker, he had many opponents, especially among the traditionalists of his own party. Chamberlain, doubtless with an eye to the support of staid back-benchers when future leadership was discussed, was determined to peg the kites of Churchillian initiative to political terra firma. In the de-rating scheme he saw dangers to the funding and local autonomy of Britain's town halls and he requested a cabinet sub-committee to look more closely into the workings of the proposed scheme. The Agriculture Minister was an essential member of this group. Over the first three months of 1928 the complex issues were argued out in committee and full cabinet, not without frequent outbursts of bad temper. Throughout the exchanges Walter Guinness showed himself to be no mere follower of Churchill. Indeed, more often than not he came down on the side of Chamberlain.

In May 1929 the life of the Baldwin government reached its end. Leaving aside the artificially prolonged parliament of 1911, that of 1924 had been the only one since 1886 to run its full term. The election of 1929, the first based on complete adult suffrage, removed the Tories from office. The Guinness MPs retained their seats comfortably. On Rupert's succession as Earl of Iveagh in 1927 his wife, Lady Gwendolin, had taken his place as member for Southend. Now she was back in the Commons with a clear 6000 majority. Still no one was prepared to set up in opposition to Walter at Bury St Edmunds. However, around the country 159 Conservative seats changed hands and Ramsay MacDonald was back in office with a workable majority.

Given a calm sea and a fair wind, the next two years, during which

Walter remained a member of the shadow cabinet, should have seen the beginnings of a Socialist political programme. Unfortunately for MacDonald, violent storms broke overhead before his administration was six months old. The Wall Street Crash of October 1929 and the depression which followed set the helm veering wildly. Ministers introduced panic measures and short-term policies in their efforts to support the pound, stabilise the economy and protect the more vulnerable from job losses and rising prices. Among the items of cargo now hastily jettisoned were the gold standard and the de-rating programme. With the support of a diminishing band of friends, Churchill protested against these measures. He also opposed the government's proposal to grant dominion status to India and began to issue warnings about Hitler's rise to power in Germany. In all these matters he was strongly supported by Walter Guinness. In August 1931, with the crisis worsening by the day, it was decided to apply the solution which had worked in wartime; the formation of a coalition government. Baldwin agreed to serve under MacDonald and a cabinet was formed from leading members of the three parties. Churchill was not offered a position. Nor was Guinness. The ex-Chancellor remained in the Commons, but devoted more of his time to writing books and newspaper articles. The ex-Minister for Agriculture and Fisheries resigned his parliamentary seat and pursued his other varied interests with greater vigour. In the New Year's Honours List he was raised to the peerage as Baron Moyne. The coat of arms granted to him was based on the family achievement, but with some interesting variations. The supporters were two Singhalese macaques, signifying Walter's travels and his interest in exotic fauna. The choice of these animals annoyed some members of the family, who considered them undignified. They were even more upset by his motto: in place of his father's, *Spes Mea In Deo*, Lord Moyne chose the more enigmatic *Noli Judicare*, Judge Not. The words were a wry warning to critics. Walter was a man who charted his own course, which often veered from the sea lanes of family tradition, party dogma and conventional morality, and he had no regard for the censorious and small-minded.

16

'THE DAYS WHEN WE WERE ALL SO HAPPY, AND DID NOT KNOW IT'*

The decade which trundled with increasing acceleration towards Hitler's war posed many problems for those who possessed the leisure and intelligence to ponder them. Worrying developments on the Continent and the intricacies of economic recovery at home were only the surface encrustations covering the social turbulence which bubbled beneath. Young men and women who had no memories of 1914–18 partied frenetically, while scorning the social distinctions which permitted them their privileged lives. Some declared they would not fight for King and Country, while their friends went off to enlist in the causes of foreign patriots. New thinking varied from the revolutionary state planning and rejection of capitalism proposed by Oswald Mosley, expelled from the Labour party in 1931 to the cynical mockery of Edith Sitwell, a friend of Lord Moyne's family:

> I saw the County Families
> Advance and sit and take their teas;
> I saw the County gaze askance
> At my thin insignificance:
> Small thoughts like frightened fishes glide
> Beneath their eyes' pale glassy tide:
> They said: 'Poor thing! we must be nice!'
> They said: 'We know your father!' – twice.

The elderly ex-bankers were firmly ensconced among the 'County Families'. Gerald Seymour and Arthur Eustace moved freely among the

*R. R. James (ed.), *Chips: The Diaries of Sir Henry Channon*, 1967, p.397.

leading clans of the hunting shires, particularly the de Capell-Brookes, to whom Gerald was related by marriage. They were seen in the right places, were guests of and hosts to the right people and were generous supporters of the Conservative party (Gerald Seymour's elder son married the daughter of a Tory MP). And they looked to gain materially from their titled kindred. Sir Arthur de Capell-Brooke, Bart had no direct heir and the Guinnesses knew that, if they played their cards right, Great Oakley Hall and its extensive Northamptonshire acres would come to the children of Eleanor de Capell-Brooke and Gerald Seymour Guinness. Arthur Eustace (who had no sons of his own) was very close to the baronet and worked on him assiduously to bring about this desired objective.

He was not helped by the circumstances of his elder brother's death. After Eleanor died suddenly in 1926 Gerald Seymour retreated within himself. But it was not grief that pushed him over the edge. This intensely proud man, who considered himself an astute financier, became involved in the machinations of the 'Match King'. Ivar Kreuger had inherited a fortune based on the manufacture of safety matches but his Phaethonic ambition could not be satisfied by the running of a successful Swedish business; he aspired to be the greatest financier of his day, the banker of governments, the arbiter of national destinies. The economic dislocation of the post-war world enabled him to create this role for himself and perform it with bravura. Scores of struggling states became his debtors as he magnificently distributed loans totalling tens of millions. The backing for this prodigality was a labyrinthine complex of over 400 companies, which sucked in investment from large and small shareholders dazzled by the king's gilded career and desirous of sharing his success. They were destined, like Kreuger himself, to become victims of his megalomania. As the twenties advanced he rushed frenetically around behind the impressive façade of his financial mansion making structural repairs with increasingly shady deals. It was impossible that Kreuger could survive the crash of 1929. Company after interlinked company collapsed in bankruptcy and, in March 1932, Kreuger shot himself in his Paris luxury apartment. Gerald Seymour was only one among hundreds of experts who had been taken in by the spectacular fraudster, but the humiliation affected him deeply. In September 1933 he took his own life.

This came as a great shock to the landed Guinnesses and their respectable kith and kin. Sir Arthur de Capell-Brooke was a stickler for proprieties. If he was going to will his estate away to distant relatives he wanted to be sure that it would be in the hands of a strong and healthy male line, untinged by mental weakness – or moral depravity. The elderly baronet made clear to Arthur Eustace that he would only consider Gerald or Anthony Guinness as principal beneficiary if they had sons of their own brought up in stable homes where the parents were firmly Anglican and eschewed divorce. In 1936 Anthony ruled himself out by leaving his wife and going off to Canada with her best friend. Sir Arthur was a wealthy man who believed he could use his money to hold together a dis-integrating society and he was very annoyed when Gerald and Desirée, members of a more emancipated generation, refused to accept his condi-tions. Gerald was prepared, as the old man wished, to change his name by deed poll, but beyond that he would not go. Eventually Sir Arthur gave in. When he died in 1939 Gerald Richard de Capell-Brooke Guinness acquired a fortune which usefully supplemented the depleted inheritance he had received from his unfortunate father.

Sir Arthur's concerns about the stability of the Guinnesses may well have been inspired by the much-publicised matrimonial misadventures of Benjamin Seymour's children. Benjamin, the high-profile younger brother of Robert Darley, Gerald Seymour and Arthur Eustace, had brought up his one son and two daughters to share his glittering globe-trotting existence. In the world of fast cars, all-night parties and Riviera escapades they readily fell in love with beautiful consorts and just as easily fell out of love again. By the mid-thirties (Thomas) Loel and Tanis had already been divorced and remarried, and would both repeat the experience once more.

Loel, however, was far from being an empty-headed young man who lived only for pleasure. Part of him identified with the 'England home and beauty' philosophy of his uncles. He, too, made his country home in the Midland shires, choosing Arthingworth Manor in Leicestershire. In 1929, at the age of twenty-three, he decided to take a leaf out of Rupert Guinness's book: he stood as a Tory candidate for the rock-solid Labour seat of Whitechapel. He lost, and lost heavily, his prospects among the tenements and terraces of the East End not being helped by the fact that his father had just given him the Carlton House Terrace mansion as a town residence. Benjamin was the first of a growing number of wealthy Guinnesses who gave up British residence to avoid their estates being encumbered by heavy death duties. Undeterred by his trouncing, Loel contested the same seat in a by-election the next year – with a similar result. Having been twice blooded in Whitechapel, Loel was acceptable to the Tory high command, who put him up for the safe seat of Bath in the 1931 general election. Loel joined his older relatives on the Conservative benches and immediately gave evidence of rapid progress through the political ranks.

Entering the Commons just as Walter left, Loel seemed to be about to occupy the niche vacated by the ex-minister. He associated himself with those supporting Churchill in his fervent opposition to Socialism and his demands for greater military preparedness. Political commentators watched his début expectantly and greeted with enthusiasm his maiden speech on the Finance Bill. Possibly their judgement was coloured by their anticipation of another brilliant extrovert Guinness parliamentary career. Loel's congratulations of the chancellor and suggestions for modest changes to the measure do not, today, read like the incisive observations of a precocious tiro. Nor, in subsequent years, did his parliamentary performance rise above the mediocre. However, he had powerful contacts and these gained him early preferment. At the very outset of his Commons career he was appointed private secretary to Sir Philip Sassoon, Bart. Sassoon was one of the political fixers of the day. He had entered the Commons in 1912, served as Field Marshal Haig's secretary during the First World War, been Lloyd George's PPS in the coalition government of 1919–22 and, by 1931 was Under-Secretary of State for Air. Equally important as his work in Whitehall and Westminster was his behind-the-scenes activity. He was a great giver of parties. At his town and country houses he brought together many of the leading Tory figures and their allies to sound out opinion, compare notes and plan strategies. Many of Sassoon's gatherings were for the Churchillian group and frequently included Walter Guinness. Loel and Sir Philip shared a passion for aeroplanes. They were both aviators (Loel easily having graduated from the love affair with motor cars he shared with his father) and members of the same Auxiliary Royal Air Force squadron. For six years Loel worked closely with Sassoon, though behind the scenes, to raise public awareness of the reality of aerial warfare and to obtain increased Treasury commitment to aircraft production and aircrew training.

His first marriage came to an end – very publicly – in 1935. It may be that his wife, Joan, found unacceptable the transition from companion of a carefree playboy to consort of an MP who kept long hours and was frequently away on government business. She was readily swept off her feet by the dashing gambler and womaniser, Prince Aly Khan. She made no defence against Loel's petitions for divorce and custody of their son and, as soon as the decree came through, she married the prince. Within a year Loel had taken a second wife eleven years his junior. Isabel Manners was the daughter of one of England's leading peers, the Duke of Rutland and as such she was, perhaps, better acquainted with the responsibilities of men prominent in British public life. In any event the marriage lasted through fifteen years of peace and war.

During the thirties Guinness Mahon continued to be in the capable hands of (Henry) Samuel, Edward and Arthur Rundell. Thanks to their close links with America, they were able to foresee the Wall Street Crash and make plans accordingly. Cautious advance and the seeking of new markets was the appropriate strategy during the recovery years. Here Samuel's family connections proved invaluable. During his Oxford days he had fallen in love with Alfhild Holten, a Norwegian girl of good family. They were subsequently married and Samuel built up important Scandinavian friendships (including several with members of the Norwegian royal family) and business contacts. The most important was that with Viking Whaling. Guinness Mahon became bankers to this expanding maritime enterprise, which took advantage of America's withdrawal from the whaling industry to develop a virtual monopoly. With funding organised from Bishopsgate the Oslo-based company grew into one of the largest working in the Atlantic and in Arctic and Antarctic waters, and was the first to commission a factory ship. But markets were changing. It was the mounting demand for petroleum products that had caused the Americans to divert their attention from whale oil production and the Norwegians calculated that they would eventually have to follow suit. In the late thirties Viking Whaling switched to bulk oil carriers. Skilful diversification aided by advice from their bankers had turned Viking Tankers into one of the most profitable transatlantic fleets by the eve of the Second World War.

In Dublin the Guinness bank paralleled the development of its London sister, albeit in a more subdued tone. Henry Eustace was the man who dragged the College Green office into the twentieth century. He had arrived in 1922 intending to 'help out' temporarily in the reorganisation. In the event he stayed there until 1971 and was largely responsible for the expansion of several areas of activity including the organisation of share issues for the government, Dublin corporation and several industrial concerns.

Samuel and Arthur Rundell were energetic travellers. While their yachting relatives were cruising the world for pleasure and the satisfying of curiosity, the bankers were tirelessly touring economic centres in search of business. Gone were the days when London financiers could rely on their reputation and let clients come to them. Survival in the difficult inter-war years relied on active internationalism, seeking out those concerns which had the products and the management skills which were worth backing.

For a few years Nazi Germany seemed to fall into that category. Many British men and women who visited Hitler's Reich were impressed by the

transformation of a bankrupt and dispirited people into a nation where
the wheels of commerce and industry were once more turning. Samuel
and Arthur were among them. They encouraged British investment in
German companies and, in a speech delivered in Berlin to the
International Chamber of Commerce, Arthur advocated, 'a large gold
credit or loan at a reasonable rate of interest should be granted by the
United States and Great Britain to Germany to allow her to get rid of
exchange control, get back to freedom of currency and abolish the
restrictions which hindered German tree trade'.[1]

Visitors to Germany or to the Soviet Union only saw what their hosts
wanted them to see and tended to believe what they wanted to believe.
Many for whom idealism was an escape hatch from reality rather than a
firm platform upon which to come to terms with it declared themselves
enamoured of the systems emanating from Berlin or Moscow. Because
problems were complex, simple answers – scapegoating the Jews, confis-
cating the property of the idle rich, programmes of national discipline –
were doubly attractive.

Walter, ever independent of thought and critical of authority, continued to support the Churchillian minority. Rupert and his family
remained staunchly Conservative and loyal to Neville Chamberlain when
he became Prime Minister in 1937. During her years in parliament
(1927–35) Gwendolin was a star and the darling of the party. She was
widely acknowledged as the leading female orator with a style very
different from that of that other notable lady MP, the excitable and un-
predictable Lady Astor. When Lady Iveagh addressed the house she did so
in beautifully constructed sentences delivered in a mellifluous voice.
Members enjoyed listening to her, whether or not they agreed with what
she was saying. Her political philosophy was tap-root Conservatism: the
British Empire and institutions represented the pinnacle of civilisation;
little needed changing and state 'interference' with capitalist enterprise
was a thing abhorrent. She and Rupert had a loathing for Socialism which
deepened over the years. It was this which induced in them, as in many
Tories, a sneaking regard for the right-wing dictators of Europe. Their
favourite personal haven was in Mussolini's Italy. They owned a house,
Casa del'Arco, at Asolo, on the lower slopes of the Dolomites within easy
reach of Treviso, Padua, Vicenza and Venice, and it was to this peaceful
spot that they retreated from the multitudinous demands and pressures
of life in Britain. Here they enjoyed the company of the young Freya
Stark, the traveller and writer, whose family had also discovered the
delights of an uncluttered life among the vineyards, olive groves and
gentle hills. But Rupert could not content himself with being the

Englishman abroad. He identified with the local people and was especially concerned about peasant poverty. As in his own constituency and on his estate, he regarded it as his responsibility to do what he could for the more needy members of society. He made several contributions to the regional economy of which the most impressive was a boot factory, which he built to provide employment. All the instincts of Rupert and his wife lay in the preservation of peace and the encouragement of strong, non-Communist governments.

Rupert and his brothers were too old to participate in the gay society of the twenties and thirties. After his father's death Lord Iveagh only continued for a couple of seasons the tradition of royal shooting parties at Elveden. The perspectives of the children, however, were very different. The new generation of Guinnesses, growing up in an age of uncertainty, possessed the wealth and the social connections to give themselves totally to the enjoyment of the London season, summers on the Riviera and winter house parties for shooting and hunting. And they were cosmopolitan. They spent spring holidays in Paris, where Lord Moyne kept an apartment on the rue de Poitiers. They stayed at the Asolo villa. They visited Berlin for its deliciously decadent night-life. Yachting parties took them all around the Mediterranean and sometimes farther afield.

The family's love of boats continued. Indeed it may be said to have burgeoned in the inter-war years when restrictions were few and travel was easy for people with money. In 1936 Loel took his young bride on an ocean voyage in his 216-ton *Atlantis*. Ernest was especially proud of his *Fantôme*. He owned in succession three craft of this name, two of which he bought from the Duke of Westminster. In 1923 he took his family on a round-the-world cruise in the first of his magnificent yachts. The finest, which he sailed throughout most of the thirties, was a handsome French barque, which he had enlarged to carry an impressive spread of canvas and a crew of thirty-six. She was Ernest's pride and joy, and became the centre of his increasingly eccentric life – a life which would have furnished wonderful material for a P. G. Wodehouse novel. Many stories are told about this large and amiable man whose total absorption in his own interests insulated him from what were, for most other people, the realities of life. On one occasion, while touring the Caribbean, he went in search of a rum distillery on a remote island. *Fantôme* was anchored in deep water, and the owner and his companions made their way by launch to a ramshackle quay. Ernest now despatched his bowler-hatted valet to make the necessary arrangements: 'On the jetty the only signs of life were two hoboes lying fast asleep on coils of rope. Harris shook the first of these into life and in Jeeves-like imperious tones said, "Kindly conduct these gentlemen to the First Class Waiting Room"'.[2]

Arrived at Blackpool for an air display and unable to secure a taxi, Ernest found himself in the unique position of having to travel by tram. When the conductor approached to collect the fares, Ernest smilingly held out a crisp white five-pound note (which would have represented two or three times the man's weekly wage), at which the official demanded to know whether his passenger wanted 'to buy the bloody tram'.[3]

The sequel to that incident is that, in order to avoid similar embarrassment in future, Ernest acquired a cumbersome metal 'purse' with different compartments for various denominations of coins. Gadgets small and large fascinated him. Just as he would rush off at a moment's notice to observe some invention that might be adapted for use in the brewery, so he filled his house with modern devices. His country home in England was at Holmbury, Surrey, chosen for its proximity to an airfield. It boasted a system of concealed loudspeakers, which piped music all over the house. He was one of the first to own a cinematograph projector with which he 'entertained' after-dinner guests, usually with old newsreels. Real events, in his opinion, were much more interesting than mere stories and he was a compulsive collector of data. On car journeys he constantly checked the speedometer and made calculations about times and distances, and he never travelled by air without a pocket altimeter.

Ernest, who was a martinet like his father, lived in an all-female household with a lively wife and three effervescent daughters. Aileen, Maureen and Oonagh loved partying, perhaps in reaction to the rigid regimentation of the parental home where everything kept time with a regular, strict rhythm of daily routine. In later years Maureen recalled that she and her sisters received no affection from their father, who, she claimed, cared more about the brewery than about his family. If true, this goes a long way towards explaining the tragic difficulty they experienced in forming stable relationships in adult life. It goes without saying that materially they lacked for nothing. After 'coming out', the 'Golden Guinness Girls' took London society by storm. Titled young men fell over themselves to win their favours. But while they devoted themselves to fun and frivolity Ernest, who had long abandoned any attempt at understanding them, could only look on bemused.

Rupert, similarly, had a largely female environment. Gwendolin's first child, Richard, died soon after birth. Subsequently she produced three daughters and a son. Arthur Onslow, the only boy, was a 'solid' young man very much after the pattern of his father. From his earliest years he knew that his destiny was to shoulder, in his turn, all the responsibilities

Edward Cecil = Adelaide Guinness
1st Lord Iveagh 1847-1927   1873-1916

Sir Rupert Edward Cecil Lee Guinness, = Lady Gwendolin Onslow, CBE
Bart, KG, CB, CMG, FRS,   1903-1966
2nd Earl of Iveagh 1874-1967

Henry Channon, MP (1) = Lady Honor = (2) Flt-Lt Frantisek
Dorothy Mary   Svejdar
Guinness
1909-1976

Hon. Arthur Onslow = Lady Elizabeth
Edward Guinness,   Cecilia Hare
Viscount Elveden   e. dau. of 4th
1912-1945   Earl of Listowel

Rt. Hon. Alan Tindal = Lady Patricia Florence
Lennox-Boyd PC, CH, DL   Susan Guinness
Viscount Boyd of Merton   1918-
1904-1983

(1) HRH Prince Friedrich = Lady Brigid Katherine = Major Anthony
Georg Wilhelm Christoph   Rachel Guinness 1920-   Patrick Ness
von Preussen 1911-1966

Hon. Arthur Ernest Guinness = Marie Clothilde Russell
1876-1949   dau. of Sir George Russell, Bart 1880-1953

Hon. Brinsley (1) = Aileen Sibell = (2) Valerian
Sheridan Bushe   Mary Guinness   Stux-Rylar
Plunket, 2nd s.   1904-
of Baron Plunket

Sir Sheridan Hamilton (1) = Maureen = (2) Major H.A. = (3) Judge John
Temple- Blackwood, Bart   Constance   Desmond   Cyril Maude
4th Marquess of Dufferin   Guinness   Buchanan
and Ava   -1945   1907-1998

Philip (1) = Oonagh = (2) Dominick = (3) Miguel
Leyland   Guinness   Geoffrey   Ferrera
Kindersley   1910-1995   Edward Browne,
4th Baron Oranmore
and Browne

Hon. Walter Edward Guinness, DSO = Lady Evelyn H.S. Erskine
1st Baron Moyne 1880-1944   1883-1939

Hon. Diana Freeman- (1) = Hon. Bryan Walter Guinness = (2) Elizabeth Nelson
Mitford 1905-1992   2nd Baron Moyne 1905-1992

Hon. Murtogh = Anne Tarbolton
David Guinness
1913-

Oswald Constantine John Phipps = Hon. Grania Meve Rosaura
MBE, 4th Marquess of Normanby   Guinness 1920-1951

connected with the Iveagh title, a fate he seems to have accepted with equanimity. In 1935, when he was twenty-three, he was taken on to the board of the brewery and, the following year, he made a suitable marriage to Lady Elizabeth Hare, younger sister of the Earl of Listowel. At least, it was suitable from the point of view of status, if not of politics. Elizabeth's brother was an extremely intelligent, radical politician who sat on the Labour benches in the House of Lords and was a Socialist member of the LCC. Arthur's older sisters, Honor and Patricia, were of an age to be caught up in the 'flapper' culture of the jazz age. The life of parties, balls and tea dances was immensely diverting and became even more so when 'Chips' Channon entered their lives.

Henry Channon was a young American of independent means who, as he freely confessed, 'put my whole life's work into my anglicization'.[4] In the period when America was, for men of enterprise, industry and ruthlessness, a yellow-brick road to limitless wealth his grandfather had established a shipping and chandlering empire based in Chicago. Chips inherited the fortune generated by his family without any affection for the country in which it had been accumulated. 'The more I know of American civilization,' he wrote, 'the more I despise it. It is a menace to the peace and future of the world. If it triumphs, the old civilizations, which love beauty and peace and the arts and rank and privilege will pass from the picture.'[5] Penned in the year of *The Jazz Singer*, the words had a certain prophetic quality. Channon moved to Europe at the first opportunity, living first in Paris, then Oxford, then London, where he deliberately cultivated 'the quality'. He possessed that air of brash snobbery unique to those Americans who were obsessed by ancestry, culture, heritage and style, but incapable of understanding or emulating the emotional restraint and disdain of 'vulgar' display affected by the British upper class. However, he exuded a combination of sycophantic charm and ebullient bonhomie that gained him entrée to all the salons of fashionable London and to not a few of its boudoirs. The Iveaghs were delighted with him, as were their girls. In the summer of 1933 Chips married Honor Guinness, when he was thirty-six and she a few days short of her twenty-fourth birthday. The union had the full blessing of Rupert and Gwendolin, and within months plans were made for Lady Iveagh to stand down from parliament in time for Chips to woo and win the Southend electorate in the 1935 election.

Having achieved this position in Britain's political and social life (he held the Southend seat until his death in 1958), Channon became a behind-the-scenes parliamentarian. He rarely tried to catch the Speaker's eye in the chamber, but bent many an ear in the corridors and committee rooms, and enjoyed exercising influence through his sumptuous hospitality. He and Honor set out to invite anyone and everyone who 'mattered' to their fine houses, Kelvedon Hall, Essex, and 5 Belgrave Square (once the home of Lord Shaftesbury) described thus by Harold Nicolson:

> Oh my God how rich and powerful Lord Channon has become! There is his house in Belgrave Square next door to Prince George, Duke of Kent, and Duchess of ditto and little Prince Edward. The house is all Regency upstairs with very carefully draped curtains and Madame Récamier sofas and wall-paintings. Then the dining-room is entered through an orange lobby and discloses itself suddenly as a copy of the blue room of the Amalienburg near Munich – baroque and rococo and what-ho and oh-no-no and all that. Very fine indeed.[6]

Channon was fascinated by the royal families of Europe, both those still in possession of their thrones and those who had been deposed. He was never happier than when enjoying the intimacy of crowned or un-crowned heads:

> The Ball was the best spectacle so far of the summer; we were ushered into an improved ballroom hung with tapestries, with, at one end, an enormous dais of red baize where all the Royalties of the earth seemed congregated. We had barely arrived when the King and Queen entered with the Sutherlands. All four were gay, smiling and impressive, and I noticed how both the King and Queen have gained greatly in presence and dignity. They went to the queue of Royalties and greeted them all, kissing many. The Queen was in white, with an ugly spiked tiara, and she showed no sign of her supposed pregnancy, which I am beginning to doubt. The King followed her, showing his teeth. Queen Mary was in icy blue; soon the ball began. Honor and I were dancing near the dais when we caught Queen Mary's eye, and we stopped to curtsey and bow as she held out her hand. Then Honor and I became separated and I danced with Lady Iveagh. Later I danced with Alice Hofmannsthal, and we went up on the dais to talk to Princess Olga who was wearing her mother's ruby parure. We chatted with her for a few minutes, and as we turned we saw the King and Queen coming up to us, and they very smilingly talked to us. Both Alice and I were thrilled, which was unreasonable as we have both known them for years, and at one time intimately.[7]

For a few years Honor whirled gaily in this exalted society. She and Henry had many German friends, both those of the new regime and the old royalty. They were courted by the ambassador to London, Joachim von Ribbentrop, who saw his mission as winning Britain's 'ruling class' over to the Nazis. They also counted among their intimate circle members of the deposed Kaiser's family. Principal among them was 'Fritzi', Prince Friedrich Georg Wilhelm Christoph of Prussia. 'Very young, fair, Nordic and dripping with decorations' was Chips's way of describing (in 1937) the twenty-six-year-old grandson of Wilhelm II. Friedrich worked hard to restore relationships between his family and George V's. He was on very good terms with the Prince of Wales and Mrs Simpson, and was accused of inclining Edward towards Nazism. Friedrich, in fact, held no torch for Hitler, particularly as the Führer's ambitions became more blatant. In the late 1930s, however, subtle political distinctions were not appreciated in Britain; one was either pro-German or anti-German.

In 1936 Ribbentrop invited Chips and Honor to Berlin for the Olympic Games and they accepted with alacrity. The athletics bored them, but they vastly enjoyed being fêted by Ribbentrop, Goering, Goebbels and various Hohenzollerns. They were shown the regime's proud achievements and were duly impressed. 'There has never been anything like this since the days of Louis Quatorze,' a fellow guest enthusiastically suggested. 'Not since Nero,' Channon promptly replied.[8]

Walter and Evelyn Guinness's children were separated by gaps of several years, Bryan being born in 1905, Murtogh in 1913 and Grania in 1920. This meant that each of them grew up as virtually an only child. When Murtogh was born his brother was already at boarding-school and by the time their sister became aware of them both brothers were being educated away from home. Bryan went from Eton to Christ Church, Oxford, where having already become fluent in French and German, he took a degree in modern languages. From there he progressed to the Inner Temple and, for a while, practised as a barrister, but his heart was never in it. Bryan's reaction against the previous generation took the form of poetic introversion. He did not excel in and would not cultivate those skills and attitudes considered appropriate for a nobleman's son. He had not enjoyed Eton for, unlike his father and uncles he was a failure at sports. Neither his co-ordination nor his eyesight was keen and an attack of poliomyelitis as a child slowed his development, but his aversion went deeper than his physical limitations. Once, staying with friends in the country, he went on a shoot and performed dismally. Bryan's reaction was to make light of the affair but his father, whose prowess with a gun was prodigious, viewed the young man's ineptitude very differently and wrote him a stern letter about the importance of field sports.[9] It was no use; Bryan was a dreamer, an observer, an intuitive, a lover of theatre and music, and books and bookish people. The realisation came to him in adolescence that what really mattered was trying to see to the soul of things:

> I remember one morning looking out of the window at Rue de Poitiers and experiencing a moment of illumination which I was unable to express. There was an old woman with a besom chasing a flood of water and jetsam down the gutters of the Rue de Verneuil. The early morning sunlight flashed from the running water as the old woman swished it along with her broom. I had heard about free verse and tried to put what I had experienced into a poem. It was not a success.[10]

He went on, for the rest of his life, wrestling with words, refusing to loose his hold until they blessed him. His happiest memories of childhood and teenage years were of visits to the theatre in London and Dublin. At the Abbey Theatre he early became acquainted with the works of Yeats and Synge, and they fostered in him an appreciation of the Irish aspect of his heritage, which he probed more deeply over the years.

At university he was contemporary with Evelyn Waugh, Harold (later Sir Harold) Acton, Tom Driberg and Louis MacNeice. Later he numbered among his friends the Sitwells, John Betjeman, Augustus John, Lytton Strachey, Lord Berners and several of the lesser lights of the Bloomsbury set. In London, while waiting vainly for briefs, it was thrilling to pass the time with kindred spirits and 'real' writers. Bryan was by now more adept at poetry and his first book of verse was published in 1931. This was the precursor of around thirty volumes of poetry, fiction, memoirs and plays.

It was in the inward-looking, arty-aristocratic world of 1920s' London that Bryan became caught up in the eccentric life of the Mitford clan. David Freeman-Mitford, 2nd Baron Redesdale, and his wife Sydney were closely related to Clementine Churchill. They had one son and six daughters, three of whom, Nancy, Unity and Diana, were destined to achieve celebrity or notoriety. The eldest, Nancy the novelist, referred in one of her books to her contemporaries as a 'lost generation'. By this she meant that, sandwiched between two world wars, they would be regarded by posterity as having no distinct identity, but the word 'lost' could with greater truth be taken to refer to a *search* for identity, an attempt to come to terms with the rival ideologies of the age. Certainly, the word could be so applied to Nancy's own family. In their teenage and early adult years, when Bryan first joined their circle, they were a close and ebullient set of siblings. They attracted around them a self-defining literary and artistic élite with its own jargon, pet names and amused intolerance of those who were not party to the mysteries of the guild. This was a brittle-gay world of gossip, verbal pyrotechnics and enthusiastic debate on all that was new on the stage, in the galleries and upon the printed page. In politics they were united only in their impatience with the unimaginative pragmatism of Westminster, which seemed unable to solve current problems, let alone give the nation a vision for the future. The leaders and revolutionaries of Germany, Russia, Spain and Italy were, by contrast, men who had a cleanly cut template for the world they wished to shape.

Bryan fell in love with the eighteen-year-old Diana Mitford in 1928 and they were married within the year at the obligatory society wedding in St Margaret's Westminster. For four years they were very happy. Walter provided them with a country estate, Biddesdon House, Wiltshire, and the couple divided their time between there and their town residence in Buckingham Street (now Buckingham Gate), close by the palace, and, later, Cheyne Walk, Chelsea. They entertained enthusiastically and were among the darlings of the gossip columnists. All the 'bright young things' attended their dances, dinners and house parties. Writers came to read from their works and compare notes with Bryan. Politicians of all persuasions argued as they feasted, or sat and watched fellow guests play tennis.

The Guinnesses' most elaborate entertainment was a great ball given in Chelsea in June 1932. Diana described it thus:

> We invited everyone we knew, young and old, poor and rich, clever and silly. It was a warm night and the garden looked twice its real size with the trees lit from beneath. A few things about this party dwell in my memory: myself managing to propel Augustus John, rather the worse for wear, out of the house into a taxi; Winston Churchill inveighing against a large picture by Stanley Spencer of Cookham war memorial which hung on the staircase, and Eddie Marsh defending it against his onslaught. I wore a pale grey dress of chiffon and tulle, and all the diamonds I could lay my hands on. We danced until day broke, a pink and orange sunrise which gilded the river.[11]

Yet, while being very much a part of the London scene they could be iconoclastic towards prevailing establishments, as their son records:

> Bryan and Diana staged a spoof exhibition of paintings at their house in Buckingham Street. The idea, and most of the paintings, were Brian Howard's. The artist was given the name 'Bruno Hat'. Howard painted some twenty pictures on cork bathmats, in surrealist style; one was an 'Adoration of the Magi' in which each of the figures, instead of a head, had three finger-like antennae. The style struck Diana as being 'something between Picasso and Miro; rather decorative', but we see in it also more than a little of John Banting, another artist friend. Banting was in the Bruno Hat secret; Brian Howard painted most of the pictures in his studio, while Banting himself

painted one or two. Evelyn Waugh wrote a preface to the catalogue, entitled 'Approach to Hat'. Bruno Hat was supposed to be an avant-garde artist, tragically crippled and of German extraction. Tom Mitford impersonated him at the opening party, sitting in a wheelchair and sporting a black wig and moustache.[12]

The hoax was a complete success. The critics came and pontificated upon Hat's work in their columns and a few pictures were sold. To those in the know it was side-splittingly hilarious. Significantly, it was Bryan who decided when the joke had gone far enough and revealed all to the press. There was that in his nature which was no more at home among the bitchy verbal sniping of the Bloomsbury arties than among the blazing shotguns of the Suffolk hearties. He could never totally suppress the more serious side of his nature. It might be amusing to make fun of artistic pretentiousness, but as one who himself struggled with creativity, he was aware of the problems involved in the quest for originality. He found it more satisfying to encourage painters by buying their work than to mock them for their perceived failures. Bryan shunned the extremisms, aesthetic and political, into which some around him rushed headlong – most notably his wife.

By 1933 Diana had brought two sons into the world, Jonathan and Desmond. She had also grown from a teenage bride recently emancipated from the cloistered life of a very close family into a young woman aware of the wider world and stimulated by the ideas of clever men. Sensible now of the sufferings of many of her fellow human beings, of the seeming inability of politicians to get to the root of society's ills and also of the frivolity of her own life-style, she went in pursuit of the simple answer and, when she had tracked it down, she committed herself to it body and soul. That 'answer' for her was the Union of British Fascists and its leader Oswald Mosley. Having been excluded from the Labour party and subsequently failing to win a seat in 1931, Mosley decided to follow the non-democratic path pursued by Mussolini and Hitler. He founded the UBF in 1932, dressed his followers in black shirts, trained them in the arts of coercion, and relied on force and oratory to swell the ranks of his supporters. His policies were complex, but his appeal was simple: the people of Britain must place themselves under Fascist discipline in order to counteract the ineffectiveness of the government which, by failing to address the misery and hopelessness of the working class, was driving them into the open arms of Communism. Diana was overwhelmed by the man and his message. She left her husband, petitioned for a divorce, became Mosley's mistress and, in 1936, his wife.

This came as a great shock to the Guinnesses, who were naturally distressed for Bryan and the boys, but also profoundly disturbed to see ideological wedges being driven into the close grain of kith and kin. In Conservative circles there was a widespread fear of Communism and, therefore, a degree of sympathy with those totalitarian regimes which were bulwarking Europe against the red menace. 'Appeasement', which was to become such a dirty word by the end of the decade, was a natural attitude of many who loathed equally the idea of another war and the spread of Socialism. Channon once defended Lady Astor, whom he loathed, against the charge that she and the Cliveden set were pro-Hitler. They were not, he insisted; they were just 'pro-Chamberlain and pro-sense'. But political para-militarism ran counter to the system built up in Britain since the seventeenth century. The vicious career of the Nazis was something few wanted to see emulated in the UK. Diana and, more notoriously, her sister Unity, were open admirers of Hitler. They paid frequent visits to Germany, were intimate friends of the Führer and were seen by him as important links with the British ruling class.

Walter Guinness, in particular, had no time for the antics of his ex-daughter-in-law and her sister. As Churchill became more and more isolated within the Conservative party and viewed by many as an irritant in the process of securing Anglo-German accord, Walter was among those who remained close to him. Lord Moyne, like Lord Beaverbrook and others of the élite group of Churchillian intimates, possessed three things the ex-Chancellor especially valued: wealth, independent judgement and fearlessness in expressing his views. Walter had by now been elected to the Other Club, an exclusive confraternity set up by Winston in 1911 to bring together parliamentarians of all shades of opinion. One of its few rules was that members must not be inhibited from frankly expressing their opinions. There was no better way of keeping an ear close to the political ground than dining with fellow 'Otherers'.

Not that Walter's parliamentary activities had ceased with his departure from the Commons. He spoke occasionally in Lords debates and was active on various commissions. In 1932 he spent some months in Kenya over-seeing the colony's finances. The following year he chaired a departmental inquiry into housing and slum clearance. In 1934 his services were required on the royal commission on the University of Durham and as soon as that report was ready he was asked to lead a committee examining the British film industry.

This workaholic needed an occasional escape from speeches, research and round-table discussion, but even his hobbies were pursued with an enthusiasm bordering on the frenetic. His travels to exotic, little-known regions became more frequent. 'My own instinct', he wrote, has always been to get away from the great ports and centres of modern life and to visit human races, birds and beasts, rivers, mountains and forests where they still remain untouched by Western development ... For many of my journeys in other continents since the War I have been so fortunate as to be able to reach the less accessible regions by using my yacht as a base of operations. I have made six such expeditions to the Pacific, three times by Panama and three times by Suez, and my interest has concentrated more and more on that Western fringe of islands which separates it from the Indian Ocean. [Lord Moyne, op.cit., pp.1–2]

He had never lost his fascination with boats but, unlike his father and brothers who enjoyed the social paraphernalia of smart yacht clubs, his interest was not confined to participation in a fashionable sport. Adventure and scientific inquiry provided his motivation. The exploits of Livingstone, Stanley and his own missionary cousins had thrilled him as a boy and, as a young man they had stirred him to trek for himself into the interior of Africa and Asia. Hunting and exploring safaris had eventually lost their interest for him when the motor car and aeroplane penetrated the mysteries of remote regions and travel on foot was 'no longer imposed by necessity'.[14] His search for other regions rarely or never visited by white men and areas which could be explored in weeks or months rather than years led him to use his yacht as a base for riverain travel. He was one of the last wealthy amateur scientists, able to choose his own fields of study, establish his own methodology, select his own professional companions, and bring back reports, observations and specimens for presentation to museums and zoos.

Lord Moyne's conception of a 'yacht' was not that of a graceful schooner cutting through sparkling waters under a full spread of excurvate canvas. His vessels had to be powerful workhorses with sufficient luxury accommodation for passengers and crew, as well as storage for supplies, and zoological and anthropological specimens. *Roussalka*, in which he carried out his earlier voyages, was a sturdy, converted cross-Channel steamer. When she was wrecked off the Irish coast in 1933, Walter immediately acquired and refitted a 700-ton Newhaven–Dieppe ferry and named her *Rosaura*.

In September 1934 he took her on a proving voyage to the eastern Mediterranean. His guests of honour were the Churchills, who came aboard at Marseilles. As the yacht progressed sedately to Athens, Cyprus, the coast of southern Turkey and thence to Beirut, Winston worked on a film script on the reign of George V, commissioned by Alexander Korda, and Walter regaled the rest of the company with stories of his voyages and adventures. It was a time to relax, away from the problems and frustrations of Westminster politics. The party swam and explored the unspoilt, little-visited ruins of every major early civilisation from Hittite to Saracen. But inevitably the friends discussed the European situation and in Jerusalem, when they were dining at the luxurious King David Hotel as guests of the acting High Commissioner, their host mischievously plied Churchill with excellent Napoleon brandy in order to loosen his inhibitions. As a result, Churchill expatiated on international issues and national personalities 'with devastating wit and in superb prose'.[15] Walter took great delight in introducing his guests to those Levantine sights and experiences which he knew so well – old Jericho, 'rose-red' Petra, Akaba and Cairo. His knowledge of the history, peoples and age-old problems of the fertile crescent impressed Churchill and would be remembered eight years later when, as Prime Minister, he had an important and sensitive diplomatic post to fill. Clementine Churchill so enjoyed the trip that she agreed to accompany Moyne on a six-month voyage to the Far East planned for mid-December.

This latter trip was a reconnoitring exercise for a science-oriented voyage to New Guinea. In November 1935 Walter flew to Singapore to join the *Rosaura* with his nephew Arthur, Rupert's only son, who, he thought, should see something of the real world before settling to the restricting life of an English landowner. Their companions were Vera, Lady Broughton, estranged wife of Sir Henry Broughton, Bart, and her daughter Rosamond. Lady Broughton was a seasoned traveller and enthusiastic amateur photographer, and her official designation was expedition camerawoman. Walter never took his wife on their voyages. Lady Evelyn Guinness did not share her husband's passions for the sea and primitive peoples. Her interests were artistic. Much of her time in the early 1930s was spent in creating a replica medieval house in Sussex. Bailiffscourt was built almost entirely from period stone and timber, and incorporated several authentic fourteenth–fifteenth-century features. Though the house included every comfort and convenience deemed necessary for 1930s living, it managed to achieve a genuine feel and merged with the adjoining thirteenth-century chapel to create the illusion of a venerable ensemble. The professional members of the New Guinea expedition were ornithologists Anthony and Alvida Chaplin and Mr Lanworn, keeper of the reptile house at London Zoo.

The next few months carried the travellers to various parts of the Malay mainland and to islands as far apart as the Philippines and Andamans, as well as to New Guinea, their primary objective. If the younger members of the expedition were looking for thrills they certainly found them, in the form of spear-brandishing pygmies uncertain how to react to the strange invaders, impenetrable forests harbouring poisonous snakes, and unseen creatures that rustled and roared in the dripping undergrowth. The most hazardous incident, however, and one which could have put a sudden end to the Iveagh dynasty, occurred when the expedition was 120 miles up the Ramu river. Both the ship's launches in which they were travelling were holed and the party was forced to pitch camp ashore. They had enough provisions for five days and only one way of making contact with the *Rosaura*: a perilous journey downstream in a flimsy dinghy through whirl-pools, rapids, floating debris and crocodiles. Arthur volunteered for the task. He and the local guide travelled night and day, taking it in turns to row and keep watch. It took them nearly four days of sweating and anxious labour, in the sticky riverain heat, to get back to the coast and organise a relief expedition. This heir to one of Britain's largest fortunes accepted the hazards with becoming *sangfroid*. He seemed more concerned about the novel attentions of fleas than the prospect of sudden death. His uncle, however, spent several sleepless nights worrying about Arthur's safety.

Walter's attitude towards the 'hidden' tribes he visited was a mixture of fatalism and Rousseauesque romanticism. He deplored the relentless incursion of western civilisation:

> One could wish that some of the ancient races might be protected in their purity as in the case of the Ongé of Little Andaman, who maintain their vigour and fertility while tribes on the other Andaman Islands have withered in contact with the whites. Missionaries, too, are so entrenched in many parts of New Guinea that at present it seems hardly practical to suggest that they should be restrained from exterminating native customs and beliefs in order to impose their own.[16]

(That sentiment would hardly have pleased his Grattan Guinness cousins.) Walter wrestled with the problem of how best to integrate primitive peoples into the modern world without wrecking their cultures and came to no conclusions. He saw himself as a privileged and fascinated observer of natives 'in the raw'. Yet he was inevitably a part of that very process he abhorred. He paid for local labour and artefacts with brass rings and trinkets from his 'trade box', just like the missionary-explorers of the previous century. He showed Stone Age pygmies how to clear camp sites with steel tools. He amazed them by bringing down birds with rifle and shotgun. Brief though his visits were, they could not be without effect on the host peoples.

His very attitude of fascinated observer and specimen collector assumed a detached superiority. He was interested, as were many men of science and psychiatric medicine of the time, in 'racial characteristics'. Among the 'trophies' of this expedition were the crania and other skeletal remains of some forty New Guineans, which were presented to the Royal College of Surgeons. They and the photographs of men, women and children were just as much objects of study as the brightly plumaged birds, the gibbons and langurs, the hundred reptiles and the newly discovered species of tree kangaroo brought back for the London Zoo, or the tools, pots and carvings collected for the British Museum. Walter made observations about the effects of tribal interbreeding and the different ways native groups related to their environment. He adopted the same attitude in his reflections on Arabs, Jews and Turks and their problems. If he had known of the experiments soon to be carried out by Nazi scientists on living human guinea-pigs he would have been appalled, but Walter's underlying assumptions about racial superiority and the Svengali of the genes which imposed intellectual limitations on other peoples sprang from the same stock as full-blown Aryanism.

Lord Moyne accurately identified the challenge which colonial administrators and, later, international aid workers and indigenous governments had to take up – how to introduce primitive peoples to the blessings of 'civilisation' while avoiding the curses and, indeed, how to tell the difference:

> The future of the native population remains a problem for which no satisfactory solution has as yet been suggested ... Primitive populations ... have not been exterminated merely by the more obvious agencies of slaughter and disease. In many cases, the reasons for natives dying out in contact with Western civilisation are due to deeper causes which are unfortunately but little understood ...
>
> On the credit side, civilisation will no doubt deal effectively with diseases such as tropical ulcers, yaws and malaria. We must not, however, assume that customs healthy in the temperate zone are necessarily applicable to the tropics. Steps should therefore be taken to restrain the destruction of health from evaporation and sudden chills due to wearing clothes in a hot, rainy climate. The standard of nourishment and resistance to disease can also be greatly assisted by spreading better knowledge of cultivation.
>
> Unfortunately, psychological problems cannot so easily be solved. Different races probably need different rules of life, and what suits one may be fatal for another ... No one can foretell the results of transforming the age-long habits of people of such different race and customs from ourselves.[17]

Lord Moyne was able to make one more epic voyage of scientific exploration. Having devoted several cruises to the Pacific rim, in 1937 he transferred his attention to the Atlantic, travelling from Greenland, along the American seaboard to Honduras. There were other outings in *Rosaura*, but they were connected with his government responsibilities. From the middle of 1938 he was caught up in the gathering pace of world events.

Early in September he invited the Churchills on a Christmas Caribbean cruise. Regretfully declining, Winston drew attention to the government's mishandling of Hitler, thus creating a situation which, at any moment, might erupt into major conflict. 'We seem to be very near the bleak choice between War and Shame,' he wrote. 'My feeling is that we shall choose Shame, and then have War thrown in a little later on even more adverse terms than at present'.[18] The Führer was demanding independence for the Sudetan Germans of Czechoslovakia. Churchill insisted that the time had come to take a stand by threatening military intervention if Hitler took the step of 'protecting' his fellow nationals. Walter was not quite so bold, but he was appalled at the way Prime Minister Chamberlain scuttled around Europe making concession after concession in an effort to maintain peace.

On 29 September Walter was present at what must have been the most uncomfortable gathering of the Other Club. That same morning Chamberlain had set out for a conference in Munich with Hitler, Mussolini and Daladier, the French Premier, to settle the Czechoslovak problem. Each man in the sombre group gathered around the table at the Savoy in the evening shared Churchill's apprehension about the summit, including Lloyd George, Bob Boothby MP, Brendan Bracken MP, J. L. Garvin, editor of the *Observer*, Duff Cooper, First Lord of the Admiralty, Walter Elliot, Secretary for Scotland and Churchill's principal information gatherer, and Lord Moyne. Winston ranted and raved, venting his spleen on the two government ministers present and demanding to know how they could support a policy that was 'sordid, squalid, sub-human and suicidal'.[19] Heated debate went on beyond midnight. As soon as the first newspapers were available carrying details of the Munich agreement they were brought in to the diners, who absorbed in stricken silence the humiliating terms to which Chamberlain had agreed. Then the meeting broke up and its leaden-hearted members went to their homes. Hours later the Prime Minister returned to wave his notorious piece of paper and proclaim 'peace for our time'.

That morning, Chips Channon had awoken in his bed at Kelvedon. He was now PPS to 'Rab' Butler, the Under-Secretary of State at the Foreign Office. When he read the news he was euphoric. 'It is peace,' he wrote in his diary, 'a Chamberlain, respectable gentleman's peace.' 'I consider Neville the Man of our Age,' he declared. The Prime Minister's accomplishment was one in which, 'the whole world rejoices whilst only a few malcontents jeer'.[20]

17

'WHAT IS THE GAIN OF OUR COMING AND GOING?'*

At the end of August 1939 Lady Iveagh sent a telegram to her friend Freya Stark at Asolo to warn her of the rapidly deteriorating international situation. Freya hurriedly packed a bag, drove to Venice and was able to secure the last berth on the last Orient Express to leave Italy before the opening of hostilities. If Gwendolin were tempted to regard this as an omen that somehow the Guinnesses would escape the worst effects of the avalanche about to loose itself on the world, events would cruelly disillusion her. She and hers had, till then, lived a charmed existence. The horrors of the Kaiser's war had not come nigh them. Wealth and influence had held away from their lives the drabness of the thirties. But Hitler's war and its aftermath would rain bitter blows on the family, which would weaken for all time their political, social and commercial standing.

Lord Moyne had suffered a cruel stroke before the conflict even began. In the summer of 1939 his wife Evelyn died while staying in their Paris apartment. She was fifty-six. Theirs had been an unconventional marriage during which they had spent long periods apart. They had their own separate interests and there were undoubtedly other women in Walter's life. Yet they were close. Bryan Guinness's account of his childhood (*Dairy Not Kept*) is of a happy time spent with loving parents. Walter and Evelyn certainly expressed their feelings for each other and their children more openly than Walter's father and mother had. They exchanged tender letters when they were separated and Walter kept those that he received. In later years husband and wife shared a passion for medievalism and

*From the *Rubáiyát of Omar Khayyám*, a favourite poem of Walter, Lord Moyne.

gave expression to it in the Gothic extravaganza of Bailiffscourt, which became their principal home.

Work now helped to staunch Walter's grief. He was, as ever, extremely busy and had actually taken *Rosaura* to the West Indies, where he was chairing a royal commission, when Evelyn fell ill. War hugely increased his responsibilities. His first thoughts on the fall of Poland were for the people of that country. He chaired the Polish Relief Fund and provided accommodation for its officers in his Grosvenor Place house. In the following drear months, when Axis armies spread inexorably across Europe and Britain's merchant convoys were being savaged by the German navy, Walter considered it his duty to support the Chamberlain government despite his own conviction that, in A. J. P. Taylor's later words, they were 'moving into war backwards, with their eyes tightly closed'.[1] The crisis which eventually shoehorned Chamberlain out of office was the Norwegian campaign fiasco. British forces were sent across the North Sea when the Scandinavian kingdom was invaded. The campaign was a failure from the start, doomed as much by divided political and military counsels as by superior German air and land power. In a parliamentary debate on 7–8 May Chamberlain's own back benches turned on him and Labour determined to use the issue to oust a prime minister whose stock in the country had run out. In the Commons Churchill, who, as First Lord of the Admiralty, bore much of the responsibility for military failure, was in a difficult position. Longing to see Chamberlain fall, but not wishing to be dragged down with him, he was obliged to defend the government from the two-pronged attack. Walter, having watched the Commons debate, took the same line in the Lords: 'There is a great danger in the middle of this war effort', he declared, 'that two entirely different elements of criticism may combine to produce results which are contrary to the public advantage'.[2] However, it was the seventy-seven-year-old Lloyd George who, in his last celebrated Commons speech, caught the mood of parliament. Chamberlain had called for sacrifice, he reminded the house. Well, there was nothing which would contribute more to victory than the Prime Minister's sacrifice of the seals of office. Two days later Chamberlain resigned and Churchill kissed hands.

Walter Guinness was among those the new leader immediately brought back into government. At first he was returned to the Ministry of Agriculture and Fisheries, though in the subordinate role of joint parliamentary secretary. However, in the following February Winston further refined his cabinet team and in the reshuffle Walter became Colonial Secretary and government leader in the House of Lords.

From the very moment that he was back in parliamentary harness Lord Moyne strained every intellectual muscle to haul the government war effort forward. This included impeaching those of his own acquaintance whom he considered to be security risks. He may well have felt a certain satisfaction in moving against Diana, Lady Mosley, who had caused his son such pain (Bryan was by now happily married again, to Elisabeth Nelson, with whom he brought up a large family). Walter interviewed his grandsons' governess and made this the basis of a report to the head of the Security Executive. He listed Diana's and Unity's visits to Germany and their alleged pro-Nazi sentiments. At this time (June 1940) Sir Oswald had already been imprisoned (though the BUF was not proscribed), but his wife was being kept at liberty so that MI5 could watch her movements and contacts. Walter urged that this 'extremely dangerous character' should be interned. A few days later, while Bryan was serving in the Royal Sussex Regiment, his ex-wife was locked up in Holloway prison.

These disruptions to anything vaguely resembling a normal family life were particularly hard on Bryan's and Diana's sons though, with the stoicism of childhood, they accepted that this was the way life was. Jonathan and Desmond were nine and eight respectively at the outbreak of war. They were permitted to visit their mother occasionally, for twenty minutes at a time. Jonathan later described these outings in the third person:

> Visitors would be first shown to a waiting room near the main gate. The yellow walls and benches resembled those in waiting rooms everywhere, though in a station there would have been graffiti, and in a hospital some dog-eared magazines. There were one or two other people there, women in headscarves and sad, shapeless clothes, sometimes a disconsolate soldier. Nobody talked much. In due course one would be escorted through a yard to a similar, smaller, room where Diana would appear. She looked much as usual, though the absence of make-up made her seem rather washed out and insubstantial. A wardress would sit there; her presence did not seem to matter. In any case Jonathan was later to make friends with several of the wardresses. Everyone chatted quite cheerfully and normally; Jonathan does not remember these first occasions as poignant, though he was sorry when the twenty minutes was up. It was all part of the war: mother in prison, father away in the Army, no sweets, food on the ration, gasmasks.[3]

After a couple of years and much importuning of friends at the Churchillian court Diana and Oswald were permitted shared quarters in Holloway. They had a tiny, bleak flat and were able to prepare their own food. They could also have their children with them for whole-day visits.

The boys could now be treated to prison rations, cooked imaginatively by Diana, augmented by what guests had brought in and also by such exotic vegetables as kohlrabi which Mosley grew in a little plot of ground allocated to him. Jonathan and Desmond liked their stepfather. He was an intelligent and widely read man, and knew how to keep youngsters entertained with stories about ancient heroes, lessons in human biology and bawdy songs. The incarcerated couple put on a bold front and refused to be cowed by punitive, sometimes insanitary conditions, or by bouts of ill health. When, in November 1943, Oswald's condition gave real cause for alarm and raised the prospect of his dying in prison and, thereby, becoming a martyr, he and his wife were released. The few fashionable friends and relatives who had stuck by them celebrated. One of the many oddities about the upper class's war was the toings and froings of society leaders between Holloway cells and Mayfair salons. On one occasion Diana's brother visited her in the morning and dined with Churchill in the evening. The press and most members of parliament were scandalised by the Mosleys' deliverance. Lord Moyne's comments are not recorded.

He was frantically busy, both in Westminster and Whitehall. He had to organise the business of the upper house and explain government policy on a wide range of issues. Just how wide may be illustrated by his activity in one period of a hundred days between July and November 1942, when he addressed their lordships on matters relating to aerodromes, agriculture, Anglo-American relations, civil defence, colonial administration, factories, the Far East, food supplies, hospitals, Pearl Harbor, Jewish affairs, sundry military events, Palestine, pensions, the pottery industry, Rhodesia and Nyasaland, and the Soviet Union. He was not a member of Churchill's small war cabinet, but he was often involved with the PM in discussions of vital issues.

Two of the most vital engaged him and his colleagues in the spring of 1941. One was lend-lease, the scheme by which Britain received war material and financial credits from the USA in return for economic and political concessions. Churchill was determined to press it through as the only means of obtaining the 'tools' to 'finish the job' of defeating Hitler, but colleagues were worried about the terms America was extracting for the deal. Walter was particularly concerned about the demand for certain Caribbean naval bases in exchange for a fleet of old warships. Moyne told the Prime Minister that West Indian governments resented the proposed handover. Churchill saw the point of Walter's comment, but feared a backlash from American isolationists. He insisted, in a secret minute, that current exigencies made subtlety essential. 'I am anxious ... by one means or another to keep this business as quiet as possible till the [Lend-lease]

Bill is through [the US legislature]. We shall then have only the President to deal with, and not be in danger of giving ammunition to our enemies in the Senate'.[4] Churchill, as usual, got his own way and his instinct was undoubtedly right not only about the need for war supplies, but also about dragging a reluctant America into the conflict.

The other matter under consideration at the same time resolved itself less happily. Lord Moyne was brought into discussions on the desirability of the Allies going to the aid of the Greeks. Their country was about to be overrun by the *Wehrmacht*. The problem was twofold, political and military: would British prestige suffer throughout the eastern Mediterranean if the country failed to go to Greece's aid, and if troops were committed what was the prospect of success? Walter's advice was called for because of his expertise in Levantine affairs and also because the first forces to be sent in would be Australians and New Zealanders. On both counts his mind must have gone back to the Gallipoli fiasco and he urged the necessity of an accurate military assessment of the situation. In the end a unanimous cabinet decision was reached without just such a soldierly evaluation. Sixty-two thousand allied troops landed on the Greek mainland. They never seriously engaged the enemy, who swept down from the north in superior numbers, and had to be evacuated. Another friendly nation had fallen to the Nazis after a totally ineffectual attempt at protection by the British Empire. It was Norway all over again.

Nor was there any good news in domestic Guinness affairs. The Park Royal brewery was damaged several times during the blitz, the worst incident being a daylight raid in October 1940 when a direct hit destroyed the ice house and killed four employees. Bombs also affected production and distribution. During the winter of 1940–1 storage facilities in Bristol, Manchester and Liverpool were hit, and railway lines were often put out of action. The enemy targeted ports and coastal shipping, and thousands of casks of stout ended up on the Channel sea bed. Finding ways of minimising disruption was a constant intellectual challenge to management. The old canal network of Britain was revivified and, where practicable, beer was sent by this slower but more secure means of transport. Surprisingly, the three Guinness-owned vessels plying between Dublin, Manchester and Liverpool survived the war unscathed, but whether this had anything to do with giving them security code names – *Matthew, John* and *Thomas* – is questionable. Undoubtedly, what cushioned Arthur Guinness Sons and Co. most effectively was the existence of the St James's Gate brewery. The plant in neutral Ireland was safe from enemy attack, and production there was deliberately stepped up to offset losses and delays in Britain. This largely explains the company's relatively healthy trading figures throughout the war. In 1938–9 profits after tax had been £1.6 million. Despite a low of £1.2 million in 1941–2, lost production, distribution problems and expenditure on plant repairs, by the last year of the war profits stood at £1.4 million and during the following twelve months they recovered to pre-war levels.

Arthur Guinness, Son and Co. Ltd may be said to have played their part in boosting public morale between 1939 and 1945. They provided stout to military and civil hospitals, often free or at discounted prices. The War Office ensured a regular supply of beer to NAAFI outlets. After D Day this became a problem. The military command insisted that home-brewed beer was essential in maintaining the spirits of the advancing armies. Government responded with emergency legislation which ordained that five per cent of total production must be reserved for the troops. This placed an almost intolerable burden on supply logistics, especially as they related to the availability of bottles and casks, but it indicates how far Guinness had become an essential ingredient of Britishness – in a sense it was part of what the servicemen were fighting for. The company made use of this in its advertising. Churchill's speeches, heroic war films and cheerful wireless programmes were major elements in a propaganda scheme designed to boost morale, but the by now familiar Guinness posters also contributed to the raising of spirits. Bensons produced many wartime variants on established themes. The Guinness strong man was shown wheeling a barrowload of Brobdingnagian vegetables, which associated the product with the government's 'dig for victory' campaign. Another advertisement depicted a soldier and a sailor playing draughts over a glass of stout. 'I have Guinness for strength; that's strategy,' the man in khaki declared. 'I have it on you,' his companion replied. 'That's tactics.' Another variation on an old theme was a poster headed 'What the Situation Demands' and pictorially depicted common aphorisms such as 'Wheel – for putting shoulder to' and 'Brass Tacks – for getting down to' and ending with 'Guinness – for strength'. Such advertisements, frequently changed, worked by cheering passers-by and by reinforcing a comforting sense of continuity.

Of the ten grandchildren of the first Lord Iveagh alive in 1939 only three were boys. One of them (Murtogh, Lord Moyne's younger son) elected to live abroad. The heirs to the Iveagh and Moyne titles were both in uniform and, therefore, at risk. This made the continuance of the senior Guinness line in the family business very precarious. Rupert's sons-in-law, Chips Channon and Alan Lennox-Boyd (see below, pp.246ff), had already been brought on to the board, but there was a question mark over the preservation of a tradition reaching back to the first Arthur. There was, of course, no justification for the head of the family occupying the chairmanship as of inherited right, since he did not have a majority shareholding, but no one had ever challenged the custom and AGMs tended to be intimate gatherings attended almost exclusively by members of the family.

All of the Guinness husbands and fathers who were of call-up age served in the armed forces. The most distinguished was John Slessor, who was married to Hermione, elder daughter of Gerald Seymour Guinness and sister of Gerald de Capell-Brooke Guinness. Hermione's first husband, a Lieutenant-Colonel in the King's Own Yorkshire Light Infantry, had died tragically in February 1919, only seven months after their wedding. When she married again in 1923 at the age of twenty-five she chose another serving officer, Wing-Commander John Slessor. By 1939 he was one of the most experienced pilots in the RAF and, as Assistant Chief of British Air Staff, he made a valuable contribution to policy development. But he was constantly frustrated by the failure of politicians to understand the rudiments of combined operations warfare. Not until February 1943 did he have the freedom to implement his own strategy. That was when Churchill designated him C.-in-C. Coastal Air Command. It was one of the really significant appointments of the war. Up to that point German submarines were winning the battle of the Atlantic. In March 1943 they sent almost half a million tons of convoy shipping to the bottom. Slessor now insisted on the diversion of bombers from blanket attacks on Germany to the defence of Britain's vital supply lanes. He had to argue his case against Arthur 'Bomber' Harris, who was very close to Churchill, but he gained his point, with immediate and dramatic effect. Shipping losses fell rapidly and by the end of the year well over a hundred U-boats had been sunk. Control of coastal waters was wrested from the enemy in good time for the D-Day invasion of 1944.

Loel Guinness also served in the air defence of Britain. His reserve squadron was made operational in 1940, and equipped with Spitfires and Hurricanes. He was mentioned in despatches five times and received the Croix de Guerre. Loel continued to represent Bath in the Commons between missions. He was one of the fortunate pilots who returned intact from every sortie and by the end of hostilities he had reached the rank of group-captain.

Bryan spent most of the war in the Middle East. His linguistic fluency fitted him ideally for a liaison role. In the spring of 1941 he was with the Anglo-Free French force which wrested Syria from the hands of a government loyal to Vichy and thus denied the country to Germany as a potential air base. The eastern Mediterranean was a sensitive area criss-crossed by military and diplomatic trip wires. The conflict involving British, French, German and Italian forces was overlaid on animosities far more ancient and potentially destructive: Turk v. Greek, Arab v. Jew, Arab v. Arab. Add to this the existence of nationalist groups opposed to the protectorate mandates set up by international agreement, the mutual suspicion of the colonial powers, and the European and American companies exploiting the region's oil wealth and you have a situation of Byzantine complexity. In Cairo, Damascus and Jerusalem local issues of competing nationalisms constituted the reality; issues such as Jewish settlement and freedom from European control were slow fires, flaring up occasionally but always smouldering. The immediate pre-war months had seen a fresh eruption of terrorist attacks, prompting a contemporary analyst to observe:

A final settlement of the Palestine question is essential if the growing soli-darity of the Arab world is not to become a force actively hostile to Great Britain, in an area of great importance to her imperial communications. While the rulers of Arabia, Transjordan, and Iraq are naturally well-disposed to England, the policy of the Balfour Declaration, and its effect in delaying or denying the emancipation of Palestine from foreign control, excite the united and implacable hostility of the whole Arab world. It is of course essential that faith should be kept with the Jews, but, unless an acceptable solution can be quickly reached, the prospect for the future is far from reassuring.[5]

The view from London was very different. War had imposed new priorities. The Levant was seen as a crossroads where a land bridge between the battlefields of Africa and Europe intersected with vital imperial sea lanes. Britain's representative on the spot was, thus, a man who carried enormous authority and responsibility, on whom were fixed the hopes, fears, ambitions and hatreds of several races. So important was the post of British Resident in Cairo that it carried automatic membership of the war cabinet. In the summer of 1942 the Australian diplomat Richard Casey (later Lord Casey and Governor-General of Australia) was appointed to this position, with Lord Moyne as his deputy. In January 1944 Walter moved up to the top job. He was now the most powerful man in the Middle East.

The turning point of the war had arrived. When Churchill and Roosevelt met in Cairo in November 1943 in preparation for the Tehran conference with Stalin it was to plan the invasion of Germany and to begin thinking about post-war reconstruction. After days of hard bargaining in the Persian capital Churchill returned to Cairo and Walter was shocked to see his old friend looking exhausted and ill. Much had changed in the decade since he had introduced Winston and Clementine to the ancient and modern delights of this city.

Of all the problems Walter had to deal with the most intractable was that of partitioning between two hostile peoples a land to which each laid claim as of right. The fundamental issues were similar to those with which he had been all too familiar in Ireland, but here the contending parties were the Arabs and Jews of Palestine. In the Balfour Declaration (1917) Britain had recognised the Jews' right to their own homeland and made clear that the realisation of this objective should not interfere with the 'civil and religious rights of existing non-Jewish communities'. By this statement the government of the day had clamped its successors into a vice, which pressed ever tighter. Both ethnic groups believed that the occupying power favoured the other side, or that it was only interested in keeping power in its own hands.

Lord Moyne was not partisan; throughout his time as Colonial Secretary and in the Cairo residency he made frequent visits to Palestine in order to negotiate with both Zionists and Arabs. However, the more dramatic events of his years in office involved him in attempts to thwart the Jews from forcing the pace of change. Illegal immigration into Palestine was a constant problem to the authorities. Every time a group was discovered and deported, world Zionism branded the British government as repressive and unfeeling. The worst calamity occurred in the early weeks of 1942. The SS *Struma*, a decrepit old tramp steamer, arrived in Istanbul vastly overloaded with a human cargo of more than 700 Romanian Jews fleeing Nazi persecution. They were refused permission to land and *Struma's* captain declined to take his ship back to sea, on the grounds that it simply would not survive another voyage. For almost eight weeks the stinking hulk lay moored in the harbour, while Turkish and British authorities argued about the passengers' fate. The High Commissioner in Jerusalem, Sir Harold MacMichael, backed by his superiors, refused the refugees onward transit to Palestine. Eventually he relented as far as to allow entry permits to all children under eleven. It was too late; the Turks had already forced the *Struma* back out into the Black Sea where, on 24 February, she broke up with the loss of all but one of the passengers and crew.

Such events played into the hands of the extremists. Jewish nationalism inevitably had its guerrilla fringe – lunatic and dangerous – of angry, frustrated, impatient inadequates who believed or persuaded themselves, against evidence to the contrary, that a stable, free nation could be built on foundations of death and destruction. One of the rag-bag of terrorist organisations, calling itself the Lohmey Heruth Israel (Israel Freedom Fighters), was known to the authorities as the Stern Gang after one of its leaders, Abraham Stern, who was killed in Italy in February 1942. After the *Struma* the spate of demonstrations, bombings, kidnappings and shootings increased and there were several attempts on MacMichael's life. Zionist leaders, engaged in negotiations with Britain, publicly deplored the wave of fanaticism while making political capital out of it.

Lord Moyne went quietly about his work, a large part of which involved trying to square the circle of conflicting Arab and Jewish interests. Never, in all his incredibly varied life, had he been busier or carried more responsibility. There was something unreal about Cairo, a city where diplomats, wealthy Egyptians, foreign visitors and Allied officers on leave lived as if there were no war, throwing parties, dining at exclusive clubs and restaurants, swimming, going to the races, playing or watching polo, cricket and tennis, gossiping and being gossiped about. Walter did his share of entertaining and, of course, did it very well. His office was in the British embassy, but his residence was at Zamalek on the comparatively cool Nile island of Gezira and he also had a villa near the pyramids to which he could escape at weekends. In his homes he received Churchill and other government colleagues on their sporadic visits, laid on duty receptions and dinners for members of King Farouk's court, Arab and Jewish delegations, royals in exile and diplomats, and sometimes was able to relax with friends like Freya Stark (also in Cairo on important war work) or Joyce Grenfell (who stayed with him in 1944 while on a tour entertaining the troops). Occasionally Bryan would come, snatching a few days' leave from his office in Damascus.

Walter's diary for the last quarter of 1944 was very full. With victory in Europe now clearly visible on the horizon diplomatic agendas were being set for tackling the complexities of peace-making. On 20 October he had a breakfast meeting with Churchill, who had touched down in Cairo for a few hours on his way home from several days of hard bargaining in Moscow. The two friends discussed Winston's forthcoming meeting with Chaim Weizmann, president of the World Zionist Association. Only weeks before, the full horrors of Auschwitz had broken upon a shocked world. This had added a new, moral dimension to the settlement of the Palestinian question. As well as publicly declaring his outrage over the death camps, Churchill reaffirmed his support for Zionist aspirations. Among the immediate practical steps he had taken had been the raising of a Jewish brigade to take part in the final push into Germany and the recalling of the hated Sir Harold MacMichael.

For his part, Walter had to report on the bizarre business of Joel Brand, a Hungarian Jew picked up in Damascus *en route* from Berlin to Tel Aviv. He bore a message from the infamous SS chief, Adolf Eichmann, offering to spare a million Jewish lives in return for ten thousand lorries carrying essential food supplies to the beleaguered German capital. Brand had been brought to Cairo for interrogation by Walter's intelligence officers. They concluded that the offer was genuine and reflected the desperation of Hitler's high command. They recommended that it could safely be ignored, on the grounds that all the concentration camps would be liberated within weeks and that, in any case, there could be no negotiation with the Nazis.

At the conclusion of the brief meeting it was arranged that the Prime Minister would discuss in outline plans for the creation of a state of Israel with Dr Weizmann, then invite him to hammer out the details with Walter in Cairo. When the Premier put the suggestion to the Jewish leader at Chequers on 4 November Weizmann was hesitant. It was generally believed, he said, that Lord Moyne was no well-wisher of Zionism. Churchill assured his guest that any reservations his old friend might once have harboured were now well in the past; Walter was committed to achieving a permanent settlement.

Meanwhile Lord Moyne had to deal with a more pressing problem. The expulsion of the Germans from Greece had left a power vacuum, which Communist resistance fighters and supporters of King George were vying to fill. Churchill was determined to prevent the country falling under Soviet influence and ordered troops in to support the government. On 26 October 1944 the Foreign Secretary, Anthony Eden, arrived in Cairo, and the next day he and Moyne flew to Athens to update themselves on the situation. They surveyed the devastation wrought by civil war in the aftermath of enemy occupation and retreat. They saw the ruined infrastructure, devastated farmland and starving people. They felt the intensity of mutual hatreds. To prepare for the cabinet a summary of the state of affairs and to propose recommendations about this shattered and divided country took the ministers long hours of discussion and interviews with government officials. It was with some relief that Walter returned to his post on 1 November. In comparison with the ancient Greek capital, where snipers lurked among ruined buildings, Cairo seemed like a paradisal haven.

Walter Guinness had never been overly concerned for his own safety. He had risked death in South Africa, the Dardanelles, the French trenches, the storms of empty oceans and untamed wildernesses. At sixty-four he had no intention of changing the habits of a lifetime. Despite comparisons with Athens, he knew that dangers stalked the streets of Cairo where the British presence was, at best, only tolerated. That made little impression on him. He refused to surround himself with bodyguards and sometimes he walked home alone from the security-stockaded embassy.

On Monday, 6 November he returned to the residency for lunch in his chauffeur-driven Humber with his aide and his devoted secretary, Dorothy Osmond, who had been with him for more than twenty years. It was routine – a routine that members of the Stern Gang had learned well. The car stopped in front of Moyne's house and the chauffeur opened the rear door for the minister. Before Walter could step out two assassins brandishing revolvers ran from the shrubbery and fired a volley of shots. The driver died instantly. Lord Moyne was rushed to hospital where, despite all the efforts of King Farouk's personal physician, he too died, at 8.40 p.m.

In Damascus news reached Bryan at about 3 p.m. that his father had been injured. He immediately set out on what proved to be a nightmare car journey. By midnight he had reached Jerusalem and was desperately searching in the dark for the British High Commission building:

Lost. Arab guard on a building nearly shot me, but afterwards told me the way. Blackness. Rain. Despair. Empty road. No sign post. Military camps: barbed wire: no one to ask. Light ahead. It was the gate, which I remembered, of the grounds. Scottish policeman would not let us through in the car. He did not know if I was expected, and could not get answer from the house with his telephone. Allowed me through with Arab guard. Fiercely challenged as we went. Rang front door bell. Butler came – said I was expected. 'It is very sad about his Lordship.' Very anxious – drawing-room – Lord Gort: kind looking person with two officers. I told him I had had no news since 3. He told me at once that my father had died. He took me to the dining-room. Gave me green pea soup. Butler brought other things – but soup had warmed me up and I asked to go to bed. Lord Gort said I was to travel on by air with Giels of Palestine police. ADC showed me my room. Alone at last and able to cry.[6]

18

GUINNESS TIME*

While the dead man's son was going to Cairo to look his last upon his father and make arrangements to convey the body back to England, the world was recording its shock. Chaim Weizmann was among the first to offer condolences and to assure the world that Zionism would go to the utmost limit of its power to cut out this evil from its midst. His distress, he insisted, was even greater than that he had felt when his own son had gone missing on an RAF mission over Germany. In the event it was Egyptian police who arrested the murderers and Egyptian justice which delivered them to the hangman. The newspaper *Telaviv Ha'aretz* expressed the anxiety that followed immediately on the sense of outrage: '[The assassins] have done more by this single, reprehensible crime to demolish the edifice erected by three generations of Jewish pioneers than is imaginable.'[1] In the Commons Churchill could not bring himself to make the formal announcement of his friend's death: that was left to Eden, but subsequently the PM, one of the few men who knew the efforts Walter Guinness was making for Palestinian peace and could appreciate the tragic irony of his death, underscored Zionist concerns: 'If our dreams for Zionism are to end in the smoke of assassins' pistols and our labours for its future to produce only a new set of gangsters worthy of Nazi Germany, many like myself will have to reconsider the position we have maintained so consistently and so long in the past.'[2]

For all the family it was a devastating blow. The most distinguished and, at the same time, the most unorthodox Guinness of his generation

*Title of the Park Royal house magazine issued quarterly from 1946 to 1975.

had been torn suddenly and brutally from their midst. Henry Channon recorded his immediate reaction in his diary, with a characteristic mixture of sensitivity and bitchiness:

> I went to sleep last night with strange emotions. Walter Moyne was an extra-ordinary man, colossally rich, well-meaning, intelligent, scrupulous, yet a viveur, and the only modern Guinness to play a social or political role, being far less detached than most of his family. He collected yachts, fish, monkeys and women. He had a passion for the sea, and for long expeditions to remote places ... Walter with his steely-grey hair, turquoise eyes, had a distinguished appearance, and also the curious Guinness money traits. He was careful of his huge fortune, though he had probably about three millions.[3]

The Guinness family was given little time to recover from the Cairo outrage before other sadnesses came upon them. Twelve weeks later news reached Britain of a tragedy that was more poignant and more far-reaching in its effects. Arthur Onslow Guinness, heir to the Iveagh earldom, had begun to learn about farming and the brewery, and had resolved in the late thirties to contest a parliamentary seat at the next election. When war cut across his plans he obtained an anti-tank commission in the Suffolk and Norfolk Yeomanry. By the end of 1944 he had risen to the rank of major and was stationed at Nijmegen, in territory occupied by the Allies after the initial push from Normandy. In the last days of the year Hitler threw everything into a western counter-offensive that took the British and American generals by surprise. During the course of what was to be the last major battle of the war in northern Europe Major Guinness was killed. There was about the tragedy something of almost malevolent chance: on 8 February 1945 he was some distance from any military action when a German V2 rocket failed well short of its target and fell upon the farmhouse where he was lodged. He was thirty-two. He left a widow and three children. Six weeks later it was the turn of Ernest's family to be overwhelmed by tragedy. Maureen's husband, the Marquis of Dufferin and Ava, was killed on active service in Burma.

Life for the Iveaghs was falling apart. In the space of a few weeks Rupert had lost his two closest male relatives in tragic circumstances. At the same time his daughters were adding to his store of sorrows. Honor's marriage to Chips Channon had broken down and her parents sided with their son-in-law. Life had been fun in 1930s high society, but in the changed atmosphere of the war years Honor, it seems, tired of Chips's frivolous, effeminate self-indulgence. She walked out on him at the end of 1940, having fallen for a young war hero, a Czech fighter pilot named Frantisek

Svejdar. Channon filed for divorce on the grounds of his wife's desertion and obtained custody of their son, a boy on whom he doted. The decree absolute came through within days of his brother-in-law's death. After her remarriage, Honor became the first Guinness to convert to Catholicism. She and her husband lived devoutly, simply and happily near Dublin. So far from severing the family's links with Chips, the Iveaghs continued to support his parliamentary career and his place on the Guinness board, where he served until 1953.

The impending marriage of their youngest daughter, Brigid, should have introduced a ray of happiness into Rupert's and Gwendolin's life. In fact it brought embarrassment and a degree of pain. It was in December 1944 that Brigid's engagement was announced to a man who, in happier times had been a family friend – Prince Friedrich of Prussia. Fritzi had done his utmost to keep one foot on ship and one on shore, as the gap between Britain and Germany widened. His family estates and economic interests were in the Fatherland, but his sympathies lay with England, where he had attended university (Cambridge) and had many friends. On the outbreak of hostilities he chose to remain in London and was interned for several months in 1940. Pressure from the royal family secured his release and he spent most of the war doing farm work in Hertfordshire under the pseudonym of 'George Mansfield'. The secret was well kept and Fritzi, some of whose male relatives had died fighting under the swastika, was anxious that it should remain so. The news of his marriage to a Guinness girl effectively torpedoed his anonymity.

Brigid was the most serious of the Iveagh children. She had been too young to join the gay social scene of the thirties and early in the war she enlisted as a nursing auxiliary. Her contact with the handsome Prussian eight years her senior was sporadic and it is not clear what drew her to him. It may have been the attraction of opposites, or youthful rebellious-ness, or pity for one dispossessed of his country and family by the fortunes of war. Possibly Chips Channon played Cupid; he certainly declared himself delighted at the news of their engagement in December 1944. The response of Brigid's parents could only be mixed. A German rocket had killed their son and here was their daughter marrying a German. They did what they could to hush up the facts. The wedding took place quietly in a country church a few weeks after the end of the European war and George Mansfield's real name was not released. In fact, the very low-key nature of the ceremony attracted the newshounds. Guinnesses had always entered the state of holy matrimony in style, in a fashionable church packed with fashionable guests. Why was this one being conducted almost clandestinely? The truth was brandished to the world in outraged headlines the following day. The couple had no alternative but to retreat from the glare of publicity and live quietly in the country. They acquired Patmore Hall, Hertfordshire, with its 350-acre estate and Fritzi, who took up British nationality in 1946, began emulating his father-in-law by applying scientific methods to farming.

War both encouraged and hampered the development of Rupert's East Anglian farms. In 1940 he lost his base at Elveden Hall when the house was requisitioned first by the British army and, subsequently, by the American air force. Lord and Lady Iveagh adapted one of the cottages for their use when in residence. Part of the estate was turned into a tank range. Yet, in the midst of these difficulties Lord Iveagh, like all land-owners, was being required to increase agricultural production. His first response was to protest: he was being ordered to make more bricks while being deprived of straw. There had been a time when government depart-ments capitulated to the wishes of a man of Lord Iveagh's eminence. Those days had gone. The War Office was unmoved by his arguments. *Faute de mieux*, his lordship knuckled down to the task in hand. He reclaimed every acre not actually being used by the military, making savage inroads into the pheasant coverts. He stepped up the pace of mechanisation and increased his dairy herds. To replace high-quality imported cattle feed he planted more protein-rich lucerne and devised improved methods of silaging and haymaking. These changes completed the transformation of Elveden from a sporting estate to an economically viable agricultural concern. The Iveaghs knew that this was an irreversible metamorphosis. Talking with Channon on a visit to Pyrford in 1942, Gwendolin observed wistfully that country house parties were things of the past. No more would she or any of her friends play hostess to a royal contingent including twenty or more servants. In fact, she and her husband never again lived in the Elveden mansion.

At the close of World War Two the second Lord Iveagh was seventy-one, an age when he might have expected to be relinquishing his brewery responsibilities into younger hands. This he could not do, at least not in the terms of what had become family tradition, which dictated that the chairmanship should be held by a member of the senior line of the Lee Guinness family. This continuation never seems to have been questioned. Rupert sometimes expressed his weariness in later years, but everyone accepted that he was keeping the chairman's seat warm for his nearest direct descendant. If any sideways move to his brothers' families were considered it was probably rejected on the basis of the personalities concerned and their situations. Ernest was still mentally vigorous and visited St James's Gate religiously every day from his home on the edge of

Dublin, and Park Royal twice a week when he was resident in Surrey, but the arthritis which had plagued him for years was taking a firmer hold on his septuagenarian body and he had no son to succeed him. As for Bryan, Rupert did not understand his 'arty' nephew and had no regard for his business acumen, in which judgement he was largely right. During the years that he worked at St James's Gate Bryan concerned himself almost entirely with the recreational aspects of brewery life. Therefore, of all the male Guinnesses available to head the family business – the suggestion that a woman might take on this role would have been considered distinctly odd – the only one left was Rupert's grandson and heir (Arthur) Benjamin – and he had just celebrated his eighth birthday. The other family members on the board apart from Bryan Guinness, who had come on in 1935 and shared the vice-chairmanship with Ernest, were Henry Channon and another of Lord Iveagh's sons-in-law, Alan Lennox-Boyd.

Lennox-Boyd was a young Tory politician, a member of the Chamberlain fan club and an occasional drinking partner of Chips Channon when he came into the Iveaghs' ambit in the late 1930s. Lady Astor, as famous for her aggressive teetotalism as for her ready wit, once saw the two friends outside the Houses of Parliament about to climb into their respective Rolls-Royces. 'Well,' she observed, 'Guinness is certainly good for you.' Alan was an obviously up-and-coming parliamentarian with an informed interest in colonial affairs, though his membership of the RNVR probably did as much as his politics to commend him to Rupert. He won the heart of the second Iveagh daughter, Patricia, and they were wed at the end of 1938 soon after Alan had been appointed PPS to the Minister of Labour. She was twenty and he thirty-four, and theirs was to be a long and very happy marriage. Churchill had no place in his team for one who had been such a staunch supporter of the late Prime Minister and Alan spent most of the years 1940–3 on active service with torpedo-boat patrols in the Channel. It was in 1942 that he was brought on to the Guinness board, but he was obliged to resign the following year when, having made his peace with Churchill, he returned to government as a junior minister in the department of aircraft production. The Tory defeat of 1945 sent him to the opposition benches and he resumed his Guinness directorship. Despite his insistence that he had no business experience his quiet wisdom proved invaluable to the company in the years of post-war recovery (see below pp.252–3).

The fiction of a family business began to break down seriously in the immediate post-war years. The majority shareholding was already spread between various Guinnesses and although the first Lord Iveagh had stipulated that it should not pass out of family control it was only a

matter of time before this happened. There was a dearth of male descendants of Lord Iveagh's three sons and those who were available had neither
the need nor the sense of loyalty to go into the business. They were
wealthy enough to follow their own interests and would have found a
tough apprenticeship at Park Royal or St James's Gate decidedly
'unamusing'. When members were brought in from other parts of the
extensive family they were regarded as distinctly second-class Guinnesses
and were never permitted to share the social world of their 'mainstream'
cousins.

Management directors continued to respect the family members of the
board, but such a gap of knowledge had opened up that frustrations were
inevitable. The senior brewery staff were men of high calibre. Most of
them were Oxbridge 'firsts' in science subjects. The company's ethos was
entirely product based so that even those who ended up in 'marketing',
'personnel' or 'finance' had all started out as brewers and had a practical
knowledge of the manufacturing of stout. The majority of them gave long
years of service and some were descended from long lines of brewers.
They understood the plant, the product and the market better than their
board colleagues, who sat alongside them by virtue of birth or marriage.
Nevertheless, up till and including the time of Edward Cecil the chairmanship commanded great respect. The first Lord Iveagh knew the
business from the bottom up and had the personality to enforce his
views. He was able to set a clear course for the company based upon
principles and objectives that, to him at least, were perfectly clear. The
same was not true of Rupert: he so far left matters in the hands of the
managers that even his AGM speeches were written for him. On one
occasion, when there had been a recent change of MD, Lord Iveagh stood
up to address the meeting, ran his eyes over the script and observed 'It
appears that my style has changed'.[4] The brewery staff had an enormous
affection for Ernest and appreciated his contribution to modernising the
operation. Bryan took his responsibilities seriously, but the managers
never quite knew what to make of the quiet young man who often rode
to work across Phoenix Park and had a special stable built to house his
horse.

Two appointments in 1945 very clearly flagged the attempt to hold
together the business and also to keep it in the family. The first was that
of Edward Guinness as junior brewer. Rupert and Ernest were casting their
eyes around the family for anyone who might be trained for an executive
role. Therein lay a problem. While the Lee line was suffering from an
imbalance of daughters other branches of the Guinness tree were sprout-
ing copious male leaves. The descendants of the first Arthur by now ran

into hundreds, a fecundity producing phenomena that were anathema to the Iveaghs and Moynes – poor relations. Earlier attempts to provide for cousins and nephews at the brewery had sometimes produced successful results, but other experiments had been disastrous. It was with extreme caution, therefore, that Rupert and Ernest explored the possibilities of some of their less distant relatives. In the event, there may have been an element of chance in the circumstances that drew (Cecil) Edward to their attention.

Edward was the great-grandson of 'Old Pel', the MP of dubious reputation, whose daughter Adelaide had married the first Lord Iveagh. At the end of the nineteenth century, when the brewery had been in need of fresh Guinness blood, Adelaide's younger brothers, Reginald and Claude, had been brought into management, but her older brothers had been passed over. Charles Wolfran was a serving army officer. As for Arthur Cope (always known as Cecil), he was revealing some of his father's less commendable traits. As a young man he had gone to seek his fortune in Australia and had done very well for himself. By the age of twenty-one he was manager of a large sheep station and had married the boss's daughter, Marion Forlonge. His wife, doubtless impressed by Arthur's stories of his noble-born mother and his wealthy Irish relatives, aspired to the grand life. The couple returned to London, took a house in a fashionable quarter and lived in some style. But just as Richard Samuel's pretentious wife had contributed to his ruin, so the extravagance of Marion and the demands of their two daughters ran through his son's money. After Marion's death in 1885 he migrated again, this time to try his luck on North America's booming west coast and taking with him his new bride, Agnes, who according to family tradition was a barmaid. Clearly, Arthur Cope would not have been a suitable choice for a leadership role in the world's biggest brewery.

However, Lady Iveagh did maintain an interest in her brother's second clutch of children – or, rather, in one of them. Arthur Cope died in 1898, leaving his widow to bring up a boy and a girl, both under the age of ten. They lived in fairly squalid conditions in Earls Court. Now, history repeated itself. Just as Adelaide had come within the ambit of her rich relatives, so she now took her niece, (Agnes) Mildred, under her wing. The girl was provided with clothes and taught how to behave as a lady. She was invited to Elveden house parties and even presented to the king and queen. Meanwhile her brother's most exalted pleasure was looking after a few homing pigeons in a hutch in the backyard. As for John Cecil Cope's education, it was virtually non-existent. Ironically, it was the First World War which, to some extent, reversed the fortunes of brother and sister.

John Cecil Cope became a lieutenant in the Coldstream Guards and this was the making of him. Mildred made a disastrous wartime marriage with a serving officer, which came to an end in 1921, after which she never remarried.

John Cecil Cope moved to Lancashire and made his career in the cotton industry. He had very little contact with his brewing relatives, although Ernest did stay in touch and occasionally invited him on yachting excursions. When John Cecil Cope's first son, (Cecil) Edward was born, Ernest consented to be godfather – and presented the baby with a pair of binoculars. The boy grew up with only the haziest knowledge of his wealthy relatives, but in the summer of 1945, when he was twenty-one, he made an impulse call on his godfather. Edward was at the time being treated in a military hospital at Aldershot for a serious arm injury and decided to travel the twenty miles as a means of breaking the tedium of convalescence. Possibly his appearance on Ernest's doorstep, clad in hospital 'blues', made an immediate impact on the old man who had so recently lost a young nephew and a son-in-law in the war. He gave Edward a warm welcome and invited him back for a weekend. Edward duly arrived at Holmbury St Mary and it soon became obvious that he was under scrutiny. When Ernest had finished quizzing him Rupert arrived on a 'surprise' visit and took up the interrogations. A few days later the young man was asked to attend an interview, after which he was offered a post as junior brewer at Park Royal. He was thrilled to be offered an opening in the family business, which his distant cousins disdained. Then began the forty-five year career of the last of the brewing Guinnesses.

The other newcomer in 1946 was Sir Hugh Beaver, who was engaged as assistant managing director and took over as MD the following year. He was no stranger to the brewery for, as a member of a leading firm of consulting engineers, he had been the brains behind the construction of the Park Royal plant. Sir Hugh was a high-profile figure in the business world and had valuable government contacts. His impressive career to date had included a spell as a policeman in India, several years in engineering, and wartime service as Director General of Works and Buildings for the Ministry of Works. He had been an adviser to governments and major companies around the world, his most impressive achievement being the reconstruction of St John's harbour, New Brunswick, which had been destroyed by fire in 1931. This was the man – autocratic, impatient and brimming with ideas – who joined the board in 1945 as the first manager to be recruited from outside the brewing industry.

One member of the family whose life-style altered radically in the aftermath of war was Loel. He simply reverted to his playboy habits of two decades before. In 1945 he lost his Commons seat. No one was more shocked than he at the British public's 'great betrayal'. He may well have felt that, after fourteen years in parliament and five years risking life and limb in the sky above, his country owed him something – and that it had welshed on the debt. As he approached his fortieth birthday he resolved to spend more time enjoying himself. New horizons opened up for him in 1947 with the death of his immensely wealthy father, though he was involved for several months in a legal battle with his stepmother over the division of Benjamin's estate.

Just as his radical change of life-style in 1930 had involved a change of matrimonial partner, so now a new commitment to gaiety seemed to require a different companion. In 1949 he met the exotic Gloria Rubio, a woman whose contrast to the very English Isabel could not have been more marked. Mexican by birth, this Latin beauty had been a Paris fashion model, and the wife by turns of a pro-Nazi Prussian aristocrat and the Egyptian ambassador to France. Princess Gloria Fakry, as she was then known, offered romance, glamour and excitement to a man entering middle age and looking back wistfully to the escapades of his youth. Loel obtained an amicable divorce from Isabel in 1951 and immediately married Gloria aboard one of his yachts in the Caribbean. The couple became founder members of the international jet set, mixing with beautiful people in all the world's fashionable pleasure centres.

On the evening of 2 April 1949 a large crowd gathered in Piccadilly Circus to watch a simple but symbolic ceremony. While the music-hall star Zoë Gail sang 'I'm going to get lit up when the lights go on in London' all the neon signs circling the 'hub of empire' which had been unillumined for almost a decade sprang into garish light. Londoners could now feel that life had returned to normal after the bleakness of the war years. Central to the bright display was the famous Guinness Clock, one of the city's landmarks. The name had become more than ever a national institution thanks almost entirely to the advertising campaign begun in the thirties. Bensons' brilliant and innovative posters had continued throughout the war and several of them were morale-boosting in tone, urging people to dig for victory or poking fun at Hitler and his 'cronies'.

However, sadness tinged the celebrations and euphoria at St James's Gate and Park Royal. Only a few days before Ernest Guinness had died suddenly. Laid low by an attack of phlebitis he had refused to follow his doctor's order for complete rest. It was his own impatience to be constantly active that had hastened his death. That same impatience showed itself in his anxiety and concern for the family business. Edward Guinness recalls how the Vice-Chairman frequently invited him to stay at Holmbury. Almost every other weekend when Ernest was in residence the young man was expected to present himself at the Surrey house. Always there would be long walks after breakfast, during which Ernest poured out information, anecdotes and experiences, eager that a new generation of leaders should be fully equipped to carry on what he saw as a proud tradition. Probably, he felt he was cramming into a concentrated course of 'lectures' the instruction which he would have imparted over the years to the son he never had. He must have been aware of the widening gulf between family amateurs and brewery professionals, and apprehensive about what that might mean for the future.

For the present, around the mid-century, everything in the garden could not have been lovelier. Profits had risen from £1.6 million in the first post-war year to £4.6 million in 1950–1 and £8.2 million a decade later. Family shareholders saw their fortunes grow very agreeably. Technical improvements and expert marketing had their parts to play in this dramatic business development, but the major contributory factor was overseas expansion. Before the war foreign sales had never accounted for more than ten per cent of the brewery's output and expanding this area of operations was not a priority for management. Indeed, in 1932 their response to poor performance had been to get rid of their travelling representative: they argued that he was now redundant due to 'shrinkage of trade'. Beyond the British Isles the company was largely in the hands of bottling firms with which it had long-standing contracts. Until it was prepared to adopt a more flexible policy dictated by the different and changing conditions in its various markets it could only watch, while local brewers and major rivals with more aggressive policies nibbled away at Guinness's market share.

The transformation that overcame the business in a few years was staggering. By 1950 sales in all traditional foreign markets had multiplied many times over and those in what was beginning to be called the 'Third World' accounted for eighty per cent of total turnover. It was Ernest who signposted a new direction for Guinness in the middle of the war. E. and J. Burke Inc., who had been bottling Guinness in America for almost a century, had begun their own brewery in the 1920s and there had been frequent instances of friction between the two companies. In 1943 Burke needed to sell and Guinness stepped in quickly to buy up their competitor. Soon, for the first time, Guinness stout was being brewed outside the British Isles. But it was *not* Guinness stout, at least as far as the proprietors of thousands of American-Irish bars were concerned. Descendants of immigrants from the 'emerald isle', as it was romantically identified in folklore, made up most of the customers for the black beer. Advertisers cashed in on this nostalgia. Shillelaghs, shamrocks and leprechauns featured prominently on the hoardings, but the target audience put up a strong resistance to what was widely considered a 'bastard' brew. 'Real' Guinness, according to popular perception, could only be brewed from Liffey water and many bar-room connoisseurs asserted that they could taste the peat in the genuine article. Moreover, manufacturing on the 'wrong' side of the Atlantic, so it was said, deprived good Irishmen of jobs. This resistance added to the problem of building new markets. Had the company really persevered with coast-to-coast advertising they could almost certainly have overcome the moment of inertia, but the expense involved was too daunting and, after a few years, they capitulated, sold the Long Island brewery and went back to selling imported beer.

It took very little political foresight in the late 1940s, to see that western imperialism was in retreat and that in the emerging Third World capitalism and democracy would be competing with Communist collectivism for the hearts and minds of newly-independent peoples. India and Pakistan were granted independence in 1947 and though there was a reluctance in London, Paris, Brussels and Lisbon to see other colonies following the same path until they were 'ready' and an entrenched belief that decolonisation would occupy several decades, no informed observer doubted the eventual outcome of nationalist demands in Africa, Asia and the Americas. Under the circumstances it made excellent political and commercial sense for western companies to win friends and influence people in countries which would, sooner or later, be important trading partners. Such facts were certainly obvious to the new leaders of Arthur Guinness, Son and Co. Ltd.

Alan Lennox-Boyd was responsible for establishing valuable contacts overseas. During his years on the opposition front bench (1945–51) Patricia Guinness's husband was the Tory spokesman on colonial and Commonwealth affairs. His wealth, most of which derived from the breweries, enabled him to visit several developing countries in the era when they were struggling for independence. Both party and company benefited from these fact-finding tours. Lennox-Boyd had a genius for making friends. He was that rare phenomenon in political circles – a good listener. He took trouble to understand other people's points of view, studied hard to ensure that he was well briefed for every situation and was always supremely courteous. Without the relationships he established the end of empire would have been a more combative process in some areas than it was. Meanwhile, as a Guinness director Lennox-Boyd provided useful introductions in Africa, Malaysia and the Caribbean.

Meanwhile, the M.D. Sir Hugh Beaver had been shaking up the organisation so that it could take the best advantage of new trading opportunities. He restructured the enterprise by turning St James's Gate and Park Royal into separate subsidiaries of the parent company. He introduced Guinness to the mysteries of budgeting control, work study, job evaluation and market analysis. Eventually, in 1957, the company established its own consumer research unit, Public Attitude Surveys. Complementary to this was the setting up of Guinness Exports Ltd in 1950 to replace the scores of agencies and bottling companies with which the breweries had previously dealt. No longer was Arthur Guinness, Son and Co. Ltd a company which did one thing – making stout – and left all other aspects of trade to those who were experts in their various fields. Now, the organisation had centralised control over all branches of marketing as well as production. In the 1950s 'diversification' was a buzz-word and Sir Hugh persuaded the board of the advantages of investing surplus capital in other concerns. The first to be acquired was the William Nuttall confectionary group, famous for Callard and Bowser boiled sweets, made at a factory close to Guinness's at Park Royal. Major Allnatt, the chairman, was a friend of Lord Iveagh and it was as a personal favour that Rupert considered seriously Allnatt's request to be bought up. Beaver and the board looked carefully at their neighbour's operation, decided that it could be made to work as a Guinness subsidiary and took it over. During the following years the company acquired a number of small Irish breweries and also entered the fields of plastics and pharmaceuticals. Some of these acquisitions worked better than others.

What was important for the Guinness business and family was that the commercial operation was becoming much more complex. The company had turned into a small player in a big international league in which the rewards for success were vast and the hazards commensurate. No Queensbury Rules existed in this game, whose only principle was that enunciated by the American commentator Malcolm Forbes: 'If you don't drive your business you'll be driven out of business.' This did not square with the genteel image the major shareholders still indulged and the dichotomy was the cause of frequent headaches for Sir Hugh Beaver. On one occasion it came to his attention that Bryan Guinness had dealt with a sudden emergency in Dublin because there was no one else present to make the necessary urgent decision. Sir Hugh's response was to send a memo to St James's Gate instructing that there must always be an executive director on duty.[5] He tried to bring home to family members the reality that they were not the only fish in the company pond. To this end he prefaced the AGM with a luncheon in order to encourage more share-holders to attend. This, he planned, would put an end to the cosy family gatherings that annual meetings had become. Unfortunately, the initiative was too successful; such a crowd turned up to enjoy free hospitality that the experiment had to be abandoned.

A similar brilliant idea coupled with miscalculation brought into being Guinness's most successful non-brewing subsidiary. The story has entered publishing folklore and various versions of it are current. This seems to be the most reliable: Sir Hugh was enjoying a shooting weekend at Castlebride House, Co. Wexford in 1951. Having failed lamentably to bring down a golden plover he fell to musing whether this was Europe's fastest game bird. He later checked through encyclopaedias and other reference books, but could find nothing to confirm or refute his theory. The irritating query obviously nagged away at his unconscious because it emerged again some three years later. Speed records were then very much in the news. Chris Chataway, who had competed for Britain in the 1952 Olympics, had joined the company and was often to be seen training on the Guinness sports ground. Sometimes he was accompanied by his friend Roger Bannister. Bannister had already conceived the ambition to be the first athlete to break the four-minute-mile barrier and when he achieved this in May 1954 Chataway was a pacemaker. One of Guinness's major disadvantages was that it had no tied houses and had to persuade brewery chains to stock their product. Sir Hugh thought that a slim volume dedicated to all manner of superlatives and bearing the Guinness logo might be placed in public houses to help customers settle arguments about who or what were the best, fastest, longest, oldest, most expensive, etc., etc., etc. in various fields. It was a gimmick worth trying, to see if it would encourage pubs to sell more stout, but could anyone be found to compile such a collection of intriguing but useless statistics? Chataway had in mind the very people – the McWhirter twins, Ross and Norris, old Oxford friends who were obsessed by *outré* facts and figures, and had set up a tiny research outfit which provided obscure data to publishers, businesses and the press. Over lunch at Park Royal, in September, the two young men faced a barrage of questions from the director, ranging from the world's pole-squatting record to the only irregular verb in Turkish. The discussion ended with Sir Hugh engaging the McWhirters and telling them to pop into the accountant's office and let him know 'how much money you need to get started'.[6] The *Guinness Book of Records* went on sale, very modestly priced, in 1955 and proved an immediate and spectacular winner. Within a few years it had to appear in its own pages as the best selling copyright book of all time. Sir Hugh, however, could not immediately grasp the significance of the golden egg Guinness's publishing goose had laid. He persisted in regarding the *Book of Records* purely as an advertising gimmick, until growing sales world-wide proved that Guinness Superlatives was a successful and permanent business operation in its own right.

Another lap-marker in the Guinness image marathon had just been passed. On 31 July 1953 Lord Moyne followed in his grandfather's footsteps when, in a letter to *The Times*, he castigated the proposed introduction of commercial television as 'an unnecessary and extravagant extension which the snowball effect of competition would oblige all advertisers to use if once it were open'. When the Television Bill came before the upper house Bryan continued his opposition to what he dubbed 'this circus', although he did not go as far as Lord Reith, who catalogued commercial TV with such disasters for human civilisation as 'dog-racing, smallpox and bubonic plague'. They were, of course, latter-day Canutes trying to resist the irresistible and Bryan's attitude was an embarrassment to the professional directors. When ITV went on air on 22 September 1955 the first advertisement the viewers saw was for SR toothpaste. The second was for Guinness stout.

Nine months later, on 18 June 1956 Lord Iveagh reached the summit of personal achievement when he went to Windsor Castle for his investiture as a Knight of the Garter. He could scarcely have been in more exalted company, for his two fellow recipients were a previous prime minister, Lord Atlee, and the current holder of that office, Sir Anthony Eden. It was the highest honour ever achieved by a member of the family, the culmination in personal terms of all that Sir Benjamin and the first Lord Iveagh had reached for. On that day of panoply and splendour none of Rupert's relatives would have reflected that from this peak there was only one direction the family could take.

19

'NEW MEN, STRANGE FACES, OTHER MINDS'

Our Chairman is a new young Lord. Elveden, tenderly aged by 25 summers and there was much maternal clucking as he rapped the table three times and said that it has been company policy to take the notice of convening the meeting as read. Would we take it so?

Anyway in the background one could hear the glasses being arranged. Of course we would take it as read ...

Lord Elveden then told us in a thin, clipped upper-class voice for which the three microphones were able to do very little that this was his first year as chairman. He looked up fractionally from his notes, lost his place, fluffed the next line and clutched at his heavily-rimmed glasses with his right hand ...

The amplified faltering monotone gave us quick glimpses of his empire. Higher sales, increased consumption, satisfactory production, preliminary brewings in Nigeria going well, and as he spoke he relaxed, his spectacle catching mellowed to an occasional adjustment of the tortoiseshell frame.

And so, he said, it is time for us to vote on the report. He looked up.

Those in favour, he read, looked up again; raise your hands he said absolutely without reference to the script.

We all raised our hands. It was that sort of meeting and if it hadn't been there would have been all those ex-employees and probably several buildings full of proxy cards.

Those against; he looked around, we looked around.

Carried unanimously, he said.

Two people began to clap.

It is customary, Lord Elveden now informed us, that directors retire in rotation and offer themselves for re-election. This year, he said deprecatingly, it is the turn of myself and three of my colleagues. I will step down from the chair and leave this part of the business to a slightly older Etonian.

He did so, and the older man said: do we vote for Lord Elveden, do we now?

Well, it was obvious, and there was a great clinking of bottles outside in the bar, so we all proposed him and seconded him and voted for him and didn't vote against him and then gave him a big cheer as he came back and sat down in the middle chair, rather like a man coming back intact after a conjuror had just sawn him in half.[1]

Clement Freud's humorous account of a Guinness AGM in 1963 is only a slight parody of reality. The public business of the world's largest brewing concern was still managed like the personal fiefdom of an aristocratic family whose confidence in its ability to govern was reflected by its grateful subjects. To have doubted the capacity of Benjamin Guinness, Lord Iveagh's heir, to step into his grandfather's shoes would have been little short of lese-majesty. Rupert took the first possible opportunity to have Benjamin proclaimed. The young man was brought on to the board soon after his twenty-first birthday and was appointed chairman in 1962. There was no questioning of the right of primogeniture. Other members of the family were senior in terms of age and experience, but as next in line to the earldom and head of the senior line descended from the first Lord Iveagh chairmanship of the business was considered to be his birthright. However, the mysterious rules of genetics are not subject to the dictates of wealthy peers of the realm. Benjamin was not equipped by nature for the responsibilities thrust upon him.

As the head of a major international company Sir Arthur Francis Benjamin Guinness, Bart, third Earl of Iveagh, had three major defects. The first was that he was directed from childhood towards the shouldering of considerable responsibilities for which he had little aptitude. Instead of being allowed to develop his own interests he was groomed to assume those of his grandfather. His cousin Bryan, heir to the other Guinness peerage, also experienced the pressure of family expectations, but he had been able to go his own way. That was not true of Benjamin. Lord Iveagh had lost two sons, one in infancy and one in war. He was determined that his grandson should take their place. More than that, he looked to Benjamin to fulfil those ambitions he himself had failed to accomplish. In his early years the boy was dominated by Rupert and constantly indoctrinated with information about agriculture, science and brewing. At Cambridge he was obliged to take the science degree his grandfather had not taken even though he would have preferred to study history. Thereafter, he was shown how to run Elveden and continue its

Directors of Arthur Guinness, Son and Co. Ltd indicated thus: Rupert

Walter
1st Baron Moyne

Arthur Ernest

Rupert
2nd Earl of Iveagh

Honor = Henry Channon

Paul Channon

Arthur = Elizabeth Hare
Viscount Elveden

Benjamin
3rd Earl of Iveagh

Patricia = Alan
Viscount Boyd

Simon
2nd Viscount Boyd

Brigid = (1) Prince Friedrich von Preussen = (2) Anthony Ness

Oonagh = (1) Philip Kindersley = (2) Dominick 4th Baron Oranmore and Browne = (3) Miguel Ferrera

Aileen = (1) Brinsley = (2) Valerian Stux-Rylar
Sheridan Bushe Plunket

Maureen = (1) Sheridan 4th Marquess of Dufferin and Ava = (2) Desmond Buchanan = (3) John Maude

Sheridan
5th Marquess of Dufferin and Ava

Bryan
2nd Baron Moyne
= (1) Diana Freeman-Mitford = (2) Elisabeth Nelson

Jonathan
3rd Baron Moyne
(1) = Ingrid Wyndham (2) = Suzanne Phillips

Murtogh = Anne Tarbolton

Desmond = (1) Princess Marie Gabrielle = (2) Penelope Cuthbertson

Grania = Oswald Phipps

Paul Channon

Rosaleen   Diarmid   Fiona   Finn   Thomasin   Kieran   Catriona   Erskine   Mirabel transformation into a modern, highly productive agricultural concern. He was initiated into the maritime and social mysteries of yachting. From the late fifties, as Lord Iveagh retired from various boards, organisations and trusts, Benjamin was insinuated into the vacancies. A man of strong mental constitution might have been able to adapt to such a life, but Benjamin's second shortcoming was that he was almost pathologically shy. Like his great-grandfather, he was a very private man who found it difficult to make friends. He could relax with small groups of people, but whereas the first Lord Iveagh also had an extrovert side to his nature which came to his aid on public occasions, Benjamin loathed making speeches and appearances. A company AGM or even a board meeting was an ordeal for which colleagues had to brief him minutely, prepare answers for any questions that might be asked and be on hand to support him. Benjamin's extreme diffidence made him appear distant, a man who preferred books (he was a prodigious collector) to people. His third disadvantage as a Guinness director was that he knew nothing about the details of the brewing process. He inherited from his grandfather the attitude that this was the work of paid minions. In order to give him some involvement he was put in charge of the metal barrel department, but as his second-in-command observed it was quite useless asking the chairman for a decision on anything: he would be bound to say 'yes' because he did not know enough to say 'no'. Inevitably, he relied wholly on the brewing and managerial professionals and laid himself open to manipulation by any executive minded to push his own authority and power to the limit.[2] In later years declining health and the necessity of enforced residence in Ireland added to Benjamin's problems.

There was no immediate family member available to help with Ben's initiation. Alan Lennox-Boyd was a valued support in the early years, but after his departure the chairman felt isolated and vulnerable. The most senior member on the Guinness board was Bryan, Lord Moyne, the Vice-Chairman, who was no businessman. His casual attitude to matters financial is well illustrated by a story about the blackcurrant cordial, Ribena. Inspired, apparently, by his children's love of the drink, he instructed his broker to acquire some shares in the manufacturing company. 'How many?' the agent enquired. 'Oh, I suppose about 50,000,' Lord Moyne replied vaguely. Shortly afterwards he decided it would be interesting for his family to be shown around the factory and made arrangements for a visit. Much to his surprise the entire board turned out to welcome the Moynes, who were treated almost as visiting royalty. When he expressed his appreciation of and bewilderment at this red-carpet treatment the MD explained, 'Well you are our major shareholder, you know'.[3] Rupert was irritated by his nephew's casual air and his refusal to regard money making as a prime activity.

Bryan took his role as vice-chairman seriously, but his contributions to board meetings were always those of an amateur. His real commitment was to his writing – novels, plays and poetry. His *Riverside Charade* had its première at the Abbey Theatre, of which he continued to be an active patron, in 1954 and his *Collected Poems* were published in 1956, the same year as his most engaging story, *A Fugue of Cinderellas*. The flow of elegant verse and prose continued throughout the sixties and seventies, as did his eager support for artists and authors. From 1955 he was Governor of the National Gallery of Ireland. In 1956 he became president of the Irish centre of PEN, the international writers' association. He received honorary Ph.D.s from Trinity College, Dublin, and the National University of Ireland. His social connections and his family name had both beneficial and maleficent influences on his literary career. They undoubtedly helped him to get published; and he was fêted by the academic and artistic establishments. The obverse of the coin was that it was almost impossible for his works to be assessed objectively. Bryan was too intelligent to accept the flattery with which the élite greeted each new offering and longed to know what standing his books enjoyed among informed and disinterested critics. Byran was unique among all the Guinnesses of his generation in his sensitivity and passionate devotion to the humanities. Of all his antecedents he came closest to Sam Ferguson, with whom, of course, there was no blood relationship. Like the archivist-poet, Bryan loved to entertain writers, artists and scholars at Biddesden House and, more especially, at Knockmaroon, where he held regular play readings to which brewery workers were frequently invited.

It was Bryan who began the drift back to Ireland. Since Edward Cecil had become an English gentleman the Lee Guinness homes in and around Dublin had been maintained largely as residences for family members in Ireland on brewery or estate business. Bryan was the first of his generation to enjoy life in the Irish capital for its own sake, even though his wife had no taste for it. The stresses and strains of the years before and after independence had been eased away by the establishment of normal intergovernmental relations. The old social life of Ascendancy days had given way to something altogether more modest, but it was a life in which all Dubliners of means, whether Protestant or Catholic, could share and it was one with which Bryan readily identified. He loathed pretentiousness and found the less stratified society of Ireland more to his liking than that of class-ridden England. Nothing better illustrates the attitudes Bryan tried to inculcate in his children than his practice of taking them on annual hop-picking holidays. Traditionally this work was done in the Kent and Sussex hopfields by parties of London's East Enders, for whom it provided an opportunity to get some country air into their lungs and be paid for it. Lord Moyne believed that his sons and daughters should labour alongside the urban poor to see 'how the other half lived'. What made this rehabilitation easier was the cachet which the name 'Guinness' still carried. Despite all the blood spilt in the struggle for freedom; despite Edward Cecil's relocation; despite the opening of the Park Royal brewery; despite the family's uncompromising Unionism; despite the constant irritant of Ulster, members of the brewery family were always welcomed and respected in Ireland. Mere mention of the name secured the best theatre seats; the best restaurant tables, and the most attentive service in shops and offices.

Having said that, Lord Moyne had several interests on the eastern side of the Irish Sea to keep him well occupied. He farmed his Wiltshire estate; he was a trustee of his family's charitable foundations; and, although never the devoted parliamentarian his father had been, he was fairly active in the House of Lords. Apart from all this he was the father of a large family. As well as his two boys by Diana Mitford, he had nine more children with his second wife, Elizabeth, between 1937 and 1956. It was his family which this most genial of men enjoyed most. Someone who knew him in the years when his sons and daughters were growing up commented, 'to see him in either of his homes is to be struck instantly by the enormous importance attached to home in his eyes'.[4]

Bryan's eldest son, Jonathan, was brought on to the board in 1961. While at Eton he had actually contemplated going into the brewery, but he received no encouragement from his father and accepted that his talents lay in a different direction. After a spell in Reuters he took to merchant banking. Jonathan's career in the City lasted until 1968, when he went to live in the Midlands shires, joined a building ceramics company and took a leading role in local politics. His business experience might have been valuable to the company, but he never held an executive position. Jonathan's eldest half-brother, Diarmid (born 1938), made good the deficiency when he started at Park Royal after leaving university. However, in 1971 his father decided that, for tax reasons, Diarmid should take up residence in Malaysia, so he was lost to the central councils of the company.

The problem for the other two brewing Guinness families, the descendants of Rupert and Ernest, was a dearth of men. This led to the necessary evil (at least in the eyes of some traditionalists) of women on the board. Rupert's daughters, Honor Svejdar and Patricia Lennox-Boyd, and Ernest's middle daughter, Maureen Marchioness of Dufferin and Ava, were appointed – all as non-executive directors. The same was true of Paul Channon, who became a Guinness director at the same time as Jonathan. The son of Honor Guinness and her one-time husband, Sir Henry Channon, the twenty-five-year-old Paul was introduced in succession to his father to maintain the representation of Rupert's line. When Chips died in 1958 his son walked into his father's Southend West seat and set out to become a career politician. He thus kept alive a family connection with the constituency which had already lasted almost half a century.

The family member who knew most about brewing was Edward. Since joining the company in 1945 his rise had been steady. By 1956 he was personnel manager. From there he moved to northern sales manager, then trade manager, and when the Harp Lager subsidiary was set up in 1960 (see below) Edward was appointed chairman and managing director. He understood the business thoroughly, was excellent with personal relationships at all levels and built up very valuable contacts within the brewing trade. In 1967 he joined the board of the parent company as marketing director. By 1961 he had been followed into the company by his youngest brother Richard. Just as Claude and Reginald had come to the aid of Edward Cecil in the 1880s and 1890s, once again the descendants of Old Pel were making up deficiencies in the brewing line.

For the first time an important link was forged between the brewing and banking families when in 1964 (Anthony) Peter Guinness came on to the board first of the Dublin brewery and, subsequently, of the parent company (Benjamin Seymour Guinness had briefly been a director between the wars). Peter was the son of one Guinness and Mahon chairman, Henry Eustace, and the brother of another, John Henry. He had for some time been a financial consultant to the brewery. He now became, in effect, finance director, but without the power that title suggests in modern corporate parlance. The top executives (the chairman, managing directors in London and Dublin and their deputies) made the major policy decisions which their directorial subordinates had to carry out.

The relationship between the family and the company in the 1960s was thus idiosyncratic in the extreme. The main board of Arthur Guinness, Son and Co. Ltd gave every appearance of being the executive body of a family business. It was chaired by Benjamin, who became Lord Iveagh on the death of his grandfather in 1967. It was filled with the children and grandchildren, and their spouses, of the three brothers who had inherited between them a majority shareholding in 1927. These 'inner' family members held their positions irrespective of talent and despite the fact that they no longer represented a controlling interest, some of their close relatives having sold their inherited shares. Their power was more apparent than real because all important decisions were made by the professional managers. However, because of their connections with the first Lord Iveagh, they carried more weight than their two relatives, Edward and Peter, who really were 'brewing Guinnesses' in the traditional mould, but came from 'wrong' branches of the family. The company which was now embarked on its third century had the appearance of an imposing Palladian mansion. From the outside it was a highly impressive feature of the commercial landscape. Its venerable history as a British institution gave it an air of permanence. Its continuing, innovative advertising campaigns made it appear vigorous and up-to-date. The antics of family members, who were seldom out of the gossip columns, intrigued the punters, who regarded it as more than just a cold edifice. Inside, however, rot and beetle were working with silent industriousness and the foundations were seriously in need of attention.

The man who set in hand certain vital renovations was Alan Lennox-Boyd. In 1954 he had finally achieved his political goal, the colonial secretaryship. The next five years had been frantically busy and had called for all his diplomatic skills. Preparing former dependencies for orderly transition to self-government meant dealing tactfully with white settlers, former terrorist leaders, rival chieftains and Communist ideologues. Relationships established during his opposition years were vital in enabling him to win the confidence of emerging Third World élites. His travels took him from Cyprus to Singapore, from Kenya to Jamaica. In the midst of all this activity he found himself at loggerheads over policy with the new Prime Minister, Harold Macmillan, and made up his mind to leave politics at the next general election in 1959. He was immediately offered a viscountcy. Many major companies and international organisations clamoured to have Lord Boyd in their boardrooms, but his first loyalty was to Arthur Guinness, Son and Co. and he returned firstly as joint managing director, then in 1961–7 as MD and finally in 1967–79 as joint vice-chairman.

It was in no small measure the industry, popularity and wide-ranging contacts of Alan Lennox-Boyd that resulted in a rise in pre-tax profits over this period from £8 million to £44 million. He had great personal charm and the very rare ability to make anyone who was talking to him feel himself to be the most interesting person in the world. As well as his extensive overseas connections and his various company directorships, he was very active in the Institute of Directors, the Royal Exchange, the Brewers' Society and the Goldsmiths Company. As to his boundless energy, Edward recalls an occasion when Lord Boyd was not far short of his seventieth birthday. The two men met one evening to discuss matters connected with a visit to Tokyo for which Alan was setting out next morning at 6 a.m. The visitor was alarmed to see that his host's face was badly swollen as the result of a bee sting and offered to leave. Boyd would not hear of it and they got down to work. They had not finished when other dinner guests arrived. After the meal someone else turned up to discuss Brewers' Society business and stayed until gone midnight. The two directors then resumed their meeting which went on for another half-hour. The tired visitor at last returned home and had just got off to sleep at 1.30 a.m. when the phone rang. It was Lord Boyd, who had recalled another matter that needed going over.[5]

The main reason for business expansion in the sixties and seventies was the increased role of lager and draught Guinness, but there was also a dramatic rise in overseas trade. Manufacturing and service companies were stampeding to set up subsidiaries and agencies in the newly opening markets. Lord Boyd's contacts gave Guinness a head start in several areas. He travelled all over the world, often with Peter Guinness at his side, to sort out the financial aspects of foreign deals. Under the aegis of Guinness Overseas Ltd breweries were established at Ikeja, Nigeria (1963) and Sungei Way, Malaysia (1966). By 1979 the experiment had been repeated in Cameroon, Ghana and Jamaica. Stout was brewed under licence in Australia, New Zealand, Canada, Mauritius, Thailand, the Seychelles, Liberia and Sierra Leone. Extensive advertising and modern promotion methods had significantly expanded traditional markets in Europe and the USA.

At home, drinking habits were changing. Overseas travel was inspiring British people to experiment with wine, shorts and cooled foreign lagers. Emancipated women were invading the once-male preserve of the pub. Guinness advertising responded to the complexities of the rapidly changing market. 'Red, White or Black' read one slogan accompanying a picture of three beverages in goblets. And the text of an ad in a woman's magazine read:

> It takes a bold girl to ask for a Guinness in a bar full of men. Try it next time you're in your local. Watch the raised eyebrows. And ignore them. After all, if men had had their way, girls would never have been allowed in pubs at all. So demand your rights ... And who knows? If enough girls start drinking Guinness in pubs, it might even become respectable. Then you'll have to think of something even more daring to do.

The time had come to break a 200-year-old tradition. From the beginning Guinness had been a one-product company; it had built and maintained its reputation on stout. Now there was little that could be done to increase consumption dramatically. If home sales were to grow, Guinness would have to offer their customers greater variety. The answer was to challenge the fashionable light beers that were invading Britain's pubs and bars. The impetus for the new development was the old problem of getting more product into tied houses. Edward had concentrated effectively on this, raising sales of draught Guinness from 30,000 barrels in 1960 to one million barrels in 1970. Lager was chosen as another means of infiltration because, in 1960, consumption was insignificant. Rival brewers, therefore, could be persuaded to stock it in their outlets because it presented no apparent challenge.

Guinness formed a consortium with three other breweries to secure a stronger capital base and to use their partners' stock of tied houses to get the product launched as widely as possible. The new company head-hunted a German brewer, bought a brewery at Dundalk and began to manufacture Harp lager in 1961. They launched a massive advertising campaign and built more breweries in England and Scotland, but the real breakthrough came in 1966 with the introduction of draught lager. Harp rapidly established itself as the brand leader and by 1976 sales had reached 2.2 million barrels. In 1971 Edward Guinness became Chairman and Joint Managing Director of Harp Lager Ltd.

Throughout the commercial world at this time successful companies were using excess profits to establish diverse empires on the principle that in uncertain economic times it was advisable to distribute one's eggs among as many baskets as possible. This was the exact antithesis of the long-standing Guinness ethos, which took it as axiomatic that success resulted in doing one thing better than anyone else. The philosophical contradiction largely explains why Guinness entered the acquisitions market so cautiously and without the conviction of major commercial predators. Thus, while Cadbury Schweppes, United Biscuits and other confectionary giants gobbled up smaller firms, Guinness were content to see their sweets subsidiary turn in modest profits year on year and gave no thought to enlarging this aspect of the business. Crookes, a pharma-ceutical company taken over jointly by Guinness and Philips, lost money largely due to poor managerial direction and was sold to Boots in 1971. However, another chemicals concern, J. Morison Son and Jones Holdings Ltd was a success story and Guinness's plastics subsidiary was turning in satisfactory profits. At one time it was the second most successful plastics company in the country. By the mid-1970s the Guinness group's non-brewing activities accounted for about fifteen per cent of profits and this figure was rising.

To most people on the outside, and quite a few on the inside, everything at Guinness seemed *couleur de rose*. But the weaknesses at the centre were affecting the company's competitiveness at the very time when rivals were becoming stronger and more ruthless. This was the era of take-overs and mergers. The market arena never did have its Queensbury Rules, but the new, fat multinationals who came to dominate the game in the sixties and seventies were like sumo wrestlers, menacing each other with size and weight, and ominous grunts. In these two decades there were at least two dozen major mergers and take-overs in the drinks industry alone.

The banking Guinnesses had to live in the same world. The evil-smelling cauldron of ruthlessness and greed which the City of London had now become was presided over by a new breed of alchemists – men and women bringing innovation and panache to the arcane pseudo-science of financial services. There were clients in plenty demanding the casting of corporate horoscopes and the arrangement of deals that would transmute the base metal of small companies into the gold of prodigious combines. There were fortunes to be made by bankers adaptable and resilient enough to reinvent themselves for a changed world. By the same token, there were millions to be lost as powerful rivals from Europe, America, the oil-rich sheikdoms of the Gulf and, eventually, the Far East elbowed their way into the lucrative market. Guinness Mahon proved equal to the task. In 1961 the partnership structure was abandoned and the London bank became a limited company. Two years later it received a valuable infusion of cash on merger with its old associates, Viking Tankers. The bank was soon active in several areas of finance, organising take-overs, raising capital for local government authorities and most notably helping to establish IBM in the UK market.

In 1973 the bank was strengthened by a major merger. Lewis and Peat Ltd were a venerable and respected City firm specialising in commodity markets and merchanting (facilitating the international exchange of goods). Combining with Guinness Mahon and Co. to form Guinness Peat made a great deal of sense because it extended the scope of the company at a time when versatility was seen as the key to success in increasingly complex markets.

The vastly enlarged London bank, like the vastly enlarged brewing organisation, now relied on high-powered professionals bought on the executive market rather than inherited Guinness flair. Henry Samuel remained at the helm until 1966. By then he had been joined by Sir Arthur's son, James, the only member of the next generation to be prominent in Guinness Mahon. Henry's only son George had died at the age of sixteen in what was adjudged at the inquest to be a tragic accident with a gun and Sir Arthur's younger son, Ivan, at twenty-nine, became a victim of alcohol poisoning. Henry's brother Edward had opted out of banking, taken his capital and invested it in building up a chain of bicycle repair shops. Cycling, as well as being a convenient form of urban transport, was a hobby and sport growing in popularity in the years before and after World War Two, and Edward became yet another of the Rundell Guinnesses to build an individual fortune. James was, therefore, the only member of the family to be represented on the board, but he was the linchpin. As well as owning almost a third of Guinness Peat Group's shares, he was Joint Chairman of the holding company from 1973 to 1977 and Deputy Chairman thereafter. In addition he remained a director of the subsidiaries, Guinness Mahon and Co. and Guinness Mahon Holdings.

Sex discrimination had scarcely begun to break down in the fifties and sixties, and would survive longer in the City than in most other professional centres. This doubtless explains why it never occurred to the banking Guinnesses to introduce their daughters into Guinness Peak. Had they done so the relationship between the family and the business would very probably have continued longer, for several of the Guinness girls were highly accomplished. In a more open society they escaped from the stereotype image of the Guinness woman as a wife, mother and society hostess. Two of Samuel's daughters became highly successful businesswomen. Marit married a Swedish artist and set up her own studio, producing jewellery and *objets d'art* in enamel and precious metals. Helga became involved in the world of books and book people through her first husband who was the brother of Graham Greene. In the fifties she started her own literary agency.

In this capacity she met and came within an ace of marrying Raymond Chandler. Their first encounter was in London in 1955, when the author was sixty-seven and Helga a committed career woman of thirty-nine. Chandler's time as a Hollywood screenwriter had come to an end in 1951 and he had returned to his first love – crime fiction. But he had an alcohol problem which seriously interfered with the flow of his creativity. The American widower was strongly attracted to Helga and asked her to become his agent. She, of course, was thrilled; she liked Chandler and was excited at the prospect of being able to handle one of the hottest properties in the fiction market, and for the next couple of years she used every stratagem she could muster to help and encourage him to complete his current Philip Marlowe novel, *Playback*. It was no easy task. At one time she had to spend weeks in a California clinic helping him to dry out. Her attitude towards Chandler was professional, but pleasant and caring. For his part, the American believed himself to be in love with his agent and frequently pressed offers of marriage upon her. A pattern soon developed to this bizarre relationship. When the couple were together in London, California or on foreign trips Chandler would be happy and write fluently. Once separated, he returned to the bottle and was able to compose nothing but maudlin, despairing letters. *Playback* was at last finished and received inevitable acclaim in 1958. But publication was a disaster for the author, who suffered from post-natal depression. Alarmed at the possibility of his rapid deterioration, Helga did, at last, agree to marry the American. It was too late. The old demon regained possession and Raymond Chandler died in a Californian hospital in March 1959. When his will was published it was revealed that one of the century's most remarkable authors had bequeathed his personal and literary estate to the woman who had befriended and supported him in his last years.

In 1953, James married Pauline Mander, a top fashion model and over the next six years they had five children, including two sets of twins. As the family grew up, life revolved around their town house in Kensington, their estate near Basingstoke and their villa outside St Tropez. By the late 1970s it was obvious to James that his only son, Hugo (twin brother of Julia), was not interested in the family bank and he did not exert any pressure on the young man. He was himself in his fifties and began to devote more time to his other interests. These centred round his Hampshire estate, where he enjoyed shooting and fishing. It was also convenient for Cowes where, like so many of his relatives, he was a member of the yachting fraternity.

His contemporaries in the Irish bank also shared the Guinness passion for the sea. John was Commodore of the Howth Yacht Club and his brother Peter had won the Royal Cruising Club's Founders Cup for a particularly fast and adventurous round trip from Falmouth to Vigo in his boat, *Rob Roy MacGregor*. Both young men joined their father Henry Eustace at Guinness and Mahon, though, as we have seen, Peter subsequently moved to England in order to devote most of his time to the expansion of the brewery. Henry Eustace decided that the continuance of the family bank depended on his sons' commitment to it. They would not be able to afford his own semi-detached attitude. He ensured that both boys' thorough training included spells in European and American financial institutions. John began at Guinness and Mahon in 1960. During the ensuing decade he gradually took over from his father and became chairman in 1971, the year before Henry Eustace's death. It was a decade during which the bank, like its London associate, came under increasing foreign pressure thanks, in part, to Ireland's comparatively relaxed commercial laws. Suddenly Guinness and Mahon's virtually un-challenged supremacy in Dublin was under attack.

The firm was able to respond vigorously because the directors under-stood the international markets and the connection with Guinness Peat gave it additional muscle in those markets. The Dublin bank quadrupled in size in as many years. By 1972 its premises had increased sixfold by the incorporation of adjoining buildings in College Green and Trinity Street, and a new office block constructed in the brash, functional style typical of the age scowled haughtily down on its more sedate neighbours. It was symbolic of the personnel changes taking place within. Like every forward-looking business, Guinness and Mahon had to recruit talented career executives who had proved their toughness in the service of other organisations. The first of several non-family directors joined the board in 1968. However, no one at that stage thought in terms of the Guinnesses relinquishing control of the family bank. Guinness and Mahon's historian, writing in 1974, observed, 'John Henry Guinness is a young, vigorous man and as great a lover of the sea as was his grandfather and, hopefully, will preside over many successful years as head of the company'.[6] It was one of the many tragedies that befell the Guinnesses in the 1980s that this hope was not fulfilled.

There are, in broad terms, three ways that the members of a commercial dynasty can react to the inheritance of vast wealth: they may devote themselves to the continuance of the business; they may employ their riches creatively and make their own contributions to the sum of human well-being; they may pursue their own pleasures with lavish abandon. There is no immutable law of human nature that dictates that these options shall be mutually exclusive, but in practice that is very often what happens. By the 1960s there were a lot of young Guinnesses with a lot of money. While their business-orientated relatives were labouring in malt store, counting-house or boardroom they were, in the parlance of the age, doing their own thing. And because they were the gilded darlings of society their successes, excesses and freakishnesses were always of immense interest to the media.

The 1960s have often been twinned with the 'flapper' years of the 1920s. It is a superficial comparison and it takes no account of the unique features of the era following years of war and austerity. The gay young things of the twenties were a small élite of men and women who had lost fathers and brothers in the Great Carnage and were set upon recapturing a pre-war life-style as a means of overcoming grief and coping with the threat of social dislocation. What their counterparts of the next generation were reacting against was restraint. They wanted to have fun and have it while they were still young. That meant not recapturing a past golden age, but establishing a new culture of pleasure, and rebelling against those who threatened their lives with atom bombs and expected them to go and fight in places like Korea and Vietnam, where they were still waging their senseless wars. There was about the totally unprecedented youth culture a defiance, a rebelliousness and an arrogance often shading into violence. This culture, internationalised through television, the record player and continent-hopping planes, affected all young people and not just the glamorous jet setters. It had a classlessness – more apparent than real – in that teenagers and young adults with money in their pockets could all follow the same fashions, dance to the same pop records, drink heavily, fornicate and dabble in drugs; pastimes hitherto associated almost exclusively with the upper classes. Exploiters such as music moguls, boutique owners and narcotics pushers were better at encouraging excess than parents, teachers and politicians were at containing it. Whatever was possible became permissible. Of course, for the rich more things were possible and it was their exploits that regularly hit the headlines, but behaviour patterns between rich and not-so-rich brats differed in degree rather than kind. Many families experienced the trauma of daughters going through abortions or overdosing on drugs, of sons driving cars to destruction or (later) succumbing to AIDS.

In the genealogical tree of wealthy Guinnesses there were only two branches seriously diseased by wealth; two families rendered dysfunctional by their inability to cope with inordinate riches. These were the immediate descendants of Ernest the brewer and Benjamin the independent financier. We have already traced the tangled matrimonial careers of two of Benjamin's three children. For Loel it was a case of third time lucky. By 1960 he had found a wife ready to abandon her own interests and fall in with his every whim. He had been happily married for nine years and living the jet-set life *par excellence*. From their New York base he and his Mexican-born wife Gloria met the obligations of a full social calendar. Their three private jets, three yachts and helicopter conveyed them between homes in London, Paris, Deauville, Lausanne, Florida and their Leicestershire estate. They were seen at all the most amusing functions from Royal Ascot to the Cannes Film Festival, from gala opening nights at the Met to the major grand prix race meetings (Loel's love of fast cars had never abated). They entertained and were entertained by the Kennedys, the Rothschilds, the Windsors and the more socially extrovert stars of stage and screen such as Noel Coward, Errol Flynn, David Niven, Orson Welles and Anthony Quinn. Part of the price Gloria paid for her commitment to the good time was the abandonment of her own creativity. She wrote very little after her marriage and when, in the mid-sixties, one of her plays was accepted for West End production she set aside the project, rather than create domestic friction by shining in her own right instead of as Loel's accomplished and ever-smiling hostess.

Loel had three children by his earlier marriages, only one of whom was destined to find any kind of fulfilment in life. The eldest, Patrick, fell in love with his stepmother's daughter. Dolores Von Fürstenberg was one of Gloria's two children by her former Prussian aristocrat husband. The couple married in October 1955 when Patrick was twenty-four and his bride nineteen. It was a happy 'in' family occasion, after which the young couple settled to a life in which they had to do nothing except enjoy themselves and raise children. They based themselves in Switzerland although, like their parents, 'home' was simply a nodal point from which to move into partying orbit. This charmed life lasted a little short of ten years. It came to an end on 5 October 1965 when Patrick, who had either inherited or sought to emulate his father's reckless passion for speed and daring, smashed up his sports car and himself on a mountain road near Lausanne. For Loel this tragedy was especially devastating for he had only recently exerted his influence to have lifted a police ban imposed on his son for dangerous driving.

Twelve months earlier his only daughter Serena Belinda (Lindy) had also married a relative. Sheridan, fifth Marquess of Dufferin and Ava was the only son of Maureen Guinness by her first husband, who had been killed in Burma in 1945. Maureen's subsequent marriages had produced no other children in addition to the three who bore the Hamilton-Temple-Blackwood name. At the time of her father's death in 1949 Maureen was already a millionairess in her own right, so she made over to her children her share of Ernest's fortune. It was a typically impulsive and indulgent gesture from a mother who had habitually spoiled her children. She had always given Sheridan, Caroline and Perdita the free-dom she had been denied in her own early years. Now she deliberately set them up with the wealth that would enable them to become both secure and delightfully irresponsible young people.

She particularly pampered Sheridan, a living memorial of her first love. He received from his upbringing everything except the guidance a father could have provided for he was only eleven when the fourth marquess perished in the Burmese jungle and he never had very much to do with Desmond Buchanan, Maureen's second husband. Effectively Sheridan's

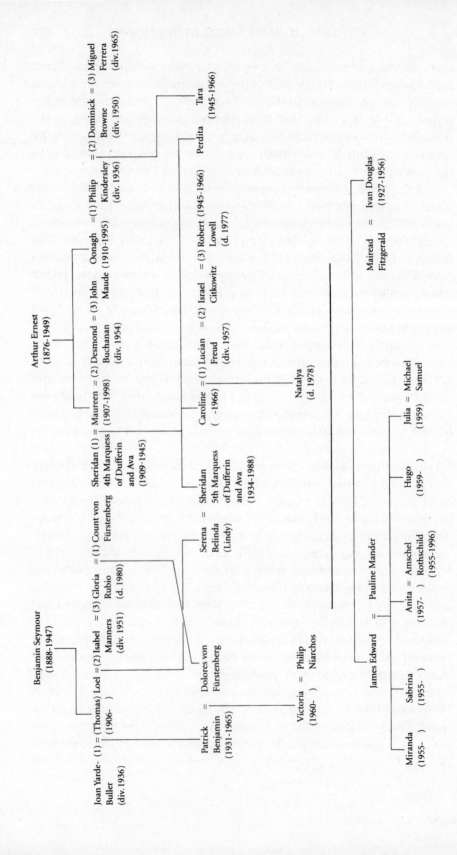

teenage years were divided between Eton and the all-female households of Clandeboye and Mayfair, where he was smothered with maternal love and brought up in the gay atmosphere of constant parties and entertainments. At university in the fifties he became the doyen of the arrogantly wealthy. At a time when only a tiny minority of undergraduates possessed and were permitted to keep a motor car Sheridan had four. He was generous with his hospitality and hugely popular. Later, in the London of the sixties, he continued to be at the centre of the 'swinging' scene, friendly with the Beatles, the Rolling Stones and other idols of the generation which espoused a breakaway culture. Sheridan had several friends in the *avant-garde* art world and he became the joint proprietor of a Bond Street gallery, which helped to launch several new names, including David Hockney. But underneath the very public life-style there was a very private secret – something that even in the permissive sixties could not be openly acknowledged. Sheridan was homosexual. Whether Lindy knew this at the time of their marriage – whether Sheridan was, in fact, bisexual – no one knows, but there was at the heart of the relationship a truth that could only be corrosive. All that the outside world saw was an almost unsurpassed display of Guinness magnificence. The union of the two branches of the family was celebrated on 21 October 1964 at Westminster Abbey with several royals in the congregation. As yet another grandiloquent gesture (involving not a little personal sacrifice) Maureen made over Clandeboye to the newly-weds. There they continued the traditional glittering Guinness life; as far as outsiders could tell, a happy couple – though childless.

The difficulty of establishing and maintaining meaningful relationships afflicted all Maureen's family in one way or another. Rightly or wrongly, Caroline and Perdita felt cut off from their mother's affection. By the time they came of age they were certainly sated with the hollow world of balls, cocktail parties and aristocratic beaux. It may have been something in the Protestant Guinness genes that rebelled against the mindless promiscuity of their social set and provoked inner conflicts. Perdita was the lucky one; she knew what she wanted. In 1960 she quit society for rural Ireland, where her serious-minded Uncle Bryan, Lord Moyne helped her to set up a stud farm for the breeding and rearing of eventers and show jumpers. Caroline, by contrast, was introverted and unsure of herself. She had considerable literary talent, but no understanding of her real worth. In the London of the fifties she fell in with a Bohemian set and found herself particularly attracted to the painter Lucian Freud. Modelling for him soon led to an affair and, when he had divorced his wife, Kathleen Epstein, they were married. Life with Freud was frenetic, intense and punctuated by parties at which drink flowed freely. It was scarcely the best environment for an insecure young woman whose father had had an alcohol problem. The marriage ended in 1957 and Caroline rebounded into a relationship with Israel Citkowitz, an American composer of Russian extraction. She now made her principal home in New York's Greenwich Village, where she gave birth in fairly quick succession to three daughters. Despite the bond of children this marriage could not survive the misunderstandings arising from Caroline's bouts of depression and her husband's preoccupation with his career.

In New York she met one of the lions of the American literary scene, Robert Lowell. This remarkable poet gave voice, both in his writings and his membership of protest groups, to the racial and generational conflicts scissoring American sixties society. Equally powerful forces were eviscerating his own mental and physical constitution and he had spent time in a mental hospital. When Lowell came to England for a spell of university teaching in 1970 he looked up Caroline and thus began a turbulent seven-year relationship in which the formality of marriage, when it came, was an irrelevance. Their periods of angry, reproachful separation and mutually absorbed reconciliation at last unlocked the chastity belt of Caroline's inhibited creativity. She began to write – and write well, dredging truth and honesty painfully from her own experience. She now spent most of her time in Ireland and it was there that Lowell visited her in September 1977 in an effort to heal their latest estrangement. They rowed and, while flying back to the USA, Robert suffered a fatal heart attack. The funeral in Boston, attended by the élite of American letters, was a guilt-laced ordeal for Caroline. Worse was to follow: nine months later her eighteen-year-old daughter, a drug addict, died accidentally while under the influence of heroin. From this point Caroline's bouts of depression became worse and were exacerbated by the alcohol in which she increasingly sought refuge.

While Sheridan was managing his gallery in Bond Street his cousin Tara was running a fashionable boutique on the King's Road. Tara was, at least as far as the tabloids were concerned, the most effulgent of the 'Gilded Guinnesses'. He was a friend of the Beatles, a popular, rich, wilful, high-profile Adonis at the very heart of the youth scene who, by the age of twenty-one, had already provided the gossip columnists with one good, long-running story. Tara was a son of Oonagh's second marriage to Dominick, Baron Oranmore and Browne. Oonagh's third matrimonial adventure to fashion designer Miguel Ferrera, whom she set up in his own salon, came to an end in 1965 with the collapse of her husband's business and the couple's subsequent divorce, but she was much more concerned about her third son than about her own situation. The previous year he had got married without her knowledge or permission. There could scarcely have been a more marked contrast than that between the Westminster Abbey ceremony which united Sheridan and Lindy and the brief, clandestine register office rite in which Tara took to wife Noreen (Nicky) Macsherry, an Irish farmer's daughter three years his senior. When the news was broken to Oonagh she was furious that some 'opportunist gold digger' had seduced her too-trusting boy. Tara found himself torn between two women he genuinely loved, but he settled with his wife in a mews house off Knightsbridge, from where it was an easy drive to Chelsea in his shiny Lotus. The couple soon had two sons. Far from softening Oonagh's heart, the birth of grandchildren made her even more determined to oppose the match. Whether her attempts at sabotage were successful, or whether Tara simply exhibited an inherited waywardness is not clear, but one autumn day in 1966 he walked out on Nicky and took the children to stay with Oonagh in Ireland. Divorce and custody proceedings were instituted. Then, just as the society pages were filling very satisfactorily with the details, something occurred which took the story straight to the front pages: Tara crashed his sports car in Chelsea and was killed. The postscript to this Guinness tragedy was that fifty-six-year-old Oonagh obtained custody of her infant grandsons, who were permanently removed from their mother.

Handling wealth, a famous name and media attention was difficult for Guinness youngsters in the sixties and seventies but some – in fact, the majority – coped better than those whose misadventures we have already recorded. To underscore the contrast we might consider the children of James, the banker. It was the second half of the seventies when the two sets of twins – Miranda and Sabrina, and Hugo and Julia – with their sister Anita burst upon the London scene. Inflation following the OPEC oil price rise in 1973 had taken some of the shine off England's 'big apple', but there was still a lot of pleasure and heartache to be bought by young people with cash in their pockets. James's children did not have cash in their pockets. By the standards of Maureen's offspring they were veritable paupers. Their father was determined that they should learn the value of money and not lay hands on the bulk of their trust funds until they were mature enough to employ them sensibly. James allowed them freedom and certainly made no attempt to dictate the course of their lives, but by the same token ensured that they would learn the pleasures and the irksomeness of honest labour, at least until such time as they became masters of their own fortunes. The Protestant work ethic survived strongly among most of the banking Guinnesses, who had never been promoted from the bourgeoisie to the aristocracy.

The two older girls trained as infant teachers. Miranda worked for a while in the slums of Glasgow, which at that time were among the worst in Europe, Sabrina in a distinctly more salubrious London school. They numbered several pop stars and actors among their friends, and through influential contacts both sisters spent some time in America, Sabrina landing a job as a production assistant in Hollywood. It was all very exciting, but it did not go to their heads. Nor did they play up to the gossip columnists who had fun linking their names with various celebrities. By the late 1970s Guinness girls had become fair game for the paparazzi and all of James's daughters were photographed at one time or another with Mick Jagger, Jonathan Aitken MP, Robert Powell, Prince Andrew and other eligible bachelors.

The story that provoked banner headlines in the summer of 1979 was rather more serious. The Prince of Wales dated Sabrina on a number of occasions and even took her home for an interview with the queen. Charles, as we now know, was under family pressure to find a wife. Inevitably, media speculation was frenetic. However, the moment passed and so did whatever was between Sabrina Guinness and the heir to the throne. One or both parties decided that the relationship had no future and, two years later, Prince Charles found himself another infants' school teacher. As for her siblings: Hugo went into an advertising agency; Miranda joined the staff of a fashion magazine; and Anita and Julia both married into Jewish banking families, which were already closely connected with the Guinnesses. Julia's husband, Michael Samuel, was the son of Peter Samuel, Deputy Chairman of the merchant bank Hill Samuel. Anita's choice was Amschel Rothschild, younger son of Victor, Baron Rothschild. They were to have fifteen years of happiness before stresses and tensions in his own family and the Rothschild bank drove Amschel to suicide in 1996.

Lord Iveagh's family had their share of sorrows. On May Day 1966 the marriage of Brigid Guinness and 'Fritzi' came to a tragic and mysterious end. The conclusion of the war, the rapid economic recovery of West Germany and the normalisation of relations with her old enemies induced Brigid's husband to reconsider his position. As 'George Mansfield' he had identified fully with his chosen country of residence, turned his back on the land of his birth and definitely renounced all imperial pretensions. He lived the life of a wealthy English gentleman, thanks to his wife's money. Naturally, he visited his relatives from time to time and kept abreast of events in divided Germany. He was well aware that there were those who, like some of the post-1918 generation, resented the humiliation of the fatherland and dreamed of a restoration of its greatness. Some spoke to him about his Hohenzollern blood and the leadership of a renascent Reich. It is doubtful in the extreme whether Friedrich entertained any serious political plans, but romantic ideas and sentiments of family pride stirred within him. In 1951 his father died and, whether as an emotional response or as a piece of cool calculation relating to estates and titles he might one day wish to claim, he immediately dropped his English name and legally established his right to be known as Friedrich Georg Wilhelm Christoph von Preussen. It signalled to friends in Germany that he wished to be recognised as a prince of the imperial blood. Two years later he applied for dual nationality. He had now reverted almost entirely to the position he had occupied in 1939, that of a German royal living abroad.

Fritzi's changed status and the reaction to it by Brigid's family and friends, linked with his behaviour in the home, soon began to undermine the marriage. Brigid was not estranged from her brother and sisters, but there was a coolness and awkwardness about their relationships. She was the only one of Rupert's children not invited on to the board of Arthur Guinness, Son and Co. Ltd. At home Friedrich felt the need to assert his mastery over his own household. He insisted not only that he should be addressed as 'Prince' and 'Your Highness' but that Brigid, also, should be accorded similar honorifics. His concern about his ancestry and possible future destiny became an obsession. Casting about for understanding friends, Brigid turned to a neighbour, Patrick Ness. Their relationship developed into intimacy, an outcome made easy by Fritzi's frequent visits to South-West Africa (now Namibia) where he had business interests and to Germany where his multifarious activities included meetings with a mistress.

On the face of it what is surprising is not that the marriage failed, but that it lasted so long. It became increasingly difficult for either party to keep up appearances and the attempt to do so added considerably to the agony of alienation. Brigid certainly wanted her freedom from a man whose behaviour was boorish to the point of violence. Friedrich wanted to break the shackles that prevented him taking up his proper place in German society. But he could not do that without money. It was his reluctance to be parted from Guinness wealth that prevented him consenting to a divorce. Not until 1965 did the couple agree to go their separate ways. They decided to untie the marital knot in a Frankfurt court the following April.

In preparation Friedrich von Preussen went to stay at Rheinhartshausen Castle a few kilometres away on the banks of the Rhine, a luxury hotel which had originally been one of his family's more imposing residences.

He had a series of meetings with relatives and associates concerning his future and, late on the night of 19 April 1966, he walked out of the hotel. The following morning, when it became obvious so important a guest had not returned, the police were informed. They searched the river and its environs, while the international press speculated about kidnap, murder and suicide. It was not until 1 May that the prince's fully clothed body was pulled from the Rhine a few kilometres down river from the hotel. There was nothing about the corpse to suggest violence, nor had any valuables been removed from the pockets. Since Fritzi was known to be an excellent swimmer and the river at that point was not particularly treacherous misadventure was ruled out. The official verdict was that Prince von Preussen had taken his own life. If that was the case it certainly surprised most people who knew him intimately. He had not appeared to be in low spirits in his last days. He left no explanatory note. Furthermore, for Fritzi a quick pistol shot would have been far more characteristic a method of self-destruction than the slow, cold agony of drowning. Mystery is the mother of conspiracy theories and there will always be those who refuse to accept the simple solution in a closed police file. As for the prince's widow, after a decent interval she married Patrick Ness and was able at last to enjoy a quiet, rural life out of the public eye.

Secrecy and an unwillingness to expose themselves to the probings of researchers are characteristic of many members of the family. Given the misfortunes that have befallen the Guinnesses over the last half-century it is understandable that this should be so. Not only are some memories painful for them, but the reiteration of sensational and tragic incidents, they believe, creates a distorted impression of the dynasty. They are correct in the latter observation. A catalogue of suicides, divorces, scandals and violent deaths cannot be an accurate picture of any family's life. Yet nor can an account of its achievements and successes. The banking and brewing Guinnesses were immensely wealthy. That wealth made them different from the rest of us. It is this difference that makes them interesting.

An account of the last and most poignant Guinness tragedy of the sixties and seventies, the death of Lady Henrietta, is included because it points up most vividly the confusion and disorientation that can so easily afflict members of a 'different' family, symptoms which, as we have seen, displayed themselves in many of the younger Guinnesses of the 'liberated' generation. Their misfortunes stemmed as much from the mores of the age as from their genes and their bank balances.

'I want to be with real people'.[7] The following account is based largely on pp.220–4 of this book). That *cri de coeur* most excruciatingly expressed Henrietta's sense of being isolated, cut off, ring-fenced by riches and 'Guinnessness'. She grew up with no memory of her father, who died when she was two and a half. Her stepfather from the age of six was Rory O'Ferrall, a breeder of Irish racing thoroughbreds and her formative years were, therefore, divided between the relaxed atmosphere of the Kildare stud farm, where she could mix with grooms and stable lads, and her mother's London house, which provided access to the capital's swinging youth *demi-monde*. Henrietta was not close to her brother and her sister, Elizabeth, had her own life to live after her marriage in 1960 when Henrietta was eighteen.

The mainstay of this lonely girl's life was her distant relative Mildred Guinness, known affectionately in the family as 'Aunt Gunn' (she never married after her disastrous brief marriage to Captain Eric Gunning). Ever since she had been brought into the brewing family by Adelaide she exercised a role as permanent guest-cum-governess-cum-confidante and had brought a touch of normality into the gilded halls of her wealthy relatives. Aunt Gunn actually *worked* for a living, as an interior design consultant. In this capacity she refurbished Ernest's yacht. During the war, when a hospital operated in the grounds of Ernest's house at Holmbury St Mary, Mildred acted as quartermaster. She was a capable, sympathetic woman and Henrietta came to rely on her. Aunt Gunn was always there, a steadying influence when, in her late teens, the girl was caught up in a life of parties and wild romances, meeting her cousins' exciting and glamorous friends, experiencing all that the sixties Chelsea set had to offer. With one of her lovers she was involved in a car crash – something almost obligatory in a generation for which James Dean was a role model. The incident scarred her mentally as well as physically.

Henrietta had always been profligate with her money. The immature girl found it an easy way of attracting 'friends'. Her mother and brother saw more clearly that she was being exploited by unscrupulous hangers-on and persuaded her to put her capital into an unbreakable trust. Financially this was doubtless a wise precaution; emotionally it was disastrous. After her accident, Henrietta became obsessed with the idea of using her wealth creatively to help talented people less fortunate than herself. She bought the works of struggling young artists. She set up a young chef in his own restaurant and provided the money for her hair-dresser to open his own salon. These business ventures were extremely important to her. Encouraged by Aunt Gunn and by a genuine business talent she discovered in herself, she pursued them with enthusiasm. She bitterly resented the restraints on her generosity which, she convinced herself, were typical of the upper class's conspiracy against the 'real' people. Her brother and his talentless friends were determined to keep money for their own frivolous pursuits and the enhancement of their own prestige, and to deny it to those who could make better use of it. She explored every legal avenue which might lead to the breaking of the trust and by the early seventies was only communicating with her family via lawyers. Almost as bad in her eyes as the aristocratic establishment were the government, who battened on to her income. In 1975 Henrietta's life began to fall apart. On 2 January her beloved Aunt Gunn died. She lost interest in the businesses and was at a loose end. Shortly afterwards Benjamin announced his decision, for tax reasons, to become domiciled in Ireland. Henrietta, too, felt there was nothing to keep her in England. She would move to Italy where the people were 'real' and the British authorities could not touch her money. In Rome's artists' quarter she mingled with painters, musicians and writers who, she convinced herself, were more 'real' than the stuffy English. Her new Latin friends had the warm natural exuberance of the simple Irish folk she had known in her childhood.

In 1976 she met and moved in with one of these 'uncomplicated' people, an unemployed ex-medical student seven years her junior. Then, in a final gesture of defiance to her family and all they stood for, she became a Roman Catholic. After the birth of a daughter in October 1977 she married her lover, Luigi Marinori. She suffered a bout of post-natal depression, but seemed to be recovering. She and her husband had set up home in Spoleto and were making enthusiastic plans for their future life together. Emotionally Henrietta had invested everything in Luigi and their child, Sarah. Exactly what went wrong on the morning of 3 May 1978 either happened entirely inside Henrietta's head or is known only to Luigi. After keeping a dentist's appointment she walked on to the Ponte della Turin aqueduct, climbed over the parapet and plunged seventy-five metres to her death.

Benjamin, Lord Iveagh, had never been close enough to his sister to be devastated by this tragedy and, in any case, he had problems enough of his own to occupy his mind. The advent in 1974 of a Labour government pledged to introducing a swingeing wealth tax had forced him to move to Dublin and stay there for five years until his residence (and therefore exemption from UK taxation) had been established. He sold his London homes and spent almost the rest of his life at Farmleigh, even after the government, in 1978, permitted him occasional visits to oversee his English interests. This enforced move was far from being distasteful to

Benjamin as it distanced him from the affairs of the brewery, which he found increasingly stressful. He had already been diagnosed as suffering from diverticulitis, a painful irritation of the intestines, and over the ensuing years would endure thirteen operations until, as he confided once to Edward Guinness, 'They can't take any more away'.[8] At Farmleigh he could be at peace with his beloved books and also indulge his passion for horseflesh. He had invested in his stepfather's stud farm at Kildangan and was never happier than when watching the magnificent animals being exercised, or attending a race meeting on some obscure Irish course. It was typical of the man that although his own horses won prestigious races at Ascot, Deauville and other important meetings, he preferred those aspects of the sport which had nothing to do with fashion-conscious crowds or presentations of gleaming trophies. As far as the business was concerned, he preferred not to interfere with the professional management who, he believed, knew best how to run things. Ben sheltered behind these other men. Alan Boyd was a first class vice chairman and his colleague, Lord Moyne, was an excellent front man and when, in 1979, Simon Boyd succeeded to his father's position on the board, he too, filled the post with distinction. Yet there was always another side to these relationships. Although Benjamin was content to see his relatives involved in running the business there was that in his upbringing that told him that it was really *his* business. The result of this tension was that Ben lived in what was almost a fantasy world. He sometimes spoke of the brewery as though he was in charge and others were his junior executives or employees. This was to show itself particularly strongly when Ernest Saunders came along; Ben was at one and the same time in awe of the new man's talent and off-hand in his attitude towards him. But at the end of the seventies, Lord Iveagh enjoyed his semi-seclusion at Farmleigh and convinced himself that all was well with the family business. This was a miscalculation or, at best, wishful thinking. All was not well with the running of the business and the family's active participation in its affairs was becoming progressively weaker.

On the surface everything still looked fine. Profits rose steadily through the second half of the seventies from £28.9 million to £54.8 million, an increase of over forty-seven per cent. But in this period of rising inflation the cost of living soared by sixty-five per cent. The company was not holding its own. The major weakness lay in its diversification programme. The existing management was not equipped to run a many-faceted, multinational conglomerate. This was demonstrated most clearly by the history of the subsidiary Morison Son and Jones. The former pharmaceuticals company had 'growed' Topsy-like under its exuberant management team into a general trading operation organised under two operating groups, Guinness Morison International Ltd and MSJ Overseas Ltd. Their activities covered the manufacture and distribution of, 'auto engineering and fire prevention equipment, confectionery and food manufacture, branded baby products, toiletries and sunglasses, photographic equipment, lighting and heating products'.[9] In addition it had recently entered the leisure business and film finance. Enormous amounts of group money were poured into this expanding and successful part of the empire. Optimism proved ill-founded. In 1979 non-brewing profits slumped, suddenly and drastically.

In the same year the Harp consortium fell apart. The major pub-owning partners no longer needed Guinness and resented paying them a major share of profits. The success of lager had been proved. Now they could go their own way with their own brands. They continued to make and sell Harp under licence through their own outlets, but were under no obligation to promote it alongside their own products. As a result the consortium contracted: Guinness and its smaller partners sold a beer now brewed exclusively at Park Royal.

The year 1979 witnessed some major boardroom changes. Alan Boyd and Bryan Guinness retired as vice-chairmen. Alan's son Simon Lennox-Boyd was appointed to occupy the position vacated by both men. Jonathan Guinness felt that he, too, should have been promoted and that he was passed over for personal and political reasons. He espoused right-wing views, was a member of the Conservative Monday Club and had unsuccessfully contested two by-elections for the party. Benjamin disliked his cousin's politics and believed that attitudes he regarded as 'racist' would be a handicap in the company's expanding Third World markets. He had even tried to force Jonathan to stand down from the board when he became chairman of the Monday Club. The most obvious person to fill the directoral vacancy left by Bryan would have been his son Diarmid, who had worked in the company for a decade. Unfortunately, this last of the genuine brewing Guinnesses had died suddenly of cancer in 1977. This meant that another outsider, Dr Finn Guinness, was brought in to maintain the Moyne representation. Maureen, at seventy-two, took the opportunity to resign in favour of her son Sheridan. There was some opposition to him in the family because Sheridan was an art dealer who knew nothing about brewing. He was also, now, openly homosexual. Furthermore, he and his sisters had sold most of their shares so that it was difficult to see any reason for his inclusion. However, Maureen was adamant; the family discussed the matter; and Sheridan was 'in'. That was the way the Guinnesses still did things in a public company of which they now owned less than a quarter of the shares.

Thus 1979 was in many ways a watershed year. Yet, perhaps the most symbolic event which marked the passing of the world in which the Guinnesses had been so influential was the one that occurred almost 4000 kilometres away and commanded far less media space than the peccadilloes of the family's wilder and younger members. In Tel Aviv the assassins of Walter, Lord Moyne were acclaimed as national heroes. Their bodies were removed from Cairo, in the new spirit of accord following the Camp David talks, and reburied with full military honours. The Israeli prime minister who organised this piece of nationalist triumphalism was Menachem Begin, one-time leader of Irgun Zvai Leumi, the largest terrorist organisation of the forties. The Speaker of the Knesset in 1979 and Begin's eventual successor was Yitzhak Shamir, who, as leader of the Stern Gang, had ordered Lord Moyne's killing.

The following year the management of Arthur Guinness, Son and Co. Ltd went head-hunting for a top executive capable of rescuing the company from its predicament. The man they eventually found was a high-flyer from Nestlé called Ernest Saunders.

20

AN ENTERPRISE OF DECEPTION

In 1982 around twenty per cent of Guinness shares were held by members of the family of whom there were eight on the board. Ten years later descendants of the founder owned less than two per cent of the company and were not represented among the directors. This situation would almost certainly have come about by the natural continuation of trends we have already identified, but the final separation of the family and business might have been delayed had it not been for the complex series of bizarre events which came to be known as the 'Guinness Affair'.

The financial scandal which began in 1985 sent top businessmen to prison, put millions of pounds into the pockets of lawyers and barristers, shook several City reputations, called in question Thatcherite policies of market emancipation, precipitated the enactment of new protective legislation, provided acres of copy for moralising journalists, cost the tax payers dear, and was not finally wound up until 1997. Few of the people involved came out of the mêlée with any credit, although the fact that most family directors had, by the eighties, become marginalised meant that little blame could be attached to them for what the Department of Trade and Industry inspectors called 'an enterprise of deception'.[1] The business survived the scandal and was, indeed, to go from strength to strength, but it would do so unaided by any Guinness. Since this period also witnessed the departure of the last family members from the Guinness banks the year 1990 provides us with an obvious cut-off point for this account of the family.

'A company run by Anglo-Irish aristocrats and enthusiastic amateurs engaged among other things in snake farming, orchid growing and the manufacture of babies' plastic potties'.[2] That description of Guinness by

Ernest Saunders's defence counsel in the later trial was a piece of courtroom bombast. City insiders in 1980 had a less cynical if more enthusiastic appreciation of Arthur Guinness, Son and Co. Ltd: it was a one-time market leader currently in the doldrums largely as a result of hide-bound management; in other words, a company ripe for take-over. Inside the Guinness boardroom the perception was less stark, but there was no doubt that something had to be done; Camelot needed a new Merlin. The imagery is not so very fanciful. This was the age of the high-flyer; the market magician who possessed arcane knowledge of complex financial networking and real power derived from ambition and ruthlessness. No one in Guinness knew such a wizard, so the board had recourse to head-hunters. The most suitable candidate produced by the experts was Ernest Walter (propitious forenames, some may have thought) Saunders, a forty-five-year-old Cambridge law graduate who had spent fourteen years in senior management with international companies and had recently come to prominence by helping the food giant Nestlé out of a PR quagmire into which it had stumbled as a result of its marketing of baby food in Third World countries. He was appointed managing director in the autumn of 1981.

From the beginning Saunders and the family directors were oil and water. The new MD was surprised to discover the degree of respect accorded to a little group of titled people who, in his opinion, were completely out of touch with market realities and had no concept of just how dire the company's situation was. More than that, he felt that these grandees looked down on him as an object of patronage. For their part, family members who met the new executive were not slow to sense in him considerable ambition and personal animosity. Maureen told a television interviewer that Saunders 'hated us'. In a *Guardian* article the new man averred that one day the company would be known not as Guinness and Son but as 'Guinness and Saunders'.[3]

Two incidents illustrate the gulf that existed between Saunders and the Guinnesses. In August 1983, when a memorial service was held for Viscount Boyd in Westminster Abbey and attended by 2000 of the great and the good, several family members were distressed that Saunders insisted on very prominent seats being allocated to himself and his wife. Eleven months later, at the wedding of one of Lord Moyne's grand-daughters the Saunderses were seated with the company secretary and the Moyne estate manager, and Ernest was introduced to other guests as 'the new brewery manager'.[4] Jonathan Guinness's recollection of the same event is that there were 'no important or unimportant seats', that the arrangements were much more fluid and that guests were encouraged to mingle. As to the other complaint, he concedes that his family had always referred proprietorially to Arthur Guinness, Son and Co. Ltd as 'the brewery' and that, for ease of communication to the uninitiated Saunders may have been referred to as 'manager' rather than 'MD', but that no slight was intended.[5] What matters is not whether the mutual suspicions and animosities were justified but that they existed.

Snobbery, inverted snobbery and class feelings were all at play and coloured boardroom relationships. However, in practical day-to-day terms there was little change, certainly in the early days of Saunders's tenure of office. The new man tended to make decisions off his own bat and to be uncommunicative, but family directors had grown accustomed to not being closely involved and Lord Iveagh by conviction and incli-nation deliberately left business affairs to the professionals. Only when things went wrong was this relationship called into question. 'Mr Saunders managed the affairs of Guinness in a form which was autocratic, and did so with the approval of his fellow directors, particularly the Chairman, Lord Iveagh,' so one observer testified in later legal proceedings.[6]

Whatever the family directors thought of Saunders, they had one very good reason for letting him get on with the job: he was outstandingly successful. He threw himself into his reforming task with intense energy and what bordered on religious zeal. Every example of old-fashioned fuddy-duddyism and unthinking traditionalism was to him almost a personal affront: Guinness had to be transformed into a new, aggressive, market-leading multinational. To this end Saunders wielded his icono-clastic axe with abandon and the old guard frequently winced as familiar aspects of the business toppled. His attitude towards advertising was symbolic of his approach to every aspect of company life. The media representation of the core product was a national institution. The J. Walter Thompson agency, who had had the advertising account for a dozen years, had shown innovative flair and a degree of sophistication in seeking to commend the product to the seventies smart set. In 1979 they brought out of retirement the toucan who had been the star of Guinness promotions for more than twenty years before, during and after the war. For Saunders this throwback to the 'good old days' was precisely the kind of attitude he loathed and, to do them justice, other board members were also unhappy with what seemed to them unfocused appeals to nostalgia and indulgence in cleverness for its own sake. The Saunders axe fell swiftly on JWT. 'Advertising – even at Guinness – is not just an art form, but a vital part of communications and business strategy. We need a totally fresh look at the advertising question'.[7] With that apologia

Saunders transferred the account to a rival agency, Allen, Brady and Marsh Ltd, who soon made a breakthrough with a series of poster and TV ads based on the slogan 'Guinnless isn't good for you'. The famous black-and-white drink was once again a national talking point.

It was not long before the company's performance was also attracting attention in the City. Saunders initiated a five-year plan; the first two to be devoted to rationalisation and retrenchment and the subsequent three to advancement. He carried out a thorough review of Guinness's one hundred and fifty non-core activities and disposed of every subsidiary which was not performing satisfactorily. He applied tighter internal controls and launched a ruthless attack on outdated, inefficient practices. In an astonishing twelve months the company was seen to have turned round. Pre-tax profits were up from £41.8 million to £50.9 million, share values were rising and investors received an increased dividend. By early 1984 Guinness was able to go on the prowl in the acquisitions jungle. The progress of the next year was scarcely less remarkable than that of the two which had preceded it. By July 1985 Guinness had become the largest national retailer in the newsagent, tobacco and confectionary sector, having taken over Martins, Meesons and Neighbourhood Stores. It pursued its voracious path, gobbling up food retailers, health product manufacturers and spas in Britain, France and America. The group's appetite seemed insatiable and, in August 1985, it swallowed its largest prey to date. After a brief, hard-fought battle Guinness acquired Bell's Distilleries, which brought with it the prestigious Gleneagles hotel. The business had come a very long way since the first Arthur had defended the brewing of beer against moralising critics on the grounds that it provided the working class with a wholesome alternative to the evils of drinking spirits.

The company's rapid growth was not without risk and family board members were sometimes alarmed at the speed with which their vehicle was being driven. But while they might sometimes gasp or shout a warning as a hazard was negotiated, they were by now mere passengers who could be and were ignored by the man at the wheel. And Saunders might well reflect that since the value of each Guinness share had risen from 60p in the doldrum year of 1981 to 320p by December 1985, gratitude would be a more fitting response than criticism.

Saunders's remarkable achievements could not have been made without the assumption of virtually dictatorial powers. As in days of yore, when Sir Benjamin's or Edward Cecil's writ ran large, so now Saunders made the major decisions and handed down policy. Where did this leave Lord Iveagh? He insisted right up to the time of the crisis that he was in charge and it is probable that he persuaded himself that he was an 'absentee landlord' in the style of his grandfather and great-grandfather. This perception was certainly shared in those sections of society not closely involved with corporate and financial affairs. Benjamin had inherited the mystique of the Guinness name and the respect that went with it – particularly in Ireland, where he had been a senator from 1973 to 1977, thus enjoying the perhaps unique privilege of belonging to the upper houses of both the United Kingdom and Irish parliaments. He was also very conscious of his duty to the family concern, which did not admit of him being sidelined by a company 'employee'. However, the notion that Lord Iveagh was in any way in control of the destiny of Arthur Guinness, Son and Co. Ltd was a fantasy. Though it was sometimes useful for Saunders to claim that his decisions had the chairman's backing this was not always the case and he found it increasingly irksome to be theoretically answerable to a man who spent most of his time in the draughty fastnesses of Farmleigh and was distracted by illness and personal problems. Edward Guinness recalls Iveagh confiding in him that, from as early as 1984, the MD was pressing him to stand down as chairman in favour of the one who had the real power and the knowledge to support it.[8]

Yet another family tragedy had further depleted Guinness influence in the company and had come as a personal disaster to the Earl of Iveagh. Since 1979 Lord Boyd had been sorely missed as the chairman's right-hand man, but he had continued on the board, where his wisdom and experience had been highly valued. One day in March 1983 he was lunching with Lord Moyne at a restaurant in the Fulham Road. As they were leaving after the meal Bryan crossed the street to look at something in a shop window. Alan stepped off the pavement to follow – right into the path of an oncoming car and was killed.

By 1985 Saunders was ready to take on the rump of the family directors. He called a meeting of the Guinness executives and told them that Benjamin would soon be fulfilling a purely presidential role and that it had been decided that Finn and Sheridan should stand down. Before the meeting Saunders was at pains to point out to Edward that he was not included in this purge. It would, indeed, have been unthinkable to jettison the man who was now Vice-Chairman of both Arthur Guinness, Son and Co. Ltd and Guinness Brewing Worldwide Ltd, as well as holding other important positions with the corporate complex. This Guinness from the 'wrong' branch of the family had risen to a position of considerable prestige in the commercial world and established an unassailable right to be placed alongside the great brewing Guinnesses. He was the first member of the family ever to become Master of the Brewers' Company (1977–8) and would be only the fourth to be Chairman of the Brewers' Society (1986). His prominence in the City had led to his involvement with several charities and brought him the Freedom of the City. For several years he had been chairman of the trustees of the Duke of Edinburgh's Commonwealth Studies Conferences and for this he was created a Commander of the Victorian Order in the Birthday Honours list of 1986. Ever since 1969 he had occupied on the governing body of the Lister Institute one of the places reserved for Lord Iveagh's nominees, but this was only one of an extensive portfolio of charities for educational, medical and disabled-persons concerns in which Edward invested considerable time and effort. Several Guinnesses followed the philanthropic trail blazed by their Victorian forebears, but none with more dedication than Edward. Saunders's lack of respect for members of the family who enjoyed status without responsibility certainly did not extend to him. On one occasion Saunders told Edward, 'I see you as the conscience of this company'.

Easing out Finn and Sheridan was, in reality, only recognising the fact that neither had much to contribute to the business and could not justify continued membership of the board. Jonathan remained as a board member as, briefly, did Simon Boyd, who had taken over from his father as Vice-Chairman. A few months later Simon abruptly resigned, unwilling to continue working with Saunders.

The effect of this pressure on Benjamin was to increase his anxiety and nervousness. He retreated more and more from his English responsibilities. He and Miranda found the relaxed pace of life in Ireland much more congenial. Elveden held no attractions for them. Though they maintained an upper-floor apartment in the hall, they seldom stayed there and, in 1984, Benjamin sold off the contents of the buildings. An increasing number of family members made their sole or principal homes in Ireland in the post-war decades. The financial advantages were obvious, as was the celebrity – now quite unsullied by Nationalist–Unionist ill will – which they enjoyed. Doubtless there was for some a sense of getting in touch with their roots. Beyond all that there was, and is, the indefinable quality of upper-class life, possessing an unselfconscious tranquillity quite distinct from its counterpart on the other side of 'the pond'. The Guinnesses and their friends were no Ascendancy rump, pathetically clinging to the forms of a lost way of life. Independence had drawn a line under all that. The pressures of attaining or maintaining élite status were largely absent. The cultural difference between the Dublin and London *hauts mondes* was apparent from Saunders's observations about Farmleigh.

He was puzzled at and dismissive of its 'decayed gentility'. He could not understand how a spacious entrance hall could be suffered to be littered with wellington boots or a kitten be permitted to stalk across the luncheon table. The atmosphere of Farmleigh was an affront to his sense of social proprieties. To Benjamin it was home and haven.

By this time Benjamin's condition, exacerbated by the pressures of being titular head of a vigorously expanding company that was consistently hitting the headlines of the financial press, had reached the point where surgery could do no more for him. He began drinking heavily and inevitably this took a toll of his family and business life. His marriage came to an end in 1984. Company board meetings were an embarrassing ordeal not only for himself, but for his colleagues. He needed cups of the strongest coffee to see him through and the air rapidly thickened with the smoke from his black cheroots.

Dictators have a tendency to rely on their own court favourites rather than the advisers with whom they find themselves saddled. In the mid-eighties friction was created in Mrs Thatcher's cabinet by her preference for the counsels of economics gurus to those of her own ministers. Like her, Ernest Saunders was not a team player. As he embarked on his own majestic progress, he turned to experts outside the company rather than strengthening the management he inherited. Indeed, a large part of Saunders's genius lay in attracting to Guinness the best brains to serve in a permanent or temporary capacity. The management consultants Bain and Co. prepared the ground for all the Guinness take-overs. From Bain came Olivier Roux, a brilliant money wizard, gradually drawn more and more into Guinness until be became Saunders's right-hand man in all financial negotiations. From a Washington firm of attorneys the MD brought in Thomas Ward, an expert in international commercial law. Sir Jack Lyons, a financial consultant on friendly terms with Mrs Thatcher and with the Carlton Club grandees, became a close companion of Saunders and was entrusted with an important company investment portfolio. By the same token Saunders paid little attention to the company's own senior and middle management. He saw no discourtesy in keeping directors waiting an hour or more for board meetings and no deviousness in 'consulting' them on policies that had already been decided and implemented by his own cabal.

This was the situation in early 1985 when the Distillers Co. Ltd came within the range of Saunders's artillery. DCL was the largest producer of spirits in Britain, marketing several leading brands of Scotch whisky and gin. It was a much bigger group than Guinness and the idea of a take-over was audacious, but the company was on a roll and had on its throne a

Midas whose auriferous touch seemed irresistible. Despite its size, Distillers was vulnerable because of its ramshackle organisation and the bad press it had attracted over many years. One of its subsidiaries had been responsible for producing a tranquilliser whose trade name was Thalidomide and which was widely prescribed for pregnant women. When several of these women were delivered of appallingly misshapen babies Thalidomide hit the headlines and stayed there for a long time. The furore cost Distillers millions in legal actions and compensation, and seriously bedaubed its public image. To the most informed spectators of the City's sawdust ring it was obvious that DCL was a marked take-over victim. Over the next few months two slavering predators entered the arena and began to prowl around the defiant DCL. Guinness put forth its claws, knowing that the conflict would be hard and bloody, and would require all its guile and financial muscle. It was not long before the cage doors opened to admit Argyll PLC into the arena. Argyll was a food-retailing conglomerate whose growth in the early eighties had closely paralleled that of Guinness. What now took place was one of the bloodiest take-over battles the market had ever seen.

To understand the frenzied activities of the following months and the ultimate reactions of the City, government and public opinion it is necessary to recall the general atmosphere of the time. Britain was em-barking on the 'yuppie years'. London, like other financial centres, was in the grip of manic hypertrophy. Rumours of bids, mergers and take-overs fuelled a market excitement deliberately blown into white heat by government expansionism. Thatcher's privatisation bandwagon was rolling unstoppably; the Channel tunnel (publicly agreed by heads of government in January 1986) was designed to be the jewel in her crown; and the 'big bang' planned for October, when the stock exchange and major financial institutions would be deregulated, would free the City of its last vestiges of gentlemanly restraint and allow British operators to pitch in with the bully boys of Tokyo and New York. The oft-repeated, if never formally acknowledged, slogan 'Greed is Good' challenged all the canons of traditional morality, but despite the mounting protests of church leaders it carried all before it – for the time being. No major commercial player could distance himself from the prevailing mood. Bankers, accountants, arbitrageurs and a range of new financial fixers were ever at his elbow urging him to keep a wary eye open for potential victims and raptors.

Ernest Saunders's later recollection was that he was pushed into the Distillers take-over contest by his coterie of advisers, all of whom stood to gain substantially from it. The Department of Trade and Industry investi-

gators concluded that he had long been contemplating this major coup
which, if successful, would put him on the throne of an international
commercial empire.[9] What is significant for our story is that all discussions
were carried out in confidential meetings and phone calls by Saunders and
his personal advisers and that the Guinness directors were not put in the
picture until they were summoned to company headquarters on the
evening of Sunday, 19 July 1986. By this time negotiations had reached an
advanced stage and the board's ratification was needed urgently. Reactions
of the remaining family members were mixed. Jonathan and Edward were
persuaded that the proposed aggrandisement of the company was an
exciting advance. Simon Boyd was unhappy but he had already resigned.
As for Lord Iveagh, Saunders later claimed that the Chairman saw the
merger as a means of matching the achievements of his ancestors: 'if the
Guinness family had done in its second hundred years what it had done
in its first hundred years we would have been up there with the
Rothschilds and people like that'.[10] Weeks of frantic and often bitter
activity followed as Guinness and Argyll made bids and counterbids,
sought government support, ran press campaigns and used the courts to
challenge each other's tactics. It was, perhaps, the most controversial
campaign the City had ever seen.

While this high-profile battle was commanding daily space in the
financial columns another Guinness story hit the front pages. The fifty-
first birthday of John Guinness, Chairman and Chief Executive of
Guinness and Mahon was on 8 April 1986, the day after his twenty-
seventh wedding anniversary. On that day three armed men burst into
his family home, Censure House overlooking Dublin Bay at Howth, and
held at gunpoint his wife Jennifer and his elder daughter Gillian. The
women were bound and gagged, while the intruders ransacked the house
for cash. But it was soon clear that this was no simple robbery. The gang
leader, who spoke with a cultured accent and was referred to by his subordinates as the 'Colonel', told Mrs Guinness that they intended holding
her and her daughter for ransom. They were still there a couple of hours
later when John arrived home. He struggled with the men but soon found
himself also tied to a chair. The Colonel now made his demand known –
Ir£2million, to be paid in sterling and dollars, for the safe return of the
two women. It was a terrifying situation, made all the more frightening
by the realisation that the gunmen were highly strung amateurs at
kidnapping who might at any moment lose their nerve. The endurance
and self-discipline learned sailing the family's forty-foot *Deerhound*
through Atlantic storms came to Jennifer's aid as she reasoned quietly

with the thugs and persuaded them that they had nothing to gain by abducting Gillian. Eventually the men left with her alone in a battered old Toyota. It was two and a half hours before John could break free and raise the alarm.

This was the kind of outrage wealthy Dubliners living in the fashionable suburbs north and south of the city constantly feared. Violent crime was increasing on both sides of the water, as was drug trafficking, but the terrorist situation in Ulster added another anxiety-provoking dimension. Nationalist and Loyalist desperadoes craved money, publicity and vengeance. They resorted to narcotics peddling and bank raids to finance their operations and although they restricted most of their activities to Northern Ireland and the UK mainland, there was always the feeling that the wealthy Protestant community in the South might become soft targets for extortion. In fact, the police soon established that Jennifer's kidnappers had no political agenda. They were a criminal gang with a reputation for violence whose main activity was drug running.

Jennifer's first nightmare ride was brief. She was driven into the city, to a sparsely furnished house, where she was strapped to a bed in an upstairs room. With a display of *sang-froid* which would doubtless have pleased her military ancestors she remained calm, reasoning with her jittery captors and trying to defuse the situation by establishing a rapport with them. She tried to make them understand that, despite her name, she was not a member of the legendary, rich 'Guinnasty' but the distinction was obviously lost on them. Perhaps they were dazzled by the newspaper stories about the £2.8 billion the Guinness group were on the point of paying for Distillers. 'Jesus, Mrs, you're worth millions,' was the response of one of the young men.

The police, in the meantime, were conducting a campaign on two fronts. They had every available officer manning road blocks, searching city streets and probing their information sources. For such a high-profile case they had to pull out all the stops. At the same time they had to bring pressure to bear on John Guinness and his family to dissuade them from paying the demanded ransom. The distraught husband was frantically worried by telephoned threats from the Colonel, which became more blood-curdling as the days passed. His own relatives and the bank board offered to help raise the money, and John was determined to hand over the demanded two million. Only with difficulty did the police convince him that they were closing the net on the villains. This was, in fact, the case. After five days they had located the house to which Jennifer had been taken. They stormed it, only to discover that the criminals and their hostage had already left for another location. The search began again. It focused on the Ballsbridge suburb of Dublin and a block of flats in Waterloo Road.

Now the most hazardous part of Jennifer's captivity began. As soon as the criminals knew that they were surrounded they became very excitable, shouting hysterically, brandishing their guns and making wild threats. When a police inspector hailed them from the street and told them to give themselves up their response was to push Jennifer to the window with a pistol held to her head. The police agreed to hold off. Stalemate.

Inside the flat Jennifer was, amazingly, able to keep her wits about her. It was obvious to her that her captors had reached the end of the road. Sooner or later and dead or alive they would be taken by the *garda*. She set about persuading them to accept the inevitable without making their situation any worse than it already was. It took her five and a half hours, but she eventually succeeded. On the afternoon of 16 April the kidnappers surrendered and Jennifer was restored to her family.

There has to be some significance in the fact that over the 200 years during which the Guinnesses had been wealthy leaders of Dublin society this was the only occasion on which a family member had been targeted by criminals or malcontents. In years of rebellion, famine, land war and struggle for independence there had been murders, robberies and arson attacks in plenty inflicted on unpopular landlords and men who were seen to represent British dominance, but no Guinness had ever come to harm. There was an aura about the name, which protectively enveloped everyone who bore it. The Guinnesses always enjoyed a unique position in Ireland, so that the editorials and letters to the press which condemned Jennifer's abduction were more than expressions of conventional anger against another violent crime.

Two days after the happy outcome of Jennifer's and John's ordeal the Guinness group gained control of Distillers. The DCL board accepted the Guinness offer in preference to that of Argyll because Guinness shares (with which Distillers shareholders would largely be paid) were riding high on the market and Distillers directors were promised influential positions in the merged company. It was a remarkable coup and Saunders became the man of the hour in financial circles. The tide in the affairs of men was running in his favour and he resolved to take it at the flood. The moment had come for him to assume absolute mastery of the enlarged company. He repudiated commitments given to DCL directors and proposed a constitution which made him chairman. Lord Iveagh was to be appointed president, a figurehead from whom the last vestiges of real power had been removed.

The British love nothing more than putting people on pedestals and then knocking them off. Several City leaders and financial journalists who had hailed Saunders as a brilliant tactition now attacked him for hubris and dishonesty. No one was very concerned about Benjamin Guinness, who, in public, supported 'his' chairman to the hilt, but commentators were incensed by Saunders's cavalier treatment of the Distillers directors. Government, in the form of the Department of Trade and Industry, were quick to intervene. This was particularly embarrassing for the recently appointed Secretary of State at the DTI, Paul Channon, who had to field questions from the Labour benches. His department instructed the Bank of England and the Stock Exchange to act promptly. As a result of negotiations with these bodies the board proposed the addition of four new non-executive directors (Ian Maclaurin, Anthony Greener, Sir Norman MacFarlane and Sir David Plastow – the 'four wise men') who would exercise a supervisory role and who would, in the last analysis, have the authority to dismiss the chairman. This arrangement was enthusiastically promoted by Benjamin at an extraordinary shareholders' meeting (his last) in September 1986 and received unanimous backing, despite the fact that the crisis had given Guinness share values a severe mauling. It had been an uncomfortable summer, during which Saunders had lost several friends and erstwhile colleagues. But the new company had emerged relatively unscathed and might hope that the worst was over. It was not.

In December 1985 a *Daily Mail* journalist had coined the phrase, 'the unacceptable face of capitalism'.[11] He was referring to incidences of fraud and profiteering in the City, and pointing out that unless systems were put in place to curb the unscrupulousness and greed of financial operators when deregulation occurred the following autumn the Thatcher government could face an electoral backlash in 1987. A few days later a Financial Services Bill was presented to parliament and it was making its often tempestuous way through both houses during the Distillers take-over and its aftermath. Its object was to protect investors by setting up a mechanism of self-regulation capable of dealing effectively with any alleged misconduct. The Tory administration was vulnerable and jittery about the implementation of its leading free market reform, which meant that any alarm bells ringing in the market would reverberate in Downing Street. In the aftermath of the Guinness directorial brouhaha a *Times* leader, somewhat naïvely quoting the stock exchange motto 'my word is my bond', apostrophised 'If the impression were to be given that the rules can be broken and the situation patched up – or apologised for – later, then the City's revolution and its new form of self-regulation would get off to a bad start ... It must be hoped that the Guinness case is a lesson, not an omen, for the future'.[12] Events in New York were soon to disappoint that optimistic wish.

On the evening of 1 December two parties were held in London. Ernest Saunders was hosting a reception at the National Gallery to mark the presentation of an important Raeburn painting which had belonged to Distillers. Several members of the art and social establishments were present for what should have been a glittering, highly prestigious event. Less than a mile away Benjamin and Jonathan were dinner guests of Sir David Plastow, Chairman of Vickers Engineering and Rolls-Royce Motors, in his suite on the thirtieth floor of Millbank Towers. It had been planned as a social gathering at which the family directors were to become closer acquainted with Sir David and three other newly appointed non-executive directors in advance of a Guinness board meeting the following day. In the event, a more pressing matter intruded into the relaxed conversation. Less than twelve hours before, DTI inspectors had arrived unannounced on the doorstep of Guinness HQ with accreditation stating that they had powers to impound documents and submit staff to exhaustive examination. There was considerable alarm and mystification around the dinner-table, which was only heightened when the name Ivan Boesky entered the conversation. Boesky, 'the shark of Wall Street', who had for years been a leading player in the international merger business, had just been arrested in New York for insider dealing and was now 'singing' fluently to the authorities about all deals and associates as part of a plea-bargaining arrangement. What could this unscrupulous American operator possibly reveal about Guinness that would be detrimental? Directors recalled that at a meeting in July Saunders and his advisers had urged the desirability of locating funds in New York, which could readily be available for possible future take-over deals and that they had recommended one of Boesky's investment companies as a recipient of such funds. What now transpired was that a deal had already been done on 24 May, whereby $100 million of Guinness money had been transferred to America. Boesky had not at that time been exposed as a fraudster, but he was already under investigation, including electronic surveillance, and the deposit of moneys the company could ill afford in a Boesky concern within weeks of the DCL take-over suggested the kind of suspicions about rule bending or downright fraud that might be harboured at the Department of Trade and Industry. The immediate response of the more established board members, including those of the family, was to remain loyal to their chief executive. They suspected that the investigation was prompted by sour grapes; some DTI officials were known to feel that Guinness had got off too lightly the previous summer and there were several parliamentarians who were on the look-out for a City victim to be thrust into the pillory *pour encourager les autres*.

That Christmas there was a spectre flitting between many Guinness festal boards. Its name was Secrecy. For five years family members had been excluded from the inner councils of the business that bore their name. They did not know the complex manoeuvrings behind the Distillers coup. Ignorance had been bliss as long as things had gone well. Now it was an embarrassment. DTI staff were still doggedly fine-tooth-combing company files and databases. What were they finding? What nefarious activities might the family's compliance in the Saunders regime have led them into? The press, of course, were making the most of every rumour. Saunders's imminent resignation and the possibility of criminal charges were hinted at and columnists were doing their own eager probing. Guinness, like some American revivalist claiming to have performed a spectacular miracle, was now being held up to obloquy for having deceived the financial world with a fraud. Former associates in the City were scrambling to put distance between themselves and Guinness. But still no one, especially the Guinness board, knew the truth.

The comforting screen of ignorance was torn down on 4 January. Olivier Roux, one of Saunders's closest associates in the take-over operation, set out to the directors in an eight-page letter the tactics that had been employed in bringing off the Distillers coup. What emerged was a massive share support operation, which had involved eleven corporate institutions and wealthy individuals, including Boesky, in buying blocks of Guinness shares (thereby boosting their market price and making the Guinness offer more acceptable to Distillers shareholders) and being indemnified from company funds for any loss they might thereby incur. The revelation was a solar-plexus blow, but not an inevitable knock-out punch. At a hastily convened board meeting Saunders was confronted with Roux's revelations. He denied involvement in nefarious activities. Macfarlane had foreseen this reaction and now produced Roux who had been waiting in a nearby room. There was a highly charged confrontation in which the two men's versions of events clashed. Who was to be believed? In the fast-moving activities of the next few days the remaining family directors found themselves, bewildered, on centre stage rather like actors from whom the audience and other members of the cast expected something but who had not been provided with a script. They were not only denied frank information from Saunders's office, they were also not fully consulted by the four leading non-executive directors who had been put in place to keep an eye on the Chief Executive.

The strain on all board members was now almost intolerable. Benjamin, Jonathan and Edward wanted to believe Saunders or, at least, to support him publicly as long as it remained credible to do so. On 8 January Jonathan gave an interview to the *Evening Standard* in which he expressed confidence in Saunders, but conceded that he was a man under stress who might resign the chairmanship, while remaining Chief Executive. He had actually discussed with Ernest this possible solution to the crisis, but it is astonishing that he did not foresee the way the newspaper was likely to handle it. Next day his words were reported accurately, but under the emotive headline SAUNDERS MUST GO. The Chief Executive interpreted the report as betrayal. His enemies on the board saw it as the catalyst that would remove the embarrassment from the company. Another hurried meeting was called that afternoon at Lazard's bank. Five board members, including Jonathan and Edward, met the company's City advisers. They agreed that Saunders would have to stand down, a decision confirmed by telephone discussions with several of their colleagues. Four of them then set off for Guinness's Portman Square office to confront Saunders.

It was Edward who became the last family member to perform a major service for the company. As their taxi containing four executive directors, Edward Guinness, Vic Steele, Brian Baldock and Shaun Dowling, threaded its way through the rush-hour traffic Steel urged Edward, as a Guinness who had seen over forty years' service in the brewery, to be the herald of bad tidings to Saunders. Edward ruefully recollected that, had he not agreed, at Saunders's insistence, to stay on to help with the reorganis-ation, he would by now be six months into a well-earned retirement. Characteristically, he stoically undertook this last painful duty. Quietly he took the beleaguered Chairman on one side and informed him of the executives' decision. After a few hours, during which he spoke with his wife and his lawyer, Saunders agreed, on condition that his salary would continue to be paid and that this should be ratified by a full board meeting. The following day, a Saturday, he flew to Dublin to ensure him-self of Lord Iveagh's continuing support. Benjamin said that he would do all he could for him, a promise which Saunders interpreted as a guarantee that the President would hold the board to the decisions reached on Friday evening. Benjamin had no power to do this, although he may well have convinced himself that he had.

By now there were very few who had a good word to say for Ernest Saunders. Other members of his inner circle were following Roux in a *sauve qui peut* scramble, throwing their share of the blame on to him. Throughout the City fear and hypocrisy cowered behind the ramparts of indignation as dealers, backers, fixers and journalists clamoured for 'truth' and 'justice'. Not many were in a position to cast the first stone. In the fevered mid-eighties 'buy-or-be-bought' atmosphere in which the rules were not always clear and when they were, were frequently evaded, share support operations were common. One of Saunders's colleagues later claimed quite reasonably that while the Distillers take-over was in train at least fifty other similar transactions were taking place in the City, though none were on so extravagant a scale.

Somewhere in the middle of this fog of anxiety and hysteria the family board members and their supporters made a belated attempt to grasp the helm of the company. On Sunday, 11 January Benjamin flew over from Ireland for a hastily convened board meeting summoned for that evening. The executive directors hoped to persuade their colleagues to agree a modest set of proposals concerning the selection of a new chairman and a package of damage limitation procedures. Their efforts were doomed to failure; the four wise men had determined on a more drastic course. When the board gathered in the offices of Sir David Plastow, where Lord Iveagh and his colleagues had first discussed the emerging crisis six weeks before, it immediately became clear that there was no room for policies of moderation. The directors were angry at the way they had been deceived and resolved not only to throw the captain overboard but to do so with as resounding a splash as possible. Any lingering misgivings were swept aside on 13 January when a report from Price Waterhouse, the company's accountants confirmed the scale of the misdemeanours. At the board meeting the following day a unanimous decision was taken to deprive Saunders of his position and all remuneration attached to it. It was Benjamin who had to brace himself to face the media posse and tell them that the man in whom he had reposed full confidence and who, he still insisted, was a friend, had been sacked.

Saunders may well have reflected that with friends like that he had no need of enemies. He believed that Lord Iveagh and his ilk were prominent among his betrayers, a conviction not abated when, in 1990, he was at last able to argue his case in open court. Family directors were among many witnesses who helped to convict him. Saunders never ceased protesting his innocence, through the English appeals procedure and right up to the European Court of Human Rights which, in December 1996 (ten years after the instigation of the DTI inquiry), adjudged that his trial had been a shambles.

The Guinness Affair was a market disaster of *Titanic* proportions, but it is by no means easy accurately to identify the icebergs. The DTI report, which was little more than an historical postscript by the time it shuffled into the public domain in November 1997, managed to find a formula which distributed blame between the morality of the City, the ambition of Saunders and the ill advice of his evil geniuses:

> It would be easy to regard Mr Saunders as a man corrupted by a milieu. Such an assessment would contain an element of truth. It was not Mr Saunders who conceived the techniques used in the support operation to distort the share price: he learned of them from advisers and acquaintances, and the struggle for Distillers cannot have been the first takeover battle in which they were deployed. On the other hand, it was Mr Saunders ... who decided what company he should keep, and what advice he should accept. Impressed by success – particularly of a financial nature – he listened increasingly to those who cut corners to achieve it. Far from resisting the sirens, he adopted their song. The success of the bid corrupted him further, leading thereafter to unjustifiable favours for cronies and self, and a dubious attitude to truth.[13]

A government-sponsored report could scarcely blame the vindictiveness of the administration in power at the time, the judicial process impugned by the European judges, or the flawed tactics of the Serious Fraud Office. All were involved in turning the Distillers take-over into a financial scandal ranking, at least in journalistic rhetoric, alongside the South Sea Bubble and the Kreuger Match swindle. One group of people fingered by no commentator, with the exception of Saunders himself, was the Guinness family. Yet, if one goes far enough back along the sequence of cause and effect one encounters the management vacuum into which the man from Nestlé was sucked.

Despite the brake applied to his promising career in corporate management and ten unpleasant months spent in an open prison, Saunders survived. Arthur Guinness, Son and Co. Ltd did more than survive. In 1997 they announced a merger with Grand Metropolitan (owner of such brands as Smirnoff vodka, Cinzano and Bailey's Irish Cream) which made the Distillers take-over look like a positively Lilliputian transaction. At a valuation of £23.8 billion the new conglomerate, Diageo, became the world's largest drinks company. Months later the company chairman, Tony Greener, emerged as the spiritual heir of the first Lord Iveagh when he announced a massive development of sixty acres of spare land beside the Park Royal brewery. The scheme to provide shops, housing, offices, bars and a health spa, as well as a new underground and bus station, was exactly the kind of project that would have appealed to Edward Cecil. It testifies to the emergence of corporate man as today's aristocrat.

All this will take place without benefit of Guinnessess. Benjamin died in June 1992, tended at the end by his ex-wife. The company now has no

Guinness board members and the family's financial stake in it is reckoned currently at less than two per cent. After years of largely undesired celebrity the descendants of Edward Cecil are now able to pursue their very varied lives away from the public gaze. Benjamin's son, Arthur Edward (Ned), is an active member of the House of Lords, as is Jonathan, who succeeded to the Moyne title in 1992.

The connection of the Rundell line with the banks founded in London and Dublin also came to an end around the time that the Guinness Affair was making frequent reappearances in the headlines, in conditions which were at times hardly less turbulent and even more tragic. John Henry and his family recovered quickly from Jennifer's kidnapping in April 1986. As Chairman and Chief Executive of Guinness and Mahon, John was an important player in the world of international finance. He was also the Norwegian consul in Dublin. With his passion for yachting and his comfortable home in Howth he enjoyed what most people would have considered a well-balanced life. In February 1988 he was attending a sailing club conference in Llandudno, where he was due to address the gathering in the evening. In the afternoon, accompanied by his son Ian and three friends, he climbed to the summit of Snowdon and turned to make the return journey. It had been snowing and the party was inadequately equipped for the wintry conditions. As they descended along a narrow ridge John suddenly felt his unsuitable shoes slipping on the icy surface. He called out in alarm, but before anyone could grab him he fell over the edge and plunged 700 feet to his death. No family member succeeded him in the Irish bank.

In London James still held directorial positions in the Guinness Peat conglomerate. The group had a turbulent ride through the eighties. A series of heavy losses and write-offs during the early years of the decade resulted in several spectacular boardroom rows and seriously shook confidence. Then came the 'big bang' and GPG was inevitably caught up in the rush to acquire stockbroking and securities trading houses in order to participate in a wide range of financial services. Guinness Mahon had tended to remain fairly distinct from the rest of the group, but was now drawn in to the new, aggressive corporate strategy. In 1987 GPG became the victim of a take-over by the New Zealand finance group Equiticorp. Within months the stock market crashed and Equiticorp went to the wall. During the following difficult months Guinness Mahon salvaged its own position by demerging from GPG, but when the Bank of Yokohama acquired the group in 1989 the business was restructured and Guinness Mahon became a wholly owned subsidiary of the Japanese organisation. In 1990 the City was a very different place from that in which James's gentlemen-banker ancestors had found a niche. It was time to leave the financial world to a new breed of men.

In 1958 Desmond Guinness, Jonathan's brother, returned to his roots. Having decided to live in Ireland, he and his wife went house hunting. They wanted to be reasonably near Dublin, but not in a fashionable suburb of the city. They also had a genuine desire to rescue one of the many fine old buildings that were rapidly falling into decay or being bulldozed by insensitive developers. They discovered a thirteenth-century castle in Co. Kildare, built by one of the Norman conquerors, founder of Anglo-Irishness. But the building had more than architectural appeal: it stood at Leixlip, where the first Arthur had entered the brewing business almost exactly 200 years before. While his relatives were fighting their boardroom battles, Desmond was renovating his home and also founding the Irish Georgian Society, dedicated to preserving as many as possible of the splendid Ascendancy residences, which were suffering such appalling neglect. Over the next three decades he campaigned locally, organised seminars and visits, and made regular lecture tours in America. The IGS attracted considerable funding and became one of the 'in' societies of the Irish élite.

Leixlip Castle provides an elegant yet comfortable setting which proclaims the romanticism and nostalgia of its owner. Desmond loves everything Irish – its folklore, landscape, poetry, drama and people. He has inherited much of this Hibernianism from his father, but it goes back much further – to Sam Ferguson, the Reverend Hosea and the first two Arthurs. Of all the many strands one can unravel from the Guinness tapestry this is the most fundamental. More recently, Desmond's brother, Jonathon, Lord Moyne, has reinforced the historical connection by acquiring a home at Celbridge, where the patriarch, Richard Guinness, established himself almost three centuries ago. Several other members of the family have maintained or established Irish residence. If they have more than a sneaking regard for Ascendancy values and life-style, as they gaze out from mullioned windows over their modest gardens and parkland, this is tempered by a thankfulness that they have been purged of that cultural superiority, which wrought such havoc in the past and continues to spill blood north of the border. They can now unashamedly enjoy 'their' Ireland, just as Ireland unashamedly still holds the name of Guinness in affectionate regard and shows respect to those who bear it.

Hibernianism may be the basic strand in the tapestry, but it is not the most widely distributed. If Ireland's greatest son was right when he wrote 'People will not look forward to posterity, who never look backward to their ancestors', the Guinnesses may not have a rosy future. Few of them are, like Desmond, interested in their inherited past. The traumas of recent decades and the intrusiveness of journalists have made them wary. The family name may be something of a halo in Ireland; elsewhere it has slipped down to become a restricting collar. A famous surname can be a liability when all you want to do is get on and lead your own life. Benjamin and his sister Henrietta were both pursued by tragedy – one attempting to live up to Guinnessness and the other desperately trying to escape from it. They were not the first to wrestle unsuccessfully with their inheritance: Arthur Lee, the second Arthur's ne'er-do-well brother, Edward, Old Pel and Gerald Seymour are among the many who would have been able to sympathise with them. Others whose destinies have not been so extreme have experienced frustration and annoyance at the attentions of the media and the expectations of society. It is not surprising, therefore, that most modern Guinnesses know little and care less about their family history.

It is left to the outside observer to trace other threads in the polychromatic fabric. Entrepreneurial flair is obviously the brightest. The Guinnesses have been, over three centuries, people who have grasped the opportunities provided by buoyant markets, technical innovation and western expansion across the globe. With an enthusiasm often bordering on recklessness, perhaps inherited from their Irish forebears, they have, over and again, grabbed Fortune by the hem. Some succeeded spectacularly, others failed dramatically, but they did it with style. Sir Kenelm Guinness, fourth baronet, became a highly successful consultant engineer in the USA. Sir Howard (knighted 1981) Guinness left Guinness Mahon and made a distinguished career in Warburgs. Timothy Guinness's economic brilliance in founding Guinness Flight was no less remarkable. Public service stands out nobly from the pattern. In recent decades we might single out the activities of John Ralph Guinness who held several top civil service posts at home and abroad before becoming the head of British Nuclear Fuels. Guinness money and the Guinness name enabled several individuals to attain high office, indulge discreet charity or bestow headline-grabbing benefactions. Then there is religion. There have been far more ecclesiastics than brewers, bankers and playboys in the Guinness lineage; more missionaries than millionaires, more pastors than politicians, more humble servants of God than haughty slaves of Mammon. Michele Guinness.[14] has chronicled many of their lives and it would have been superfluous to retell their stories here.

Then there were those members of the family whose lives simply brightened the world through which they passed. As this book was going into production the death was announced of Maureen Guinness, Marchioness of Dufferin and Ava, at the age of 91. The middle daughter of Ernest Guinness was the last of the clan to live with that dazzling, flamboyant élan which had made several members of the family such prominent figures in the years before 1939. Her party-giving never ceased from the pre-war extravaganzas at Clandeboys to her ninetieth birthday celebration ball at Claridges (a white tie and tiara affair). Despite the many tragedies and sadnesses of her personal life she never ceased in public to be an ebullient and vastly amusing hostess – and an unrepentant practitioner of conspicuous consumption.

In the preceding pages it has been possible to give only a flavour of this remarkable dynasty, to illuminate the lives of the more prominent Guinnesses and to set them in the context of changing events – social, political and economic. People are two-way mirrors. Depending on the angle of the light, we can either see through them into what lies within, or catch glimpses of their reflected surroundings. History is really only understood in the lives of individuals who enact it and suffer it. The Guinnesses stand before us as men and women who provide new viewpoints on Anglo-Irish relations, public policy, social frivolity and international commerce. They are also a gallery of remarkable individuals, fascinating for their own sakes. A Guinnless world would be a poorer world.

BIBLIOGRAPHICAL NOTE

The only authoritative works on the Guinness family have been privately published and are not available to the general public. They are:

P. Brendan, *Head of Guinness*, 1979
B. Guinness (ed.), *The Guinness Family* (official genealogy), 1985
H. S. Guinness, *Richard Guinness of Celbridge*, 1934
I. F. Jones, *The Rise of a Merchant Bank: A short history of Guinness Mahon*, 1974
G. Martelli, *A Man of His Time: A life of the first Earl of Iveagh, KP, GCVO*
G. Martelli, *Rupert Guinness: A life of the second Earl of Iveagh, KG, CB, CMG, FRS*

Principal published books by or about members of the family:

Lady Ferguson, *Sir Samuel Ferguson in the Ireland of His Day*, 1896
G. Frank, *The Deed*, New York, 1963 (The assassination of Lord Moyne)
B. Guinness, *Dairy Not Kept: Essays in Recollection*, 1975
B. Guinness, *A Personal Patchwork*, 1986
H. Grattan Guinness, *The Approaching End of the Age*, 1878
H. Grattan Guinness, *The Divine Programme of the World's History*, 1888
J. Guinness (with C. Guinness), *The House of Mitford*, 1984
J. Guinness, *Requiem for a Family Business*, 1997
M. Guinness, *The Guinness Legend, The Changing Fortunes of a Great Family*, 1989 (Despite its title this is primarily a detailed account of H. Grattan Guinness and his descendants.)
G. Martelli, *The Elveden Enterprise*, 1932
G. Martelli, *The Elveden Estate 1953–1963*, 1965

Lord Moyne, *Walkabout, A Journey in Lands between the Pacific and Indian Oceans,* 1936

Lord Moyne, *Atlantic Circle,* 1938

F. Mullally, *The Silver Salver,* 1981

'Septima' (Grace Hurditch), *Peculiar People,* 1934

The early history of the Guinness brewery is to be found in:

P. Lynch and J. Vaizey, *The Guinness Brewery in the Irish Economy 1759–1876,* Cambridge, 1960

The later history is only in MS form held at the Park Lane brewery:

S. R. Dennison and O. MacDonagh, *The History of Guinness 1886–1939,* 1976

C. E. Guinness, The Guinness Book of Guinness 1935–1985, 1988 is an anthology on the history of the Park Royal brewery.

B. Sibley, *The Book of Guinness Advertising,* 1985 is a fully-illustrated account of the promotional campaigns from 1927 to the 1980s.

Much has been written, perhaps too much, on the brewery scandal of 1986–7 and the subsequent trials:

N. Kochan and H. Pym, *The Guinness Affair: Anatomy of a Scandal,* 1987 was published too close to the events for mature reflection.

J. Saunders, *Nightmare,* 1989, is an account by Ernest Saunders' son.

J. Guinness, *Requiem for a Family Business* (see above) is remarkably fair for one so closely involved.

The best (though not the most readable) treatment is the official DTI report:

D. Donaldson and I. Watt, *Guinness PLC Investigation Under Section 432(2) and 442 of the Companies Act 1985,* 1997

Manuscript sources available in public archives are referenced in the text.

NOTES

Chapter 1

1. cf. D. C. Boulger, *The Battle of the Boyne*, 1911, pp.234–94
2. T. Bartlett, *The Fall and Rise of the Irish Nation*, Dublin, 1952, p.10
3. cf. J. C. O'Callaghan, *A History of Irish Brigades in the Service of France*, 1870, p.159
4. N. Curnock (ed.), *The Journal of the Rev. John Wesley, A.M.*, 1938. IV, p.259
5. ibid., VII, p.260
6. ibid., VII, p.259
7. J. Warburton, J. Whitelaw and R. Walsh, *History of the City of Dublin*, 1818, I, p.444

Chapter 2

1. *The Guinness Family*, a pedigree compiled by Henry Seymour Guinness and Brian Guinness, 1953, third edition 1985; cf. also F. Mullay, *The Silver Salver*, 1981, pp.226ff; also J. Guinness, *Requiem for a Family Business*, 1997, pp.361–7
2. E. Burke, *Reflections on the Revolution in France*, ed. C. Cruise O'Brien, 1969, p.52
3. cf. M. McConville, *Ascendancy to Oblivion*, 1986, p.151
4. R. B. McDowell, *Ireland in the Age of Imperialism and Revolution 1760–1801*, Oxford, 1979, p.153
5. J. Wesley, op.cit., III, p.314
6. *DNB*

7. cf. R. B. McDowell, op.cit., p.284
8. cf. P. Lynch and J. Vaizey, *Guinness's Brewery in the Irish Economy 1759–1876*, Cambridge, 1960, pp.54ff
9. J. Wesley, op.cit., VII, p.485
10. cf. T. Bartlett, op.cit., p.143

Chapter 3

1. R. Watson, *A Defence of Revealed Religion in Two Sermons Preached in the Cathedral Church of Llandaff, 1795*, 1806 ed, p.400
2. cf. T. Bartlett, op.cit., p.140
3. cf. P. Lynch and J. Vaizey, op.cit., p.125
4. P. Lynch and J. Vaizey, op.cit., p.108
5. ibid., p.109
6. ibid., p.112
7. G. Martelli, *A Man of His Time; A Life of the First Earl of Iveagh, IP., GCVO*, 1957 pp.23–4

Chapter 4

1. G. Martelli, op.cit., p.24
2. cf. P. Lynch and J. Vaizey, op.cit., p.106
3. R. B. McDowell, *Public Opinion and Government Policy in Ireland 1801–1846*, 1952, p.232
4. P. Lynch and J. Vaizey, op.cit., pp. 113–4
5. Lady Ferguson, *Sir Samuel Ferguson in the Ireland of His Day*, 1896, Vol. 1, pp.249–54
6. ibid., p.245, quoting C. G. Duffy, preface to *Young Ireland 1840–5*, 2 vols 1880–3
7. P. Lynch and J. Vaizey, op.cit., p.167
8. quoted in R. D. C. Black, *Economic Thought and the Irish Question 1817–70*, Cambridge, 1970, p.112
9. P. Lynch and J. Vaizey, op.cit., p.108

Chapter 5

1. J. Lynch and P. Vaizey, op.cit., p.109
2. ibid., pp.158–9

3. *North Devon Journal*, 7 June 1855
4. ibid., 21 December 1854
5. ibid., 19 July 1855
6. I. F. Jones, *The Rise of a Merchant Bank, A Short History of Guinness Mahon*, Dublin, 1974
7. P. Lynch and J. Vaizey, op.cit., p.178
8. cf. G. Parsons (ed.), *Religion in Victorian Britain*, Manchester, 1988, III, p.116

Chapter 6

1. *Hansard*, 31 May 1869
2. P. Lynch and J. Vaizey, op.cit., p. 180
3. J. Morley, *Life of William Ewart Gladstone*, 1903, II, pp.246–7
4. cf. M. Guinness, *The Guinness Legend*, 1989, p.53
5. The Irish *Daily Express*, 15 February 1858, cited in ibid., p.63
6. H. Grattan Guinness, *The Approaching End of the Age in the Light of History, Prophecy and Science*, 1886, ed, pp.459–60
7. M. Guinness, op.cit., p.75

Chapter 7

1. F. D. How, *William Conyngham Plunket, Fourth Baron Plunket and Sixty-first Archbishop of Dublin – A Memoir*, 1900, p.50
2. ibid., p.42
3. ibid., p.132
4. ibid., p.67
5. P. Lynch and J. Vaizey, op.cit., p.184
6. ibid., p.188
7. Lady Ferguson, op.cit., I, p.270
8. ibid., I, p.189
9. ibid., I, p.159

Chapter 8

1. J. Morley, op.cit., II, pp.390–1
2. cf. M. Bence-Jones, *Twilight of the Ascendancy*, 1987, p.23
3. ibid., p.31

4. ibid., pp.34–5
5. Lady Ferguson, op.cit., I, pp. 258–9
6. H. Grattan Guinness, *Romanism and the Reformation*, 1887, pp.240–1
7. F. D. How, op.cit., pp.197–8
8. Lady Ferguson, op.cit., I, pp.254–5
9. ibid., I, p.254–5
10. ibid., I, p.267

Chapter 9

1. J. Guinness, op.cit., p.21
2. cf. G. Martelli, op.cit., p.73
3. ibid., p.72 quotation from the Whitehall Review, 1881
4. ibid., op.cit., pp. 93–4
5. ibid., op.cit., p.96
6. ibid., p.121
7. ibid., p.122
8. S. R. Dennison and O. MacDonagh, *The History of Guinness, 1886–1939* (in MS only), 1972, Ch.2, p.14
9. ibid., Ch.2, p.2
10. ibid.
11. ibid., Ch.2, p.4
12. cf. J. Bryant, *The Iveagh Bequest: Kenwood*, p.76
13. R. Gathorne-Hardy (ed.), *Ottoline – the Early Memoirs of Lady Ottoline Morell*, 1963, p.291
14. G. Martelli, op.cit., pp. 340–41
15. cf. J. White, *Rothschild Buildings: Life in an East End Tenement Block, 1887–1920*, 1980, pp.17, 24
16. G. Martelli, op.cit., pp.167–8
17. ibid., pp.146–7
18. B. Guinness, *Dairy Not Kept, Essays in Recollection*, 1975, pp.68–9
19. S. R. Dennison and O. MacDonagh, op.cit., Ch.4, p.52

Chapter 10

1. *Hansard*, 4th ser. 127, 21
2. ibid., 4th ser. 101, 866
3. Elizabeth, Countess of Fingall, *Seventy Years Young*, 1937, p.93
4. I. F. Jones, op.cit., p.36

5. Henry Mayhew, *London Labour and the London Poor*, 1862, III, p.27
6. J. Pollock, *Moody Without Sankey*, 1963, p.96
7. ibid., p.151
8. F. Guinness, *East London Institute Reports*; cf. M. Guinness, op.cit., p.123

Chapter 11

1. *Hastings Observer*, 7 July 1903
2. 'Septima' (Grace Hurditch), *Peculiar People*, 1935, p.30
3. cf. T. Pakenham, *The Boer War*, 1979, p.252

Chapter 12

1. cf. M. Guinness, op.cit., p.261
2. *Hansard*, 5th ser. 22, 311ff
3. ibid., 5th ser. 19, 116
4. ibid., 5th ser. 39, 1129
5. *Southend Observer*, 22 November 1911
6. cf. G. Martelli, *The Elveden Enterprise*, 1952, p.71
7. Hansard, 5th ser. 58, 250–1
8. Lord Moyne, *Walkabout, A Journey in Lands between the Pacific and Indian Ocean*, 1936, p.1
9. S. R. Dennison and O. MacDonagh, op.cit., Chapter 5, p.52

Chapter 13

1. K. Everett, *Bricks and Flowers*, 1950; cf. M. Bence-Jones, op.cit., p.181
2. *Hansard*, 4th ser. 180, 1548
3. *Hansard*, 5th ser. 84, 658, 1023, 2159
4. Sir William Russell in G. Martelli, *The Elveden Enterprise*, 1952, p.17
5. J. Bryant. op.cit., p.59
6. S. R. Dennison and O. MacDonagh, op.cit., ch.11, p.16
7. cf. D. Wilson, *The Astors: The Life and Times of the Astor Dynasty, 1763–1992*, 1993, p.187ff

Chapter 14

1. *The Times*, 13 February, 1919
2. ibid., 14 February, 1919
3. *Southend Observer*, 15 November 1922
4. cf. J. M. Nankivell and S. Loch, *Ireland in Travail*, 1922, p.68
5. F. Mullally, op.cit., pp.29–30
6. M. Bence-Jones, op.cit., p.243
7. E. Guinness, *The Guinness Book of Guinness, 1935–1985*, 1988, p.151
8. *Hansard*, 5th ser. 153, 2330; *The Times*, 17 February, 4 March 1922
9. *Southend Observer*, 6 December 1923

Chapter 15

1. cf. G. Martelli, *The Elveden Enterprise*, 1952, p.56
2. S. R. Dennison and O. MacDonagh, op.cit., Ch.12, p.16
3. ibid., Ch.12, p.24
4. ibid., Ch.13, p.43
5. ibid., Ch.19, p.6
6. ibid., Ch.18, p.7
7. E. Guinness, op.cit., p.8
8. ibid., p.7
9. M. Gilbert, *Churchil, A Life*, 1991, p.463
10. ibid., p.468
11. ibid., p.471

Chapter 16

1. *The Times*, 2 July 1937
2. E. Guinness, op.cit., p.151
3. ibid.
4. R. R. James (ed.), *Chips: The Diaries of Sir Henry Channon*, 1967, p.4
5. ibid., pp. 3–4
6. N. Nicolson (ed.), *Harold Nicolson, Diaries and Letters, 1930–39*, 1966, p.244
7. R. R. James (ed.), op.cit., pp 126–7
8. ibid., p.111
9. J. Guinness, op.cit., p.70
10. B. Guinness, op.cit., p.15

11. J. Guinness with C. Guinness, *The House of Mitford*, 1984, p.32
12. ibid., p.318
13. Lord Moyne, op.cit., pp. 1–2
14. ibid., p.2
15. M. Gilbert, *Prophet of Truth: Winston S. Churchill 1922–1939*, 1990, p.563
16. Lord Moyne, op.cit., p.289
17. ibid., pp.288–90
18. M. Gilbert, *Prophet of Truth*, p.972
19. ibid., p.989
20. R. R. James (ed.), op.cit., pp.172–3

Chapter 17

1. A. J. P. Taylor, *English History 1944–45*, Oxford, 1965, p.466
2. *Hansard*, 5th ser. 116, 331
3. J. Guinness with C. Guinness, op.cit., p.497
4. M. Gilbert, *Finest Hour: Winston S. Churchill 1939–41*, 1983, p.1019
5. G. M. Gathorne-Hardy, *A Short History of International Affairs 1920–1938*, Oxford, 1938, p.300
6. B. Guinness, *Personal Patchwork 1939–1945*, 1986, p.212

Chapter 18

1. *The Times*, 9 November 1944
2. M. Gilbert, *Churchill, A Life*, 1991, p.803
3. R. R. James (ed.), op.cit., pp.396–7
4. E. Guinness, op.cit., p.175
5. J. Guinness, op.cit., p.71
6. E. Guinness, op.cit., pp.232–4

Chapter 19

1. *Sunday Telegraph*, 20 January 1963; cf. E. Guinness, op.cit., pp.362–3
2. Edward Guinness in conversation with the author
3. E. Guinness, op.cit., p.256
4. *The Times*, 23 June 1992
5. E. Guinness, op.cit., p.322
6. I. F. Jones, op.cit., 1974, p.52

7. quoted in F. Mullaly, op.cit., p.223. The following account is based largely on pp.220–4 of this book.
8. Edward Guinness in conversation with the author
9. A. Guinness, Son and Co. Ltd., Annual Report 1979, quoted by J. Guinness, op.cit., p.113

Chapter 20

1. D. Donaldson and Ian Watt, Guinness plc – Investigation under Sections 432(2) and 442 of the Companies Act 1985, 1997, p.304
2. *Independent*, 28 August 1990, p.17
3. Edward Guinness in conversation with the author
4. J. Saunders, *Nightmare*, 1989, p.109
5. J. Guinness, op.cit., pp.163–4
6. N. Kochan and H. Pym, *The Guinness Affair: Anatomy of a Scandal*, 1987, p.152
7. B. Sibley, *The Book of Guinness Advertising*, 1985, p.209
8. Edward Guinness in conversation with the author
9. J. Saunders, op.cit., p.138; D. Donaldson and I. Watt, op.cit., p.41
10. *Independent*, 28 August 1990, p.17
11. A. Alexander, *Daily Mail*, 4 December 1985
12. *The Times*, 12 September 1986
13. D. Donaldson and I. Watt, op.cit., p.303
14. M. Guinness, op.cit.

NOTES